WEBSTER'S SPELLER

Edited by
Liz Kauffman

Proofread by
Marsha Tischner

Staff
Kim Nichols
Kathleen Flickinger
Cindy Carter
Marsha Tischner

WEBSTER'S SPELLER

This WEBSTER'S SPELLER is designed for use in the school, in the office, and in the home, as a Quick Referance Guide to spelling and proper word hyphenation.

Words that contain double dashes (--) between letters indicates a hyphenated word. Single dashes (-) show syllabic division.

A

aard-vark
a-back
ab-a-cus
  ab-a-cus-es
  ab-a-ci
a-baft
  abaft-ment
  abaft-ed
ab-a-lo-ne
a-ban-don
  aban-doned
  aban-don-er
  aban-don-ment
a-base
  a-based
  a-bas-ing
  a-base-ment
a-bash
  a-bash-ment
a-bate
  a-bat-ed
  a-bat-ing
  a-bat-a-ble
  a-bate-ment
aba-tis
ab-at-oir
ab-ba-cy
  ab-ba-tial
ab-bess
ab-bey
  ab-beys
ab-bot
ab-bre-vi-a-tion
  ab-bre-vi-ate
  ab-bre-vi-at-ed
  ab-bre-vi-at-ing
  ab-bre-vi-a-tor
ab-di-cate
  ab-di-cat-ed
  ab-di-cat-ing
  ab-di-ca-tion
ab-do-men
  ab-dom-i-nal
  ab-dom-i-nal-ly
ab-duce
ab-duct
  ab-duc-tion
  ab-duc-tor
  ab-duct-ing
a-beam
a-bed
ab-er-rance
  ab-er-ran-cy
ab-er-rant
  ab-er-rant-ly
ab-er-ra-tion

ab-er-ra-tion-al
a-bet
  a-bet-ted
  a-bet-ting
  a-bet-ment
  a-bet-tor
  a-bet-ter
a-bey-ance
ab-hor
  ab-horred
  ab-hor-ring
  ab-hor-rence
  ab-hor-er
ab-hor-rence
ab-hor-rent
  ab-hor-rent-ly
a-bide
  a-bid-er
  a-bi-ded
  a-bid-ing
  a-bid-ance
a-bid-ing
  a-bid-ing-ly
a-bil-i-ty
  a-bil-i-ties
ab-ject
  ab-ject-ly
  ab-ject-ness
  ab-jec-tion
ab-jure
  ab-jured
  ab-jur-ing
  ab-ju-ra-tion
  ab-jur-er
ab-late
  ab-lat-ed
  ab-lat-ing
  ab-la-tion
  ab-la-tive
  ab-la-tive-ly
ab-laut
a-blaze
a-ble
  a-bler
  a-blest
  a-bly
a-ble-bod-ied
a-bloom
ab-lu-tion
  ab-lu-tion-ar-y
ab-ne-gate
  ab-ne-gat-ed
  ab-ne-gat-ing
  ab-ne-ga-tor
  ab-ne-ga-tion
ab-nor-mal

ab-nor-mal-ly
ab-nor-mal-i-ty
ab-nor-mal-i-ties
a-board
a-bode
a-boil
a-bol-ish
  a-bol-ish-a-ble
  a-bol-ish-er
  a-bol-ish-ment
ab-o-li-tion
  ab-o-li-tion-ary
  ab-o-li-tion-ism
  ab-o-li-tion-ist
a-b-oma-sum
  a-b-oma-sal
a-bom-i-na-ble
  a-bom-i-na-bly
a-bom-i-nate
  a-bom-i-nat-ed
  a-bom-i-nat-ing
  a-bom-i-na-tion
  a-bom-i-na-tor
ab-o-rig-i-ne
  ab-o-rig-i-nal
  ab-o-rig-i-nal-ly
a-born-ing
a-bort
  a-bort-er
a-bor-ti-fa-cient
a-bor-tion
a-bor-tion-ist
a-bor-tive
  a-bor-tive-ness
  a-bor-tive-ly
a-bout-face
a-bove-board
ab-ra-ca-dab-ra
abrad-ant
a-brade
  a-brad-ed
  a-brad-ing
  a-brad-a-ble
  a-brad-er
a-bra-sion
a-bra-sive
  a-bra-sive-ness
  a-bra-sive-ly
ab-re-act
a-breast
a-bridge
  a-bridged
  a-bridg-ing
  a-bridg-er
  a-bridg-a-ble
  a-bridg-ment

a-bridge-ment
a-broach
a-broad
ab-ro-gate
  ab-ro-gat-ed
  ab-ro-gat-ing
  ab-ro-ga-tion
ab-rupt
  abrupt-ness
  abrupt-ly
ab-scess
  ab-scessed
ab-scis-sa
  ab-scis-sas
  ab-scis-sae
ab-scis-sion
ab-scond
  ab-scond-er
ab-sence
ab-sent
  ab-sent-ly
ab-sen-tee
  ab-sen-tee-ism
ab-sent-mind-ed
  ab-sent-mind-ed-ly
  ab-sent-mind-ed-ness
ab-sinthe
ab-so-lute
  ab-so-lute-ness
  ab-so-lute-ly
  ab-so-lu-tion
  ab-so-lut-ism
  ab-so-lut-ist
ab-solve
  ab-solved
  ab-solv-ing
  ab-solv-a-ble
  ab-solv-er
ab-sorb
  ab-sorb-er
  ab-sorb-a-bil-i-ty
  ab-sorb-a-ble
  ab-sorb-en-cy
  ab-sorb-ent
  ab-sorb-tion
  ab-sorb-tive
  ab-sorp-tiv-i-ty
ab-sorb-ing
  ab-sorb-ing-ly
ab-stain
  ab-stain-er
  ab-sten-tion
  ab-sti-nence
  ab-sti-nent
ab-ste-mi-ous
  ab-ste-mi-ous-ly

ab-stract
  ab-stract-ly
  ab-strac-tion
  ab-strac-tive
ab-stract-ed
  ab-stract-ed-ly
  ab-stract-ed-ness
ab-strac-tion-ism
  ab-strac-tion-ist
ab-struse
  ab-struse-ness
  ab-struse-ly
  ab-stru-si-ty
ab-surd
  ab-surd-ness
  ab-surd-i-ty
  ab-surd-i-ties
  ab-surd-ly
a-bub-ble
a-build-ing
a-bud-dance
a-bun-dant
  a-bun-dant-ly
a-buse
  a-bused
  a-bus-ing
  a-bus-er
  a-bus-a-ble
a-bu-sive
  a-bu-sive-ly
  a-bu-sive-ness
a-but
  a-but-ter
  a-but-ted
  a-but-ting
a-but-ment
a-but-tals
a-but-ting
a-buzz
a-bye
a-bysm
a-bys-mal
  a-bys-mal-ly
a-byss
  a-bys-sal
a-ca-cia
ac-a-deme
ac-a-dem-ic
  ac-a-dem-i-cal-ly
  ac-a-dem-i-cal
acad-e-mi-cian
a-cad-e-my
  a-cad-e-mies
a-can-thus
  a-can-thus-es
  a-can-thi

a cap-pel-la
ac-cede
  ac-ced-ed
  ac-ced-ing
ac-ce-le-ran-do
ac-cel-er-ate
  ac-cel-er-at-ed
  ac-cel-er-at-ing
  ac-cel-er-a-tive
  ac-cel-er-at-ing-ly
ac-cel-er-a-tion
ac-cel-er-a-tor
ac-cel-er-om-e-ter
ac-cent
  ac-cent-less
ac-cen-tu-al
  ac-cen-tu-al-ly
ac-cen-tu-ate
  ac-cen-tu-at-ed
  ac-cen-tu-at-ing
  ac-cen-tu-a-tion
ac-cept
  ac-cept-ing-ly
  ac-cept-ing-ness
  ac-cept-ance
  ac-cept-er
  ac-cept-or
ac-cept-a-ble
  ac-cept-a-bil-i-ty
  ac-cept-a-bly
  ac-cept-a-ble-ness
ac-cept-ed
  ac-cept-ed-ly
ac-cess
ac-ces-si-ble
  ac-ces-si-bil-i-ty
  ac-ces-si-ble-ness
  ac-ces-si-bly
ac-ces-sion
  ac-ces-sion-al
ac-ces-so-ry
  ac-ces-so-ri-ly
  ac-ces-so-ri-ness
ac-ci-dent
  ac-ci-dent-ly
  ac-ci-den-tal
  ac-ci-den-tal-ness
  ac-ci-den-tal-ly
ac-ci-dent--prone
ac-cip-i-ter
  ac-cip-i-trine
ac-claim
  ac-claim-er
ac-cla-ma-tion
ac-clam-a-to-ry
ac-cli-mate

4

ac-cli-mat-ed
ac-cli-mat-ing
ac-cli-ma-tion
ac-cli-ma-ti-za-tion
ac-cli-ma-tize
ac-cli-ma-tized
ac-cli-ma-tiz-er
ac-cli-ma-tiz-ing
ac-cli-ma-ti-za-tion
ac-cliv-i-ty
ac-cliv-i-ties
ac-co-lade
ac-com-mo-date
ac-com-mo-dat-ed
ac-com-mo-dat-ing
ac-com-mo-da-tive
ac-com-mo-dat-er
ac-com-mo-da-tion
ac-com-pa-ni-ment
ac-com-pa-nist
ac-com-pa-ny
ac-com-pa-nied
ac-com-pa-ny-ing
ac-com-pa-nies
ac-com-plice
ac-com-plish
ac-com-plish-a-ble
ac-com-plish-ment
ac-com-plish-er
ac-com-plished
ac-cord
ac-cord-ance
ac-cord-ing
ac-cord-ing-ly
ac-cor-dant
ac-cor-dant-ly
ac-cor-di-on
ac-cor-di-on-ist
ac-cost
ac-couche-ment
ac-cou-cheur
ac-count
ac-count-a-ble
ac-count-a-bil-i-ty
ac-count-a-bly
ac-count-a-ble-ness
ac-count-an-cy
ac-count-ant
ac-coun-tant-ship
ac-count-ing
ac-cou-tre-ment
ac-cred-it
ac-cred-i-table
ac-cred-i-ta-tion
ac-crete
ac-creting

ac-creted
ac-cre-tion
ac-cre-tive
ac-cre-tion-ary
ac-cru-al
ac-crue
ac-crued
ac-cru-ing
ac-cru-a-ble
ac-crue-ment
ac-cul-tur-ate
ac-cul-tur-ating
ac-cul-tur-ated
ac-cul-tur-a-tion
ac-cul-tur-a-tion-al
ac-cul-tur-a-tive
ac-cum-u-late
ac-cum-u-lat-ed
ac-cum-u-lat-ing
ac-cum-u-la-tion
ac-cu-mu-la-tive
ac-cu-mu-la-tive-ness
ac-cu-mu-la-tive-ly
ac-cum-u-la-tor
ac-cu-ra-cy
ac-cu-ra-cies
ac-cu-rate
ac-cu-rate-ly
ac-cu-rate-ness
ac-curs-ed
ac-curst
ac-curs-ed-ness
ac-curs-ed-ly
ac-cus-al
ac-cu-sa-tion
ac-cu-sa-tive
ac-cuse
ac-cus-er
ac-cus-ed
ac-cus-ing
ac-cu-sa-tion
ac-cu-sa-to-ry
ac-cus-ing-ly
ac-cus-tom
ac-cus-tom-a-tion
ac-cus-tomed
ac-cus-tomed-ness
ace-dia
a-cel-da-ma
a-cel-lu-lar
a-cen-tric
a-ceph-a-lous
a-ce-quia
a-cerb
a-cer-bi-ty
ac-er-o-la

ac-er-vate
ac-er-vate-ly
ac-er-va-tion
ac-e-tab-u-lar-ia
ac-e-tab-u-lum
ac-e-tab-u-lar
ac-et-al-de-hyde
ac-et-amide
ac-et-amin-o-phen
ac-et-an-i-lide
ac-e-tate
a-ce-tic
a-cet-i-fy
a-cet-i-fied
a-cet-i-fy-ing
a-ce-ti-fi-ca-tion
a-ce-ti-fi-er
ac-e-tone
ac-e-ton-ic
ac-e-to-phe-net-i-din
a-ce-tous
a-cet-y-late
a-cet-y-lat-ing
a-cet-y-lat-ed
a-cet-y-la-tion
a-cet-y-la-tive
a-ce-tyl-cho-line
a-ce-tyl-cho-lin-ic
a-cet-y-lene
a-cet-y-le-nic
ache
ached
ach-ing
ach-ing-ly
a-chene
a-chieve
a-chiev-ed
a-chiev-ing
a-chiev-a-ble
a-chiev-er
a-chieve-ment
a-chla-myd-e-ous
a-chlor-hy-dric
a-chon-drite
a-chon-drit-ic
a-chon-dro-pla-sia
a-chon-dro-plas-tic
ach-ro-mat-ic
ach-ro-ma-tic-i-ty
ach-ro-mat-i-cal-ly
ach-ro-ma-tize
a-cic-u-la
a-cic-u-late
a-cic-u-lar
ac-id
ac-id-ness

ac-id-ly
ac-id-ic
a-cid-i-fy
a-cid-i-fied
a-cid-i-fy-ing
a-cid-i-fi-ca-tion
a-cid-i-fi-er
a-cid-i-ty
ac-i-do-phile
ac-i-do-phil-ic
ac-i-do-sis
ac-i-dot-ic
a-cid-u-late
a-cid-u-lat-ed
a-cid-u-lat-ing
a-cid-u-la-tion
a-cid-u-lent
a-cid-u-lous
ac-i-nar
ac-i-nus
ac-i-nous
ac-knowl-edge
ac-knowl-edged
ac-knowl-edg-ing
ac-knowl-edge-a-ble
ac-knowl-edg-er
ac-knowl-edg-ment
ac-knowl-edge-ment
ac-me
ac-ne
ac-ned
ac-o-lyte
ac-o-nite
a-corn
a-cous-tic
a-cous-ti-cal
a-cous-ti-cal-ly
a-cous-tics
ac-quaint
ac-quaint-ance
ac-quaint-ance-ship
ac-qui-esce
ac-qui-esc-ed
ac-qui-esc-ing
ac-qui-es-cence
ac-qui-es-cent
ac-qui-es-cent-ly
ac-quire
ac-quired
ac-quir-ing
ac-quir-er
ac-quir-a-ble
ac-quire-ment
ac-qui-si-tion
ac-quit
ac-quit-ted

ac-quit-ting
ac-quit-tal
a-cre
a-cre-age
ac-rid
acrid-i-ty
ac-ri-mo-ni-ous
ac-ri-mo-ni-ous-ness
ac-ri-mo-ni-ous-ly
ac-ri-mo-ny
ac-ro-bat
ac-ro-bat-ic
ac-ro-nym
ac-ro-pho-bi-a
a-crop-o-lis
a-cros-tic
a-cros-ti-cal-ly
a-cryl-ic
ac-ry-lo-ni-trile
act-ing
ac-tin-i-a
ac-tin-i-an
ac-tin-ic
ac-tin-i-cal-ly
ac-tin-ism
ac-tin-i-um
ac-ti-nom-e-ter
ac-ti-nom-e-try
ac-ti-no-mor-phic
ac-ti-no-mor-phy
ac-ti-no-my-ces
ac-ti-no-my-ce-tal
ac-ti-no-my-co-sis
ac-ti-no-my-cot-ic
ac-ti-non
ac-ti-no-zo-an
ac-tion
ac-tion-a-ble
ac-tion-a-bly
ac-ti-vate
ac-ti-vat-ed
ac-ti-vat-ing
ac-ti-va-tion
ac-ti-va-tor
ac-tive
ac-tive-ly
ac-tive-ness
ac-tiv-ism
ac-tiv-ist
ac-tiv-i-ty
ac-tiv-i-ties
ac-tor
ac-tress
ac-tu-al
ac-tu-al-ly
ac-tu-al-i-ty

ac-tu-al-i-ties
ac-tu-al-ize
ac-tu-al-ized
ac-tu-al-iz-ing
ac-tu-al-i-za-tion
ac-tu-ar-y
ac-tu-ar-ies
ac-tu-ar-i-al
ac-tu-ate
ac-tu-at-ed
ac-tu-at-ing
ac-tu-a-tion
ac-tu-a-tor
a-cu-i-ty
a-cu-i-ties
a-cu-men
a-cu-mi-nate
ac-u-punc-ture
a-cute
a-cute-ly
a-cute-ness
a-cut-est
a-cut-er
a-cy-clic
ac-yl
ad-age
a-da-gio
ad-a-mant
ad-a-mant-ly
ad-a-man-tine
a-dapt
a-dapt-er
a-dapt-ed-ness
a-dapt-a-ble
a-dapt-a-bil-i-ty
ad-ap-ta-tion
ad-ap-ta-tion-al
ad-ap-ta-tion-al-ly
a-dap-tive
a-dap-tive-ly
a-d-ap-tiv-i-ty
add
add-a-ble
add-i-ble
ad-dax
ad-dax-es
ad-dend
ad-den-dum
ad-den-da
ad-der
ad-dict
ad-dic-tion
ad-dict-ed
ad-dic-tive
Ad-dis Ab-a-ba
Ad-di-son's dis-ease

6

ad-di-tion
ad-di-tion-al
ad-di-tion-al-ly
ad-di-tive
ad-di-tive-ly
ad-di-tiv-i-ty
ad-dle
ad-dress
ad-dress-er
ad-dress-ee
ad-dress-a-ble
ad-duce
ad-duc-ing
ad-duced
ad-duc-er
ad-duct
ad-duc-tion
ad-duc-tive
a-de-lan-ta-do
a-demp-tion
ad-e-nine
ad-e-ni-tis
ad-e-no-car-ci-no-ma
ad-e-no-hy-poph-y-sis
ad-e-noid
ad-e-noi-dal
ad-e-no-ma
aden-o-sine
a-dept
a-dept-ly
a-dept-ness
ad-e-qua-cy
ad-e-quate
ad-e-quate-ly
ad-e-quate-ness
ad-here
ad-hered
ad-her-ing
ad-her-ence
ad-her-ent
ad-her-ent-ly
ad-he-sion
ad-he-sion-al
ad-he-sive
ad-he-sive-ly
ad-he-sive-ness
ad hoc
ad ho-mi-nem
ad-i-a-bat-ic
a-dieu
ad in-fi-ni-tum
a-di-os
ad-i-pose
ad-i-pos-i-ty
ad-ja-cen-cy
ad-ja-cen-cies

ad-ja-cent
ad-ja-cent-ly
ad-jec-tive
ad-jec-ti-val
ad-join
ad-join-ing
ad-journ
ad-journ-ment
ad-judge
ad-judged
ad-judg-ing
ad-ju-di-cate
ad-ju-di-cat-ed
ad-ju-di-cat-ing
ad-ju-di-ca-tion
ad-ju-di-ca-tor
ad-junct
ad-junc-tive
ad-jure
ad-jured
ad-jur-ing
ad-ju-ra-tion
ad-ju-ra-to-ry
ad-jur-er
ad-just
ad-just-a-ble
ad-just-er
ad-jus-tor
ad-just-ment
ad-ju-tan-cy
ad-ju-tant
ad lib
ad libbed
ad lib-bing
ad-man
ad-men
ad-min-is-ter
ad-min-is-ter-ing
ad-min-is-tered
ad-min-is-trate
ad-min-is-trat-ing
ad-min-is-trated
ad-min-is-tra-tion
ad-min-is-tra-tive
ad-min-is-tra-tor
ad-min-is-tra-tive-ly
ad-min-is-tra-tion-al
ad-mi-ral
ad-mi-ral-ty
ad-mire
ad-mired
ad-mir-ing
ad-mi-ra-ble
ad-mi-ra-bly
ad-mi-ra-tion
ad-mi-rer

ad-mir-ing-ly
ad-mis-si-ble
ad-mis-si-bil-i-ty
ad-mis-sion
ad-mis-sive
ad-mit
ad-mit-ted
ad-mit-ting
ad-mit-ted-ly
ad-mit-tance
ad-mix
ad-mix-ture
ad-mon-ish
ad-mon-ish-er
ad-mo-ni-tion
ad-mon-i-to-ry
ad-mon-ish-ing-ly
ad-mon-ish-ment
a-do
a-do-be
ad-o-les-cence
ad-o-les-cent
ad-o-les-cent-ly
a-dopt
a-dopt-a-ble
a-dopt-er
a-dop-tion
a-dop-tive
a-dopt-a-bil-i-ty
a-dore
a-dored
a-dor-ing
a-dor-a-ble
ador-ing-ly
ad-o-ra-tion
a-dorn
a-dorn-ment
a-doze
ad-re-nal
ad-re-nal-ly
a-dren-a-line
a-drift
a-droit
a-droit-ly
a-droit-ness
ad-sorb
ad-sor-bent
ad-sorp-tion
ad-u-late
ad-u-lat-ed
ad-u-lat-ing
ad-u-la-tor
ad-u-la-to-ry
a-dult
a-dult-hood
a-dul-ter-ate

7

a-dul-ter-at-ed
a-dul-ter-at-ing
a-dul-ter-ant
a-dul-ter-a-tion
a-dul-ter-y
a-dul-ter-ies
a-dul-ter-er
a-dul-ter-ess
a-dul-ter-ous
ad-um-brate
ad-um-brat-ed
ad-um-brat-ing
ad va-lo-rem
ad-vance
ad-vanced
ad-vanc-ing
ad-vance-ment
ad-van-tage
ad-van-taged
ad-van-tag-ing
ad-van-ta-geous
ad-van-ta-geous-ly
ad-vent
ad-ven-ti-tious
ad-ven-tive
ad-ven-ture
ad-ven-tured
ad-ven-tur-ing
ad-ven-tur-er
ad-ven-tur-ess
ad-ven-tur-ous
ad-ven-ture-some
ad-verb
ad-ver-bi-al
ad-ver-sar-y
ad-ver-sar-ies
ad-verse
ad-verse-ly
ad-verse-ness
ad-ver-si-ty
ad-ver-si-ties
ad-vert
ad-vert-ence
ad-vert-ent
ad-ver-tise
ad-ver-tised
ad-ver-tis-ing
ad-ver-tis-er
ad-ver-tise-ment
ad-vice
ad-vise
ad-vised
ad-vis-ing
ad-vis-a-bil-i-ty
ad-vis-a-ble
ad-vis-a-bly

ad-vis-er
ad-vi-sor
ad-vis-ed-ly
ad-vise-ment
ad-vi-so-ry
ad-vo-ca-cy
ad-vo-ca-cies
ad-vo-cate
ad-vo-cat-ed
ad-vo-cat-ing
ad-vo-ca-tion
ae-gis
ae-on
aer-ate
aer-at-ed
aer-at-ing
aer-a-tion
aer-a-tor
aer-en-chy-ma
aer-i-al
aer-i-al-ly
aer-i-al-ist
aer-ie
aer-i-fy
aer-i-fi-ca-tion
aer-obe
aero-me-chan-ics
aero-naut-ics
aero-nau-ti-cal
aero-nau-tic
aero-pause
aer-o-plane
aer-o-sol
aero-sol-ize
aero-sol-iza-tion
aero-sol-iz-ing
aero-sol-ized
aer-o-space
aero-sphere
aero-stat
aero-stat-ics
aes-thete
aes-thet-ic
aes-thet-i-cal-ly
aes-thet-i-cal
afar
afeard
af-fa-ble
af-fa-bil-i-ty
af-fa-bly
af-fair
af-fect
af-fect-ing
af-fect-ing-ly
af-fec-tive
af-fec-ta-tion

af-fect-ed
af-fect-ed-ly
af-fect-ed-ness
af-fec-tion
af-fec-tion-ate
af-fec-tion-ate-ly
af-fec-tion-ate-ness
af-fer-ent
af-fer-ent-ly
af-fi-ance
af-fi-anced
af-fi-anc-ing
af-fi-da-vit
af-fil-i-ate
af-fil-i-at-ed
af-fil-i-at-ing
af-fin-i-ty
af-fin-i-ties
af-firm
af-firm-a-ble
af-firm-a-bly
af-fir-ma-tion
af-firm-a-tive
af-fix
af-fix-a-ble
af-fix-ment
af-fix-a-tion
af-fla-tus
af-flict
af-flic-tion
af-flu-ence
af-flu-ent
af-flu-ent-ly
af-fray
af-fri-cate
af-fric-a-tive
af-fri-ca-tion
af-front
af-ghan
afield
afire
aflame
af-la-tox-in
afloat
aflut-ter
afoot
afore
afore-men-tioned
afore-said
afore-thought
a for-ti-o-ri
afoul
afraid
afreet
afresh
af-ter

8

af-ter-ef-fect
af-ter-glow
af-ter--hours
af-ter-life
af-ter-most
af-ter-noon
af-ter-taste
af-ter-thought
af-ter-time
af-ter-ward
 af-ter-wards
again
against
agape
 aga-pe-ic
agar
ag-ate
ag-ate-ware
aga-ve
agaze
age
 aged
 ag-ing
 age-ing
 aged
 age-less
 age-long
agen-cy
 agen-cies
agen-da
 agen-da-less
agent
 agen-tial
ag-glom-er-ate
 ag-glom-er-at-ed
 ag-glom-er-at-ing
 ag-glom-er-a-tion
 ag-glom-er-a-tive
ag-glu-ti-nate
 ag-glu-ti-nat-ed
 ag-glu-tin-at-ing
 ag-glu-ti-na-tion
 ag-glu-ti-na-tive
ag-gran-dize
 ag-gran-dized
 ag-gran-diz-ing
 ag-gran-dize-ment
 ag-gran-diz-er
ag-gra-vate
 ag-gra-vat-ed
 ag-gra-vat-ing
 ag-gra-va-tion
ag-gre-gate
 ag-gre-gat-ed
 ag-gre-gat-ing
 ag-gre-ga-tion

ag-gre-ga-tive
ag-gress
 ag-gress-ive
 ag-gress-ive-ly
 ag-gress-ive-ness
 ag-gres-sor
 ag-gres-sion
ag-grieve
 ag-grieved
 ag-griev-ing
aghast
ag-ile
 ag-ile-ly
 agil-i-ty
agin-ner
agio
ag-i-tate
 ag-i-tat-ed
 ag-i-tat-ing
 ag-i-tat-ed-ly
 ag-i-ta-tion
 ag-i-ta-tor
 ag-i-ta-tion-al
agleam
aglow
agly-con
ag-nail
ag-nate
 ag-na-tion
 ag-nat-i-cal-ly
 ag-nat-ic
ag-nize
 ag-niz-ing
 ag-nized
ag-no-men
 ag-nom-i-na
ag-nos-tic
 ag-nos-ti-cism
agog
ag-o-nal
agon-ic
ag-o-nist
ag-o-nis-tic
 ag-o-nis-ti-cal-ly
 ag-o-nis-ti-cal
ag-o-nize
 ag-o-nized
 ag-o-niz-ing
 ag-o-niz-ing-ly
ag-o-ny
 ag-o-nies
ag-o-ra-pho-bia
 ag-o-ra-pho-bic
 ag-o-ra-pho-bi-ac
agrar-i-an
agrar-i-an-ism

agree
 agreed
 agree-ing
 agree-a-bil-i-ty
 agree-a-ble
 agree-a-ble-ness
 agree-a-bly
 agree-ment
ag-ri-busi-ness
ag-ri-cul-ture
 ag-ri-cul-tur-al
 ag-ri-cul-tur-ist
agron-o-my
 ag-ro-nom-ic
 ag-ro-nom-i-cal
 agron-o-mist
 ag-ro-nom-i-cal-ly
aground
ague
 agu-ish-ly
 agu-ish
aha
ahead
ahem
ahoy
aide-de-camp
ai-grette
ai-guille
ai-guil-lette
ai-ki-do
ail
 ail-ing
 ail-ment
ai-lan-thus
ai-ler-on
aim-less
air-less
 air-less-ness
air-borne
air-brush
air-con-di-tion
 air-con-di-tioned
 air con-di-tion-er
 air con-di-tion-ing
air-craft
air-field
air-mail
air-man
 air-men
air-plane
air-port
air pres-sure
air-sick-ness
air-space
air-wave
airy

9

air-i-er
air-i-est
air-i-ness
air-i-ly
aisle
ajar
akim-bo
akin
al-a-bas-ter
al-a-bas-trine
a la carte
alack
alac-ri-ty
alac-ri-tous
alarm
alarm-ing
alarm-ing-ly
alarm-ist
alarm-ism
alas
alate
alat-ed
al-ba-core
al-ba-cores
al-ba-tross
al-ba-tross-es
al-be-do
al-be-it
al-bi-no
al-bi-nos
al-bi-nism
al-bum
al-bu-men
al-bu-min
al-bu-mi-nous
al-che-my
al-che-mist
al-che-mize
al-che-miz-ing
al-che-mized
al-co-hol
al-co-hol-ic
al-co-hol-ism
al-co-hol-i-cal-ly
al-cove
al-de-hyde
al-de-hy-dic
al-der
al-der-man
al-der-man-ic
ale-a-to-ry
alee
alert
alert-ness
alert-ly
ale-wife

ale-wives
al-ex-an-drine
al-ex-an-drite
alex-ia
al-fal-fa
al-fil-a-ria
al-for-ja
al-fres-co
al-ga
al-gae
al-gal
al-goid
al-ge-bra
al-ge-bra-ic
al-ge-bra-ic-al
al-ge-bra-ic-al-ly
al-ge-bra-ist
al-go-rithm
al-go-rith-mic
ali-as
ali-as-es
al-i-bi
al-i-bi-ing
al-i-bied
alien
alien-a-ble
alien-a-bil-i-ty
alien-ate
alien-at-ed
alien-at-ing
alien-ator
alien-ist
alien-ism
ali-form
alight
alight-ed
alit
alight-ing
alight-ment
align
align-ment
alike
al-i-ment
al-i-men-tal
al-i-men-tal-ly
al-i-men-ta-tion
al-i-men-ta-ry
al-i-men-ta-ry ca-nal
al-i-mo-ny
al-i-mo-nies
aline-ment
al-i-quant
al-i-quot
alive
alive-ness
al-ka-li

al-ka-lies
al-ka-lis
al-ka-line
al-ka-lin-i-ty
al-ka-lize
al-ka-lized
al-ka-liz-ing
al-ka-li-za-tion
al-ka-loid
al-ka-loi-dal
all-Amer-i-can
all-a-round
al-lay
al-layed
al-lay-ing
al-lay-er
al-le-ga-tion
al-lege
al-leged
al-leg-ing
al-lege-a-ble
al-leg-ed-ly
al-le-giance
al-le-go-ry
al-le-go-ries
al-le-gor-ic
al-le-gor-i-cal
al-le-gor-i-cal-ly
al-le-gor-ist
al-le-gret-to
al-le-gro
al-le-gros
al-ler-gen
al-ler-gen-ic
al-ler-gy
al-ler-gies
al-ler-gic
al-ler-gist
al-le-vi-ate
al-le-vi-at-ed
al-le-vi-at-ing
al-le-vi-a-tion
al-le-vi-a-tor
al-le-vi-a-tive
al-le-vi-a-to-ry
al-ley
al-leys
al-li-ance
al-lied
al-li-ga-tor
all--in-clu-sive
all--in-cul-sive-ness
al-lit-er-ate
al-lit-er-at-ed
al-lit-er-at-ing
al-lit-er-a-tive

al-lit-er-a-tive-ly
al-lit-er-a-tive-ness
al-lit-er-a-tion
al-lo-ca-ble
al-lo-cate
  al-lo-cat-ed
  al-lo-cat-ing
  al-lo-ca-tion
al-lo-cu-tion
al-log-a-mous
  al-log-a-my
al-lo-ge-ne-ic
al-lo-graph
  al-lo-graph-ic
al-lom-er-ism
  al-lom-er-ous
al-lo-path
al-lop-a-thy
  al-lo-path-ic
  al-lo-path-i-cal-ly
al-lop-a-thist
al-lo-phone
  al-lo-phon-ic
al-lo-pu-ri-nol
al-lo-ste-ric
  al-lo-ste-ri-cal-ly
al-lot
  al-lot-ted
  al-lot-ting
  al-lot-ment
  al-lot-ta-ble
  al-lot-ter
al-lo-trope
  al-lo-trop-ic
  al-lo-trop-cal-ly
al-lot-ro-py
  al-lot-ro-pism
al-lo-trope
  al-lo-trop-ic
  al-lo-trop-i-cal-ly
al-low
  al-low-a-ble
  al-low-a-bly
  al-low-ed-ly
al-low-ance
  al-low-anced
  al-low-anc-ing
al-loy
all--pow-er-ful
all--pur-pose
all right
all-spice
al-lude
  al-lud-ed
  al-lud-ing
al-lure

al-lured
al-lur-ing
al-lure-ment
al-lur-er
al-lur-ing-ly
al-lu-sion
  al-lu-sive
  al-lu-sive-ly
  al-lu-sive-ness
al-lu-via
al-lu-vi-al
al-lu-vi-um
  al-lu-viums
al-ly
al-lies
al-lied
  al-ly-ing
al-ma mat-er
al-ma-nac
al-man-dine
al-man-dite
al-mighty
  al-mighti-ness
al-mond
al-mo-ner
al-most
alms-giv-er
  alms-giv-ing
alms-house
al-ni-co
al-oe
aloft
alo-ha
alone
  alone-ness
along
along-shore
along-side
aloof
  aloof-ly
  aloof-ness
al-o-pe-cia
al-paca
al-pen-glow
al-pen-stock
al-pes-trine
al-pha
al-pha-bet
  al-pha-bet-ic
  al-pha-bet-i-cal
  al-pha-bet-i-cal-ly
  al-pha-bet-i-za-tion
  al-pha-bet-ize
  al-pha-bet-ized
  al-pha-bet-iz-ing
al-ready

al-so
al-tar
al-ter
  al-ter-a-bil-ity
  al-ter-a-ble
  al-ter-ant
  al-ter-a-tion
  al-ter-a-tive
al-ter-cate
  al-ter-cat-ing
  al-ter-cat-ed
al-ter-ca-tion
al-ter e-go
al-ter-nate
  al-ter-nat-ed
  al-ter-nat-ing
  al-ter-nate-ly
  al-ter-na-tion
al-ter-na-tive
  al-ter-na-tive-ly
  al-ter-na-tive-ness
al-ter-na-tor
al-though
al-tim-e-ter
al-tim-e-try
al-ti-pla-no
al-ti-tude
al-to
al-to-cu-mu-lus
al-to-gether
al-to-re-lie-vo
al-to-stra-tus
al-tru-ism
  al-tru-is-tic
  al-tru-is-ti-cal-ly
  al-tru-ist
al-lu-mi-na
alu-mi-nate
alu-mi-nif-er-ous
al-u-min-i-um
alu-mi-nous
alu-mi-num
alum-na
  alum-nae
alum-nus
  alum-ni
al-ve-o-lar
  al-ve-o-lus
  al-ve-o-li
al-ways
alys-sum
amain
amal-gam
  amal-gam-a-ble
  amal-gam-ate
  amal-gam-at-ed

amal-gam-at-ing
amal-gam-a-tion
aman-u-en-ses
aman-u-en-ses
am-a-ryl-lis
amass
amass-ment
amass-er
am-a-teur
am-a-teur-ism
am-a-teur-ish
am-a-teur-ish-ly
am-a-teur-ish-ness
am-a-tive
am-a-tive-ness
am-a-tive-ly
am-a-to-ry
am-au-ro-sis
amaze
amazed
amaz-ing
amaz-ed-ly
amaz-ed-ness
amaze-ment
amaz-ing-ly
am-bas-sa-do-ri-al
am-ber
amber-gris
am-ber-jack
am-bi-dex-trous
am-bi-dex-trous-ly
am-bi-dex-ter-i-ty
am-bi-ance
am-bi-ence
am-bi-ent
am-big-u-ous
am-big-u-ous-ly
am-big-u-ous-ness
am-bi-gu-i-ty
am-bit
am-bi-tion
am-bi-tion-less
am-bi-tious
am-bi-tious-ly
am-bi-tious-ness
am-biv-a-lence
am-biv-a-lent
am-biv-a-lent-ly
am-bi-ver-sion
am-bi-ver-sive
am-bi-vert
am-ble
am-bled
am-bling
am-bler
am-blyg-o-nite

am-bly-opia
am-bo-cep-tor
am-bro-sia
am-bro-sial-ly
am-bro-sial
am-bro-type
ambs-ace
am-bu-la-crum
am-bu-lance
am-bu-la-to-ry
am-bu-lant
am-bu-late
am-bu-lat-ed
am-bu-lat-ing
am-bu-la-tion
am-bus-cade
am-bus-cad-ed
am-bus-cad-ing
am-bus-cad-er
am-bush
am-bush-ment
am-bush-er
ameba
amel-io-rate
amel-io-rat-ed
amel-io-rat-ing
amel-io-ra-ble
amel-io-ra-tion
amel-ior-a-tive
amel-io-ra-tor
amen
ame-na-ble
ame-na-bil-i-ty
ame-na-ble-ness
ame-na-bly
amend
amend-a-ble
amend-er
amend-ment
amends
amend-i-ty
amend-i-ties
amerce
amerced
amerc-ing
amerce-a-ble
amerce-ment
amerce-er
Amer-i-ca
Amer-i-can
Amer-i-cana
Amer-i-can-ism
am-e-thyst
am-e-thys-tine
am-e-tro-pia
ami-a-ble

ami-a-bil-i-ty
ami-a-bly
ami-a-ble-ness
ami-ca-ble
am-i-ca-bil-i-ty
am-i-ca-bly
am-i-ca-ble-ness
am-ice
amid
amidst
am-ide
amid-ic
amid-ships
ami-go
amine
amino acid
ami-no-ac-id-uria
ami-no-py-rine
amir
amiss
am-i-to-sis
am-i-tot-ic
am-i-tot-i-cal-ly
am-i-ty
am-me-ter
am-mi-no
am-mon-nia
am-mon-ic
am-mo-ni-ac
am-mo-ni-um
am-mo-ni-un chlo-ride
am-mu-ni-tion
am-ne-sia
am-ne-sic
am-nes-tic
am-nes-ty
am-ni-on
am-ni-ons
am-ni-on-ic
am-nia
am-ni-ot-ic
a-moe-ba
a-moe-bae
a-moe-bas
a-moe-bic
a-moe-ban
a-moe-boid
a-mok
a-mong
a-mongst
a-mon-til-la-do
a-mor-al
a-mo-ral-i-ty
a-mor-al-ism
a-mor-al-ly
amo-ret-to

am-or-ist
am-o-rous
  am-o-rous-ly
  am-o-rous-ness
a-mor-phism
a-mor-phous
  a-mor-phous-ness
  a-mor-phous-ly
am-or-tize
  am-or-tized
  am-or-tiz-ing
  am-or-ti-za-tion
  am-or-tiz-able
a-mount
a-mour
am-per-age
am-pere
am-per-sand
am-phet-a-mine
am-phib-ia
am-phib-i-an
am-phib-i-ous
  am-phib-i-ous-ly
  am-phib-i-ous-ness
am-phi-the-a-ter
  am-phi-the-at-ric
am-pho-ra
  am-phe-rae
  am-phe-ras
am-ple
  am-pler
  am-plest
  am-ple-ness
  am-ply
am-pli-fy
  am-pli-fied
  am-pli-fy-ing
  am-pli-fi-ca-tion
  am-pli-fi-er
am-pli-tude
am-pul
am-pu-tate
  am-pu-tat-ed
  am-pu-tat-ing
  am-pu-ta-tion
  am-pu-tee
a-muck
am-u-let
a-muse
  a-mused
  a-mus-ing
  a-muse-ment
  a-mus-ed
am-yl-ase
a-nach-ro-nism
  a-nach-ro-nis-tik

a-nach-ro-nis-ti-cal-ly
a-nach-ro-nous
an-a-con-da
an-aer-obe
an-aes-the-sia
an-aes-thet-ic
an-a-gram
  an-a-gram-mat-ic
  an-a-gram-mat-i-cal
  ana-gram-ma-tize
  ana-gram-ma-tized
  ana-gram-ma-tiz-ing
a-nal
an-a-lects
an-al-ge-sic
al-a-log
  an-a-log-i-cal
  an-a-log-i-cal-ly
a-nal-o-gize
  a-nal-o-gized
  a-nal-o-giz-ing
a-nal-o-gy
  a-nal-o-gies
  a-nal-o-gous
a-nal-y-sis
  a-nal-y-ses
an-a-lyst
  an-a-lyt-ic
  an-a-lyt-ics
an-a-lyze
  an-a-lyzed
  an-a-lyz-ing
  an-a-lyz-a-ble
  an-a-ly-za-tion
  an-a-lyz-er
an-a-pest
an-a-pes-tic
an-ar-chism
an-ar-chis-tic
an-ar-chy
  an-ar-chic
  an-ar-chi-cal
a-nath-e-ma
  a-nath-e-mas
  a-nath-e-ma-tize
  a-nath-e-ma-tized
  a-nath-e-ma-tiz-ing
  a-nath-e-mat-iz-a-tion
a-nat-o-mize
  a-nat-o-mized
  a-nat-o-mizing
  a-nat-o-mi-za-tion
a-nat-o-my
  a-nat-o-mies
  an-a-tom-i-cal
  an-a-tom-i-cal-ly

a-nat-o-mist
an-ces-tor
  an-ces-tral
  an-ces-tress
  an-ces-try
an-chor
  an-chor-age
an-cho-ress
an-cho-rite
an-cho-vy
an-cient
  an-cient-ly
  an-cient-ness
an-cil-lary
an-dan-te
and-i-ron
an-dro-gen
  an-drog-y-nous
  an-drog-y-ny
an-dros-ter-one
an-ec-dote
  an-ec-dot-age
  an-ec-do-tal
  an-ec-dot-ist
a-ne-mia
  a-ne-mic
an-e-mom-e-ter
an-e-mom-e-try
a-nem-o-ne
an-er-oid
an-es-the-sia
  an-es-thet-ic
  an-es-the-tize
  an-es-the-tized
  an-es-the-tiz-ing
an-eu-rysm
  an-eu-rism
  an-eu-rys-mal
a-new
an-ga-ry
an-gel
  an-gel-ic
  an-gel-i-cal
  an-gel-i-cal-ly
an-gel-i-ca
an-ger
an-gi-na
  an-gi-na pec-to-ris
an-gi-o-sperm
  an-gi-o-sper-mous
an-gle
an-gler
an-gle-worm
an-gling
an-go-ra
an-gos-tu-ra bark

an-gry
an-gri-ly
an-gri-ness
ang-strom u-nit
an-guish
an-gu-lar
an-gu-lar-i-ty
an-gu-lar-ly
an-gu-lar-ness
an-hy-dride
an-hy-drous
an-i-line
an-i-mad-vert
an-i-mad-ver-sion
an-i-mal
an-i-mal-cule
an-i-mal-cu-lar
an-i-mal-ism
an-i-mal-i-ty
an-i-mal-ize
an-i-mal-ized
an-i-mal-iz-ing
an-i-mate
an-i-mat-ed
an-i-mat-ing
an-i-ma-tion
a-ni-ma-to
an-i-mism
an-i-mis-tic
an-i-mos-i-ty
an-i-mus
an-i-on
an-ise
an-i-seed
an-i-sette
an-kle
an-kle-bone
an-klet
an-ky-lose
an-ky-losed
an-ky-los-ing
an-ky-lo-sis
an-ky-lot-ic
an-nal-ist
an-nal-is-tic
an-nals
an-neal
an-ne-lid
an-nel-i-dan
an-nex
an-nex-a-tion
an-nex-a-tion-ist
an-ni-hi-late
an-ni-hi-lat-ed
an-ni-hi-lat-ing
an-ni-hi-la-tion

an-ni-hi-la-tor
an-ni-ver-sa-ry
an-ni-ver-sa-ries
an-no Dom-i-ni
an-no-tate
an-no-tat-ed
an-no-tat-ing
an-no-ta-tion
an-no-ta-tor
an-nounce
an-nounced
an-nounc-ing
an-nounce-ment
an-nounc-er
an-noy
an-noy-ance
an-noy-er
an-nu-al
an-nu-i-ty
an-nu-i-tant
an-nul
an-nulled
an-nul-ling
an-nul-ment
an-nu-lar
an-nu-lar-i-ty
an-nu-lar-ly
an-nu-late
an-nu-let
an-nu-lus
an-nu-lus-es
an-nun-ci-a-tion
an-nun-ci-ate
an-nun-ci-at-ed
an-nun-ci-at-ing
an-nun-ci-a-tor
an-ode
an-od-ic
an-o-dyne
a-noint
a-noint-er
a-noint-ment
a-nom-a-ly
a-nom-a-lism
a-nom-a-lous
a-nom-a-lous-ly
a-nom-a-lous-ness
an-o-mie
an-o-my
an-o-nym
a-non-y-mous
a-non-y-nym-i-ty
a-non-y-mous-ly
a-non-y-mous-ness
a-noph-e-les
an-oth-er

an-ox-ia
an-ser-ine
an-swer
an-swer-a-ble
ant-ac-id
an-tag-o-nist
an-tag-o-nism
an-tag-o-nis-tic
an-tag-o-nis-ti-cal-ly
an-tag-o-nize
an-tag-o-nized
an-tag-o-niz-ing
ant-arc-tic
an-te
an-ted
an-te-ing
ant-eat-er
an-te--bel-lum
an-te-ced-ence
an-te-ced-ent
an-te-cede
an-te-ced-ed
an-te-ced-ing
an-te-ce-dent-ly
an-te-cham-ber
an-te-choir
an-te-date
an-te-dat-ed
an-te-dat-ing
an-te-di-lu-vi-an
an-te-lope
an-te-lopes
an-te me-rid-i-em
an-ten-na
an-ten-nae
an-ten-nas
an-te-pe-nult
an-te-pe-nul-ti-mate
an-te-ri-or
an-te-room
an-them
an-ther
an-ther-id-i-um
an-thol-o-gy
an-thol-o-gies
an-thol-o-gist
an-thol-o-gize
an-thol-o-giz-ing
an-tho-zo-an
an-thra-cene
an-thra-cite
an-thra-cit-ic
an-thrax
an-thra-ces
an-thro-po-cen-tric
an-thro-po-gen-e-sis

14

an-thro-poid
an-thro-pol-o-gy
  an-thro-po-log-ic
  an-thro-po-log-i-cal
  an-thro-pol-o-gist
an-thr-pom-e-try
  an-thro-po-met-ric
an-ti-air-craft
an-ti-bi-o-sis
an-ti-bi-ot-ic
  an-ti-bod-y
  an-ti-bod-ies
an-tic
an-ti-christ
an-tic-i-pate
  an-tic-i-pat-ed
  an-tic-i-pat-ing
  an-tic-i-pa-tion
  an-tic-i-pa-tive
  an-tic-i-pa-to-ry
an-ti-cler-i-cal
  an-ti-cler-i-cal-ism
an-ti-cli-max
  an-ti-cli-mac-tic
an-ti-cli-nal
  an-ti-cline
an-ti-cy-clone
an-ti-dote
  an-ti-dot-al
an-ti-fed-er-al
  an-ti-fed-er-al-ist
  an-ti-fed-er-al-ism
an-ti-freeze
an-ti-gen
an-ti-he-ro
an-ti-his-ta-mine
an-ti-log-a-rithm
an-ti-ma-cas-sar
an-ti-mis-sile
an-ti-mo-ny
an-ti-pas-to
an-tip-a-thy
an-ti-phon
  an-tiph-o-nal
an-ti-pode
an-ti-quar-i-an
  an-ti-quar-y
  an-ti-quar-ies
an-ti-quate
  an-ti-quat-ed
  an-ti-quat-ing
  an-ti-quat-ed
an-tique
  an-tiqed
  an-tiq-uing
  an-tique-ly

an-tique-ness
an-tiq-ui-ty
  an-tiq-ui-ties
an-ti-Sem-i-tism
an-ti-sep-sis
an-ti-sep-tic
an-ti-se-rum
an-ti-slav-er-y
an-ti-so-cial
an-tith-e-sis
  an-tith-e-ses
an-ti-thet-i-cal
an-ti-tox-in
  an-ti-tox-in
an-ti-trust
ant-ler
ant-ler-ed
an-to-nym
an-trum
an-tra
a-nus
an-vil
anx-i-e-ty
  anx-i-e-ties
anx-ious
  anx-ious-ness
an-y
an-y-bod-y
  an-y-bod-ies
an-y-how
an-y-more
an-y-one
an-y-place
an-y-thing
an-y-way
an-y-where
an-y-wise
a-or-ta
  a-or-tas
  a-or-tae
  a-or-tal
  a-or-tic
a-pace
a-pache
a-part
a-part-heid
a-part-ment
ap-a-thy
  ap-a-thet-ic
  ap-a-thet-i-cal-ly
ape
a-per-ri-tif
ap-er-ture
a-pex
  a-pex-es
  a-pi-ces

ap-i-cal
a-pha-sia
a-phe-li-on
  a-phe-lia
a-phid
a-phis
a-phi-des
aph-o-rism
  aph-o-rist
aph-ro-dis-i-ac
a-pi-an
a-pi-ar-i-an
a-pi-a-rist
a-pi-ary
  a-pi-ar-ies
a-pi-cul-ture
  a-pi-cul-tur-al
  a-pi-cul-tur-ist
a-piece
ap-ish
  ap-ish-ly
  ap-ish-ness
a-plomb
a-poc-a-lypse
  a-poc-a-lyp-tic
a-poc-o-pe
a-poc-ry-phal
ap-o-gee
a-po-lit-i-cal
a-pol-o-get-ics
  a-pol-o-gist
a-pol-o-gize
  a-pol-o-gized
  a-pol-o-giz-ing
  a-pol-o-gy
  a-pol-o-gies
  a-pol-o-get-ic
  a-pol-o-get-i-cal
ap-o-plec-tic
ap-o-plex-y
a-port
a-pos-ta-sy
  a-pos-ta-sies
a-pos-tate
  a-pos-ta-tize
  a-pos-ta-tized
  a-pos-to-tiz-ing
a pos-te-ri-o-ri
a-pos-tle
  a-pos-tle-ship
a-pos-to-late
ap-os-tol-ic
  ap-os-tol-i-cal
a-pos-tro-phe
a-poth-e-cary
  a-poth-e-car-ies

ap-o-thegm
  ap-o-phthegm
  ap-o-theg-mat-ic
a-poth-e-o-sis
  a-poth-e-o-ses
  a-poth-e-o-size
  a-poth-e-o-sized
  a-poth-e-o-siz-ing
ap-pall
  ap-palled
  ap-pal-ling
  ap-pal-ling-ly
ap-pa-rat-us
  ap-pa-rat-us-es
ap-par-el
ap-par-ent
ap-pa-ri-tion
  ap-pa-ri-tion-al
ap-peal
  ap-peal-a-ble
  ap-peal-er
  ap-peal-ing-ly
ap-pear
  ap-pear-ance
ap-pease
  ap-peased
  ap-peasing
  ap-pease-ment
  ap-peas-a-ble
  ap-peas-er
ap-pel-lant
  ap-pel-late
  ap-pel-la-tion
  ap-pel-la-tive
ap-pend
  ap-pen-dage
  ap-pend-ant
ap-pen-dec-to-my
ap-pen-di-ci-tis
ap-pen-dix
  ap-pen-dix-es
  ap-pen-di-ces
ap-per-cep-tion
  ap-per-cep-tive
ap-per-tain
ap-pe-tite
ap-pe-tiz-er
  ap-pe-tiz-ing
ap-plaud
  ap-plause
ap-ple
ap-ple-jack
ap-pli-ance
ap-pli-ca-ble
  ap-pli-ca-bil-i-ty
  ap-pli-ca-ble-ness

ap-pli-cant
ap-pli-ca-tion
ap-pli-ca-tive
ap-pli-ca-to-ry
ap-pli-ca-tor
ap-plied
ap-ply
  ap-ply-ing
ap-point
  ap-point-a-ble
  ap-point-ee
  ap-point-er
  ap-point-ment
ap-por-tion
  ap-por-tion-ment
ap-pose
  ap-posed
  ap-pos-ing
ap-po-site
  ap-po-si-tion
  ap-po-si-tion-al
ap-pos-i-tive
ap-praise
  ap-prais-al
  ap-praised
  ap-praiser
  ap-prais-ing
ap-pre-ci-a-ble
  ap-pre-ci-a-bly
ap-pre-ci-ate
  ap-pre-ci-at-ed
  ap-pre-ci-at-ing
  ap-pre-ci-a-tion
  ap-pre-ci-a-tive
ap-pre-hend
  ap-pre-hen-si-ble
  ap-pre-hen-sion
  ap-pre-hen-sive
ap-pren-tice
  ap-pren-tic-ed
  ap-pren-tic-ing
  ap-pre-tice-ship
ap-prise
  ap-prised
  ap-pris-ing
ap-prize
ap-proach
  ap-proach-a-bil-i-ty
  ap-proach-a-ble
ap-pro-ba-tion
  ap-pro-ba-tive
  ap-pro-ba-to-ry
ap-pro-pri-ate
  ap-pro-pri-at-ed
  ap-pro-pri-at-ing
  ap-pro-pri-ate-ly

ap-pro-pri-a-tor
ap-pro-pri-a-tion
ap-pro-pri-a-tive
ap-prox-i-mate
  ap-prox-i-mate-ly
  ap-prox-i-ma-tion
ap-pur-te-nance
  ap-pur-te-nant
ap-ri-cot
a-pri-o-ri
a-pron
ap-ro-pos
apt
  apt-ly
  apt-ness
ap-ter-ous
ap-ti-tude
aq-ua
  aq-uas
  aq-uae
a-qua-cul-ture
aq-ua-ma-rine
aq-ua-naut
aq-ua-plane
aquar-ia
aquar-i-um
  aquar-i-ums
a-quat-ic
aq-ua-tint
aq-ue-duct
a-que-ous
aq-ui-line
ar-a-besque
ar-a-ble
a-rach-nid
  a-rach-ni-dan
ar-ba-lest
  ar-ba-lest-er
  ar-ba-list
ar-bi-ter
  ar-bi-tral
ar-bit-ra-ment
ar-bi-trar-y
  ar-bi-trar-i-ly
  ar-bi-trar-i-ness
ar-bi-trate
  ar-bi-trat-ed
  ar-bi-trat-ing
  ar-bi-tra-ble
  ar-bi-tra-tor
  ar-bi-tra-tion
ar-bor
ar-bo-re-al
ar-bo-res-cent
ar-bo-re-ta
  ar-bo-re-tum

ar-bo-re-tums
ar-bor-vi-tae
ar-bu-tus
arc
  arced
  arc-ing
ar-cade
ar-cane
arch
  arch-ly
  arch-ness
ar-cha-ic
ar-cha-ism
ar-cha-ist
ar-cha-is-tic
arch-an-gel
arch-bish-op
  arch-bish-op-ric
arch-dea-con
arch-di-o-cese
  arch-di-oc-e-san
arch-du-cal
arch-duch-ess
arch-duch-y
  arch-duch-ies
arch-duke
arch-en-e-my
  arch-en-e-mies
arch-er
  ar-cher-y
ar-che-type
  ar-che-typ-al
  ar-che-typ-i-cal
arch-fiend
ar-chi-e-pis-co-pal
  ar-chi-e-pis-co-pate
ar-chi-pel-a-goes
  ar-chi-pel-a-gos
ar-chi-tect
ar-chi-tec-ton-ic
ar-chi-tec-ture
ar-chi-trave
ar-chive
  ar-chi-val
  ar-chi-vist
ar-chon
arch-priest
arch-way
arc-tic
arc-tic cir-cle
ar-dent
  ar-dent-ly
ar-dor
ar-du-ous
  ar-du-ous-ly
  ar-du-ous-ness

ar-e-a
  ar-e-al
ar-e-a-way
a-re-na
a-re-o-la
  a-re-o-lae
  a-re-o-las
ar-gent
ar-gen-tine
ar-gil
ar-gon
ar-go-sy
  ar-go-sies
ar-got
  ar-got-ic
ar-gue
  ar-gued
  ar-gu-ing
  ar-gu-a-ble
  ar-gu-er
  ar-gu-ment
  ar-gu-men-ta-tion
  ar-gu-men-ta-tive
ar-gyle
  ar-gyll
a-ri-a
ar-id
  a-rid-i-ty
a-right
a-rise
  a-rose
  a-ris-en
  a-ris-ing
ar-is-toc-ra-cy
  ar-is-toc-ra-cies
  aris-to-crat
  aris-to-crat-ic
a-rith-me-tic
  a-rith-met-i-cal
  a-rith-met-i-cal-ly
  a-rith-me-ti-cian
ar-ma-da
ar-ma-dil-lo
ar-ma-ment
ar-ma-ture
ar-mi-stice
ar-moire
ar-mor
ar-mor-er
ar-mor-y
  ar-mor-ies
arm-pit
ar-my
  ar-mies
ar-ni-ca
a-ro-ma

ar-o-mat-ic
  ar-o-mat-i-cal
a-round
a-rouse
  a-roused
  a-rous-ing
ar-peg-gi-o
  ar-peg-gi-os
ar-raign
  ar-raign-ment
ar-range
  ar-ranged
  ar-rang-er
  ar-rang-ing
  ar-range-ment
ar-rant
  ar-rant-ly
ar-ras
ar-ray
ar-rear
ar-rest
  ar-rest-er
  ar-rest-or
ar-ri-val
ar-rive
  ar-rived
  ar-riv-ing
ar-ro-gant
  ar-ro-gat-ed
  ar-ro-gat-ing
  ar-ro-ga-tion
ar-row
ar-row-head
ar-row-root
ar-roy-o
  ar-roy-os
ar-se-nal
ar-se-nate
ar-se-nic
ar-son
  ar-son-ist
ar-te-ri-al
ar-te-ri-o-scle-ro-sis
ar-ter-y
  ar-ter-ies
ar-te-sian well
art-ful
  art-ful-ly
  art-ful-ness
ar-thri-tis
  ar-thrit-ic
ar-thro-pod
  ar-throp-o-dal
  ar-throp-o-dous
ar-ti-choke
ar-ti-cle

ar-tic-u-lar
ar-tic-u-late
  ar-tic-u-lat-ed
  ar-tic-u-lat-ing
  ar-tic-u-late-ly
  ar-tic-u-late-ness
  ar-tic-u-lar-tor
  ar-tic-u-la-tion
  ar-tic-u-la-to-ry
ar-te-fact
  ar-ti-fact
ar-ti-fice
  ar-tif-i-cer
ar-ti-fi-cial
  ar-ti-fi-ci-al-i-ty
  ar-ti-fi-cial-ly
  ar-ti-fi-cial-ness
ar-til-ler-y
  ar-til-ler-ist
ar-ti-san
art-ist
ar-tiste
  ar-tis-tic
  ar-tis-ti-cal-ly
art-ist-ry
art-less
  art-less-ly
  art-less-ness
art-y
  ar-ti-ness
as-bes-tos
  as-bes-tus
as-cend
  as-cend-ance
  as-cend-ence
  as-cend-an-cy
  as-cend-en-cy
as-cend-ant
  as-cend-ent
as-cen-sion
as-cent
as-cer-tain
  as-cer-tain-a-ble
  as-cer-tain-ment
as-cet-ic
  as-cet-is-al
  as-cet-i-cism
as-cot
as-cribe
  as-cribed
  as-crib-ing
  as-crib-a-ble
a-sep-sis
a-sep-tic
a-sex-u-al
  a-sex-u-al-i-ty

a-sex-u-al-ly
a-shamed
  a-sham-ed-ly
ash-en
ash-lar
  ash-ler
a-shore
ash-y
a-side
as-i-nine
a-skance
a-skew
a-slant
a-sleep
a-slope
a-so-cial
as-par-a-gus
as-pect
as-pen
as-per-i-ty
as-perse
  as-persed
  as-pers-ing
as-per-sion
as-phalt
  as-phal-tic
as-pho-del
as-phyx-ia
  as-phyx-i-ate
  as-phyx-i-at-ed
  as-phyx-i-at-ing
  as-phyx-i-a-tion
as-pic
as-pi-dis-tra
as-pir-ant
as-pi-rate
  as-pi-rat-ed
  as-pi-rat-ing
  as-pi-ra-tion
  as-pi-ra-tor
as-pire
  as-pired
  as-pir-ing
  as-pir-er
as-pi-rin
as-sail
  as-sail-a-ble
  as-sail-ant
as-sas-sin
as-sas-si-nate
  as-sas-si-nat-ed
  as-sas-si-na-tion
  as-sas-si-na-tor
as-sault
as-say
  as-say-er

as-sem-blage
as-sem-ble
  as-sem-bled
  as-sem-bling
  as-sem-bler
as-sem-bly
  as-sem-blies
as-sem-bly-man
  as-sem-bly-men
as-sent
  as-sent-er
as-sert
  as-sert-er
  as-ser-tion
as-ser-tive
  as-ser-tive-ly
  as-ser-tive-ness
as-sess
  as-sess-a-ble
  as-sess-ment
  as-sess-or
as-set
as-si-du-i-ty
as-sid-u-ous
  as-sid-u-ous-ly
  as-sid-u-ous-ness
as-sign
  as-sign-a-bil-i-ty
  as-sign-a-ble
  as-sign-a-bly
as-sig-na-tion
as-sign-ee
  as-sign-ment
as-sist
  as-sist-ance
as-sis-tant
as-size
as-so-ci-ate
  as-so-ci-at-ed
  as-so-ci-at-ing
  as-so-ci-a-tion
  as-so-ci-a-tive
as-so-nance
as-sort
  as-sor-ted
  as-sort-ment
as-suage
  as-suaged
  as-suag-ing
  as-suage-ment
as-sume
  as-sumed
  as-sum-ing
  as-sump-tion
as-sur-ance
as-sure

as-sured
as-sur-ing
as-sur-er
as-sur-ed-ly
as-ter
as-ter-isk
a-stern
as-ter-oid
as-ter-oi-dal
asth-ma
asth-mat-ic
a-stig-ma-tism
as-tig-mat-ic
a-stir
as-ton-ish
as-ton-ish-ing
as-ton-ish-ing-ly
as-ton-ish-ment
as-tound
as-tound-ing
a-strad-dle
as-tra-khan
as-tral
a-stray
a-stride
as-trin-gent
as-trin-gen-cy
as-tro-dome
as-tro-labe
as-trol-o-gy
as-trol-o-ger
as-tro-log-ic
as-tro-log-i-cal
as-tro-naut
as-tro-nau-tics
as-tro-nau-ti-cal
as-tro-nom-ic
as-tro-nom-i-cal-ly
as-tron-o-my
as-tron-o-mer
as-tro-phys-ics
as-tro-phys-i-cist
as-tute
as-tute-ly
as-tute-ness
a-sun-der
a-sy-lum
a-sym-me-try
asym-met-ric
asym-met-ri-cal
asym-met-ri-cal-ly
at-a-vism
at-a-vist
at-a-vis-tic
a-tax-ia
a-tax-ic

at-el-ier
ath-er-o-scle-ro-sis
a-thirst
ath-lete
ath-let-ic
ath-let-ics
a-thwart
a-tilt
at-las
at-las-es
at-mos-phere
at-oll
at-om
atom-ic
atom-i-cal
atom-i-cal-ly
ato-nal-i-ty
ato-nal
ato-nal-ly
a-tone
a-toned
a-ton-ing
a-tone-ment
a-ton-er
a-top
a-tri-um
a-tro-cious
a-tro-cious-ly
a-tro-cious-ness
a-troc-i-y
a-troc-i-ties
at-ro-phy
at-ro-phies
at-ro-phied
at-ro-pine
at-tach
at-tach-a-ble
at-tach-ment
at-tack
at-tain
at-tain-a-ble
at-tain-a-bil-i-ty
at-tain-a-ble-ness
at-tain-ment
at-tain-der
at-taint
at-tar
at-tempt
at-tempt-a-ble
at-tend
at-tend-ance
at-tend-ant
at-ten-tion
at-ten-tive
at-ten-u-ate
at-ten-u-at-ed

at-ten-u-at-ing
at-ten-u-a-tion
at-test
at-tes-ta-tion
at-tic
at-tire
at-tired
at-tir-ing
at-ti-tude
at-ti-tu-di-nize
at-ti-tu-di-nized
at-ti-tu-di-niz-ing
at-tor-ney
at-tract
at-tract-a-ble
at-trac-tive
at-tract-or
at-trac-tion
at-tri-bute
at-tri-but-ed
at-tri-but-ing
at-tri-but-a-ble
at-tri-bu-tion
at-trib-u-tive
at-tri-tion
at-tune
at-tuned
at-tun-ing
a-typ-i-cal
a-typ-ic
a-typ-i-cal-ly
au-burn
au cou-rant
auc-tion
auc-tion-eer
au-da-cious
au-da-cious-ness
au-dac-i-ty
au-di-ble
au-di-ble-ness
au-di-bly
au-di-ence
au-di-o
au-di-o-vis-u-al
au-dit
au-di-tion
au-dit-or
au-di-to-rium
au-di-to-ry
au-ger
aug-ment
aug-ment-a-ble
aug-ment-er
aug-men-ta-tion
aug-ment-a-tive
au-grat-in

au-gur
  au-gu-ry
  au-gu-ries
au-gust
  au-gust-ly
  au-gust-ness
auk
auld lang syne
au na-tu-rel
aunt
au-ra
  au-ras
  au-rae
au-ral
  au-ral-ly
au-re-ate
au-re-ole
au-re-voir
au-ri-cle
au-ric-u-lar
au-rif-er-ous
au-ro-ra
au-ro-ra bor-e-al-is
aus-cul-tate
  aus-cul-tat-ed
  aus-cul-tat-ing
  aus-cul-ta-tion
aus-tere
  aus-ter-i-ty
  aus-ter-i-ties
aus-tral
au-then-tic
  au-then-ti-cat-ed
  au-then-ti-cat-ing
  au-then-ti-ca-tion
  au-then-ti-ca-tor
au-thor
au-thor-i-tar-i-an
  au-thor-i-tar-i-an-ism
  au-thor-i-ta-tive
au-thor-i-ty
  au-thor-i-ties
au-thor-ize
  au-thor-ized
  au-thor-iz-ing
  au-thor-i-za-tion
au-thor-ship
au-to
au-to-bi-og-ra-phy
  au-to-bi-og-ra-phies
  au-to-bi-og-ra-pher
au-toc-ra-cy
  au-toc-ra-cies
au-to-crat
  au-to-crat-ic
  au-to-crat-i-cal

au-to-crat-i-cal-ly
au-toc-ra-cy
  au-toc-ra-cies
au-to-graph
au-to-mat
au-to-mat-ic
au-to-ma-tion
au-to-mate
  au-to-mat-ed
  au-to-mat-ing
au-tom-a-tism
au-tom-a-ton
  au-tom-a-tons
  au-tom-a-ta
au-to-mo-bile
au-to-mo-tive
au-to-nom-ic
  au-to-nom-i-cal-ly
au-ton-o-mous
  au-ton-o-mous-ly
au-ton-o-my
  au-ton-o-mies
  au-ton-o-mist
au-top-sy
au-to-sug-ges-tion
au-tumn
  au-tum-nal
aux-il-ia-ry
  aux-il-ia-ries
a-vail
  a-vail-a-bil-i-ty
  a-vail-a-ble-ness
  a-vail-ably
av-a-lanche
  av-a-lanched
  av-a-lanch-ing
a-vant-garde
av-a-rice
  av-a-ri-cious
  av-a-ri-cious-ly
  av-a-ri-cious-ness
a-vast
av-a-tar
a-ve
a-venge
  a-venged
  a-veng-ing
  a-veng-er
av-e-nue
a-ver
  a-verred
  a-ver-ring
  a-ver-ment
av-er-age
  av-er-aged
  av-er-ag-ing

a-verse
  a-verse-ly
a-ver-sion
a-vert
a-vi-ar-y
  avi-ar-ies
a-vi-a-tion
a-vi-a-tor
av-id
  a-vid-i-ty
  av-id-ly
av-o-ca-do
av-o-ca-tion
a-void
  avoid-a-ble
  a-void-ance
a-vow
  a-vow-er
  a-vow-al
  a-vowed
a-wait
a-wake
  a-woke
  a-wak-ed
  a-wak-ing
a-wak-en
  awak-en-ing
a-ward
a-ware
  a-ware-ness
awe
  awed
  aw-ing
a-weigh
awe-some
awe-struck
aw-ful
  aw-ful-ly
  aw-ful-ness
awk-ward
  awk-ward-ly
awl
awn
  awned
  awn-less
  awn-ing
a-wry
ax-i-al
  ax-i-al-ly
ax-i-om
ax-is
ax-le
a-zal-ea
az-i-muth
a-zo-ic
az-ure

B

bab-bitt
bab-ble
  bab-bled
  bab-bling
  bab-bler
ba-bel
ba-boon
ba-bush-ka
ba-by
  ba-bies
  ba-bied
  ba-by-ing
  ba-by-hood
  ba-by-ish
ba-by--sit
  ba-by--sat
  ba-by--sit-ting
  ba-by--sit-ter
bac-ca-lau-re-ate
bac-ca-rat
bac-cha-nal
  bac-cha-na-li-an
bac-chant
bac-chant-te
bach-e-lor
  bach-e-lor-hood
bac-il-lar-y
bac-cil-lus
  bac-cil-li
back-bite
  back-bit
  back-bit-ten
  back-bit-er
back-board
back-bone
back-drop
back-field
back-fire
  back-fired
  back-fir-ing
back-gam-mon
back-ground
back-hand
  back-hand-ed
back-ing
back-lash
back-log
back-side
back-slide
  back-slid
  back-slid-den
  back-slid-ing
  back-slid-er
back-spin
back-stage
back-stairs

back-stop
back-stretch
back-stroke
back-talk
back-up
back-ward
  back-wards
  back-ward-ness
back-wash
back-water
back-woods
  back-woods-man
ba-con
bac-ter-ia
  bac-ter-i-um
  bac-te-ri-al
  bac-te-ri-al-ly
bac-te-ri-cide
  bac-te-ri-ci-dal
bac-te-ri-ol-o-gy
  bac-te-ri-ol-o-gist
  bac-te-ri-o-log-i-cal
bac-te-ri-o-phage
bad
bade
badge
  badged
  badg-ing
  badg-er
bad-i-nage
bad-land
  bad-lands
bad-ly
bad-min-ton
bad-tem-pered
baf-fle
  baf-fled
  baf-fling
  baf-fler
bag
  bagged
  bag-ging
ba-gasse
bag-a-telle
ba-gel
bag-gage
bag-gy
  bag-gi-er
  bag-gi-est
bag-man
bagn-io
bag-pipe
  bag-pi-per
bah
bail
bail-iff

bail-i-wick
bails-man
  bails-men
bairn
bait
bake
  baked
  bak-ing
bak-er
  bak-er-y
  bak-er-ies
bak-ing pow-der
bak-ing so-da
bak-sheesh
  bak-shish
bal-a-lai-ka
bal-ance
  bal-anced
  bal-anc-ing
  bal-anc-er
bal-brig-gan
bal-co-ny
  bal-co-nies
bald
  bald-ly
  bald-ness
bal-der-dash
bald-head
bal-dric
bale
  baled
  bal-ing
ba-leen
bale-ful
  bale-ful-ly
balk
  balk-er
bal-kan-ize
  bal-kan-ized
  bal-kan-iz-ing
  bal-kan-i-za-tion
balk-y
  balk-i-er
  balk-i-est
bal-lad
  bal-lade
  bal-lad-eer
  bal-lad-ry
bal-last
ball-bear-ing
bal-le-ri-na
bal-let
bal-lis-tic
  bal-lis-tics
  bal-lis-ti-cian
bal-loon

bal-lot
  bal-lot-ed
  bal-lot-ing
ball-room
bal-ly-hoo
balm
balm-y
  balm-ier
  balm-i-est
  balm-i-ly
  balm-i-ness
ba-lo-ney
bal-sa
bal-sam
bal-us-ter
bal-us-trade
bam-bi-no
  bam-bi-nos
bam-boo
bam-boo-zle
  bam-boo-zled
  bam-boo-zling
  bam-boo-zler
ban
  banned
  ban-ning
ba-nal
  ba-nal-i-ty
ban-nan-a
band-age
  band-aged
  band-ag-ing
ban-dana
  ban-dan-na
ban-deau
  ban-deaux
ban-de-role
ban-dit
  ban-dits
  ban-dit-ti
  ban-dit-ry
band-mas-ter
band-o-leer
  ban-do-lier
bands-man
  bands-men
band-stand
band-wa-gon
ban-dy
  ban-died
  ban-dy-ing
  ban-dy--leg-ged
bane-ful
  ban-ful-ness
ban-gla-desh
ban-gle

ban-ish
  ban-ish-ment
ban-i-ster
ban-jo
bank
bank-er
bank-ing
bank-note
bank-roll
bank-rupt
  bank-rupt-cy
  bank-rupt-cies
ban-ner
banns
ban-quet
  ban-quet-ter
ban-quette
ban-shee
ban-tam
ban-tam-weight
ban-ter
  ban-ter-er
  ban-ter-ing-ly
ban-yan
ban-zal
ba-o-bab
bap-tism
  bap-tis-mal
bap-tist
  bap-tist-ery
  bap-tis-ter-ies
bap-tize
  bap-tized
  bap-tiz-er
  bap-tiz-ing
bar
  barred
  bar-ring
bar-bar-ic
bar-ba-rism
bar-bar-i-ty
  bar-bar-i-ties
bar-ba-rize
  bar-ba-rized
  bar-ba-riz-ing
bar-ba-rous
bar-be-cue
  bar-be-cued
  bar-be-cu-ing
bar-ber
bar-ber-ry
  bar-ber-ries
bar-ber-shop
bar-bi-tal
bar-bi-tu-rate
  bar-bi-tur-ic

bar-busse
bar-ca-role
bard
bare
  bar-er
  bar-est
  bare-ness
bare-back
bare-faced
bare-foot
bare-hand-ed
bare-ly
bar-gain
  bar-gain-er
barge
  barg-ed
  barg-ing
bar-i-tone
bar-i-um
bar-keep-er
bar-ken-tine
bark-er
bar-ley
bar-maid
bar-man
  bar-men
bar-mitz-vah
barm-y
bar-na-cle
barn-storm
  barn-storm-er
  barn-storm-ing
barn-yard
bar-o-graph
ba-rom-et-er
  bar-o-met-ric
  bar-o-met-ric-al
bar-on
  ba-ro-ni-al
bar-on-age
bar-on-ess
bar-on-et
  bar-on-et-age
  bar-on-et-cy
bar-o-ny
  bar-o-nies
ba-roque
barque
bar-quen-tine
bar-rack
bar-ra-cu-da
  bar-ra-cu-das
bar-rage
  bar-raged
  bar-rag-ing
bar-ra-try

bar-ra-tries
bar-ra-tor
bar-ra-trous
bar-rel
bar-reled
bar-relled
bar-rel-ling
bar-ren
bar-ren-ly
bar-ren-ness
bar-rette
bar-ri-cade
bar-ri-cad-ed
bar-ri-cad-ing
bar-ri-er
bar-ring
bar-ri-o
bar-ri-os
bar-ris-ter
bar-room
bar-row
bar-ten-der
bar-ter
bar-ter-er
ba-sal
ba-salt
base-ball
base-board
base-less
base-ment
bash-ful
bash-ful-ly
bash-ful-ness
ba-sic
ba-si-cal-ly
ba-sil
ba-sil-i-cia
bas-i-lisk
ba-sin
ba-sis
bas-ket
bas-ket-ball
bas-ket-ry
bas-re-lief
bas-si-net
bas-so
bas-soon
bass-wood
bas-tard
baste
bast-ed
bast-ing
bas-tille
bas-ti-on
bas-ti-oned
bat

bat-ted
bat-ting
bat-ter
batch
bate
bat-ed
bat-ing
bathe
bathed
bath-ing
bath-er
bath-i-nette
ba-thos
bath-robe
bath-room
bath-y-scaphe
bath-y-sphere
ba-tik
ba-tiste
bat-on
bat-ten
bat-ter
bat-tery
bat-tle
bat-tled
bat-tling
bat-tle dore
bat-tle-field
bat-tle-ment
bat-ty
bat-ti-er
bat-ti-est
bau-ble
bawd-y
bawd-i-er
bawd-i-est
bay-o-net
bay-o-net-ted
bay-o-net-ing
bay-ou
ba-zaar
ba-zoo-ka
beach
beach-comb-er
beach-head
bea-con
bead
bead-ed
bead-like
bead-y
bead-i-er
bead-i-est
beak
beaked
beak-er
beam

beam-ed
bear
bear-ing
bear-a-ble
bear-a-bly
bear-er
beard
beard-ed
beard-less
bear-skin
beast
beast-li-ness
beast-ly
beast-li-er
beast-li-est
beat
beat-en
beat-ing
beat-er
be-a-tif-ic
be-at-i-fy
be-at-i-fied
be-at-i-fi-ca-tion
be-at-i-tude
beat-nik
beau
beaus
beaux
beau geste
beau-te-ous
beau-te-ous-ly
beau-ti-cian
beau-ti-fy
beau-ti-fied
beau-ti-fy-ing
beau-ti-fi-ca-tion
beau-ti-fi-er
beau-ti-ful
beau-ti-ful-ly
beau-ty
beaux-arts
bea-ver
be-calm
be-cause
beck-on
be-cloud
be-come
be-com-ing
be-com-ing-ly
bed
bed-ded
bed-ding
be-daub
be-daz-zle
be-daz-zled
be-daz-zling

be-daz-zle-ment
bed-bug
bed-clothes
be-deck
be-dev-il
  be-dev-iled
  be-dev-il-ing
  be-dev-il-ment
be-dew
bed-fast
bed-fel-low
be-dim
  be-dimmed
  be-dim-ming
bed-lam
bed-pan
be-drag-gle
  be-drag-gled
  be-drag-gling
bed-rid-den
bed-rock
bed-room
bed-sore
bed-spread
bed-spring
bed-time
bee-bread
beech
beef
beef-eat-er
beef-steak
beef-y
  beef-i-er
  beef-i-est
bee-hive
bee-line
beer-y
  beer-i-er
  beer-i-est
beest-ings
bees-wax
bee-tle
  bee-tled
  bee-tling
bee-tle-browed
be-fall
  be-fall-en
  be-fall-ing
be-fit
  be-fit-ted
  be-fit-ting
be-fog
  be-fogged
  be-fog-ging
be-fore
be-fore-hand

be-foul
be-friend
be-fud-dle
  be-fud-dled
  be-fud-dling
beg
  beg-ged
  beg-ging
be-get
  be-get-ten
  be-got
  be-got-ten
beg-gar
  beg-gar-dom
  beg-gar-hood
  beg-gar-ly
be-gin
  be-gan
  be-gun
  be-gin-ning
  be-gin-ner
be-go-ni-a
be-grime
  be-grimed
  be-grim-ing
be-grudge
  be-grudged
  be-grudg-ing
  be-grudg-ing-ly
be-guile
  be-guiled
  be-guil-ing
  be-guil-er
be-half
be-have
  be-haved
  be-hav-ing
be-hav-ior
  be-hav-ior-ism
  be-hav-ior-ist
  be-hav-ior-is-tic
be-head
be-he-moth
be-hest
be-hind
be-hind-hand
be-hold
  be-hold-ing
  be-hold-er
  be-hold-en
be-hoove
  be-hooved
  be-hoov-ing
beige
be-ing
be-la-bor

be-lat-ed
  be-lat-ed-ly
  be-lat-ed-ness
be-lay
  be-lay-ed
  be-lay-ing
belch
bel-dam
be-lea-quer
bel-fry
  bel-fries
be-lie
  be-lied
  be-ly-ing
be-lief
be-lieve
  be-lieved
  be-liev-ing
  be-liev-a-ble
  be-liev-er
be-lit-tle
  be-lit-tled
  be-lit-tling
bel-la-don-na
bell-boy
bell bouy
belle
belles let-tres
bell-hop
bel-li-cose
  bel-li-cos-i-ty
bel-lig-er-ence
  bel-lig-er-en-cy
bel-lig-er-ent
  bel-lig-er-ent-ly
bel-low
  bel-lows
bell-weth-er
bel-ly
  bel-lies
  bel-lied
  bel-ly-ing
bel-ly-ache
  bel-ly-ach-ing
bel-ly-but-ton
be-long
  be-long-ings
be-loved
be-low
belt
  belt-ed
belt-way
be-lu-ga
be-mire
  be-mired
  be-mir-ing

be-moan
be-muse
 be-mused
 be-mus-ing
bench
bend
 bend-ing
 bend-er
be-neath
ben-e-dict
ben-e-dic-tion
ben-e-fac-tion
ben-e-fac-tor
 ben-e-fac-tress
ben-e-fice
 ben-e-ficed
 ben-e-fic-ing
be-nef-i-cence
be-nef-i-cent
be-ne-fi-cial
 ben-e-fi-cial-ly
 ben-e-fi-ci-ar-ies
ben-e-fit
 ben-e-fit-ed
 ben-e-fit-ing
be-nev-o-lence
 be-nev-o-lent
 be-nev-o-lent-ly
be-night-ed
be-nign
 be-nig-ni-ty
 be-nig-ni-ties
 be-nign-ly
be-nig-nant
 be-nig-nan-cies
 be-nig-nan-cy
ben-i-son
ben-ny
 ben-nies
be-numb
bent
ben-zene
ben-zine
ben-zo-ate
ben-zo-in
ben-zol
be-queath
be-quest
be-rate
 be-rat-ed
 be-rat-ing
be-reave
 be-reaved
 be-reav-ing
be-reft
be-ret

ber-ga-mot
ber-i-ber-i
berke-li-um
ber-ry
 ber-ries
 ber-ried
 ber-ry-ing
ber-serk
berth
ber-tha
ber-yl
be-ryl-li-um
be-seech
 be-seeched
 be-seech-ing
 be-seech-ing-ly
be-set
 be-set-ting
be-shrew
be-side
 be-sides
be-siege
 be-sieged
 be-sieg-ing
 be-sieg-er
be-smear
be-smirch
bes-om
be-sot
 be-sot-ted
 be-sot-ting
be-spat-ter
be-speak
 be-speak-ing
best
bes-tial
 bes-tial-ly
 bes-ti-al-i-ty
 bes-ti-al-i-ties
be-stir
 be-stirred
 be-stir-ring
be-stow
 be-stow-al
be-strew
be-stride
 be-strid-den
 be-strid-ing
bet
 bet-ted
 bet-ting
be-ta
be-take
 be-tak-en
 be-tak-ing
be-ta rays

be-ta-tron
be-tel
beth-el
be-tide
 be-tid-ed
 be-tid-ing
be-to-ken
be-tray
 be-tray-al
 be-tray-er
be-troth
 be-troth-al
 be-troth-ed
bet-ter
bet-ter-ment
bet-tor
be-tween
be-twixt
bev-el
 bev-eled
 bev-el-ing
bev-er-age
bev-y
 bev-ies
be-wail
be-ware
be-wil-der
 be-wil-der-ing-ly
 be-wil-der-ment
be-witch
 be-witch-er
 be-witch-ery
 be-witch-ing
 be-witch-ing-ly
 be-witch-ment
be-yond
be-zique
bi-an-nu-al
bi-as
 bi-ased
 bi-as-ing
bi-ax-i-al
 bi-ax-i-al-ly
bi-be-lot
Bi-ble
 Bib-li-cal
 Bib-li-cal-ly
bib-li-og-ra-phy
 bib-li-og-ra-phies
 bib-li-o-graphic
bib-li-o-ma-ni-a
 bib-li-o-ma-ni-ac
bib-li-o-phile
bib-u-lous
bi-cam-er-al
bi-car-bo-nate

bi-ce-te-nary
  bi-cen-te-nar-ies
bi-cen-ten-ni-al
bi-ceps
bi-chlo-ride
bick-er
bi-con-cave
bi-con-vex
bi-cus-pid
  bi-cus-pi-dal
  bi-cus-pi-date
bi-cy-cle
  bi-cy-cled
  bi-cy-cling
  bi-cy-cler
  bi-cy-clist
bid
  bid-den
  bid-da-ble
  bid-der
bid-dy
  bid-dies
bide
  bid-ed
  bid-ing
bi-en-ni-al
  bi-en-ni-al-ly
bier
bi-fid
bi-fo-cal
  bi-fo-cals
bi-fur-cate
  bi-fur-cat-ed
  bi-fur-cat-ing
  bi-fur-ca-tion
big
  big-ger
  big-gest
big-a-my
  big-a-mies
  big-a-mist
  big-a-mous
big-heart-ed
big-horn
bight
big-no-ni-a
big-ot
  big-ot-ed
  big-ot-ed-ly
  big-ot-ry
  big-ot-ries
bi-jou
  bi-joux
bi-ju-gous
bi-ki-ni
bi-lat-er-al

bi-lat-er-al-ly
bil-ber-ry
  bil-ber-ries
bilge
bil-i-ary
bi-lin-gual
bil-ious
bilk
bill
  bil-led
  bil-ling
bil-la-bong
bill-board
bil-let
bil-let-doux
bill-fold
bill-hook
bil-liards
bil-lings-gate
bil-lion
  bil-lion-are
  bil-lionth
bil-low
  bil-low-y
  bil-low-ier
  bil-low-i-est
bil-ly goat
bi-met-al-lism
  bi-met-al-list
  bi-me-tal-lic
bi-month-ly
  bi-month-lies
bi-na-ry
bi-nate
bin-au-ral
bind
  bind-ing
bind-er
bind-ery
  bind-er-ies
binge
bin-go
bin-na-cle
bi-noc-u-lar
bi-no-mi-al
bio-chem-is-try
  bio-chem-i-cal
  bio-chem-ist
bi-o-cide
bi-o-e-col-o-gy
bi-o-en-gi-neer-ing
bi-o-gen-e-sis
  bi-o-ge-net-ic
bi-og-ra-phy
  bi-og-ra-pher
  bi-o-graph-ic

bi-o-graph-i-cal
  bi-o-graph-i-cal-ly
bi-ol-o-gy
  bi-o-log-i-cal
  bi-ol-o-gist
bi-o-met-rics
bi-o-nom-ics
bi-o-phys-ics
  bi-o-phys-i-cal
  bi-o-phys-i-cist
bi-op-sy
  bi-op-sies
bi-o-sphere
bi-o-tin
bi-par-ti-san
bi-par-tite
  bi-par-ti-tion
bi-ped
  bi-ped-al
bi-plane
bi-po-lar
  bi-po-lar-i-ty
birch
  birch-en
bird-bath
bird-brain
  bird-brained
bird-call
bird-ie
bird-lime
bird-man
bird's-eye
bi-ret-ta
birth-day
birth-mark
birth-place
birth-right
birth-stone
bis-cuit
bi-sect
  bi-sec-tion
  bi-sec-tor
bi-sex-u-al
bish-op
  bish-op-ric
bis-muth
bi-son
bisque
bis-ter
  bis-tered
bis-tro
  bis-tros
bi-sul-fide
bitch
bite
  bit-ten

bit-ing
bit-ing-ly
bit-stock
bit-ter
  bit-ter-ish
  bit-ter-ly
  bit-ter-ness
bit-tern
bit-ter-root
bit-ters
bit-ter-sweet
bi-tu-men
bi-tu-mi-nous coal
bi-va-lent
  bi-va-lence
bi-valve
  bi-val-vu-lar
biv-ou-ac
  biv-ou-acked
  biv-ou-ack-ing
bi-week-ly
  bi-week-lies
bi-year-ly
bi-zarre
  bi-zarre-ly
  bi-zarre-ness
blab
  blab-bed
  blab-bing
  blab-ber
  blab-ber-mouth
black-ball
black-ber-ry
  black-ber-ries
black-bird
black-board
black-en
black-guard
black-head
black-ing
black-jack
black-list
black-mail
black-out
black-smith
black-snake
black-top
blad-der
blade
  blad-ed
blame
  blamed
  blam-ing
  blam-a-ble
  blame-a-ble
  blame-ful

blame-less
  blame-less-ly
  blame-less-ness
blame-wor-thy
  blame-wor-thi-ness
blanch
  blanc-er
  blanch-ing
blanc-mange
bland
  bland-ly
  bland-ness
blan-dish
  blan-dish-er
  blan-dish-ment
blank
  blank-ly
  blank-ness
blan-ket
blare
  blared
  blar-ing
blar-ney
blas-pheme
  blas-phemed
  blas-phem-ing
  blas-phem-er
  blas-phem-ies
blas-phe-my
blast-ed
bas-tu-la
blat
  blat-ted
  blat-ting
bla-tant
  bla-tan-cy
  bla-tant-ly
blath-er
blaze
  blazed
  blaz-ing
bla-zer
bleach
  bleach-er
bleak
  bleak-ly
  bleak-ness
blear
  bleary
  blear-i-ness
bleed
  bleed-ing
  bleed-er
blem-ish
blench
blend

blend-ed
blend-ing
blend-er
bless
bless-ed
bles-sing
bless-ed-ness
blind
  blind-ing
  blind-ing-ly
  blind-ly
  blind-ness
blind-fold
blind-man's bluff
blink-er
bliss
  bliss-ful
  bliss-ful-ly
  bliss-ful-ness
blis-ter
  blis-ter-y
blithe
  blithe-ly
blithe-some
  blithe-some-ly
blitz-krieg
bliz-zard
block
  block-er
block-ade
  block-ad-ed
  block-ad-ing
  block-ad-er
block-bus-ter
block-head
block-house
block-ish
  block-ish-ly
blocky
blond
blood-curd-ling
blood bank
blood-ed
blood-hound
blood-less
  blood-less-ly
  blood-less-ness
blood-let-ting
blood pres-sure
blood re-la-tion
blood-shed
blood-shot
blood-stone
blood-suck-er
blood-thirst-y
  blood-thirst-i-ly

bloody
blood-i-er
blood-i-est
blood-ied
blood-y-ing
blood-i-ly
blood-i-ness
bloom-ers
bloom-ing
bloom-ing-ly
bloop-er
blos-som
blot
blot-ted
blot-ting
blotch
blotchy
blot-ter
blow
blown
blow-ing
blow-er
blow-fly
blow-flies
blow-gun
blow-hole
blow-out
blow-pipe
blow-torch
blow-up
blow-y
blowz-y
blub-ber
blub-bery
blu-cher
bludg-eon
blue
blu-er
blu-est
blue-ness
blue-bell
blue-ber-ry
blue-ber-ries
blue-bird
blue-blood-ed
blue-bon-net
blue-coat
blue-col-lar
blue-fish
blue-grass
blue-jac-ket
blue-nose
blue-pen-cil
blue-print
blu-et
blu-ing

blun-der
blun-der-er
blun-der-ing-ly
blun-der-buss
blunt
blunt-ly
blunt-ness
blur
blur-red
blur-ring
blur-ry
blush
blushed
blush-ing
blush-ing-ly
blus-ter
blus-ter-er
blus-ter-ing-ly
blus-ter-ous
blus-ter-y
bo-a
board-er
board-walk
boast
boas-ter
boast-ful
boast-ful-ness
boast-ing-ly
boat-house
boat-man
boat-swain
bob
bob-bed
bob-bing
bob-bin
bob-ble
bob-bled
bob-bling
bob-by-pin
bob-cat
bob-o-link
bob-sled
bob-tail
bob-white
bock
bode
bod-ed
bod-ing
bod-ice
bod-i-ly
bod-kin
bod-y
bod-ied
bod-y-ing
bod-y-guard
bog

bog-gy
bog-ging
bo-gey
bog-gle
bog-gled
bog-gling
bog-gler
bo-gus
bo-gy
boil-er
bois-ter-ous
bois-ter-ous-ly
bois-ter-ous-ness
bo-la
bo-las
bold
bold-ly
bold-ness
bold-face
bo-le-ro
bol-lix
boli-worm
boll weevil
bo-lo
bo-lo-gna
bo-lo-ney
bol-ster
bol-ster-er
bolt
bolt-ed
bolt-er
bom-bard
bom-bard-ment
bom-bar-dier
bom-bast
bom-bas-tic
bom-bas-ti-cal-ly
bomb-er
bomb-proof
bomb-shell
bomb-sight
bo-na fide
bo-nan-za
bon-bon
bond-age
bond-ed
bond-man
bond-men
bonds-men
bone
boned
bon-ing
bone-head
bon-er
bon-fire
bon-go

bon-gos
bon-gies
bon-ho-mie
bo-ni-to
bon-net
bon-ny
bon-sai
bo-nus
  bo-nus-es
bon voy-age
bon-y
  bon-i-er
  bon-i-est
boo
  booed
  boo-ing
boo-by
  boo-bies
boo-by trap
boo-dle
boo-hoo
  boo-hooed
  boo-hoo-ing
book
  book-bind-er
book-case
book-end
book-ie
book-ish
  book-ish-ness
book-keep-ing
  book-keep-er
book-let
book-mak-er
book-mark
book-mo-bile
book-plate
book-sell-er
  book-sell-ing
book-stall
book-worm
boo-me-rang
boon docks
boon-dog-gle
boor
  boor-ish
  boor-ish-ness
boost
  boost-er
boot-black
boot-ee
boot-jack
boot-leg
  boot-legged
  boot-leg-ging
  boot-leg-ger

boot-less
  boot-less-ly
  boot-less-ness
boot-lick
  boot-lick-er
boo-ty
  boo-ties
booze
  booz-er
  booz-y
  booz-i-er
  booz-i-est
bo-rax
bor-der
  bor-der-ed
  bor-der-ing
  bor-der-land
  bor-der-line
bore
  bored
  bor-ing
  bor-er
bo-re-al
bore-dom
bo-ric
bo-ron
bor-ough
bor-row
  bor-row-er
borsch
bosh
bosk-y
bos-om
boss-ism
boss-y
  boss-i-er
  boss-i-est
  boss-i-ness
bo-sun
bot-a-ny
  bo-tan-i-cal
  bot-a-nist
  bot-a-nize
botch
  botchy
  botch-i-er
  botch-i-est
both-er
  both-er-some
bot-tle
  bot-tled
  bot-tling
  bot-tle-ful
  bot-tler
bot-tle-neck
bot-tom

bot-tom-less
bot-u-lism
bou-doir
bouf-fant
bough
bought
bouil-lon
boul-der
boul-e-vard
bounce
  bounced
  bounc-ing
bound
bound-a-ry
  bound-a-ries
bound-er
bound-less
  bound-less-ness
boun-te-ous
  boun-te-ous-ness
boun-ti-ful
boun-ty
  boun-ties
bou-quet
bour-bon
bour-geois
bour-geoi-sie
bou-tique
bou-ton-niere
bo-vine
bow-el
bow-er
bow-ery
bow-ie
bow-ing
bow-knot
bowl
bow-leg
  bow-leg-ged
bowl-er
bow-line
bow-ling
bow-man
  bow-men
bow-string
box
  box-ful
  box-fuls
box-car
box-er
box-ing
box of-fice
boy
  boy-hood
  boy-ish
  boy-ish-ly

boy-ish-ness
boy-cott
boy-friend
boy-sen-ber-ry
 boy-sen-ber-ries
brace
 bra-ced
 brac-ing
brace-let
brac-er
bra-ces
brack-en
brack-et
brack-ish
 brack-ish-ness
bract
brad
 brad-ded
 brad-ding
brae
brag
 brag-ged
 brag-ging
brag-gart
braid
 braid-er
 braid-ing
braille
brain-child
brain-less
brain-pow-er
brain-storm
 brain-storm-ing
brain-wash-ing
brain-y
 brain-i-er
 brain-i-est
braise
 braised
 brais-ing
brake
 braked
 brak-ing
brake-man
 brake-men
bram-ble
 bram-bly
branch
 branch-ed
brand
 brand-er
brand-ish
brand-new
bran-dy
 bran-dies
 bran-died

bran-dy-ing
bra-sier
bras-se-rie
 bras-se-ries
bras-siere
brassy
 brass-i-er
 brass-i-est
brat
 brat-tish
 brat-ty
bra-va-do
brave
 braved
 brav-ing
 brave-ness
 brav-ery
 brav-er-ies
bra-vo
 bra-vos
bra-vu-ra
brawl
 braw-ler
brawn
 brawn-i-ness
 brawny
 brawn-i-er
 brawn-i-est
bra-zen
bra-zier
breach
bread
 bread = ed
breadth-ways
bread-win-ner
break
 break-ing
 break-a-ble
break-age
break-a-way
break-down
brak-er
break-fast
break-neck
break-through
break-up
breast-bone
breast-plate
breath
breathe
 breathed
 breath-ing
breath-er
breath-ing
breath-tak-ing
 breath-tak-ing-ly

breathy
 breath-i-er
 breath-i-est
breech-es
breech-load-er
bred
breed
 breed-ing
breeze
 breezy
 breez-i-er
 breez-i-est
 breez-i-ness
breth-ren
bre-vet
 bre-vet-ted
 bre-vet-ting
bre-vi-a-ry
 bre-vi-a-ries
brev-i-ty
brew
 brew-er
 brew-ery
 brew-er-ies
bri-ar
 bri-ary
bribe
 bribed
 brib-ing
 brib-a-ble
birb-ery
 brib-er-ies
bric-a-brac
brick-lay-er
 brick-lay-ing
brick-work
bride
 brid-al
bride-groom
brides-maid
bridge
bri-dle
 bri-dled
 bri-dling
brief
 brief-ly
 brief-ing
bri-er
bri-gade
bri-a-dier
brig-an-tine
bright
 bright-ly
 bright-ness
 bright-en
bril-liance

bril-lian-cy
bril-liant
brim
  brimmed
  brim-ming
brim-stone
brine
briny
bring
  bring-ing
brink
bri-oche
bri-quet
  bri-quette
brisk
  brisk-ly
  brisk-ness
bris-ket
bris-tle
  bris-tled
britch-es
brit-tle
broach
  broached
  broach-ing
broad-cast
  broad-cast-ed
  broad-cast-ing
broad-cloth
broad-mind-ed
broad-side
bro-cade
  bro-cad-ed
  bro-cad-ing
broc-co-li
bro-chure
broil-er
bro-ken
bro-ker
bro-ker-age
bro-mide
bro-mine
bron-chi
  bron-chi-al
  bron-chi-tis
  bron-chue
bron-co
  bron-cos
bron-to-saur
bronze
  bronz-ed
  bronz-ing
brooch
brood
  brood-ing
brook

broom-stick
broth-el
broth-er
broth-er-in-law
  broth-ers-in-law
broth-er-ly
brow-beat
  brow-beat-en
  brow-beat-ing
brown
brown-ie
browse
  browsed
  brows-ing
bru-in
bruise
  bruis-ed
  bruis-er
  bruis-ing
brunch
bru-net
brusque
bru-tal
  bru-tal-i-ty
  bru-tal-ize
  bru-tal-ized
  bru-tal-iz-ing
  bru-tal-i-za-tion
brut-ish
bub-ble
  bub-bled
  bub-bling
  bub-bler
bu-bon-ic plague
buc-ca-neer
buck-a-roo
buck-board
buck-et
  buck-et-ed
  buck-et-ing
buck-eye
buck-le
buck-saw
buck-shot
buck-skin
buck-tooth
  buck-teeth
  buck-toothed
buck-wheat
bu-col-ic
bud
  bud-ded
  bud-ding
bud-dy
budge
budg-et

buff-er
buf-fet
  buf-fet-ed
  buf-fet=ing
buf-foon
  buf-foon-ery
  buf-foon-er-ies
  buf-foon-ish
bug
  bugged
  bug-ging
bug-a-boo
bug-gy
  bug-gi-er
  bug-gi-est
bu-gle
  bu-gled
  bu-gling
  bu-gler
build
  build-er
  build-ing
built--in
built-up
bulb
bul-ba-ceous
bul-bar
bul-bous
bulge
  bulged
  bulg-ing
  bulgy
bulk-head
bulk-y
  bulk-i-er
  bulk-i-est
  bulk-i-ly
  bulk-i-ness
bull-dog
bull-doze
  bull-dozed
  bull-doz-ing
  bull-doz-er
bul-let
bul-le-tin
bul-let-proof
bull-fight
  bull-fight-er
  bull-fight-ing
bull-finch
bull-head-ed
bul-lion
bull-pen
bull's-eye
bul-ly
  bul-lies

bul-lied
bul-ly-ing
bul-rush
bul-wark
bum
 bum-mer
 bum-mest
bum-ble-bee
bump-er
bump-kin
bump-tious
 bump-tious-ness
bump-y
 bump-i-er
 bump-i-est
bunch
 bunchy
 bunch-i-er
 bunch-i-est
bun-co
bun-combe
bun-dle
 bun-dled
 bun-dling
bun-ga-low
bun-gle
 bun-gled
 bun-gling
 bun-gler
bun-ion
bunk-er
bunk-house
bun-ko
bun-kum
bun-ny
 bun-nies
bun-ting
bu-oy
buoy-an-cy
 buoy-ant
 buoy-ant-ly
bur-ble
bur-den
bur-den-some
bur-dock
bu-reau
 bu-reaus
 bu-reaux
 bu-reauc-ra-cy
 bu-reauc-ra-cies
 bu-reau-crat
 bu-reau-crat-ic
bu-rette
bur-geon
burg-er
bur-gess

bur-glar
 bur-glar-ize
 bur-glar-ized
 bur-glar-iz-ing
 bur-gla-ries
 bur-gla-ry
bur-gle
 bur-gled
 bur-gling
bur-i-al
bur-lap
bur-lesque
 bur-lesqued
 bur-les-quing
 bur-les-quer
bur-ly
 bur-li-er
 bur-li-est
 bur-li-ness
burn
 burn-ed
 burnt
 burn-ing
 burn-a-ble
burn-er
bur-nish
 bur-nish-er
bur-noose
burn-sides
burp
burr
 burred
 bur-ring
bur-ro
 bur-ros
bur-row
 bur-row-er
bur-sa
 bur-sae
 bur-sal
bur-sar
 bur-sa-ri-al
 bur-sa-ry
 bur-sa-ries
bur-si-tis
burst
 burst-ing
 burst-er
bur-y
 bur-ied
 bur-y-ing
bus
 bus-ed
 bus-ing
bus-boy
bus-by

bus-bies
bushed
bush-el
bu-shi-do
bush-ing
bush-man
 bush-men
bush-mas-ter
bush-rang-er
bush-whack
 bush-whack-er
 bush-whack-ing
bush-y
 bush-i-er
 bush-i-est
 bush-i-ness
bus-i-ly
busi-ness
busi-ness-like
busi-ness-man
 busi-ness-men
 busi-ness-wom-an
bus-kin
 bus-kined
bus-tard
bus-tle
 bus-tled
 bus-tling
 bus-tler
bus-y
 bus-i-er
 bus-i-est
 bus-ied
 bus-y-ing
bu-ta-di-ene
bu-tane
butch-er
butch-ery
 butch-er-ies
but-ler
butte
but-ter
but-tery
but-tock
but-ton
but-tress
bu-ty-ric
bux-om
buy
 bought
 buy-ing
buz-zard
buzz-er
by-gong
by-law
byte

C

ca-bal
 ca-balled
 ca-ball-ing
cab-a-la
 cab-a-lis-tic
 cab-a-lis-ti-cal
ca-bal-le-ro
ca-ba-na
cab-a-ret
cab-bage
cab-by
 cab-bies
ca-ber
cab-in
cab-i-net
cab-i-net-mak-er
cab-i-net-work
ca-ble
 ca-bled
 ca-bling
ca-ble-gram
cab-o-chon
ca-boo-dle
ca-boose
cab-ri-o-let
ca-ca-o
cach-a-lot
cache
 cached
 cach-ing
ca-chet
ca-cique
cack-le
ca-coph-o-ny
 ca-coph-o-nies
cac-tus
 cac-tus-es
cac-ti
cad
 cad-dish
ca-dav-er
 ca-dav-er-ous
cad-die
 cad-died
cad-dis fly
cad-dy
 cad-dies
ca-dence
ca-den-za
ca-det
cadge
 cadged
 cadg-ing
cad-mi-um
ca-dre
ca-du-ce-us

ca-du-cei
cea-su-ra
 cae-su-rae
ca-fe
caf-e-te-ria
caf-feine
caf-tan
cage
 caged
cai-man
cairn
cais-son
cai-tiff
ca-jole
cake
 caked
cal-a-bash
cal-a-boose
cal-a-mine
ca-lam-i-ty
 ca-lam-i-ties
 ca-lam-i-tous
cal-cic
cal-ci-fy
 cal-ci-fied
 cal-ci-fy-ing
 cal-ci-fi-ca-tion
cal-ci-mine
cal-cite
cal-ci-um
cal-cu-la-ble
 cal-cu-la-bil-i-ty
cal-cu-late
 cal-cu-lat-ed
 cal-cu-lat-ing
 cal-cu-la-tion
cal-cu-la-tor
cal-cu-lus
 cal-cu-lus-es
cal-dron
cal-en-dar
cal-ends
calf
cal-i-ber
cal-i-brate
 cal-i-brat-ed
 cal-i-brat-ing
 cal-i-bra-tion
cal-i-co
 cal-i-coes
cal-i-per
ca-liph
 cal-iph-ate
cal-is-then-ics
cal-lig-ra-pher
 cal-lig-ra-phy

call-ing
cal-li-o-pe
cal-lous
 cal-loused
cal-low
cal-lus
 cal-lus-es
calm
ca-lor-ic
cal-o-rie
 cal-o-ries
cal-o-rif-ic
cal-u-met
cal-um-ny
calve
 calved
ca-lyp-so
 ca-lyp-sos
ca-lyx
 ca-lyx-es
 cal-y-ces
ca-ma-ra-de-rie
cam-ber
cam-bi-um
cam-bric
cam-el
ca-mel-lia
cam-eo
cam-era
cam-i-sole
cam-o-mile
cam-ou-flage
 cam-ou-flaged
 cam-ou-flag-ing
cam-paign
cam-pa-ni-le
 cam-pa-ni-les
camp-er
cam-phor
cam-pus
 cam-pus-es
camp-y
cam-shaft
can
 canned
 can-ning
ca-nal
 ca-naled
 ca-nal-ing
ca-nard
ca-nar-y
ca-nas-ta
can-can
can-cel
 can-celed
 can-cel-ing

can-cel-la-tion
can-cer
can-de-la-brum
can-did
can-di-da-cy
  can-di-da-cies
  can-di-date
can-died
can-dle
can-dor
can-dy
  can-dies
  can-died
  can-dy-ing
cane
ca-nine
can-is-ter
can-ker
  can-ker-ous
can-na-bis
canned
can-ner
can-nery
  can-ner-ies
can-ni-bal
can-non
can-not
can-ny
  can-nier
ca-noe
can-on
ca-non-i-cal
can-on-ize
  can-on-ized
  can-on-i-za-tion
can-o-py
can-ta-loup
  can-ta-loupe
  can-ta-lope
can-tan-ker-ous
can-ta-ta
can-teen
can-ter
can-ti-cle
can-ti-lev-er
can-to
  can-tos
can-ton
can-tor
can-vas
can-yon
ca-pa-bil-i-ty
  cap-pa-bil-i-ties
ca-pa-ble
  ca-pa-bly
ca-pa-cious

ca-pac-i-tate
  ca-pac-i-tat-ed
  ca-pac-i-tat-ing
ca-pac-i-ty
  ca-pac-i-ties
ca-per
ca-pi-as
cap-il-lar-i-ty
cap-il-lar-y
  cap-il-lar-ies
cap-i-tal
cap-i-ta-tion
ca-pit-u-late
  ca-pit-u-lat-ed
  ca-pit-u-lat-ing
  ca-pit-u-la-tor
ca-pon
ca-pote
ca-pric-cio
ca-price
  ca-pri-cious
  ca-pri-cious-ly
cap-ri-ole
  cap-ri-oled
  cap-ri-ol-ing
cap-size
cap-stan
cap-stone
cap-sule
  cap-su-lar
cap-tain
  cap-tain-cy
cap-tion
cap-tious
  cap-tious-ness
cap-ti-vate
cap-tive
  cap-tiv-i-ty
  cap-tiv-i-ties
cap-tor
cap-ture
  cap-tured
  cap-tur-ing
  cap-tur-er
car-a-cole
  car-a-coled
  car-a-col-ing
car-a-cul
ca-rafe
car-a-mel
car-a-pace
car-at
car-a-van
car-a-van-sa-ry
  car-a-van-sa-ries
car-a-vel

car-a-way
car-bide
car-bine
car-bo-hy-drate
car-bo-lat-ed
car-bol-ic
car-bon
car-bo-na-ceous
car-bo-nate
  car-bo-na-tion
car-bon di-ox-ide
car-bon-if-er-ous
car-bon-ize
  car-bon-ized
  car-bon-iz-ing
  car-bon-i-za-tion
car-bon mon-ox-ide
car-boy
car-bun-cle
car-bu-re-tor
car-ca-jou
car-cass
car-cin-o-gen
  car-cin-o-gen-ic
car-ci-no-ma
  car-ci-no-mas
  car-ci-no-ma-ta
car-da-mom
car-di-ac
car-di-gan
car-di-nal
car-di-o-graph
  car-di-og-ra-phy
ca-reen
ca-reer
care-ful
  care-ful-ly
  care-ful-ness
care-less
  care-less-ly
  care-less-ness
ca-ress
  ca-ress-ing-ly
car-et
care-worn
car-go
  car-goes
  car-gos
car-hop
car-i-bou
car-i-ca-ture
  car-i-ca-tured
  car-i-ca-tur-ing
  car-i-ca-tur-ist
car-ies
car-il-lon

car-il-lonned
car-i-lon-ning
car-i-lon-neur
car-mine
car-nage
car-nal
car-nal-i-ty
car-nal-ly
car-na-tion
car-nel-ian
car-ni-val
car-ni-vore
car-niv-o-rous
car-niv-o-rous-ly
car-niv-o-rous-ness
car-om
ca-rot-id
ca-rous-al
ca-rouse
ca-roused
ca-rous-ing
ca-rous-er
car-ou-sel
carp
car-pen-ter
car-pen-try
car-pet
car-pet-ing
car-pus
car-riage
car-ri-er
car-ri-ole
car-rot
car-roty
car-ry
car-ried
car-ry-ing
cart
cart-age
carte-blanche
car-tel
car-ti-lage
car-ti-lag-i-nous
car-tog-ra-phy
car-tog-ra-pher
car-to-graph-ic
car-ton
car-toon
car-toon-ist
car-tridge
cart-wheel
carve
car-vel
car-y-at-id
car-y-at-ids
car-y-at-i-des

ca-sa-ba
cas-cade
cas-cad-ed
cas-cad-ing
ca-sein
case-mate
case-mat-ed
case-ment
case-ment-ed
case-work
case-work-er
cash-ew
cash-ier
cash-mere
cas-ing
ca-si-no
cas-ket
cas-sa-ba
cas-sa-va
cas-se-role
cas-sette
cas-si-no
cas-sock
cas-socked
cas-so-wary
cas-so-war-ies
cast
cast-ing
cas-ta-net
cast-a-way
caste
cas-tel-lat-ed
cast-er
cas-ti-gate
cas-ti-gat-ed
cas-ti-gat-ing
cas-ti-ga-tion
cas-ti-ga-tor
cast i-ron
cas-tle
cas-tor
cas-trate
cas-trat-ed
cas-trat-ing
cas-trat-er
cas-tra-tion
cas-u-al
cas-u-al-ty
cas-u-al-ties
cas-u-ist
cas-u-is-tic
cas-u-ist-ry
cas-ist-ries
cas-u-ist
cas-u-ist-ic
cas-u-ist-ry

cas-u-ist-ries
cat-a-clysm
cat-a-cly-mal
cat-a-comb
cat-a-falque
cat-a-lep-sy
cat-a-lep-tic
cat-a-log
cat-a-loged
cat-a-log-ing
cat-a-log-er
cat-a-log-ist
ca-tal-pa
ca-tal-y-sis
ca-tal-y-ses
cat-a-lyt-ic
cat-a-lyst
cat-a-lyze
cat-a-lyzed
cat-a-lyz-ing
cat-a-ma-ran
cat-a-pult
cat-a-ract
ca-tarrh
ca-tas-tro-phe
cat-as-troph-ic
catch
caught
catch-ing
catch-er
catch-up
catch-y
catch-i-er
catch-i-est
cat-e-chism
cat-e-chis-mal
cat-e-chiz
cat-e-chu-men
cat-e-gor-i-cal
cat-e-gor-i-cal-ly
cat-e-go-ry
cat-a-go-ries
cat-e-gor-ize
cat-e-gor-ized
cat-e-gor-iz-ing
ca-ter
ca-ter-er
cat-er-pil-lar
ca-ter-waul
cat-fish
cat-fish-es
cat-gut
ca-thar-sis
ca-thar-ses
ca-thar-tic
ca-the-dral

cath-e-ter
cath-ode
cat-i-on
cat-nap
  cat-napped
  cat-nap-ping
cat-nip
cat's-paw
cat-sup
cat-tail
cat-tle
cat-ty
  cat-tier
  cat-ti-est
  cat-ti-ly
  cat-ti-ness
cat-ty-cor-ner
cau-cus
  cau-cus-es
  cau-cused
  cau-cus-ing
cau-dal
cau-date
  cau-dat-ed
cau-dle
caul-dron
cau-li-flow-er
caulk
  caulk-er
caus-al
  caus-al-ly
cau-sal-i-ty
  cau-sal-i-ties
cause-way
caus-tic
  caus-ti-cal-ly
cau-ter-ize
  cau-ter-ized
  cau-ter-iz-ing
  cau-ter-i-za-tion
cau-ter-y
  cau-ter-ies
cau-tion
  cau-tion-ary
cau-tious
cav-al-cade
cav-a-lier
  cav-a-lier-ly
cav-al-ry
cave
ca-ve-at
cav-ern
  cav-ern-ous
cav-ier
cav-il
  cav-iled

cav-il-ing
cav-i-ty
  cav-i-ties
ca-vort
cay-enne
cay-man
  cay-mans
cay-use
ce-cum
ce-dar
cede
  ced-ed
  ced-ing
ce-dil-la
ceil-ing
cel-an-dine
cel-a-brant
cel-e-brate
  cel-e-brat-ed
  cel-e-brat-ing
  cel-e-bra-tion
  cel-e-bra-tor
ce-leb-ri-ty
  ce-leb-ri-ties
ce-ler-i-ty
cel-er-y
ce-les-tial
ce-li-ac
cel-i-ba-cy
  cel-i-bate
cel-lar
cel-lo
  cel-los
  cel-list
cel-lo-phane
cel-lu-lar
cel-lule
cel-lu-lose
ce-ment
cem-e-ter-y
ce-no-bite
cen-o-taph
cen-ser
cen-sor
  cen-so-ri-al
  cen-sor-ship
cen-so-ri-ous
  cen-so-ri-ous-ly
  cen-so-ri-ous-ness
cen-sure
  cen-sured
  cen-sur-ing
  cen-sur-er
cen-sus
  cen-sus-es
  cen-sused

cen-sus-ing
cen-tare
cen-taur
cen-te-nar-i-an
cen-te-na-ry
  cen-te-nar-ies
cen-ten-ni-al
cen-ter
cen-ti-are
cen-ti-grade
cen-ti-gram
cen-ti-li-ter
cen-ti-me-ter
cen-tral
  cen-tral-ize
  cen-tral-ized
  cen-tral-iz-ing
cen-trif-u-gal
cen-tri-fuge
cen-trip-e-tal
cen-tu-ri-an
cen-tu-ry
  cen-tu-ries
ce-ram-ic
  ce-ram-ics
ce-re-al
cer-e-bel-lum
cer-e-bral
cer-e-brum
cer-e-mo-ni-al
  cer-e-mo-no-al-ism
cer-e-mo-ny
  cer-e-mo-nies
ce-rise
ce-ric
  ce-ri-um
cer-tain
cer-tain-ty
  cer-tain-ties
cer-tif-i-cate
  cer-tif-i-ca-tion
cer-ti-fy
  cer-ti-fied
  cer-ti-fy-ing
cer-ti-tude
ce-ru-le-an
cer-vi-cal
cer-vix
  cer-vix-es
  cer-vi-ces
ces-sa-tion
ces-sion
cess-pool
ce-ta-cean
  ce-ta-ceous
chafe

chafed
chaf-ing
chaf-er
chaff
  chaf-fer
  chaff-er-er
cha-grin
  cha-grined
  cha-grin-ing
chain re-ac-tion
chair-man
  chair-men
chaise-longue
chal-et
chal-ice
chalk
  chalky
chal-lenge
  chal-lenged
  chal-leng-ing
cham-ber
cham-ber-maid
cha-me-le-on
cham-ois
cham-pagne
cham-pi-on
  cham-pi-on-ship
chance-ful
chan-cel-lor
chanc-y
  chanc-i-er
  chanc-i-est
chan-de-lier
change
  changed
  chang-ing
  chang-a-ble
chan-nel
chan-ti-cleer
cha-os
cha-ot-ic
cha-pa-re-jos
chap-ar-ral
cha-peau
  cha-peaux
chap-el
chap-e-ron
chap-fall-en
chap-lain
chap-let
chap-ter
char
  charred
  char-ring
char-ac-ter
char-ac-ter-is-tic

char-ac-ter-is-ti-cal-ly
char-ac-ter-ize
  char-ac-ter-ized
  char-ac-ter-iz-ing
  char-ac-ter-i-za-tion
  char-ac-ter-iz-er
cha-rade
char-coal
charge
  charged
  charg-ing
  charg-er
char-i-ot
  char-i-ot-eer
cha-ris-ma
char-i-ta-ble
  char-i-ta-ble-ness
  char-i-ta-bly
char-i-ty
  char-i-ties
cha-riv-a-ri
char-la-tan
  char-la-tan-ism
char-ley horse
charm
char-nel
char-ter
char-treuse
char-wom-an
chary
  char-i-er
  char-i-est
chase
  chased
  chas-ing
  chas-er
chasm
chas-sis
chaste
  chaste-ly
chas-ten
chas-tise
  chas-tised
  chas-tis-ing
  chas-tis-ment
  chas-tis-er
  chas-ti-ty
chat
  chat-ted
  chat-ting
cha-teau
  cha-teaux
chat-e-laine
chat-tel
chat-ter
chat-ter-box

chat-ty
  chat-ti-er
  chat-ti-est
  chat-ti-ly
  chat-ti-ness
chauf-feur
chau-vin-ist
  chau-vin-ism
  chau-vin-is-tic
cheap
  cheap-ly
  cheap-ness
  cheap-en
cheap-skate
cheat
check-er-board
check-list
check-mate
  check-mat-ed
  check-mat-ing
check-out
check-point
check-room
check-up
ched-dar
cheek-bone
cheek-y
  cheek-i-er
  cheek-i-est
  cheek-i-ness
cheer-ful
  cheer-ful-ly
  cheer-ful-ness
cheer-lead-er
cheer-less
  cheer-less-ly
  cheer-less-ness
chee-y
  cheer-i-er
  cheer-i-est
  cheer-i-ly
  cheer-i-ness
cheese-burg-er
cheese-cake
cheese-cloth
chees-y
  chees-i-er
  chees-i-est
  chees-i-ness
chee-tah
chem-i-cal
  chem-i-cal-ly
che-mise
chem-ist
chem-is-try
chem-o-ther-a-py

che-nille
cher-ish
che-root
cher-ry
  cher-ries
cher-ub
  cher-ubs
  cher-u-bim
  che-ru-bic
cher-vil
chess-man
  chess-men
chest-nut
chest-y
  chest-i-er
  chest-i-est
chev-ron
chew
  chew-er
chi-a-ro-scu-ro
chi-can-ery
  cha-can-er-ies
chi-chi
chick-a-dee
chic-ken
chic-ken-heart-ed
chic-le
chic-o-ry
  chic-o-ries
chide
  chid-ed
chief
  chief-ly
chief-tain
chif-fon
chif-fo-nier
chi-gnon
chil-blain
chil-dren
child-bear-ing
child-birth
child-hood
child-ish
  child-ish-ly
  child-like
chili
  chil-ies
chill
  chill-ing-ly
chill-y
  chill-i-er
  chill-i-est
  chill-i-ness
chi-me-ra
chi-mer-ic
  chi-mer-i-cal

chi-mer-i-cal-ly
chi-mer-i-cal-ness
chim-ney
chim-pan-zee
chin
  chinned
  chin-ning
chi-na
chi-no
  chi-nos
chi-noi-se-rie
chintz-y
  chintz-i-er
  chintz-i-est
chip
  chipped
  chip-ping
chip-munk
chip-per
chi-rog-ra-pher
chi-rog-ra-phy
chi-rop-o-dist
chi-ro-prac-tic
chi-ro-prac-tor
chis-el
  chis-eled
  chis-el-ing
  chis-el-er
chit-chat
chi-tin
chit-ter-ling
chiv-al-ry
  chiv-al-ries
  chiv-al-ric
  chiv-al-rous
  chiv-al-rous-ly
  chiv-al-rous-ness
chlo-rine
chlo-ro-form
clo-ro-phyll
chock-full
choc-o-late
choice
  choice-ly
  choice-ness
choir-boy
choke
  choked
  chok-ing
  chok-er
chol-er
chol-era
chol-er-ic
cho-les-te-rol
choose
  chose

cho-sen
choos-ing
choos-y
  choos-i-er
  choos-i-est
chop
  chopped
  chop-ping
chop-per
  chop-pi-ness
chop-py
  chop-pi-er
  chop-i-est
chop-sticks
chop su-ey
cho-ral
  cho-ral-ly
cho-rale
chord
  chord-al
cho-rea
cho-re-og-ra-phy
  cho-re-og-ra-pher
  cho-re-o-graph-ic
cho-ric
chor-is-ter
chor-tle
  chor-tled
  chor-tling
cho-rus
  cho-rus-es
  cho-rused
  cho-rus-ing
chos-en
chow-der
chow mein
chrism
Christ
chris-ten
  chris-ten-ing
Chris-tian
Chis-ti-an-i-ty
  Chris-ti-an-i-ties
Christ-mas
chro-mate
chro-mat-ic
  chro-mat-i-cal-ly
chro-mat-ics
chro-ma-tin
chro-mic
chro-mi-um
chro-mo
  chro-mus
chro-mo-lith-o-graph
chro-mo-some
chro-mo-sphere

chron-ic
chron-i-cal-ly
chron-i-cle
chron-i-cled
chron-i-cling
chron-i-cler
chron-o-log-i-cal
chron-o-log-i-cal-ly
chro-no-lo-gy
chro-nol-o-gies
chro-nol-o-gist
chro-nom-e-ter
chron-o-met-ric
chrys-a-lis
chry-sa-lis-es
chry-sal-i-des
chry-san-the-mum
chrys-o-lite
chub-by
chub-bi-er
chub-bi-est
chub-bi-ness
chuck-full
chuck-le
chuck-led
chuck-ling
chuk-ker
chum-my
chum-mi-er
chum-mi-est
chunk
chunky
chunk-i-er
chunk-i-est
church
church-li-ness
church-ly
church-go-er
church-man
church-men
church-war-den
church-yard
churl-ish
churl-ish-ly
churl-ish-ness
churn-er
chut-ney
chutz-pah
ci-bo-ri-um
ci-bo-ria
ci-ca-da
ci-ca-das
ci-ca-dea
cic-a-trix
cic-a-tri-ces
cic-a-trize

cic-a-trized
cic-a-triz-ing
cic-e-ro-ne
ci-der
ci-gar
cig-a-rette
cil-ia
cil-i-ar-y
cil-i-ate
cin-cho-na
cinc-ture
cin-der
cin-e-ma
cin-e-mas
cin-e-mat-ic
cin-e-ma-to-graph
cin-e-ma-tog-ra-phy
cin-e-rar-i-um
cin-na-bar
cin-na-mon
cinque-foil
ci-on
ci-pher
cir-ca
cir-ca-di-an
cir-cle
cir-cled
cir-cling
cir-clet
cir-cuit
cir-cu-i-tous
cir-cu-i-tous-ly
cir-cu-i-tous-ness
cir-cu-lar
cir-cu-lar-ize
cir-cu-lar-ized
cir-cu-lar-iz-ing
cir-cu-lar-i-za-tion
cir-cu-la-tion
cir-cu-late
cir-cu-lat-ed
cir-cu-lat-ing
cir-cu-la-tive
cir-cu-la-tor
cir-cu-la-to-ry
cir-cum-am-bi-ent
cir-cum-cise
cir-cum-cised
cir-cum-cis-ing
cir-cum-cis-er
cir-cum-ci-sion
cir-cum-fer-ence
cir-cum-fer-en-tial
cir-cum-flex
cir-cum-flu-ent
cir-cum-fuse

cir-cum-fus-ing
cir-cum-fu-sion
cir-cum-lo-cu-tion
cir-cum-lo-cu-to-ry
cir-cum-nav-i-gate
cir-cum-nav-i-gat-ed
cir-cum-nav-i-gat-ing
cir-cum-nav-i-ga-tion
cir-cum-nav-i-ga-tor
cir-cum-scribe
cir-cum-scribed
cir-cum-scrib-ing
cir-cum-scrib-er
cir-cum-scrip-tion
cir-cum-scrip-tive
cir-cum-spect
cir-cum-stance
cir-cum-stan-tial
cir-cum-stan-ti-al-i-ty
cir-cum-stan-ti-at-ed
cir-cum-stan-ti-at-ing
cir-cum-stan-ti-a-tion
cir-cum-vent
cir-cum-ven-tion
cir-cum-ven-tive
cir-cus
cir-cus-es
cir-rho-sis
cir-rhot-ic
cir-rus
cis-tern
cit-a-del
cite
cit-ed
cit-ing
ci-ta-tion
cith-a-ra
cit-i-zen
cit-i-zen-ship
cit-i-zen-ry
cit-i-zen-ries
cit-rate
cit-ric
cit-ron
cit-ron-el-la
cit-rus
cit-tern
city
cit-ies
ci-ty-state
civ-et
civ-ic
civ-ics
civ-il
ci-vil-ian
ci-vil-i-ty

ci-vil-i-ties
civ-i-li-za-tion
civ-i-lize
  civ-i-lized
  civ-i-liz-ing
clab-ber
claim
  claim-a-ble
  claim-ant
  claim-er
clair-voy-ance
  clair-voy-ant
clam
  clammed
  clam-ming
clam-bake
clam-bar
clam-my
  clam-mi-er
  clam-mi-est
  clam-mi-ly
  clam-mi-ness
clam-or
  clam-or-ous
clan
  clan-nish
clan-des-tine
clang-or
  clang-or-ous
clans-man
  clans-men
clap
  clapped
  clap-ping
clap-board
clap-per
clap-trap
claque
clar-et
clar-i-fy
  clar-i-fied
  clar-i-fy-ing
  clar-i-fi-ca-tion
clar-i-net
  clar-i-net-ist
clar-i-on
clar-i-ty
class-a-ble
clas-sic
  clas-si-cal
  clas-si-cal-ly
clas-si-cism
  clas-si-cist
clas-si-fy
  clas-si-fied
  clas-si-fy-ing

clas-si-fi-er
clas-si-fi-ca-tion
class-mate
class-room
class-y
  class-i-er
  class-i-est
clat-ter
clause
  claus-i-cle
claus-tro-pho-bia
clav-i-chord
clav-i-cle
cla-vier
clay
  clay-ey
clay-more
clean-cut
clean-er
clean-ly
  clean-li-er
  clean-li-est
  clean-li-ness
cleanse
  cleansed
  cleans-ing
  cleans-er
clean-up
clear
  clear-ly
  clear-ness
clear-ance
clear-cut
clear-ing
clear-sight-ed
cleav-age
cleave
  cleaved
  cleav-ing
cleav-er
clef
cleft
clem-en-cy
  clem-ent
clere-sto-ry
  clere-sto-riees
cler-gy
  cler-gies
cler-gy-man
  cler-gy-men
cler-ic
  cler-i-cal
  cler-i-cal-ism
  cler-i-cal-ist
clev-er
  clev-er-ly

clev-er-ness
clev-is
  clev-is-es
clew
cli-ent
cli-en-tele
cliff-hang-er
cli-mac-ter-ic
cli-mate
  cli-mat-ic
  cli-mat-i-cal
climb
  climb-a-ble
  climb-er
clinch-er
cling
  cling-ing
  cling-ing-ly
  cling-er
clin-ic
  clin-i-cal
  clin-i-cal-ly
clink-er
clip
  clipped
  clip-ping
clip-per
clique
  cliqu-ey
  cliqu-ish
clit-o-ris
clo-a-ca
  clo-a-cae
  clo-a-cal
clob-ber
clock-wise
clock-work
clod
  clod-dish
  clod-dy
clog
  clog-ged
  clog-ging
clois-ter
  clois-tral
close
  closed
  clos-ing
  clos-est
  close-ly
  close-ness
close-fist-ed
close-mouthed
clos-et
  clos-et-ed
  clos-et-ing

close-up
clo-sure
clot
  clot-ted
  clot-ting
clothe
  clothed
  cloth-ing
clothes-horse
clothes-line
clothes-pin
cloth-ier
cloth-ing
clo-ture
cloud-burst
cloud-y
  cloud-i-er
  cloud-i-est
  cloud-i-ly
  cloud-i-ness
clo-ven
clo-ver
clo-ver-leaf
clown
  clown-ish
cloy
  cloy-ing-ly
club
  clubbed
  club-bing
club-foot
club-house
clump
  clumpy
clum-sy
  clum-si-er
  clum-si-est
  clum-si-ly
  clum-si-ness
clus-ter
coach-man
  coach-men
co-ag-u-late
  co-ag-u-lat-ed
  co-ag-u-lat-ing
  co-ag-u-la-tion
co-a-lesce
  co-a-lesced
  co-a-les-cing
  co-a-les-cence
  co-a-les-cent
co-a-li-tion
coarse
  coars-er
  coars-est
  coars-en

coarse-ly
coast-er
coast-line
coat-ing
co-au-thor
coax
  coax-ing-ly
co-balt
cob-ble
  cob-bled
  cob-bling
cob-bler
cob-ble-stone
co-bra
cob-web
  cob-webbed
  cob-web-by
co-ca
co-caine
coc-cyx
  coc-cy-ges
  coc-cyg-e-al
coch-le-a
cock-ade
cock-a-too
cock-crow
cock-er span-iel
cock-eyed
cock-fight
cock-le
cock-le-bur
cock-le-shell
cock-ney
  cock-neys
cock-pit
cock-roach
cocks-comb
cock-sure
cock-tail
cocky
  cock-i-er
  cock-i-est
  cock-i-ness
co-coa
co-co-nut
co-coon
cod
  cod-fish
cod-dle
  cod-dled
  cod-dling
code
  cod-ed
  cod-ing
co-deine
codg-er

cod-i-cil
cod-i-fy
  cod-i-fied
  cod-i-fy-ing
  cod-i-fi-ca-tion
cod-liv-er oil
co-ed
co-ed-u-ca-tion
coe-len-ter-ate
co-e-qual
co-erce
  co-erced
  co-er-cing
  co-er-ci-ble
  co-er-cion
  co-er-cive
co-ex-ist
  co-ex-ist-ence
  co-ex-ist-ent
cof-fee
cof-fee-house
cof-fee-pot
cof-fer
cof-fin
co-gent
  co-gen-cy
  co-gent-ly
cog-i-tate
  cog-i-tat-ed
  cog-i-tat-ing
  cog-i-ta-ble
  cog-i-ta-tive
cog-nac
cog-nate
cog-ni-tion
  cog-ni-tive
cog-ni-zance
  cog-ni-zant
cog-wheel
co-hab-it
  co-hab-i-ta-tion
co-here
  co-hered
  co-her-ing
co-her-ent
  co-her-ence
  co-her-en-cy
  co-her-ent-ly
co-he-sion
co-he-sive
  co-hes-sive-ly
  co-hes-sive-ness
co-hort
coif-feur
coif-fure
  coif-fured

coif-fur-ing
coin-age
co-in-cide
  co-in-cid-ed
  co-in-cid-ing
co-in-ci-dence
co-in-ci-den-tal
  co-in-ci-den-tal-ly
co-i-tion
co-i-tus
  co-i-tal
coke
  coked
  cok-ing
co-la
col-an-der
cold-blood-ed
cole-slaw
col-ic
  col-icky
col-i-se-um
co-li-tis
col-lab-o-rate
  col-lab-o-rat-ed
  col-lab-o-rat-ing
  col-lab-o-ra-tion
  col-lab-o-ra-tor
col-lage
col-lapse
  col-lapsed
  col-laps-ing
  col-lap-si-ble
col-lar
col-lar-bone
col-late
  col-lat-ed
  col-lat-ing
  col-la-tion
  col-la-tor
col-lat-er-al
col-league
col-lect
  col-lect-i-ble
  col-lec-tor
  col-lect-ed
  col-lec-tion
col-lec-tive
  col-lec-tive-ly
  col-lect-tiv-i-ty
  col-lect-tiv-ism
  col-lect-tiv-ize
  col-lec-tiv-iz-ing
  col-lec-tiv-i-za-tion
col-lege
  col-le-gi-al
col-le-gian

col-le-giate
col-lide
  col-lid-ed
  col-lid-ing
  col-li-sion
col-li-mate
  col-li-mat-ed
  col-li-mat-ing
  col-li-ma-tion
col-lo-cate
  col-lo-cat-ed
  col-lo-cat-ing
  col-lo-ca-tion
col-loid
col-lo-qui-al
  col-lo-qui-al-ly
  col-lo-qui-al-ism
col-lo-quy
  col-lo-quies
col-lu-sion
  col-lu-sive
co-logne
co-lon
colo-nel
co-lo-ni-al
  co-lo-ni-al-ism
  co-lo-ni-al-ist
col-o-nist
col-o-nade
col-o-ny
  col-o-nies
  col-o-nize
  col-o-nized
  col-o-niz-ing
  col-o-niz-er
  col-o-ni-za-tion
col-or
  col-or-er
  col-or-less
col-or-a-tion
col-or-blind
  col-or-blind-ness
col-or-cast
col-ored
col-or-fast
col-or-ful
col-or-ing
co-los-sal
co-los-sus
  co-los-si
colt-ish
col-um-bine
col-umn
  co-lum-nar
  co-lumned
col-um-nist

co-ma
  co-mas
  co-ma-tose
com-bat
  com-bat-ed
  com-bat-ing
  com-bat-ant
com-ba-tive
comb-er
com-bi-na-tion
  com-bi-na-tion-al
  com-bi-na-tive
com-bine
  com-bined
  com-bin-ing
  com-bin-a-ble
  com-bin-er
com-bo
  com-bos
com-bust-ti-ble
  com-bus-ti-bil-i-ty
con-bus-tion
  com-bus-tive
come
  com-ing
come-back
co-me-di-an
  co-me-di-enne
come-down
com-e-dy
  com-e-dies
come-ly
  come-li-ness
come-on
com-er
com-et
come-up-pance
com-fort
  com-fort-a-ble
  com-fort-a-bly
  com-fort-er
com-fy
  com-fi-er
  com-fi-est
com-ic
  com-i-cal
com-ing
com-i-ty
  com-i-ties
com-ma
  com-mas
com-mand
  com-man-dant
  com-man-deer
  com-mand-er
  com-mand-er-ship

com-mand-ment
com-man-do
  com-man-dos
com-mem-o-rate
  com-mem-o-rat-ed
  com-mem-o-rat-ing
  com-mem-o-ra-ble
  com-mem-o-ra-tion
  com-mem-o-ra-tive
  com-mem-o-ra-to-ry
com-mence
  com-menced
  com-menc-ing
com-mence-ment
com-mend
  com-mend-a-ble
  com-mend-a-bly
com-men-da-tion
  com-mend-a-to-ry
com-men-su-rate
  com-men-su-rate-ly
  com-men-su-ra-tion
com-ment
com-men-tary
  com-men-tar-ies
  com-men-ta-tor
com-merce
com-mer-cial
  com-mer-cial-ism
  com-mer-cial-ize
  com-mer-cial-ized
  com-mer-cial-iz-ing
com-mie
com-mis-er-ate
  com-mis-er-at-ed
  com-mis-er-at-ing
  com-mis-er-a-tion
  com-mis-er-a-tive
com-mis-sar
com-mis-sar-y
  com-mis-sar-ies
com-mis-sion
  com-mis-sioned
com-mis-sion-er
com-mit
  com-mit-ted
  com-mit-ting
  com-mit-ment
com-mit-tee
  com-mit-tee-man
  com-mit-tee-wo-man
com-mode
com-mo-di-ous
com-mod-i-ty
  com-mod-i-ties
com-mo-dore

com-mon
com-mon-al-ty
  com-mon-al-ties
com-mon-place
com-mons
com-mon-wealth
com-mo-tion
com-mu-nal
  com-mu-nal-i-ty
com-mune
  com-muned
  com-mun-ing
com-mu-ni-cant
com-mu-ni-cate
  com-mu-ni-cat-ed
  com-mu-ni-cat-ing
  com-mu-ni-ca-ble
  com-mu-ni-ca-tive
  com-mu-ni-ca-tion
com-mun-ion
  com-mun-ism
  com-mun-ist
com-mu-ni-ty
  com-mu-ni-ties
com-mu-nize
  com-mu-nized
  com-mu-niz-ing
com-mu-ta-tion
com-mu-ta-tor
com-mute
  com-mut-ed
  com-mut-ing
  com-mut-a-ble
com-mut-er
com-pact
com-pan-ion
  com-pan-ion-a-ble
  com-pan-ion-ship
com-pa-ny
  com-pa-nies
com-par-a-ble
  com-par-a-bil-ity
com-par-a-tive
com-pare
  com-pared
  com-par-ing
com-par-i-son
com-part-ment
  com-part-men-tal
  com-part-ment-ed
  com-part-men-tal-ize
com-pass
com-pas-sion
  com-pas-sion-ate
com-pat-ible
  com-pat-i-bly

com-pat-i-bil-i-ty
com-pa-tri-ot
com-peer
com-pel
  com-pelled
  com-pel-ling
com-pem-di-ous
  com-pen-di-um
com-pen-sate
  com-pen-sat-ed
  com-pen-sat-ing
  com-pen-sa-tive
  com-pen-sa-tor
  com-pen-sa-to-ry
com-pen-sa-tion
com-pete
  com-pet-ed
  com-pet-ing
com-pet-i-tor
com-pe-tence
  com-pe-ten-cy
com-pe-tent
com-pe-ti-tion
com-pet-i-tive
com-pile
  com-piled
  com-pil-ing
  com-pi-la-tion
com-pla-cence
  com-pla-cen-cy
  com-pla-cent
com-plain
com-plain-ant
com-plaint
com-plai-sance
  com-plai-sant
com-plect-ed
com-ple-ment
  com-ple-men-tal
  com-ple-men-ta-ry
com-plete
  com-plet-ed
  com-plet-ing
  com-plet-a-ble
com-ple-tion
com-plex
com-plex-ion
  com-plex-ioned
com-plex-i-ty
  com-plex-i-ties
com-pli-ance
  com-pli-an-cy
  com-pli-ant
com-pli-cate
  com-pli-cat-ed
  com-pli-cat-ing

com-pli-ca-tion
com-plic-i-ty
  com-plic-i-ties
com-pli-ment
  com-pli-men-ta-ri-ly
com-ply
  com-plied
  com-ply-ing
com-po-nent
com-port
com-port-ment
com-pose
  com-posed
  com-pos-ing
com-pos-er
com-pos-ite
com-po-si-tion
com-post
com-po-sure
com-pote
com-pound
com-pre-hend
  com-pre-hend-i-ble
com-pre-hen-si-ble
  com-pre-hen-si-bly
com-pre-hen-sion
com-pre-hen-sive
com-press
  com-presed
  com-press-i-ble
  com-press-i-bil-ity
com-pres-sion
com-pres-sor
com-prise
  com-prised
  com-pris-ing
com-pro-mise
  com-pro-mised
  com-pro-mis-ing
comp-trol-ler
com-pul-sion
com-pul-sive
com-pul-so-ry
com-punc-tion
com-pute
  com-put-ed
  com-put-ing
  com-pu-ta-tion
com-pu-ter
com-put-er-ize
  com-put-er-ized
  com-put-er-iz-ing
  com-put-er-i-za-tion
com-rade
  com-rade-ship
com-sat

con
  conned
  con-ning
con-cave
con-ceal
  con-ceal-a-ble
  con-ceal-ment
con-cede
  con-ced-ed
  con-ced-ing
con-ceit
  con-ceit-ed
con-ceive
  con-ceived
  con-ceiv-ing
  con-ceiv-a-ble
  con-ceiv-a-bly
con-cen-trate
  con-cen-tra-ted
  con-cen-trat-ing
  con-cen-tra-tive
  con-cen-tra-tion
con-cen-tric
  con-cen-tri-cal
  con-cen-tric-i-ty
con-cept
  con-cep-tu-al
con-cep-tion
  con-cep-tive
con-cep-tu-al-ize
  con-cep-tu-al-ized
  con-cep-tu-al-iz-ing
con-cern
  con-cerned
  con-cern-ing
con-cert
  con-cert-ed
  con-cer-ti-na
con-cert-mas-ter
con-cer-to
con-ces-sion
  con-ces-sion-aire
conch
  conchs
con-cil-i-ate
  con-cil-i-at-ed
  con-cil-i-at-ing
  con-cil-i-a-tion
  con-cil-i-a-to-ry
con-cise
  con-cise-ness
  con-cise-ly
con-clave
con-clude
  con-clud-ed
  con-clud-ing

con-clu-sion
con-clu-sive
con-coct
  con-coc-tion
con-com-i-tant
  con-com-i-tance
con-cord
  con-cord-ance
  con-cord-ant
con-course
con-crete
  con-cret-ed
  con-cret-ing
con-cre-tion
  con-cre-tive
con-cu-bine
con-cur
  con-curred
  con-cur-ring
  con-cur-rence
  con-cur-rent
con-cus-sion
  con-cus-sive
con-demn
  con-dem-na-ble
  con-dem-na-tion
  con-dem-na-to-ry
con-dense
  con-densed
  con-dens-ing
  con-den-sa-ble
  con-den-sa-tion
  con-dens-er
con-de-scend
  con-de-scend-ing
  con-de-scen-sion
con-di-ment
con-di-tion
  con-di-tion-al
  con-di-tion-er
  con-di-tion-ed
con-dole
  con-doled
  con-dol-ing
  con-do-la-to-ry
  con-do-ler
con-do-lence
con-dom
con-do-min-i-um
con-done
  con-doned
  con-don-ing
  con-do-na-tion
con-dor
con-duce
  con-duced

con-duc-ing
con-duct
  con-duct-i-bil-i-ty
  con-duct-i-ble
con-duct-ance
con-duc-tion
con-fer-ence
  con-fer-en-tial
con-fess
  con-fess-ed-ly
con-fes-sion
  con-fes-sion-al
con-fes-sor
con-fet-ti
con-fi-dant
  con-fi-dante
con-fide
  con-fid-ed
  con-fid-ing
con-fi-dence
  con-fi-dent
con-fi-den-tial
con-fig-u-ra-tion
  con-fig-u-ra-tion-al
con-fine
  con-fined
  con-fin-ing
  con-fine-ment
con-firm
  con-firm-a-ble
  con-fir-ma-tion
  con-fir-ma-tive
  con-fir-ma-to-ry
con-fir-med
  con-firm-ed-ly
  con-firm-ed-ness
con-fis-cate
  con-fis-cat-ed
  con-fis-cat-ing
  con-fis-ca-tion
  con-fis-ca-tor
  con-fis-ca-to-ry
con-fla-gra-tion
con-flict
  con-flict-ing
  con-flic-tive
  con-flic-tion
con-flu-ence
  con-flu-ent
con-flux
con-form
  con-form-ist
  con-form-ism
  con-form-a-ble
  con-form-a-bly
  con-form-ance

con-for-ma-tion
con-form-i-ty
  con-form-i-ties
con-found
  con-found-ed
  con-found-ed-ly
con-front
  con-fron-ta-tion
con-fuse
  confused
  con-fus-ing
  con-fus-ed-ly
  con-fus-ed-ness
con-fu-sion
con-fute
  con-futed
  con-fut-ing
  con-fu-ta-tion
con-ga
  con-gas
con-geal
  con-geal-ment
con-gen-ial
  con-ge-ni-al-i-ty
  con-gen-ial-ly
con-gen-i-tal
con-ger
  con-ge-ries
con-gest
  con-ges-tion
  con-ges-tive
con-glom-er-ate
  con-glom-er-at-ing
  con-glom-er-a-tion
con-grat-u-late
  con-grat-u-lat-ed
  con-grat-u-lat-ing
  con-grat-u-la-tor
  con-grat-u-la-to-ry
  con-grat-u-la-tion
con-gre-gate
  con-gre-gat-ed
  con-gre-gat-ing
con-gre-ga-tion
  con-gre-ga-tion-al
con-gress
  con-gres-sion-al
con-gress-man
  con-gress-men
  con-gress-wom-an
  con-gress-wom-en
con-gru-ent
  con-gru-ent-ly
  con-gru-ence
  con-gru-en-cy
  con-gru-en-cies

con-gru-i-ty
  con-gru-i-ties
con-gru-ous
  con-gru-ous-ly
con-ic
  con-i-cal
co-ni-fer
con-jec-ture
  con-jec-tured
  con-jec-tur-ing
  con-jec-tur-al
con-join
con-joint
  con-joint-ly
con-ju-gal
  con-ju-gal-ly
con-ju-gate
  con-ju-gat-ed
  con-ju-gat-ing
  con-ju-ga-tion
  con-ju-ga-tive
con-junc-tion
  con-junc-tive
con-jur-a-tion
con-jure
  con-jured
  con-jur-ing
  con-jur-er
con-nect
con-nec-tor
con-nec-tion
con-nec-tive
con-nip-tion
con-nive
  con-nived
  con-niv-ing
  con-niv-ance
con-nois-seur
con-note
  con-not-ed
  con-not-ing
  con-no-ta-tion
  con-no-ta-tive
con-nu-bi-al
  con-ni-bi-al-ly
con-quer
  con-quer-a-ble
  con-quer-or
con-quest
con-quis-ta-dor
  con-quis-ta-dors
  con-quis-ta-dor-es
con-san-quin-e-ous
  con-san-quin-i-ty
con-science
con-sci-en-tious

con-sci-en-tious-ly
con-scious
  con-scious-ly
  con-scious-ness
con-script
  con-scrip-tion
con-se-crate
  con-se-crat-ed
  con-se-crat-ing
  con-se-cra-tive
  con-se-cra-tion
con-sec-u-tive
  con-sec-u-tive-ly
con-sen-sus
con-sent
  con-sent-er
con-se-quence
  con-se-quent
  con-se-quent-ly
con-se-quen-tial
  con-se-quen-ti-al-i-ty
  con-se-quen-tial-ly
con-ser-va-tion
  con-ser-va-tion-al
  con-ser-va-tion-ist
con-serv-a-tive
  con-serv-a-tism
  con-serv-a-tive-ly
con-serv-a-to-ry
  con-serv-a-to-ries
con-serve
  con-served
  con-serv-ing
  con-serv-a-ble
  con-serv-er
con-sid-er
  con-sid-er-a-ble
  con-sid-er-a-bly
con-sid-er-ate
  con-sid-er-a-tion
  con-sid-er-ing
con-sign
  con-sign-er
  con-sign-or
  con-sign-ment
con-sign-ee
con-sist
con-sist-en-cy
  con-sist-en-cies
  con-sist-ence
con-sist-ent
  con-sist-ent-ly
con-sis-to-ry
  con-sis-to-ries
con-so-la-tion
  con-sol-a-to-ry

con-sole
  con-soled
  con-sol-ing
  con-sol-a-ble
con-sol-i-date
  con-sol-i-dat-ed
  con-sol-i-dat-ing
  con-sol-i-da-tion
con-so-nant
  con-so-nance
  con-so-nant-ly
con-so-nan-tal
con-sort
con-sor-ti-um
  con-sor-tia
con-spic-u-ous
  con-spic-u-ous-ly
  con-spic-u-ous-ness
con-spire
  con-spired
  con-spir-ing
  con-spir-a-cy
  con-spir-a-cies
  con-spir-a-tor
  con-spir-a-to-ri-al
  con-spir-er
  con-spir-ing-ly
con-sta-ble
  con-sta-ble-ship
con-stab-u-lar-y
  con-stab-u-lar-ies
con-stant
  con-stan-cy
con-stant-ly
con-stel-la-tion
con-ster-na-tion
con-sti-pate
  con-sti-pa-tion
con-stit-u-en-cy
  con-stit-u-en-cies
con-stit-u-ent
con-sti-tute
con-sti-tu-tion
  con-sti-tu-tion-al
  con-sti-tu-tion-al-i-ty
  con-sti-tu-tion-al-ly
con-strain
  con-strain-a-ble
  con-strained
con-straint
con-strict
  con-stric-tive
  con-stric-tion
con-stric-tor
con-struct
  con-struc-tor

con-struc-tion
  con-struc-tion-al
con-struc-tive
  con-struc-tive-ly
  con-struc-tive-ness
con-strue
  con-strued
  con-stru-ing
  con-stru-a-ble
  con-stru-er
con-sul
  con-su-lar
  con-sul-ship
con-su-late
con-sult
  con-sul-ta-tion
con-sult-ant
con-sume
  con-sumed
  con-sum-ing
  con-sum-a-ble
con-sum-er
con-sum-mate
  con-sum-mat-ed
  con-sum-mat-ing
  con-sum-mate-ly
  con-sum-ma-tion
con-sump-tion
com-sump-tive
con-tact
con-ta-gion
  con-ta-gious
  con-ta-gious-ness
con-tain
  con-tain-a-ble
con-tain-er
con-tain-ment
con-tam-i-nate
  con-tam-i-nat-ed
  con-tam-i-nat-ing
  con-tam-i-nant
  con-tam-i-na-tion
  con-tam-i-na-tive
  con-tam-i-na-tor
con-tem-plate
  con-tem-plat-ed
  con-tem-plat-ing
  con-tem-pla-tion
  con-tem-pla-tive
con-tem-po-ra-ne-ous
con-tem-po-rar-y
  con-tem-po-rar-ies
con-tempt
  con-tempt-i-ble
  con-tempt-i-bly
con-temp-tu-ous

con-temp-tu-ous-ly
con-tend
  con-tend-er
con-tent
  con-tent-ment
con-tent-ed
  con-tent-ed-ly
  con-tent-ed-ness
con-ten-tion
con-ten-tious
  con-ten-tious-ly
  con-ten-tious-ness
con-ter-mi-ous
con-test
  con-test-a-ble
  con-test-er
con-test-ant
con-text
con-tig-u-ous
  con-ti-gu-i-ty
  con-ti-gu-i-ties
  con-tig-u-ous-ly
  con-tig-u-ous-ness
con-ti-nence
  con-ti-nen-cy
con-ti-nent
  con-ti-nent-ly
  con-ti-nen-tal
con-tin-gent
  con-tin-gen-cies
  con-tin-gent-ly
con-tin-u-al
  con-tin-u-al-ly
con-tin-u-ance
con-tin-ue
  con-tin-ued
  con-tin-u-ing
  con-tin-u-a-tion
  con-tin-u-er
con-ti-nu-i-ty
  con-ti-nu-i-ties
con-tin-u-ous
  con-tin-u-ous-ly
con-tin-u-um
  con-tin-ua
con-tort
  con-tor-tion
  con-tor-tive
  con-tor-tion-ist
con-tour
con-tra-band
can-tra-cep-tive
  con-tra-cep-tion
con-tract
  con-tract-ed
  con-tract-i-ble

con-trac-tu-al
con-trac-tion
  con-trac-tive
  con-trac-tile
con-trac-tor
con-tra-dict
  con-tra-dict-a-ble
  con-tra-dic-tion
  con-tra-dic-to-ry
con-tra-dis-tinc-tion
con-trail
con-tral-to
  con-tral-tos
  con-tral-ti
con-trap-tion
con-tra-pun-tal
con-tra-ri-wise
con-tra-ry
  con-tra-ries
  con-tra-ri-ly
  con-tra-ri-ness
con-trast
  con-trast-a-ble
  con-trast-ing-ly
con-tra-vene
  con-tra-vened
  con-tra-ven-ing
  con-tra-ven-er
  con-tra-ven-tion
con-trib-ute
  con-trib-ut-ed
  con-trib-ut-ing
  con-trib-ut-a-ble
  con-trib-u-tor
  con-trib-u-tory
con-tri-bu-tion
con-trite
  con-trite-ly
  con-trite-ness
  con-tri-tion
con-trive
  con-triv-ed
  con-triv-ing
  con-triv-ance
con-trol
  con-trolled
  con-trol-ling
  con-trol-la-ble
con-trol-ler
  con-trol-ler-ship
con-tro-ver-sy
  con-tro-ver-sies
  con-tro-ver-sal
  con-tro-ver-sial-ly
con-tro-vert
con-tu-me-ly

con-tu-me-lies
con-tuse
  con-tused
  con-tus-ing
  con-tu-sion
co-nun-drum
cov-va-lesce
  con-va-lesced
  con-va-les-cing
con-va-les-cence
  con-va-les-cent
con-vec-tion
con-vene
  con-vened
  con-ven-ing
  con-ven-er
con-ven-ience
con-ven-ient
  con-ven-ient-ly
con-vent
con-ven-tion
  con-ven-tion-al
  con-ven-tion-al-ism
  con-ven-tion-al-ist
  con-ven-tion-al-i-ty
  con-ven-tion-al-i-ties
  con-ven-tion-al-ize
  con-ven-tion-al-ized
  con-ven-tion-al-iz-ing
con-verge
  con-verged
  con-verg-ing
  con-ver-gence
  con-ver-gen-cy
  con-ver-gent
con-ver-sant
con-ver-sa-tion
  con-ver-sa-tion-al
  con-ver-sa-tion-al-ist
con-verse
  con-versed
  con-vers-ing
  con-verse-ly
con-ver-sion
con-vert
con-vert-er
con-vert-i-ble
  con-vert-i-bil-i-ty
  con-vert-i-bly
con-vex
  con-vex-ly
  con-vex-i-ty
con-vey
  con-vey-a-ble
con-vey-ance
con-vey-er

con-vey-or
con-vict
con-vic-tion
  con-vic-tion-al
con-vince
  con-vinced
  con-vinc-ing
  con-vinc-er
  con-vinc-i-ble
con-viv-i-al
  con-viv-i-al-i-ty
  con-viv-i-al-ly
con-vo-ca-tion
  con-vo-ca-tion-al
con-voke
  con-voked
  con-vok-ing
  con-vok-er
con-vo-lute
  con-vo-lut-ed
  con-vo-lut-ing
  con-vo-lute-ly
  con-vo-lu-tion
con-voy
con-vulse
  con-vulsed
  con-vuls-ing
con-vul-sion
  con-vul-sive
  con-vul-sive-ly
co-ny
coo
  cooed
  coo-ing
  coo-ing-ly
cook-book
cook-er-y
  cook-e-ries
cook-out
cool
  cool-ish
  cool-ly
  cool-ness
cool-ant
cool-er
coo-lie
  coo-lies
coon-skin
coop-er
coop-er-age
co-op-er-ate
  co-op-er-at-ed
  co-op-er-at-ing
co-op-er-a-tion
co-op-er-a-tive
  co-op-er-a-tive-ly

co-opt
co-op-ta-tion
co-or-di-nate
  co-or-di-nat-ed
  co-or-di-nat-ing
  co-or-di-nate-ly
  co-or-di-na-tor
  co-or-di-na-tion
coo-tie
cop
  copped
  cop-ping
cope-stone
co-pi-lot
co-pi-ous
  co-pi-ous-ly
  co-pi-ous-ness
cop-out
cop-per
  cop-per-y
cop-per-head
cop-per-plate
cop-pice
cop-ra
copse
cop-u-la
  cop-u-las
  cop-u-lae
  cop-u-lar
cop-u-late
  cop-u-lat-ed
  cop-u-lat-ing
  cop-u-la-tion
cop-u-la-tive
  cop-u-la-tive-ly
copy
  cop-ies
  cop-ied
  cop-y-ing
cop-y-book
cop-y-cat
cop-y-ist
cop-y-right
co-quet
  co-quet-ted
  co-quet-ting
co-quet-ry
  co-quet-ries
co-quette
  co-quet-tish
  co-quet-tish-ly
cor-a-cle
cor-al
cor-bel
cord-age
cor-date

cor-date-ly
cor-dial
  cor-dial-i-ty
  cor-dial-ness
  cor-dial-ly
cor-dil-le-ra
cord-ite
cor-don
cor-do-van
cor-du-roy
cord-wood
core
  cored
  cor-ing
co-re-la-tion
co-re-spond-ent
co-ri-an-der
cor-ker
cork-screw
corn-cob
cor-nea
  cor-ne-al
cor-ner
cor-ner-stone
cor-net
  cor-net-ist
corn-flow-er
cor-nice
corn-starch
cor-nu-co-pi-a
corn-y
  corn-i-er
  conr-i-est
co-rol-la
cor-ol-lar-y
  cor-ol-lar-ies
co-ro-na
  co-ro-nas
  co-ro-nae
cor-o-nar-y
cor-o-na-tion
cor-o-ner
  cor-o-ner-ship
cor-o-net
  cor-o-net-ed
cor-po-ral
cor-po-rate
  cor-po-rate-ly
  cor-po-ra-tive
cor-po-ra-tion
cor-po-rat-ism
cor-po-re-al
  cor-po-re-al-i-ty
  cor-po-re-al-ness
corps
corpse

corps-man
corps-men
cor-pu-lent
cor-pu-lence
cor-pu-len-cy
cor-pus
cor-pus-cle
cor-pus-cu-lar
cor-ral
cor-ralled
cor-ral-ling
cor-rect
cor-rect-a-ble
cor-rect-i-ble
cor-rect-ness
cor-rec-tor
cor-rec-tion
cor-rec-tion-al
cor-rec-tive
cor-re-late
cor-re-lat-ed
cor-re-lat-ing
cor-re-la-tion
cor-rel-a-tive
cor-re-spond
cor-re-spond-ing
cor-re-spond-ing-ly
cor-re-spond-ence
cor-re-spond-ent
cor-ri-dor
cor-ri-gi-ble
cor-ri-gi-bil-i-ty
cor-ri-gi-bly
cor-rob-o-rate
cor-rob-o-rat-ed
cor-rob-o-rat-ing
cor-rob-o-ra-tion
cor-rob-o-ra-tive
cor-rob-o-ra-to-ry
cor-rode
cor-rod-ed
cor-rod-ing
cor-rod-i-ble
cor-ro-sion
cor-ro-sive
cor-ru-gate
cor-ru-gat-ed
cor-ru-gat-ing
cor-ru-ga-tion
cor-rupt
cor-rupt-er
cor-rup-ti-ble
cor-rup-ti-bil-i-ty
cor-rupt-ly
cor-rupt-ness
cor-rup-tion

cor-sage
cor-sair
cor-set
cor-set-ed
cor-tex
cor-ti-ces
cor-ti-cal
cor-ti-sone
co-run-dum
co-sig-na-to-ry
cos-met-ic
cos-mic
cos-mi-cal-ly
cos-mog-o-ny
cos-mog-o-nies
cos-mo-gon-ic
cos-mog-o-nist
cos-mog-o-ny
cos-mog-o-nist
cos-mog-ra-phy
cos-mog-ra-phies
cos-mog-ra-pher
cos-mo-graph-ic
cos-mol-o-gy
cos-mol-o-gies
cos-mo-log-ic
cos-mol-o-gist
cos-mo-naut
cos-mo-pol-i-tan
cos-mo-pol-i-tan-ism
cos-mop-o-lite
cos-mos
cost-ly
cost-li-er
cost-li-est
cost-li-ness
cost--plus
cos-tume
cos-tumed
cos-tum-ing
cos-tum-er
co-sy
co-si-er
cos-i-est
co-te-rie
co-ter-mi-nous
co-til-lion
cot-tage
cot-ter
cot-ton
cot-ton-y
cot-ton-mouth
cot-ton-seed
cot-ton-tail
cot-ton-wood
couch

coun-cil
coun-cil-or
coun-cil-man
coun-cil-lor-ship
count
count-a-ble
count-down
coun-te-nance
coun-te-nanced
coun-te-nanc-ing
coun-te-nanc-er
count-er
coun-ter-act
coun-ter-ac-tion
coun-ter-ac-tive
coun-ter-at-tack
coun-ter-charge
coun-ter-charged
coun-ter-char-ging
coun-ter-claim
coun-ter-claim-ant
coun-ter-clock-wise
coun-ter-cul-ture
coun-ter-es-pi-o-nage
coun-ter-feit
coun-ter-feit-er
coun-ter-in-tel-li-gence
coun-ter-mand
coun-ter-meas-ure
coun-ter-of-fen-sive
coun-ter-pane
coun-ter-part
coun-ter-point
coun-ter-poise
coun-ter-poised
coun-ter-pois-ing
coun-ter-rev-o-lu-tion
coun-ter-sign
coun-ter-sig-na-ture
coun-ter-sink
coun-ter-sank
coun-ter-sunk
coun-ter-spy
coun-ter-spies
coun-ter-weight
coun-tees
count-less
coun-tri-fied
coun-try
coun-tries
coun-try-man
coun-try-men
coun-try-wom-an
coun-try-wom-en
coun-try-side
coun-ty

49

coun-ties
coup
  coups
coup-le
  coup-led
  coup-ling
coup-ler
cou-pon
cour-age
  cou-ra-geous
cour-i-er
course
  coursed
  cours-ing
cours-er
cour-te-ous
  cour-te-ous-ly
cour-te-sy
  cour-te-sies
court-house
cour-ti-er
court-ly
  court-li-er
  court-li-est
  court-li-ness
court-mar-tial
  courts-mar-tial
  court-mar-tialed
  court-mar-tial-ling
court-room
court-ship
court-yard
cous-in
  cous-in-hood
  cous-in-ly
cou-tu-rier
cov-e-nant
  cov-e-nan-ter
  cov-e-nan-tor
cov-er
  cov-ered
  cov-er-ing
  cov-er-less
cov-er-age
cov-er-all
cov-er-let
cov-ert
  cov-ert-ly
  cov-ert-ness
cov-er-up
cov-et
  cov-et-a-ble
  cov-et-er
cov-et-ous
  cov-et-ous-ly
cov-ey

cow-ard
  cow-ard-ly
  cow-ard-li-ness
cow-ard-ice
cow-boy
cow-er
  cow-er-ing-ly
cow-hide
cowl
  cowled
cow-lick
cowl-ing
cow-man
  cow-men
co-work-er
cow-poke
cow-pox
cow-ry
  cow-rie
  cow-ries
cox-swain
coy
  coy-ly
  coy-ness
coy-o-te
coz-en
  coz-en-age
  coz-en-er
co-zy
  co-zi-er
  co-zi-est
  co-zi-ly
  co-zi-ness
crab
  crabbed
  crab-bing
  crab-by
  crab-bed-ly
  crab-bed-ness
crack-down
crack-er
crack-ing
crack-le
  crack-led
  crack-ling
crack-up
cra-dle
  cra-dled
  cra-dling
crafts-man
  crafts-man-ship
crafty
  craft-i-er
  craft-i-est
  craft-i-ly
  craft-i-ness

crag
  crag-ged
  crag-gy
  crag-gi-ness
cram
  crammed
  cram-ming
  cram-mer
cran-ber-ry
  cran-ber-ries
crane
  craned
  cran-ing
cra-ni-um
  cra-ni-ums
  cra-nia
  cra-ni-al
  cra-ni-ate
  cra-ni-al-ly
crank-case
crank-shaft
crank-y
  crank-i-er
  crank-i-est
  crank-i-ly
  crank-i-ness
cran-ny
  cran-nies
  cran-nied
crash-land
crass
  crass-ly
  crass-ness
crate
  crat-ed
  crat-ing
cra-ter
  cra-ter-al
  cra-tered
cra-vat
crave
  craved
  crav-ing
  crav-er
  crav-ing-ly
craw-fish
crawl
  crawl-y
  crawl-ing-ly
crawl-er
cray-fish
cray-on
craze
  craz-ing
cra-zy
  cra-zi-er

cra-zi-est
cra-zi-ly
cra-zi-ness
creak
  creak-i-ly
  creak-i-ness
  creaky
  creak-i-er
  creak-i-est
cream
  cream-i-ly
  cream-i-ness
  cream-y
  cream-i-er
  cream-i-est
cream-er
cream-er-y
  cream-er-ies
crease
  creased
  creas-ing
  creas-y
  creas-i-er
  creas-i-est
cre-ate
  cre-at-ed
  cre-at-ing
cre-a-tion
  cre-a-tion-al
cre-a-tive
  cre-a-tive-i-ty
cre-a-tor
crea-ture
cre-dence
cre-den-tial
cre-den-za
cred-i-ble
  cred-i-bil-i-ty
  cred-i-bly
cred-it
  cred-it-a-ble
  cred-it-a-bil-i-ty
  cred-it-a-bly
cred-i-tor
cre-do
  cre-dos
cred-u-lous
creek
creel
creep
  crept
  creep-ing
  creepy
  creep-i-er
  creep-i-est
  creep-i-ness

creep-er
cre-mate
  cre-mat-ed
  cre-mat-ing
  cre-ma-tion
  cre-ma-tor
cre-ma-to-ry
  cre-ma-to-ri-um
cre-o-sote
crepe
  creped
  crep-ing
cre-pus-cu-lar
cres-cen-do
cres-cent
crest
  crest-ed
  crest-less
crest-fall-en
cre-ta-ceous
cre-tin-ism
cre-tonne
cre-vasse
crev-ice
crew-el
crib
  cribbed
  crib-bing
  crib-ber
crib-bage
crick-et
cri-er
crim-i-nal
  crim-i-nal-i-ty
  crim-i-nal-ly
crim-i-nol-o-gy
  crim-i-nol-o-gist
crimpy
  crimp-i-er
  crimp-i-est
crim-son
cringe
  cringed
  cring-ing
crin-kle
  crin-kled
  crin-kling
  crin-kly
  crin-kli-er
  crin-kli-est
crip-ple
  crip-pled
  crip-pling
cri-sis
  cri-ses
crisp

crisp-er
crisp-ness
crispy
  crisp-i-er
  crisp-i-est
criss-cross
cri-te-ri-on
cri-te-ria
crit-ic
crit-i-cal
  crit-i-cal-ly
  crit-i-cal-ness
crit-i-cism
crit-i-cize
  crit-i-cized
  crit-i-ciz-ing
  crit-i-ciz-a-ble
cri-tique
crit-er
croak-y
  croak-i-er
  croak-i-est
croak-er
cro-chet
  cro-cheted
  cro-chet-ing
  cro-chet-er
crock-ery
croc-o-dile
cro-cus
  cro-cus-es
crois-sant
cro-ny
  cro-nies
crook-ed
croon-er
crop
  cropped
  crop-ping
  crop-per
cro-quette
cross-bar
cross-bones
cross-bow
cross-bred
  cross-breed
  cross-breed-ing
cross-coun-try
cross-cut
cross-ex-am-ine
  cross-ex-am-ined
  cross-ex-am-in-ing
cross-fer-ti-li-za-tion
cross-ing
cross-pol-li-na-tion
  cross-pol-li-nate

51

cross-pur-pose
cross-ref-er-ence
cross-stitch
cross-ways
crotch-ety
  crotch-et-i-ness
crouch
croup
  croupy
crou-pi-er
crou-ton
crow-bar
crow's--foot
  crow's--feet
crow's--nest
cru-cial
  cru-ci-al-i-ty
  cru-cial-ly
cru-ci-ble
cru-ci-fix
cru-ci-fix-ion
cru-ci-form
cru-ci-fy
  cru-ci-fied
  cru-ci-fy-ing
crude
  crud-er
  crud-est
  crude-ly
  crude-ness
cru-di-ty
cru-di-ties
cru-el
  cru-el-ly
  cru-el-ness
  cru-el-ty
cru-et
cruise
  cruised
  cruis-ing
cruis-er
crul-ler
crum-ble
  crum-bled
  crum-bling
  crum-bly
crum-my
  crum-mi-er
  crum-mi-est
crum-pet
crum-ple
  crum-pled
  crum-pling
  crum-pler
  crum-ply
  crum-pli-er

  crum-pli-est
crunchy
  crunch-i-er
  crunch-i-est
cru-sade
  cru-sad-er
crush-er
  crush-ing
  crush-ing-ly
crus-ta-cean
crust-y
  crust-i-er
  crust-i-est
  crust-i-ly
  crust-i-ness
crux
  crux-es
  cru-ces
cry
  cried
  cry-ing
cry-ba-by
cry-o-gen-ics
cry-o-sur-gery
crypt
  crypt-al
crypt-a-nal-y-sis
crypt-ic
  cryp-ti-cal
  cryp-ti-cal-ly
cryp-to-gram
cryp-to-graph
  cryp-tog-ra-phy
  cryp-to-graph-ic
  cryp-tog-ra-pher
crys-tal
crys-tal-line
crys-tal-lize
  crys-tal-lized
  crys-tal-liz-ing
  crys-tal-liz-er
  crys-tal-liz-a-ble
  crys-tal-li-za-tion
cub-by
  cub-bies
cu-by-hole
cube
  cubed
  cub-ing
cu-bic
cu-bi-cle
cub-ism
cu-bit
cuck-old
  cuck-old-ry
cuck-oo

  cuck-oos
  cuck-ooed
  cuck-oo-ing
cu-cum-ber
cud-dle
  cud-dled
  cud-dling
  cud-dle-some
  cud-dly
  cud-dli-er
  cud-dli-est
cudg-el
  cudg-eled
  cudg-el-ing
cue
  cued
  cu-ing
cui-sine
cul-de-sac
  culs-de-sac
cu-li-nary
cul-mi-nant
cul-mi-nate
  cul-mi-nat-ed
  cul-mi-nat-ing
  cul-mi-na-tion
cu-lottes
cul-pa-ble
  cul-pa-bil-i-ty
  cul-pa-bly
cul-prit
cult
  cul-tic
cul-ti-vate
  cul-ti-vat-ed
  cul-ti-vat-ing
  cul-ti-va-tion
  cul-ti-va-ble
  cul-ti-vat-a-ble
cul-ti-va-tor
cul-tur-al
cul-ture
  cul-tured
  cul-tur-ing
cul-vert
cum-ber
  cum-ber-some
cum-brance
cum lau-de
cum-mer-bound
cum-mu-late
  cum-mu-lat-ed
  cum-mu-lat-ing
  cum-mu-la-tion
  cum-mu-la-tive
cu-mu-lo-nim-bus

cu-mu-lo-nim-bus-es
cu-mu-lus
  cu-mu-lous
cu-ne-i-form
cum-ni-lin-gus
cun-ning
  cun-ning-ly
  cun-ning-ness
cup
  cupped
  cup-ping
cup-board
cup-cake
cup-ful
  cup-fuls
cu-pid-i-ty
cu-po-la
cur-a-ble
  cur-a-bil-i-ty
  cur-a-bly
cu-rate
cur-a-tive
cu-ra-tor
  cu-ra-to-ri-al
  cu-ra-tor-ship
curb-ing
curb-stone
cur-dle
  cur-dled
  cur-dling
cure
  cured
  cur-ing
  cur-er
cure-all
cur-few
cu-ria
  cu-ri-ae
cu-ri-al
cu-rie
cu-ri-o
  cu-ri-os
cu-ri-os-i-ty
  cu-ri-os-i-ties
cu-ri-ous
cu-ri-um
curl
  curl-er
curl-i-cue
curl-ing
curly
  curl-i-er
  curl-i-est
  curl-i-ness
cur-rant
cur-ren-cy

cur-ren-cies
cur-rent
cur-ric-u-lum
  cur-ric-u-lums
  cur-ric-u-la
  cur-ri-c-u-lar
cur-rish
cur-ry
  cur-ries
  cur-ried
  cur-ry-ing
  cur-ri-er
cur-ry-comb
curse
cur-sive
  cur-sive-ly
cur-so-ry
  cur-so-ri-ly
  cur-so-ri-ness
curt
cur-tail
  cur-tail-ment
cur-tain
curt-sy
  curt-sies
  curt-sied
  curt-sy-ing
cur-va-ceous
cur-va-ture
curve
  cruved
  curv-ing
  curv-ed-nesss
cur-vi-lin-e-ar
cush-ion
cush-y
  cush-i-er
  cush-i-est
cus-pid
  cus-pi-dal
  cus-pi-date
  cus-pi-dor
cuss-ed
  cuss-ed-ly
  cuss-ed-ness
cus-tard
cus-to-dian
  cus-to-di-an-ship
cus-to-dy
  cus-to-dies
  cus-to-di-al
cus-tom
cus-tom-ary
  cus-tom-ar-ies
  cus-tom:-ar-i-ly
  cus-tom-ar-i-ness

cus-tom-built
cus-tom-er
cus-tom-ize
  cus-tom-ized
  cus-tom-iz-ing
cus-tom-made
cu-ta-ne-ous
cut-back
cute
  cut-er
  cut-est
  cute-ly
  cute-ness
cu-ti-cle
cut-lery
cut-let
cut-ting
  cut-ting-ly
cut-tle
cut-up
cy-an-ic
cy-a-nide
cy-a-no-sis
cy-ber-na-tion
cy-ber-net-ics
cyc-la-men
cy-cle
cy-clic
  cy-cli-cal
  cy-cli-cal-ly
cy-clom-e-ter
cy-clone
cy-clo-rama
  cy-clo-ram-ic
cy-clo-tron
cyg-net
cyl-in-der
  cy-lin-dric
  cy-lin-dri-cal
cym-bal
  cym-bal-ist
cyn-ic
  cyn-i-cism
cyn-i-cal
  cyn-i-cal-ly
cy-no-sure
cy-pher
cy-press
cyst
  cys-tic
cys-tic fi-bro-sis
cy-tol-o-gy
  cy-tol-o-gist
czar
czar-e-vitch
cza-ri-na

dab
 dabbed
 dab-bing
dab-ble
 dab-bled
 dab-bing
 dab-bler
dac-tyl
 dac-tyl-ic
dad-dy-long-legs
daf-fo-dil
daf-fy
 daf-fi-er
 daf-fi-est
dag-ger
da-guerre-o-type
dahl-ia
dai-ly
 dai-lies
dain-ty
 dain-ti-er
 dain-ti-est
 dain-ties
 dain-ti-ly
 dain-ti-ness
dai-qui-ri
dair-y
 dair-ies
dair-y-man
 dair-y-men
da-is
dai-sy
 dai-sies
dal-ly
 dal-lied
 dal-ly-ing
 dal-li-ance
dam-age
 dam-aged
 dam-ag-ing
 dam-age-a-ble
dam-a-scene
 dam-a-scened
 dam-a-scen-ing
dam-ask
damn
dam-na-ble
 dam-na-ble-ness
 dam-na-bly
dam-na-tion
damned
damp-en
damp-er
dam-sel
dam-son
dan-de-li-on

dan-der
dan-dle
 dan-dled
 dan-dling
dan-druff
dan-dy
 dan-dies
 dan-di-er
 dan-di-est
 dan-dy-ism
dan-ger
dan-ger-ous
 dan-ger-ous-ly
 dan-ger-ous-ness
dan-gle
 dan-gled
 dan-gling
 dan-gler
dank
 dank-ly
 dank-ness
dan-seuse
 dan-seus-es
dap-per
dap-ple
 dap-pled
 dap-pling
dare
 dared
 dar-ing
dare-dev-il
 dar-ing-ly
dark
 dark-ish
 dark-ly
 dark-ness
dark-en
dark-ling
dark-room
dar-ling
 dar-ling-ly
 dar-ling-ness
darn-er
dart-er
dash-board
dash-ing
das-tard
 das-tard-li-ness
 das-tard-ly
da-ta
date
 dat-ed
 dat-ing
 dat-a-ble
 dat-er
date-less

date-line
da-tive
da-tum
daub
 daub-er
daugh-ter
 daugh-ter-ly
daugh-ter--in--law
 daugh-ters--in--law
daunt-less
 daunt-less-ly
 daunt-less-ness
dau-phin
dav-en-port
dav-it
daw-dle
 daw-dled
 daw-dling
 daw-dler
dawn
day-break
day-dream
 day-dream-er
day-light
day-time
daze
 dazed
 daz-ing
 daz-ed-ly
daz-zle
 daz-zled
 daz-zling
 daz-zler
 daz-zling-ly
dea-con
 dea-con-ry
 dea-con-ship
dea-con-ess
dead-beat
dead-en
 dead-en-er
dead-end
dead-line
dead-lock
dead-ly
 dead-li-er
 dead-li-est
 dead-li-ness
dead-pan
dead-wood
deaf
 deaf-ly
 deaf-ness
deaf-en
 deaf-en-ing-ly
deaf-mute

deal
  dealt
  deal-ing
  deal-er
dean-ship
dear
  dear-ly
  dear-ness
dearth
death
  death-less
  death-ly
death-blow
death-trap
death-watch
de-ba-cle
de-bar
  de-barred
  de-bar-ring
  de-bar-ment
de-bark
  de-bar-ka-tion
de-base
  de-based
  de-bas-ing
  de-base-ment
  de-bas-er
de-bate
  de-bat-ed
  de-bat-ing
  de-bat-a-ble
  de-bat-er
de-bauch
  de-bauch-er
  de-bauch-ment
  de-bauch-ery
  de-bauch-er-ies
deb-au-chee
de-ben-ture
de-bil-i-tate
  de-bil-i-tat-ed
  de-bil-i-tat-ing
  de-bil-i-ta-tion
de-bil-i-ty
  de-bil-i-ties
deb-it
deb-o-nair
de-bris
debt-or
de-bunk
  de-bunk-er
de-but
deb-u-tante
de-cade
dec-a-dent
  dec-a-dence

dec-a-dent-ly
dec-a-gon
dec-a-gram
dec-a-he-dron
  dec-a-he-drons
de-cal
de-camp
  de-camp-ment
de-cant
  de-cant-er
de-cap-i-tate
  de-cap-i-tat-ed
  de-cap-i-tat-ing
  de-cap-i-ta-tion
dec-a-pod
de-cath-lon
de-cay
de-crease
  de-creased
de-ceit
  de-ceit-ful
  de-ceit-ful-ly
  de-ceit-ful-ness
de-ceive
  de-ceived
  de-ceiv-ing
  de-ceiv-er
  de-ceiv-ing-ly
  de-ceiv-a-ble
de-cel-er-ate
  de-cel-er-at-ed
  de-cel-er-at-ing
  de-cel-er-a-tion
de-cen-cy
  de-cen-cies
de-cen-ni-al
  de-cen-ni-al-ly
de-cent
  de-cent-ly
de-cen-tral-ize
  de-cen-tral-ized
  de-cen-tral-iz-ing
  de-cen-tral-i-za-tion
de-cep-tion
  de-cep-tive
  de-cep-tive-ly
  de-cep-tive-ness
dec-i-bel
de-cide
  de-cid-ed
  de-cid-ing
  de-cid-a-ble
  de-cid-ed-ly
  de-cid-ed-ness
de-cid-u-ous
  de-cid-u-ous-ly

dec-i-mal
dec-i-mate
  dec-i-mat-ed
  dec-i-mat-ing
  dec-i-ma-tion
de-ci-pher
  de-ci-pher-a-ble
de-ci-sion
de-ci-sive
  de-ci-sive-ly
  de-ci-sive-ness
deck-le edge
de-claim
  dec-la-ma-tion
  de-clam-a-tory
de-clare
  de-clared
  de-clar-ing
  de-clar-a-tive
  de-clar-a-to-ry
  de-clar-er
  dec-la-ra-tion
de-clas-si-fy
  de-clas-si-fied
  de-clas-si-fy-ing
de-clen-sion
dec-li-na-tion
de-cline
  de-clined
  de-clin-ing
  de-clin-a-ble
de-cliv-i-ty
  de-cliv-i-ties
de-code
  de-cod-ed
  de-cod-ing
  de-cod-er
de-com-pose
  de-com-posed
  de-com-pos-ing
  de-com-po-si-tion
de-com-press
  de-com-pres-sion
de-con-tam-i-nate
  de-con-tam-i-nat-ed
  de-con-tam-i-nat-ing
  de-con-tam-i-na-tion
de-con-trol
  de-con-trolled
  de-con-trol-ling
de-cor
dec-o-rate
  dec-o-rat-ed
  dec-o-rat-ing
  dec-o-ra-tion
  dec-o-ra-tive

dec-o-ra-tive-ly
dec-o-ra-tor
dec-o-rous
  dec-o-rous-ly
de-co-rum
de-coy
de-crease
  de-creased
  de-creas-ing
  de-creas-ing-ly
de-cree
  de-creed
  de-cree-ing
de-crep-it
  de-crep-i-tude
  de-crep-it-ly
de-cre-scen-do
  de-cre-scen-dos
de-cry
  de-cried
  de-cry-ing
  de-cri-al
ded-i-cate
  ded-i-cat-ed
  ded-i-cat-ing
  ded-i-ca-to-ry
  ded-i-ca-tive
  ded-i-ca-tion
de-duce
  de-duc-i-ble
de-duct
  de-duct-i-ble
de-duc-tion
  de-duc-tive
  de-duc-tive-ly
deep
  deep-ly
  deep-ness
deep-en
deep-root-ed
deep-seat-ed
deer-skin
de-es-ca-late
  de-es-ca-lat-ed
  de-es-ca-lat-ing
  de-es-ca-la-tion
de-face
  de-faced
  de-fac-ing
  de-face-ment
  de-fac-er
de fac-to
de-fame
  de-famed
  de-fam-ing
  def-a-ma-tion

de-fam-a-to-ry
  de-fam-er
de-fault
  de-fault-er
de-feat
de-feat-ism
  de-feat-ist
def-e-cate
  def-e-cat-ed
  def-e-cat-ing
  def-e-ca-tion
de-fect
de-fec-tion
  de-fec-tor
de-fec-tive
  de-fec-tive-ly
  de-fec-tive-ness
de-fend
  de-fend-er
de-fend-ant
de-fense
  de-fense-less
  de-fense-less-ly
  de-fense-less-ness
  de-fen-si-ble
  de-fen-si-bil-i-ty
  de-fen-si-bly
de-fen-sive
  de-fen-sive-ly
de-fer
  de-ferred
  de-fer-ring
  de-fer-ment
def-er-ence
  def-er-en-tial
  def-er-en-tial-ly
de-fi-ance
  de-fi-ant
  de-fi-ant-ly
de-fi-cient
  de-fi-cien-cy
  de-fi-cien-cies
  de-fi-cient-ly
def-i-cit
de-file
  de-filed
  de-fil-ing
de-fine
  de-fined
  de-fin-ing
  de-fin-er
  de-fin-a-ble
  de-fin-a-bly
def-i-nite
  def-i-nite-ly
  def-i-nite-ness

def-i-ni-tion
de-fin-i-tive
  de-fin-i-tive-ly
de-flate
  de-flat-ed
  de-flat-ing
  de-fla-tion
  de-fla-tion-ary
de-flect
  de-flec-tion
  de-flec-tive
  de-flec-tor
de-flow-er
de-fo-li-ate
  de-fo-li-at-ed
  de-fo-li-at-ing
de-for-est
  de-for-est-a-tion
de-form
  de-for-ma-tion
  de-formed
de-form-i-ty
  de-form-i-ties
de-fraud
de-fray
  de-fray-al
  de-fray-ment
  de-fray-a-ble
de-frost
  de-frost-er
deft
  deft-ly
  deft-ness
de-funct
de-fy
  de-fied
  de-fy-ing
  de-fi-er
de-gen-er-ate
  de-gen-er-at-ed
  de-gen-er-at-ing
  de-gen-er-ate-ly
  de-gen-er-a-cy
  de-gen-er-a-tion
  de-gen-er-a-tive
de-grade
  de-graded
  de-grad-ing
  deg-ra-da-tion
de-gree
de-his-cence
  de-his-cent
de-hy-drate
  de-hy-drat-ed
  de-hy-drat-ing
  de-hy-dra-tion

de-i-fy
  de-i-fied
  de-i-fy-ing
  de-i-fi-ca-tion
  de-i-fi-er
deign
de-ist
  de-ism
  de-is-tic
  de-is-ti-cal
de-i-ty
  de-i-ties
de-ject-ed
  de-jec-ted-ly
  de-jec-tion
de ju-re
de-lay
  de-lay-er
de-lec-ta-ble
  de-lec-ta-ble-ness
  de-lec-ta-bly
  de-lec-ta-tion
del-e-gate
  del-e-gat-ed
  del-e-gat-ing
del-e-ga-tion
de-lete
  de-let-ed
  de-let-ing
  de-le-tion
del-e-te-ri-ous
de-lib-er-ate
  de-lib-er-at-ed
  de-lib-er-at-ing
  de-lib-er-ate-ly
  de-lib-er-ate-ness
  de-lib-er-a-tion
  de-lib-er-a-tive
  de-lib-er-a-tor
del-i-ca-cy
  del-i-ca-cies
del-i-cate
  del-i-cate-ly
  del-i-cate-ness
del-i-ca-tes-sen
de-li-cious
  de-li-cious-ly
  de-li-cious-ness
de-lim-it
  de-lim-i-ta-tion
de-lin-e-ate
  de-lin-e-at-ed
  de-lin-e-at-ing
  de-lin-e-a-tion
  de-lin-e-a-tor
de-lin-quent

de-lin-quen-cy
  de-lin-quen-cies
de-lir-i-um
  de-lir-i-ums
  de-lir-ia
  de-lir-i-ous
  de-lir-i-ous-ly
de-liv-er
  de-liv-er-a-ble
  de-liv-er-er
de-liv-er-ance
de-liv-ery
  de-liv-er-ies
de-louse
  de-loused
  de-lous-ing
del-phin-i-um
del-ta
del-toid
de-lude
  de-lud-ed
  de-lud-ing
  de-lud-er
  de-lu-sive
  de-lu-so-ry
  de-lu-sive-ly
del-uge
  del-uged
  del-ug-ing
de-lu-sion
de-luxe
delve
  delved
  delv-ing
dem-a-gogue
  dem-a-gogu-ery
  dem-a-gog-ic
  dem-a-gog-i-cal
de-mand
  de-mand-er
de-mar-ca-tion
de-mean
de-mean-or
de-ment-ed
de-men-tia
de-mer-it
dem-i-god
de-mise
  de-mised
  de-mis-ing
dem-i-tasse
de-mo-bi-lize
  de-mo-bi-lized
  de-mo-bi-liz-ing
  de-mo-bi-li-za-tion
de-moc-ra-cy

de-moc-ra-cies
dem-o-crat
dem-o-crat-ic
  dem-o-crat-i-cal-ly
de-moc-ra-tize
  de-moc-ra-tized
  de-moc-ra-tiz-ing
  de-moc-ra-ti-za-tion
de-mog-ra-phy
  de-mog-ra-pher
  dem-o-graph-ic
de-mol-ish
  de-mol-ish-er
  dem-o-li-tion
de-mon
  de-mon-ic
de-mon-e-tize
  de-mon-e-tized
  de-mon-e-tiz-ing
  de-mon-e-ti-za-tion
de-mo-ni-ac
  de-mo-ni-a-cal
de-mon-ol-o-gy
  de-mon-ol-o-gist
dem-on-strate
  dem-on-strat-ed
  dem-on-strat-ing
  de-mon-stra-ble
  de-mon-stra-bly
  dem-on-stra-tion
de-mon-stra-tive
  de-mon-stra-tive-ly
  de-mon-stra-tive-ness
  dem-on-stra-tor
de-mor-al-ize
  de-mor-al-ized
  de-mor-al-iz-ing
  de-mor-al-i-za-tion
  de-mor-al-iz-er
de-mote
  de-mot-ed
  de-mot-ing
  de-mo-tion
de-mur
  de-murred
  de-mur-ring
  de-mur-ral
  de-mur-er
  de-mur-est
  de-mure-ly
  de-mure-ness
de-mur-rage
de-nat-u-ral-ize
  de-nat-u-ral-ized
  de-nat-u-ral-iz-ing
  de-nat-u-ral-i-za-tion

de-na-ture
  de-na-tured
  de-na-tur-ing
den-drite
den-dro-lite
den-drol-o-gy
den-e-ga-tion
de-ni-al
de-ni-er
den-im
den-i-zen
de-nom-i-nate
  de-nom-i-nat-ed
  de-nom-i-nat-ing
de-nom-i-na-tion
  de-nom-i-na-tion-al
  de-nom-i-na-tion-al-ism
de-nom-i-na-tive
de-nom-i-na-tor
de-note
  de-not-ed
  de-not-ing
  de-no-ta-tion
de-noue-ment
de-nounce
  de-nounced
  de-noun-cing
  de-nounce-ment
  de-nun-ci-a-tion
  de-nun-ci-a-to-ry
dense
  den-ser
  den-sest
  dense-ly
  dense-ness
den-si-ty
  den-si-ties
den-tal
den-tate
den-ti-frice
den-tin
den-tist
den-tist-ry
den-ti-tion
den-ture
de-nude
  de-nud-ed
  de-nud-ing
  den-u-da-tion
de-nun-ci-ate
  de-nun-ci-at-ed
  de-nun-ci-at-ing
  de-nun-ci-a-tion
  de-nun-ci-a-to-ry
de-ny
  de-nied

de-ny-ing
de-o-dor-ant
  de-o-dor-ize
  de-o-dor-ized
  de-o-dor-iz-ing
de-part
  de-part-ed
  de-part-ment
  de-part-men-tal
de-par-ture
de-pend
  de-pend-ence
de-pend-a-ble
  de-pend-a-bly
  de-pend-a-bil-i-ty
de-pend-en-cy
  de-pend-en-cies
de-pend-ent
de-pict
  de-pic-tion
de-pil-a-to-ry
  de-pil-a-to-ries
de-plete
  de-plet-ed
  de-plet-ing
  de-ple-tion
de-plor-a-ble
  de-plor-a-bly
de-plore
  de-plored
  de-plor-ing
de-ploy
  de-ploy-ment
de-po-nent
de-pop-u-late
  de-pop-u-lat-ed
  de-pop-u-lat-ing
  de-pop-u-la-tion
de-port
  de-por-ta-tion
  de-port-ment
de-pose
  de-posed
  de-pos-ing
  de-pos-a-ble
de-pos-it
  de-pos-i-tor
dep-o-si-tion
dep-os-i-to-ry
de-pot
de-prave
  de-praved
  de-prav-ing
  de-prav-i-ty
dep-re-cate
  dep-re-cat-ed

dep-re-cat-ing
  dep-re-cat-ing-ly
  dep-re-ca-tion
dep-re-ca-to-ry
de-pre-ci-ate
  de-pre-ci-at-ed
  de-pre-ci-at-ing
  de-pre-ci-a-tion
  de-pre-ci-a-to-ry
  de-pre-ci-a-tor
dep-re-date
  dep-re-dat-ed
  dep-re-dat-ing
  dep-re-da-tion
de-press
de-pres-sant
de-pressed
de-pres-sion
de-prive
  de-prived
  de-priv-ing
  dep-ri-va-tion
depth
dep-u-ta-tion
de-pute
  de-put-ed
  de-put-ing
dep-u-tize
  dep-u-tized
  dep-u-tiz-ing
dep-u-ty
  dep-u-ties
  dep-u-ty-ship
de-rail
  de-rail-ment
de-range
  de-ranged
  de-rang-ing
  de-range-ment
der-e-lict
  der-e-lic-tion
de-ride
  de-rid-ed
  de-rid-ing
de-ri-sion
de-ri-sive
  de-ri-sive-ly
  de-ri-so-ry
der-i-va-tion
de-riv-a-tive
de-rive
  de-rived
  de-riv-ing
  de-riv-a-ble
der-ma
  der-mal

der-ma-tol-o-gy
  der-ma-to-log-i-cal
  der-ma-tol-o-gist
der-mis
der-o-gate
  der-o-gat-ed
  der-o-gat-ing
  der-o-ga-tion
de-rog-a-to-ry
  de-rog-a-to-ri-ly
der-rick
der-rin-ger
der-vish
des-cant
de-scend
  de-scend-a-ble
  de-scend-ant
de-scent
de-scribe
  de-scribed
  de-scrib-ing
  de-scriba-ble
  de-scrib-er
de-scrip-tion
  de-scrip-tive
  de-scrip-tive-ly
  de-scrip-tive-ness
de-scry
  de-scried
  de-scry-ing
des-e-crate
  des-e-crat-ed
  des-e-crat-ing
  des-e-cra-tion
de-seg-re-gate
  de-seg-re-gat-ed
  de-seg-re-gat-ing
  de-seg-re-ga-tion
des-ert
de-sert
  de-sert-er
  de-ser-tion
de-serve
  de-served
  de-serv-ing
  de-serv-ed-ly
des-ha-bille
des-ic-cate
  des-ic-cat-ed
  des-ic-cat-ing
  des-ic-ca-tion
  des-ic-ca-tive
de-sid-er-a-tum
de-sign
des-ig-nate
  des-ig-nat-ed

des-ig-nat-ing
des-ig-na-tion
des-ig-na-tive
des-ig-na-tor
de-sign-ed-ly
de-sign-er
de-sign-ing
de-sire
  de-sired
  de-sir-ing
  de-sir-a-ble
  de-sir-a-bil-i-ty
  de-sir-a-bly
  de-sir-ous
de-sist
des-o-late
  des-o-lat-ed
  des-o-lat-ing
  des-o-late-ly
  des-o-la-tion
de-spair
  de-spair-ing
  de-spair-ing-ly
des-per-a-do
  des-per-a-does
des-per-ate
  des-per-ate-ly
  des-per-ate-ness
  des-per-a-tion
des-pi-ca-ble
  des-pi-ca-bly
de-spise
  de-spised
  de-spis-ing
de-spite
de-spoil
  de-spoil-er
  de-spo-li-a-tion
de-spond
  de-spond-en-cy
  de-spond-ence
  de-spond-ent
  de-spond-ent-ly
des-pot
  des-pot-ic
  des-pot-i-cal-ly
des-pot-ism
des-sert
des-ti-na-tion
des-tine
  des-tined
  des-tin-ing
des-ti-ny
  des-ti-nies
des-ti-tute
  des-ti-tu-tion

de-stroy
de-stroy-er
de-struc-tion
  de-struct-i-ble
  de-struct-i-bil-i-ty
de-struc-tive
  de-struc-tive-ly
  de-struc-tive-ness
des-ue-tude
des-ul-to-ry
  des-ul-to-ri-ly
de-tach
  de-tach-a-ble
de-tached
de-tach-ment
de-tail
  de-tailed
de-tain
  de-tain-ment
  de-tain-er
de-tect
  de-tect-a-ble
  de-tec-tion
de-tec-tive
de-tec-tor
de-ten-tion
de-ter
  de-terred
  de-ter-ring
de-ter-gent
de-te-ri-o-rate
  de-te-ri-o-rat-ed
  de-te-ri-o-rat-ing
  de-te-ri-o-ra-tion
de-ter-mi-na-ble
de-ter-mi-nant
de-ter-ni-nate
de-ter-mi-na-tion
  de-ter-mi-na-tive
de-ter-mine
  de-ter-mined
  de-ter-min-ing
  de-ter-min-er
de-ter-mined
  de-ter-mined-ly
de-ter-min-ism
  de-ter-min-ist
de-ter-rent
  de-ter-rence
de-test
  de-test-a-ble
  de-test-a-bly
de-tes-ta-tion
de-throne
  de-throned
  de-thron-ing

de-throne-ment
det-o-nate
 det-o-nat-ed
 det-o-nat-ing
 det-o-na-tion
 det-o-na-tor
de-tour
de-tract
 de-trac-tion
 de-trac-tor
det-ri-ment
 det-ri-men-tal
 det-ri-men-tal-ly
de-tri-tus
deuce
deu-te-ri-um
de-val-u-ate
 de-val-u-at-ed
 de-val-u-at-ing
 de-val-u-a-tion
dev-as-tate
 dev-as-tat-ed
 dev-as-tat-ing
 dev-as-ta-tion
de-vel-op
 de-vel-op-ment
de-vel-op-er
de-vi-ate
 de-vi-at-ed
 de-vi-at-ing
 de-vi-ant
 de-vi-a-tion
de-vice
dev-il
 dev-il-ment
 dev-il-try
 dev-il-tries
 dev-il-ry
dev-il-ish
 dev-il-ish-ly
 dev-il-ish-ness
de-vi-ous
 de-vi-ous-ly
 de-vi-ous-ness
de-vise
 de-vised
 de-vis-ing
 de-vis-a-ble
 de-vis-al
 de-vi-see
 de-vi-sor
de-void
de-volve
 de-volved
 de-volv-ing
 dev-o-lu-tion

de-vote
 de-vot-ing
de-vot-ed
 de-vot-ed-ly
dev-o-tee
de-vo-tion
 de-vo-tion-al
de-vour
 de-vour-er
 de-vour-ing-ly
de-vout
 de-vout-ly
 de-vout-ness
dew-drop
dew-lap
dewy
 dew-i-er
 dew-i-est
 dew-i-ness
dew-y-eyed
dex-ter-ous
 dex-ter-i-ty
 dex-ter-ous-ly
dex-trose
di-a-be-tes
 di-a-bet-ic
di-a-bol-ic
 di-a-bol-i-cal
 di-a-bol-i-cal-ly
di-a-crit-ic
 di-a-crit-i-cal
 di-a-crit-i-cal-ly
di-a-dem
di-ag-nose
 di-ag-nosed
 di-ag-nos-ing
 di-ag-no-sis
 di-ag-no-ses
 di-ag-nos-tic
 di-ag-nos-ti-cian
di-ag-o-nal
 di-ag-o-nal-ly
di-a-gram
 di-a-gramed
 di-a-gram-ing
 di-a-gram-mat-ic
 di-a-gram-mat-i-cal
di-al
 di-aled
 di-al-ing
di-a-lect
 di-a-lec-tal
di-a-lec-tic
 di-a-lec-ti-cal
 di-a-lec-ti-cian
di-a-logue

di-am-e-ter
di-a-met-ric
 di-a-met-ric-al
 di-a-met-ric-al-ly
dia-mond
dia-per
di-aph-a-nous
di-a-phragm
di-ar-rhea
di-a-ry
di-as-to-le
 di-as-tol-ic
di-a-ther-mic
di-a-tom
di-a-ton-ic
dib-ble
 dib-bled
 dib-bling
di-chot-o-my
 di-chot-o-mous
 di-cho-tom-ic
dic-tate
 dic-ta-tion
dic-ta-tor
dic-ta-to-ri-al
 dic-ta-to-ri-al-ly
dic-tion-ary
dic-tum
di-dac-tic
 di-dac-ti-cally
di-er-e-ses
di-e-tary
di-e-tet-ic
 di-e-tet-i-cal
 di-e-tet-i-cal-ly
di-e-tet-ics
di-e-ti-cian
dif-fer-ence
 dif-fer-enced
 dif-fer-en-cing
dif-fer-ent
 dif-fer-ent-ly
dif-fer-en-tial
 dif-fer-en-tial-ly
dif-fer-en-ti-ate
 dif-fer-en-ti-at-ed
dif-fi-cult
 dif-fi-cult-ly
dif-fi-dence
 dif-fi-dent
 dif-fi-dent-ly
dif-fuse
 dif-fused
 dif-fus-ing
 dif-fuse-ness
 dif-fu-sion

di-gest
di-gest-er
di-gest-i-ble
di-gest-i-bil-i-ty
di-ges-tion
dig-ger
dig-gings
dig-it-al
dig-i-tal-is
dig-ni-fied
dig-ni-fy
dig-ni-fy-ing
dig-ni-tary
dig-ni-tar-ies
dig-ni-ty
di-gress
di-gres-sion
di-gres-sive
di-he-dral
di-lap-i-dat-ed
di-lap-i-da-tion
dil-a-ta-tion
di-late
di-lat-ed
di-lat-ing
di-lat-a-ble
di-la-tion
dil-a-to-ry
dil-a-to-ri-ly
di-lem-ma
dil-et-tan-te
dil-et-tan-tes
dil-i-gence
dil-i-gent
dil-i-gent-ly
dil-ly-dal-ly
di-lute
di-lut-ed
di-lut-ing
di-lute-ness
di-men-sion
di-men-sion-al
di-min-ish
di-min-ish-a-ble
di-min-u-en-do
di-min-u-en-dos
dim-i-nu-tion
di-min-u-tive
di-min-u-tive-ness
dim-ple
dim-pled
dim-pling
din-er
di-nette
din-ghy
din-ghies

din-gy
din-gi-er
din-gi-est
din-gi-ness
din-ner
di-no-saur
di-o-cese
di-oc-e-san
di-o-ram-a
diph-the-ri-a
di-plo-ma
di-plo-ma-cy
di-plo-ma-cies
dip-lo-mat
dip-lo-mat-ic
dip-lo-mat-i-cal-ly
dip-per
dip-so-ma-nia
dip-so-ma-ni-ac
dire
dir-er
dir-est
dire-ness
di-rect
di-rect-ness
di-rec-tion
di-rec-tion-al
di-rec-tive
di-rect-ly
di-rec-tor
di-rec-to-ri-al
di-rec-tor-ship
di-rec-to-rate
di-rec-to-ry
di-rec-to-ries
dis-a-ble
dis-a-bling
dis-a-bil-i-ty
dis-a-ble-ment
dis-a-buse
dis-a-bused
dis-a-bus-ing
dis-ad-van-tage
dis-ad-van-taged
dis-af-fect
dis-af-fec-tion
dis-af-fect-ed
dis-a-gree
dis-a-gree-ing
dis-a-gree-a-ble
dis-a-gree-ment
dis-al-low
dis-al-low-ance
dis-ap-pear
dis-ap-pear-ance
dis-ap-point

dis-ap-point-ment
dis-ap-pro-ba-tion
dis-ap-prove
dis-ap-prov-al
dis-arm
dis-ar-ma-ment
dis-ar-range
dis-ar-ranged
dis-ar-rang-ing
dis-ar-ray
dis-as-sem-ble
dis-as-ter
dis-as-trous
dis-as-trous-ly
dis-a-vow
dis-a-vow-al
dis-band
dis-band-ment
dis-bar
dis-barred
dis-bar-ring
dis-be-lieve
dis-be-lief
dis-be-liev-er
dis-burse
dis-bursed
dis-burs-ing
dis-burs-er
dis-cern-ing
dis-cern-ment
dis-charge
dis-charged
dis-charg-ing
dis-char-ger
dis-ci-ple
dis-ci-ple-ship
dis-ci-pline
dis-ci-plines
dis-ci-pli-nary
dis-claim-er
dis-close
dis-closed
dis-clos-er
dis-clo-sure
dis-coid
dis-col-or
dis-col-or-a-tion
dis-com-fit
dis-com-fi-ture
dis-com-fort
dis-com-mode
dis-com-mod-ing
dis-com-pose
dis-com-posed
dis-com-pos-ing
dis-con-cert

dis-con-cert-ed
dis-con-nect
dis-con-nec-tion
dis-con-so-late
dis-con-tent
dis-con-tent-ed
dis-con-tin-ue
dis-con-tin-ued
dis-con-tin-u-ing
dis-con-tin-u-ous
dis-cord
dis-cord-ance
dis-cord-ant-ly
dis-count
dis-cour-age
dis-cour-ag-ing
dis-course
dis-coursed
dis-cours-ing
dis-cour-te-ous
dis-cour-te-sy
dis-cov-er
dis-cov-er-a-ble
dis-cov-er-er
dis-cov-er-y
dis-cov-er-ies
dis-cred-it
dis-cred-it-a-bly
dis-creet
dis-crep-an-cy
dis-crep-an-cies
dis-crete
dis-cre-tion
dis-cre-tion-ary
dis-crim-i-nate
dis-crim-i-nate-ly
dis-crim-i-na-to-ry
dis-crim-i-na-tor
dis-cur-sive
dis-cur-sive-ly
dis-cur-sive-ness
dis-cus
dis-cus-es
dis-cuss
dis-cuss-i-ble
dis-cus-sion
dis-dain
dis-dain-ful
dis-dain-ful-ly
dis-ease
dis-eased
dis-eas-ing
dis-em-bark
dis-em-body
dis-em-bod-ied
dis-em-bod-y-ing

dis-em-bow-el
dis-em-bow-eled
dis-em-bow-el-ing
dis-en-chant
dis-en-chant-ment
dis-en-cum-ber
dis-en-fran-chise
dis-en-fran-chised
dis-en-fran-chis-ing
dis-en-gage
dis-en-gaged
dis-en-gag-ing
dis-en-tan-gle
dis-en-tan-gled
dis-en-tan-gling
dis-es-tab-lish
dis-fa-vor
dis-fig-ure
dis-fig-ured
dis-fig-ur-ing
dis-fig-ure-ment
dis-fran-chise
dis-fran-chised
dis-fran-chis-ing
dis-gorge
dis-gorged
dis-gorg-ing
dis-grace
dis-graced
dis-grac-ing
dis-grace-ful
dis-grace-ful-ly
dis-grun-tle
dis-grun-tled
dis-grun-tling
dis-guise
dis-guised
dis-guis-ing
dis-guis-er
dis-gust
dis-gust-ed
dis-gust-ing
dis-ha-bille
dis-har-mo-ny
dis-har-mo-nies
dis-heart-en
dis-hev-eled
dis-hon-est
dis-hon-est-ly
dis-hon-es-ty
dis-hon-es-ties
dis-hon-or
dis-hon-or-a-ble
dis-hon-or-a-bly
dis-il-lu-sion
dis-in-cline

dis-in-clined
dis-in-fect
dis-in-her-it
dis-in-te-grate
dis-in-ter-es-ted
dis-in-ter-est-ed-ly
dis-junc-tion
dis-loy-al
dis-loy-al-ty
dis-o-be-di-ence
dis-or-der-ly
dis-o-ri-ent
dis-pas-sion
dis-pen-sa-tion
dis-pos-a-ble
dis-qual-i-fy
dis-qui-et
dis-re-spect
dis-re-spect-ful
dis-rup-tive
dis-rupt-er
dis-sat-is-fy
dis-sat-is-fy-ing
dis-sem-blance
dis-sem-i-nate
dis-sem-i-nat-ing
dis-sem-i-na-tor
dis-sent
dis-ser-tate
dis-ser-ta-ting
dis-ser-ta-tion
dis-serv-ice
dis-si-dent
dis-sim-i-lar
dis-sim-i-lar-i-ty
dis-sim-i-late
dis-sim-i-lat-ing
dis-sim-i-la-tive
dis-si-pate
dis-si-pa-tion
dis-so-nance
dis-so-nant
dis-suade
dis-sua-sion
dis-sua-sive
dis-tance
dis-taste
dis-taste-ful-ly
dis-tem-per
dis-til-late
dis-till-ery
dis-tinc-tion
dis-tin-guish
dis-tract
dis-tract-ing
dis-trib-ute

dis-trib-ut-ed
dis-tri-bu-tion
dis-tri-u-tor
dis-u-nite
di-van
di-verge
di-ver-gence
di-ver-gent
di-verse
di-ver-sion
div-i-dend
di-vi-sor
di-vulge
di-vulg-ing
di-vul-gence
do-a-ble
doc-tor-ate
doc-u-ment
dod-der
dog-ma
dog-mat-ic
dog-mat-i-cal
dol-drums
dol-or-ous
dol-phin
do-mes-tic
do-mes-ti-cate
do-mes-tic-i-ty
dom-i-cile
dom-i-cil-ing
dom-i-nance
dom-i-nant
dom-i-neer
do-min-ion
dop-ey
dop-i-est
dop-i-ness
dor-mant
dor-mer
dor-mi-to-ry
dos-age
dos-si-er
dou-ble-faced
dou-ble-take
dou-ble-time
doubt-a-ble
douche
dow-a-ger
dow-el
down-ward-ly
doz-ing
doz-en
drab-ness
drag-gle
drag-on
drain-age

dra-mat-ics
dra-per-y
dread-ful
drib-ble
drib-bled
drib-bling
drib-bler
drill-ing
dri-ly
driv-el
driv-eled
driv-el-ing
driz-zle
driz-zling
driz-zly
drom-e-dar-y
droop
droop-y
droop-i-er
droop-i-est
drop-per
dross
drought
drought-y
drought-i-er
drought-i-est
drowned
drowse
drowsed
drows-ing
drow-si-ness
drudge
drug-gist
dru-id
drum-mer
drunk-ard
drunk-en
drunk-en-ly
drunk-en-ness
dry-ad
du-al
du-al-i-ty
du-al-ism
du-al-ist
du-al-is-tic
du-bi-ous
du-bi-e-ty
du-bi-ous-ly
du-bi-ous-ness
du-cal
duch-ess
duck-ling
duct-less
duc-tile
du-el
du-eled

du-el-ing
du-el-ist
duke-dom
dul-cet
dum-found
dump-ling
dunce
dung
dun-ga-ree
dun-geon
dun-nage
du-o-dec-i-mal
du-o-de-num
du-o-de-na
du-o-de-nal
du-pli-cate
du-pli-cat-ing
du-pli-ca-tor
du-plic-i-ty
du-ra-ble
du-ra-bil-ity
du-ra-bly
dur-ance
du-ra-tion
dur-ing
dust-er
du-ti-a-ble
du-ti-ful
du-ti-ful-ly
du-ti-ful-ness
dwarf
dwarf-ish
dwell
dewlt
dwelled
dwell-ing
dwin-dle
dwin-dled
dwin-dling
dye-stuff
dy-ing
dy-nam-ic
dy-nam-i-cal
dy-nam-i-cal-ly
dy-na-mism
dy-na-mite
dy-na-mo
dy-nas-ty
dy-nas-ties
dyne
dys-en-tery
dys-func-tion
dys-pep-sia
dys-pep-tic
dys-pep-ti-cal
dys-tro-phy

ea-ger
  ea-ger-ly
  ea-ger-ness
ea-gle
ea-gle eyed
ea-glet
ear-ache
ear-drum
earl-dom
ear-ly
  ear-li-er
  ear-li-est
ear-mark
ear-muff
earn
  earn-er
ear-nest
  ear-nest-ly
  ear-nest-ness
earn-ings
ear-phone
ear-ring
earth-en
earth-ly
  earth-li-er
  earth-li-est
earth-quake
earth-y
ear-wax
ease
  eased
  eas-ing
ea-sel
ease-ment
eas-i-ly
  eas-i-ness
east-er-ly
east-ern
east-ern-most
east-ward
eas-y
  eas-i-er
  eas-i-est
eas-y-go-ing
eat
ebb
eb-on-y
  eb-on-ies
e-bul-lience
  e-bul-lient
  e-bul-li-tion
ec-cen-tric
  ec-cen-tri-cal-ly
ec-cen-tric-i-ty
  ec-cen-tric-i-ties
ec-cle-si-as-tic

ec-cle-si-as-ti-cal
ec-cle-si-as-ti-cal-ly
ech-e-lon
e-chi-no-derm
ech-o
e-cho-ic
e-clair
ec-lec-tic
  ec-lec-ti-cal-ly
  ec-lec-ti-cism
e-clipse
  e-clipsed
  e-clips-ing
e-clip-tic
e-col-o-gy
  e-c-o-log-ic
  e-c-o-log-i-cal
  e-col-o-gist
e-co-nom-ic
  e-co-nom-i-cal
  e-co-nom-ics
e-con-o-mist
e-con-o-mize
  e-con-o-mized
  e-con-o-miz-ing
  e-con-o-miz-er
e-con-o-my
  e-con-o-mies
ec-o-sys-tem
ec-ru
ec-sta-sy
  ec-sta-sies
ec-stat-ic
  ec-stat-i-cal
ec-to-morph
  ec-to-mor-phic
ec-to-plasm
ec-u-men-i-cal
ec-u-men-ic
  ec-u-men-i-cal-ly
  ec-u-men-ism
ec-ze-ma
e-de-ma
  e-de-ma-ta
e-den-tate
edg-y
ed-i-ble
e-dict
ed-i-fice
ed-i-fy
  ed-i-fied
  ed-i-fy-ing
  ed-i-fi-ca-tion
ed-it
e-di-tion
ed-i-tor

ed-i-tor-ship
ed-i-to-ri-al
  ed-i-to-ri-al-ly
  ed-i-to-ri-al-ize
  ed-i-to-ri-al-lized
ed-u-cate
  ed-u-cat-ed
  ed-u-cat-ing
  ed-u-ca-ble
ed-u-ca-tor
ed-u-ca-tion
  ed-u-ca-tion-al
e-duce
  e-duced
  e-duc-ing
  e-duc-i-ble
  e-duc-tion
eel
ee-rie
  ee-ri-er
  ee-ri-est
  ee-ri-ly
ef-fect
  ef-fec-tive
  ef-fec-tive-ness
  ef-fec-tive-ly
ef-fec-tu-al
  ef-fec-tu-al-i-ty
ef-fec-tu-ate
  ef-fec-tu-at-ed
  ef-fec-tu-at-ing
ef-fem-i-nate
  ef-fem-i-na-cy
  ef-fem-i-na-cies
  ef-fem-i-nate-ly
ef-fete
ef-fi-ca-cious
ef-fi-ca-cy
  ef-fi-ca-cies
ef-fi-cien-cy
  ef-fi-cien-cies
ef-fi-cient
  ef-fi-cient-ly
ef-fi-gy
  ef-fi-gies
ef-flo-resce
ef-flu-ent
  ef-flu-ence
ef-flu-vi-um
  ef-flu-via
  ef-flu-vi-ums
  ef-flu-vi-al
ef-fort
  ef-fort-less
  ef-fort-less-ly
ef-fron-ter-y

ef-fron-ter-ies
ef-ful-gent
  ef-ful-gence
ef-fuse
  ef-fused
  ef-fus-ing
ef-fu-sion
ef-fu-sive
  ef-fu-sive-ly
egal-i-tar-i-an
  egal-i-tar-i-an-ism
egg-nog
egg-plant
e-go
  e-gos
e-go-cen-tric
e-go-ism
  e-go-ist
  e-go-is-tic
  e-go-tism
  e-go-tis-tic
  e-go-tis-ti-cal
e-gre-gious
  e-gre-gious-ly
e-gress
e-gret
ei-der-down
eight
  eighth
eight-ball
eight-fold
eight-y
  eight-ies
  eight-i-eth
ei-ther
e-jac-u-late
  e-jac-u-lat-ed
  e-jac-u-lat-ing
  e-jac-u-la-tion
e-ject
  e-jec-tion
  e-ject-ment
  e-jec-tor
eke
  eked
  ek-ing
e-lab-o-rate
  e-lab-o-rat-ed
  e-lab-o-rat-ing
  e-lab-o-rate-ly
  e-lab-o-ra-tion
e-lapse
  e-lapsed
  e-laps-ing
e-las-tic
  e-las-ti-cal-ly

e-las-tic-i-ty
e-late
  e-lat-ed
  e-lat-ing
  e-la-tion
el-bow
el-bow-room
el-der
  eld-er-ship
el-der-ly
  eld-er-li-ness
eld-est
e-lect
e-lec-tion
e-lec-tion-eer
e-lec-tive
e-lec-tor
e-lec-tor-ate
e-lec-tric
  e-lec-tri-cal
  e-lec-tri-cal-ly
  e-lec-tri-cian
  e-lec-tric-i-ty
e-lec-tri-fy
  e-lec-tri-fied
  e-lec-tri-fy-ing
  e-lec-tri-fi-ca-tion
elec-tro-car-di-o-graph
e-lec-tro-cute
  e-lec-tro-cut-ed
  e-lec-tro-cut-ing
  e-lec-tro-cu-tion
e-lec-trode
e-lec-tro-dy-nam-ics
e-lec-trol-y-sis
  e-lec-tro-lyze
  e-lec-tro-lyzed
  e-lec-tro-lyz-ing
e-lec-tro-lyte
  e-lec-tro-lyt-ic
e-lec-tro-mag-net
  e-lec-tro-mag-net-ism
  e-lec-tro-mag-net-ic
e-lec-tron
e-lec-tron-ic
  e-lec-tron-ics
  e-lec-tron-i-cal-ly
e-lec-tro-plate
  e-lec-tro-plat-ed
  e-lec-tro-plat-ing
e-lec-tro-ther-a-py
e-lec-trum
el-ee-mos-y-nar-y
el-e-gant
  el-e-gance
  el-e-gan-cy

el-e-gant-ly
el-e-gy
  el-e-gies
  el-e-gi-ac
el-e-gist
  el-e-gize
  el-e-gized
  el-e-giz-ing
el-e-ment
  el-e-men-tal
  el-e-men-tal-ly
  el-e-men-ta-ry
  el-e-men-ta-ri-ly
el-e-phant
  el-e-phan-tine
el-e-vate
  el-e-vat-ed
  el-e-vat-ing
  el-e-va-tion
  el-e-va-tor
e-lev-en
  e-lev-enth
elf
e-lic-it
el-i-gi-ble
  el-i-gi-bil-i-ty
  el-i-gi-bly
e-lim-i-nate
  e-lim-i-nat-ed
  e-lim-i-nat-ing
  e-lim-i-na-tion
  e-lim-i-na-tor
e-lite
  e-lit-ism
  e-lit-ist
e-lix-ir
el-lipse
el-lip-sis
  el-lip-ses
el-lip-ti-cal
  el-lip-tic
  el-lip-ti-cal-ly
el-o-cu-tion
  el-o-cu-tion-ary
  el-o-cu-tion-ist
e-lon-gate
  e-lon-gat-ed
  e-lon-gat-ing
  e-lon-ga-tion
e-lope
el-o-quence
el-o-quent
  el-o-quent-ly
else-where
e-lu-ci-date
  e-lu-ci-dat-ed

e-lu-ci-dat-ing
e-lu-ci-da-tion
e-lu-ci-da-tor
e-lude
e-lud-ed
e-lud-ing
e-lu-sion
e-lu-sive
e-lu-sive-ly
e-lu-sive-ness
elv-ish
e-ma-ci-ate
e-ma-ci-at-ed
e-ma-ci-at-ing
e-ma-ci-a-tion
em-a-nate
em-a-nat-ed
em-a-nat-ing
em-a-na-tion
e-man-ci-pate
e-man-ci-pat-ed
e-man-ci-pat-ing
e-man-ci-pa-tor
e-mas-cu-late
e-mas-cu-lat-ed
e-mas-cu-lat-ing
e-mas-cu-la-tion
em-balm
em-balm-er
em-balm-ment
em-bank-ment
em-bar-go
em-bar-goes
em-bar-goed
em-bar-go-ing
em-bark
em-bar-ka-tion
em-bark-ment
em-bar-rass
em-bar-rass-ing-ly
em-bar-rass-ment
em-bas-sy
em-bas-sies
em-bat-tle
em-bat-tled
em-bat-tling
em-bat-tle-ment
em-bed
em-bed-ded
em-bed-ding
em-bel-lish
em-bel-lish-ment
em-ber
em-bez-zle
em-bez-zled
em-bez-zling

em-bez-zle-ment
em-bez-zler
em-bit-ter
em-bit-ter-ment
em-bla-zon
em-bla-zon-er
em-blaz-on-ment
em-bla-zon-ry
em-blem
em-blem-at-ic
em-blem-at-i-cal
em-bod-y
em-bod-ied
em-bod-y-ing
em-bod-i-ment
em-bold-en
em-bo-lism
em-bo-lus
em-bos-om
em-boss
em-boss-ment
em-bou-chure
em-brace
em-braced
em-brac-ing
em-broi-der
em-broi-dery
em-broi-der-ies
em-broil
em-broil-ment
em-bry-o
em-bry-os
em-bry-on-ic
em-bry-ol-o-gy
em-cee
em-ceed
em-cee-ing
e-mend
em-er-ald
e-merge
e-merged
e-merg-ing
e-mer-gence
e-mer-gent
e-mer-gen-cy
e-mer-gen-ies
e-mer-i-tus
em-er-y
e-met-ic
em-i-grant
em-i-grate
em-i-grat-ed
em-i-grat-ing
em-i-gra-tion
em-i-nence
em-i-nent

em-i-ent-ly
em-i-nent do-main
em-is-sary
em-is-sar-ies
e-mis-sion
e-mis-sive
e-mit
e-mit-ted
e-mit-ting
e-mit-ter
e-mol-lient
e-mol-u-ment
e-mote
e-mot-ed
e-mot-ing
e-mo-tive
emo-tion
emo-tion-al
emo-ton-al-ly
emo-tion-al-ism
em-pan-el
em-pa-thize
em-pa-thized
em-pa-thiz-ing
em-pa-thy
em-pa-thet-ic
em-path-ic
em-per-or
em-pha-sis
em-pha-ses
em-pha-size
em-pha-sized
em-pha-siz-ing
em-phat-ic
em-phat-i-cal-ly
em-phy-se-ma
em-pire
em-pir-i-cal
em-pir-i-cal-ly
em-pir-i-cism
em-pir-i-cist
em-place-ment
em-ploy
em-ploy-a-ble
em-ploy-ee
em-ploy-er
em-ploy-ment
em-pori-um
em-po-ri-ums
em-po-ria
em-pow-er
em-press
emp-ty
emp-ti-er
emp-ti-est
emp-tied

emp-ty-ing
emp-ti-ly
emp-ti-ness
emp-ty--hand-ed
emp-ty--head-ed
e-mu
em-u-late
  em-u-lat-ed
  em-u-lat-ing
  em-u-la-tion
e-mul-si-fy
  e-mul-si-fied
  e-mul-si-fy-ing
  e-mul-si-fi-ca-tion
  e-mul-si-fi-er
emul-sion
  emul-sive
en-a-ble
  en-a-bled
  en-a-bling
en-act
e-nam-el
  e-nam-eled
  e-nam-el-ing
  e-nam-el-er
e-nam-el-ware
en-am-or
  en-am-ored-ness
en-camp
  en-camp-ment
en-cap-su-late
  en-cap-su-lat-ed
  en-cap-su-lat-ing
  en-cap-sule
en-case
  en-cased
  en-cas-ing
en-ceinte
en-ceph-a-li-tis
  en-ceph-a-lit-ic
en-ceph-a-lon
  en-ceph-a-la
en-chant
  en-chant-er
  en-chant-ress
en-chant-ing
  en-chant-ing-ly
en-chant-ment
en-chi-la-da
en-cir-cle
  en-cir-cled
  en-cir-cling
  en-cir-cle-ment
en-clave
en-close
  en-closed

en-clos-ing
en-clo-sure
en-code
  en-cod-ed
  en-cod-ing
en-co-mi-ast
en-com-pass
  en-com-pass-ment
en-core
en-coun-ter
en-cour-age
  en-cour-aged
  en-cour-ag-ing
  en-cour-ag-ing-ly
en-croach
  en-croach-er
  en-croach-ment
en-crust
  en-crus-ta-tion
en-cum-ber
  en-cum-brance
en-cy-clo-pe-di-a
  en-cy-clo-pe-dic
  en-cy-clo-pe-di-cal
  en-cy-clo-pe-di-cal-ly
en-cyst
en-dan-ger
  en-dan-ger-ment
en-dear
  en-dear-ment
en-dea-vor
en-dem-ic
  en-dem-i-cal
  en-dem-i-cal-ly
end-ing
end-less
  end-less-ly
  end-less-ness
end-most
en-do-crine
  en-do-cri-nol-o-gy
  en-do-crin-o-log-ic
  en-do-crin-o-log-i-cal
  en-do-cri-nol-o-gist
en-dog-e-nous
en-dorse
  en-dorsed
  en-dors-ing
  en-dor-see
  en-dor-ser
  en-dorse-ment
en-do-sperm
en-dow
  en-dow-ment
en-due
  en-dued

en-du-ing
en-dur-ance
en-dure
  en-dured
  en-dur-ing
  en-dur-a-ble
  en-dur-a-bly
  en-dur-ing-ness
end-ways
en-e-ma
en-e-my
  en-e-mies
en-er-get-ic
  en-er-get-i-cal
  en-er-get-i-cal-ly
en-er-gize
  en-er-gized
  en-er-giz-ing
  en-er-gi-zer
en-er-gy
  en-er-gies
en-er-vate
  en-er-vat-ed
  en-er-vat-ing
  en-er-va-tion
en-fee-ble
  en-fee-bled
  en-fee-bling
  en-fee-ble-ment
en-fi-lade
  en-fi-lad-ed
  en-fi-lad-ing
en-fold
en-force
  en-forced
  en-forc-ing
  en-force-a-ble
  en-force-ment
  en-forc-er
en-fran-chise
  en-fran-chised
  en-fran-chis-ing
  en-fran-chise-ment
en-gage
  en-gaged
  en-gag-ing
  en-gage-ment
en-gen-der
en-gine
  en-gi-neer
en-gorge
  en-gorged
  en-gorg-ing
  en-gorge-ment
en-grave
  en-graved

en-grav-ing
en-grav-er
en-gross
en-grossed
en-gross-er
en-gross-ing
en-gross-ing-ly
en-gross-ment
en-gulf
en-gulf-ment
en-hance
en-hanced
en-hanc-ing
en-hance-ment
e-nig-ma
en-ig-mat-ic
en-ig-mat-i-cal
en-ig-mat-i-cal-ly
en-join
en-join-er
en-join-ment
en-joy
en-joy-a-ble
en-joy-a-ble-ness
en-joy-a-bly
en-joy-ment
en-large
en-larged
en-larg-ing
en-large-a-ble
en-larg-er
en-large-ment
en-light-en
en-light-en-ment
en-list
en-list-ed
en-list-ment
en-liv-en
en-liv-en-er
en-mesh
en-mi-ty
en-mi-ties
en-no-ble
en-no-bled
en-no-bling
en-no-ble-ment
en-no-bler
en-nui
e-nor-mi-ty
e-nor-mi-ties
e-nor-mous
e-nor-mous-ly
e-nor-mous-ness
e-nough
en-plane
en-planed

en-plan-ing
en-rage
en-raged
en-rag-ing
en-rap-ture
en-rap-tured
en-rap-tur-ing
en-rich
en-rich-er
en-rich-ment
en-roll
en-roll-ment
en route
en-sconce
en-sconced
en-sconc-ing
en-sem-ble
en-shrine
en-shrin-ing
en-shroud
en-sign
en-si-lage
en-si-laged
en-si-lag-ing
en-slave
en-slaved
en-slav-ing
en-slave-ment
en-slav-er
en-snare
en-snared
en-snar-ing
en-snare-ment
en-snar-er
en-snar-ing-ly
en-sue
en-sued
en-su-ing
en-su-ing-ly
en-sure
en-sured
en-sur-ing
en-sur-er
en-tail
en-tail-er
en-tail-ment
en-tan-gle
en-tan-gled
en-tan-gling
en-tan-gle-ment
en-tan-gler
en-tente
en-ter
en-ter-a-ble
en-ter-i-tis
en-tr-prise

en-ter-pris-ing
en-ter-pris-ing-ly
en-ter-tain
en-ter-tain-er
en-ter-tain-ing
en-ter-tain-ing-ly
en-ter-tain-ment
en-thrall
en-thralled
en-thrall-ing
en-thrall-ment
en-throne
en-throned
en-thron-ing
en-throne-ment
en-thuse
en-thused
en-thus-ing
en-thu-si-asm
en-thu-si-ast
en-thu-si-as-tic
en-thu-si-as-ti-cal-ly
en-tice
en-ticed
en-tic-ing
en-tice-ment
en-tic-er
en-tic-ig-ly
en-tire
en-tire-ly
en-tire-ness
en-tire-ty
en-tire-ties
en-ti-tle
en-ti-tled
en-ti-tling
en-ti-tle-ment
en-ti-ty
en-ti-ties
en-to-mol-o-gy
en-to-mol-o-gies
en-to-mo-log-ic
en-to-mo-log-i-cal
en-to-mo-log-i-cal-ly
en-to-mol-o-gist
en-tou-rage
en-trails
en-train
en-train-er
en-trance
en-trance-way
en-tranced
en-tranc-ing
en-trance-ment
en-tranc-ing-ly
en-trant

en-trap
  en-trapped
  en-trap-ping
  en-trap-ment
en-treat
  en-treat-ing-ly
  en-treat-ment
  en-treat-y
en-tree
en-trench
  en-trench-ment
  en-tre-pre-neur
  en-tre-pre-neur-i-al
  en-tre-pre-neur-ship
en-tro-py
en-trust
  en-trust-ment
en-try
  en-tries
en-twine
  en-twined
  en-twin-ing
e-nu-mer-ate
  e-nu-mer-at-ed
  e-nu-mer-at-ing
  e-nu-mer-a-tion
  e-nu-mer-a-tive
  e-nu-mer-a-tor
e-nun-ci-ate
  e-nun-ci-at-ed
  e-nun-ci-at-ing
  e-nun-ci-a-tion
  e-nun-ci-a-tive
  e-nun-ci-a-tor
en-u-re-sis
  en-u-ret-ic
en-vel-op
  en-vel-oped
  en-vel-op-ing
en-vi-a-ble
  en-vi-a-ble-ness
  en-vi-a-bly
en-vi-ous
  en-vi-ous-ly
  en-vi-ous-ness
en-vi-ron
en-vi-ron-ment
en-vi-ron-men-tal
  en-vi-ron-men-tal-ly
en-vi-rons
en-vis-age
  en-vis-aged
  en-vis-ag-ing
en-vi-sion
en-voy
en-vy

en-vies
en-vied
en-vy-ing
en-vi-er
en-vy-ing-ly
en-zyme
  en-zy-mat-ic
  en-zy-mat-i-cal-ly
e-on
ep-au-let
e-phed-rine
e-phem-er-al
  e-phem-er-al-ness
  e-phem-er-al-ly
ep-ic
  ep-i-cal
ep-i-cen-ter
ep-i-cure
  epi-cu-re-an
ep-i-dem-ic
  ep-i-dem-i-cal-ly
ep-i-der-mis
  ep-i-der-mal
  ep-i-der-mic
ep-i-glot-tis
ep-i-gram
ep-i-logue
  ep-i-log
epis-co-pa-cy
  epsi-co-pa-cies
epis-co-pal
epis-co-pa-lian
  epis-co-pa-lian-ism
epis-co-pate
ep-i-sode
  ep-i-sod-ic
  ep-i-sod-i-cal
  ep-i-sod-i-cal-ly
e-pis-te-mol-o-gy
  e-psi-te-mo-log-i-cal
  e-pis-te-mol-o-gist
e-pis-tle
e-pis-to-lar-y
ep-i-taph
  ep-i-taph-ic
  ep-i-taph-ist
ep-i-thet
  ep-i-thet-ic
  ep-i-thet-i-cal
e-pit-o-me
epit-o-mize
  epit-o-mized
  epit-o-miz-ing
ep-och
  ep-och-al
ep-ox-y

ep-ox-y res-in
ep-si-lon
eq-ua-ble
  eq-ua-bil-i-ty
  eq-ua-ble-ness
  eq-ua-bly
e-qual
  e-qualed
  e-qual-ling
  e-qual-ly
  e-qual-ness
e-qual-i-tar-i-an
  e-qual-i-tar-i-an-ism
e-qual-i-ty
  e-qual-i-ties
e-qual-ize
  e-qual-ized
  e-qual-iz-ing
  e-qual-i-za-tion
  e-qual-iz-er
e-qua-nim-i-ty
e-quate
  e-quat-ed
  e-quat-ing
e-qua-tion
  e-qua-tion-al
  e-qua-tion-al-ly
e-qua-tor
e-qua-to-ri-al
  e-qua-to-ri-al-ly
e-ques-tri-an
  e-ques-tri-enne
e-qui-dis-tance
  e-qui-dis-tant
  e-qui-dis-tant-ly
e-qui-lat-er-al
e-qui-li-brate
  e-qui-li-brat-ed
  e-qui-li-brat-ing
  e-qui-li-bra-tion
  e-qui-l-bra-tor
e-qui-lib-ri-um
  e-qui-lib-ri-ums
  e-qui-lib-ria
e-quine
e-qui-noc-tial
e-qui-nox
e-quip
  e-quipped
  e-quip-ping
  e-quip-per
eq-ui-page
e-quip-ment
e-qui-poise
eq-ui-ta-ble
  eq-ui-ta-ble-ness

eq-ui-ta-bly
eq-ui-ty
  eq-ui-ties
e-quiv-a-lance
  e-quiv-a-len-cy
e-quiv-a-lent
  e-quiv-a-lent-ly
e-quiv-o-cal
  e-quiv-o-cal-ly
  e-quiv-o-cal-ness
e-quiv-o-cate
  e-quiv-o-cat-ed
  e-quiv-o-cat-ing
  e-quiv-o-ca-tor
  e-quiv-o-ca-tion
e-ra
e-rad-i-cate
  e-rad-i-cat-ed
  e-rad-i-cat-ing
  e-rad-i-ca-ble
  e-rad-i-ca-tion
  e-rad-i-ca-tive
  e-rad-i-ca-tor
e-rase
  e-rased
  e-ras-ing
  e-ras-a-bil-i-ty
  e-ras-a-ble
e-ras-er
e-ras-ure
e-rect
  e-rect-a-ble
  e-rect-er
  e-rec-tive
  e-rect-ly
  e-rect-ness
e-rec-tile
  e-rec-til-i-ty
e-rec-tion
e-rec-tor
er-go
er-mine
e-rode
  e-rod-ed
  e-rod-ing
e-rog-e-nous
e-ro-sion
e-rot-ic
  e-rot-i-cal-ly
e-rot-i-cism
err
  err-ing-ly
er-rand
er-rant
  er-rant-ly
er-rat-ic

er-rat-i-cal-ly
er-ra-tum
  er-ra-ta
er-ro-ne-ous
  er-ro-ne-ous-ly
  er-ro-ne-ous-ness
er-ror
  er-ror-less
er-satz
erst-while
er-u-dite
  er-u-dite-ly
  er-u-dite-ness
er-u-di-tion
e-rupt
  e-rup-tion
  e-rup-tive
  e-rup-tive-ly
  e-rup-tive-ness
es-ca-lade
  es-ca-lad-ed
  es-ca-lad-ing
  es-ca-lad-er
es-ca-late
  es-ca-lat-ed
  es-ca-lat-ing
  es-ca-la-tion
  es-ca-la-tor
es-cal-lop
es-ca-pade
es-cape
  es-caped
  es-cap-ing
  es-cap-er
es-ca-pee
es-cap-ist
  es-cap-ism
es-carp-ment
es-chew
  es-chew-al
  es-chew-er
es-cort
es-cri-toire
es-crow
es-cutch-eon
  es-cutch-eoned
e-soph-a-gus
es-o-ter-ic
  es-o-ter-i-cal
  es-o-ter-i-cal-ly
es-pal-ier
es-pe-cial
  es-pe-cial-ly
  es-pe-cial-ness
es-pi-o-nage
es-pla-nade

es-pouse
  es-poused
  es-pous-ing
  es-pous-er
es-pous-al
es-pres-so
es-prit
es-prit de corps
es-py
  es-pied
  es-py-ing
es-quire
  es-quired
  es-quir-ing
es-say
  es-say-er
  es-say-ist
es-sence
es-sen-tial
  es-sen-ti-al-i-ty
  es-sen-tial-ly
  es-sen-tial-ness
es-tab-lish
  es-tab-lish-er
  es-tab-lish-ment
es-tate
es-teem
es-thete
  es-thet-ic
es-ti-ma-ble
  es-ti-ma-ble-ness
  es-ti-ma-bly
es-ti-mate
  es-ti-mat-ed
  es-ti-mat-ing
  es-ti-ma-tive
  es-ti-ma-tor
es-ti-ma-tion
es-trange
  es-tranged
  es-trang-ing
  es-trange-ment
  es-tran-ger
es-trus
es-tu-ar-y
  es-tu-ar-ies
  es-tu-ar-i-al
etch
  etch-er
  etch-ing
e-ter-nal
  e-ter-nal-ly
e-ter-ni-ty
e-ter-nize
  e-ter-nized
  e-ter-niz-ing

e-ter-ni-za-tion
eth-a-nol
e-ther
e-the-re-al
e-the-re-al-i-ty
e-the-re-al-ly
e-the-re-al-ness
e-the-re-al-ize
e-the-re-al-ized
e-the-re-al-iz-ing
e-the-re-al-i-za-tion
eth-ic
eth-i-cal
eth-i-cal-ly
eth-ics
eth-nic
eth-ni-cal
eth-ni-cal-ly
eth-nol-o-gy
eth-yl
eti-ol-o-gy
eti-o-log-ist
eti-o-log-i-cal
eti-o-log-i-cal-ly
et-i-quette
e-tude
et-y-mol-o-gy
et-y-mol-o-gies
et-y-mo-log-ic
et-y-mo-log-i-cal
et-y-mol-o-gist
eu-ca-lyp-tus
eu-ca-lyp-tus-es
eu-ca-lyp-ti
eu-gen-ic
eu-lo-gise
eu-lo-gized
eu-lo-giz-ing
eu-lo-gis-tic
eu-lo-gis-ti-cal-ly
eu-nuch
eu-phe-mism
eu-phe-mist
eu-phe-mis-tic
eu-phe-mis-ti-cal
eu-phe-mis-ti-cal-ly
eu-phe-mize
eu-phe-mized
eu-phe-miz-ing
eu-pho-ni-ous
eu-pho-ni-ous-ly
eu-pho-ni-ous-ness
eu-pho-ny
eu-phon-ic
eu-phon-i-cal
eu-phon-i-cal-ly

eu-pho-ria
eu-phor-ic
eu-re-ka
eu-tha-na-sia
e-vac-u-ate
e-vac-u-at-ed
e-vac-u-at-ing
e-vac-u-a-tion
e-vac-u-a-tive
e-vac-u-a-tor
e-vac-u-ee
e-vade
e-vad-ed
e-vad-ing
e-vad-a-ble
e-vad-er
e-vad-ing-ly
e-val-u-ate
e-val-u-at-ed
e-val-u-at-ing
e-val-u-a-tion
e-val-u-a-tor
ev-a-nesce
ev-a-nesced
ev-a-nesc-ing
ev-a-nes-cent
ev-a-nes-cence
ev-a-nes-cent-ly
e-van-gel
evan-gel-i-cal
evan-gel-ic
evan-gel-i-cal-ism
evan-gel-i-cal-ly
evan-gel-i-cal-ness
evan-ge-lism
evan-ge-lis-tic
evan-ge-lis-ti-cal-ly
evan-ge-list
evan-ge-lize
evan-ge-lized
evan-ge-liz-ing
evan-ge-li-za-tion
evan-ge-liz-er
e-vap-o-rate
e-vap-o-rat-ed
e-vap-o-rat-ing
e-vap-o-ra-ble
e-vap-o-ra-tion
e-vap-o-ra-tive
e-vap-o-ra-tor
e-va-sion
e-va-sive
e-va-sive-ly
e-va-sive-ness
e-ven
e-ven-ly

e-ven-ness
e-ven-hand-ed
eve-ning
e-vent
e-vent-ful
event-ful-ly
event-ful-ness
e-ven-tu-al
e-ven-tu-al-ly
e-ven-tu-al-i-ty
e-ven-tu-al-i-ties
e-ven-tu-ate
e-ven-tu-at-ed
e-ven-tu-at-ing
ev-er
ev-er-green
ev-er-last-ing
ev-er-last-ing-ly
ev-er-last-ing-ness
ev-er-more
e-vert
e-ver-si-ble
e-ver-sion
eve-ry
eve-ry-body
eve-ry-day
eve-ry-one
eve-ry-thing
eve-ry-where
e-vict
e-vic-tion
e-vic-tor
ev-i-dence
ev-i-denced
ev-i-denc-ing
ev-i-dent
ev-i-dent-ly
ev-i-den-tial
ev-i-den-tial-ly
e-vil
e-vince
e-vinced
e-vinc-ing
e-vin-ci-ble
e-vis-cer-ate
e-vis-cer-at-ed
e-vis-cer-at-ing
e-vis-cer-a-tion
e-voke
e-voked
e-vok-ing
ev-o-ca-tion
ev-o-lu-tion
ev-o-lu-tion-al
ev-o-lu-tion-ary
ev-o-lu-tion-ism

71

ev-ol-lu-tion-ist
e-volve
  e-volved
  e-volv-ing
  e-volv-a-ble
  e-volve-ment
  e-volv-er
ew-er
ex-ac-er-bate
  ex-ac-er-bat-ed
  ex-ac-er-bat-ing
  ex-ac-er-ba-tion
ex-act
  ex-act-a-ble
  ex-ac-tor
ex-act-ing
  ex-act-ing-ly
  ex-act-ing-ness
ex-act-i-tude
ex-act-ly
ex-ag-ger-ate
  ex-ag-ger-at-ed
  ex-ag-ger-at-ing
  ex-ag-ger-a-tion
  ex-ag-ger-a-tor
ex-alt
  ex-alt-er
  ex-al-ta-tion
ex-alt-ed
  ex-alt-ed-ly
  ex-alt-ed-ness
ex-am
ex-am-i-na-tion
ex-am-ine
  ex-am-ined
  ex-am-in-ing
  ex-am-in-a-ble
  ex-am-in-er
  ex-am-i-nee
ex-am-ple
  ex-am-pled
  ex-am-pling
ex-as-per-ate
  ex-as-per-at-ed
  ex-as-per-at-ing
  ex-as-per-a-tion
ex-ca-vate
  ex-ca-vat-ed
  ex-ca-cat-ing
  ex-ca-va-tion
  ex-ca-va-tor
ex-ceed
  ex-ceed-ing
  ex-ceed-ing-ly
ex-cel
  ex-celled

ex-cel-ling
ex-cel-lence
ex-cel-len-cy
  ex-cel-len-cies
ex-cel-lent
  ex-cel-lent-ly
ex-cel-si-or
ex-cept
  ex-cept-ing
  ex-cep-tion
  ex-cep-tion-a-ble
  ex-cep-tion-al
ex-cerpt
ex-cess
  ex-ces-sive
  ex-ces-sive-ly
  ex-ces-sive-ness
ex-change
  ex-changed
  ex-chang-ing
  ex-change-a-bil-i-ty
  ex-change-a-ble
  ex-chan-ger
ex-cheq-uer
ex-cise
  ex-cised
  ex-cis-ing
  ex-cis-a-ble
  ex-ci-sion
ex-cit-a-ble
  ex-cit-a-bil-i-ty
  ex-cit-a-bly
  ex-ci-ta-tion
ex-cite
  ex-cit-ed
  ex-cit-ing
ex-cit-ed
  ex-cit-ed-ly
  ex-cit-ed-ness
ex-cite-ment
ex-cit-ing
  ex-cit-ing-ly
ex-claim
ex-cla-ma-tion
  ex-clam-a-to-ry
  ex-clam-a-to-ri-ly
ex-clude
ex-clu-sion
ex-clu-sive
  ex-clu-sive-ly
  ex-clu-sive-ness
  ex-clu-siv-i-ty
ex-com-mu-ni-cate
ex-co-ri-ate
  ex-co-ri-at-ed
  ex-co-ri-at-ing

ex-co-ri-a-tion
ex-cre-ment
  ex-cre-men-tal
ex-cres-cense
  ex-cres-cent
ex-cre-ta
  ex-cre-tal
ex-crete
  ex-cret-ed
  ex-cret-ing
ex-cre-tion
ex-cru-ci-ate
  ex-cru-ci-at-ed
  ex-cru-ci-at-ing
  ex-cru-ci-at-ing-ly
  ex-cru-ci-a-tion
ex-cul-pate
  ex-cul-pat-ed
  ex-cul-pat-ing
  ex-cul-pa-tion
  ex-cul-pa-to-ry
ex-cur-sion
  ex-cur-sion-al
  ex-cur-sion-ary
  ex-cur-sion-ist
ex-cur-sive
  ex-cur-sive-ly
  ex-cur-sive-ness
ex-cus-a-to-ry
ex-cuse
ex-e-cra-ble
  ex-e-cra-ble-ness
  ex-e-çra-bly
ex-e-crate
  ex-e-crat-ed
  ex-e-crat-ing
  ex-e-cra-tive
  ex-e-cra-tor
ex-e-cra-tion
ex-e-cute
  ex-e-cut-ed
  ex-e-cut-ing
  ex-e-cut-a-ble
  ex-e-cut-er
ex-e-cu-tion
ex-e-cu-tion-er
ex-ec-u-tive
  ex-ec-u-tive-ly
ex-ec-u-tor
  ex-ec-u-tor-ship
ex-e-ge-sis
ex-em-pli-fy
  ex-em-pli-fied
  ex-em-pli-fy-ing
  ex-em-pli-fi-a-ble
  ex-em-pli-fi-ca-tion

ex-empt
ex-emp-tion
ex-er-cise
  ex-er-cised
  ex-er-cis-ing
  ex-er-cis-er
ex-ert
ex-er-tion
ex-fo-li-ate
  ex-fo-li-at-ed
  ex-fo-li-at-ing
  ex-fo-li-a-tion
ex-hal-la-tion
ex-hale
  ex-haled
  ex-hal-ing
  ex-hal-ant
ex-haust
ex-hib-it
  ex-hib-it-a-ble
  ex-hib-i-tor
  ex-hib-i-to-ry
ex-hi-bi-tion
  ex-hi-bi-tion-ism
  ex-hi-bi-tion-ist
  ex-hi-bi-tion-is-tic
ex-hil-a-rate
ex-hort
  ex-hor-ta-tive
  ex-hor-ta-to-ry
  ex-hort-er
  ex-hort-ing-ly
ex-hor-ta-tion
ex-hume
  ex-humed
  ex-hum-ing
ex-i-gen-cy
  ex-i-gen-cies
ex-i-gent
  ex-i-gent-ly
ex-ile
  ex-iled
ex-ist
  ex-ist-ence
  ex-ist-ent
ex-is-ten-tial
  ex-is-ten-tial-ly
ex-it
ex li-bris
ex-o-dus
ex of-fi-ci-o
ex-og-a-my
  ex-og-a-mous
ex-og-e-nous
  ex-og-e-nous-ly
ex-on-er-ate

ex-or-bi-tant
  ex-or-bi-tance
  ex-or-bi-tant-ly
ex-or-cise
  ex-or-cised
  ex-or-cis-ing
  ex-or-cism
  ex-or-cist
ex-o-tic
  ex-ot-i-cal-ly
  ex-ot-i-cism
ex-pand
  ex-pand-er
ex-panse
  ex-pan-si-ble
ex-pan-sion
  ex-pan-sion-ism
  ex-pan-sion-ist
ex-pan-sive
  ex-pan-sive-ly
  ex-pan-sive-ness
ex-pa-ti-ate
  ex-pa-ti-at-ed
  ex-pa-ti-at-ing
  ex-pa-ti-a-tion
ex-pa-tri-ate
  ex-pa-tri-at-ed
  ex-pa-tri-at-ing
  ex-pa-tri-a-tion
ex-pect
  ex-pect-a-ble
  ex-pect-a-bly
  ex-pect-ing-ly
ex-pect-an-cy
  ex-pect-an-cies
ex-pect-ant
  ex-pect-ant-ly
ex-pec-ta-tion
ex-pec-to-rate
  ex-pec-to-rat-ed
  ex-pec-to-rat-ing
  ex-pec-to-ra-tion
ex-pe-di-en-cy
  ex-pe-di-ent
  ex-pe-di-ent-ly
ex-pe-dite
  ex-pe-dit-ed
  ex-pe-dit-ing
  ex-pe-dit-er
ex-pe-di-tion
  ex-pe-di-tion-ary
ex-pe-di-tious
  ex-pe-di-tious-ly
ex-pel
  ex-pelled
  ex-pel-ling

ex-pend
  ex-pend-a-ble
  ex-pend-a-bil-i-ty
ex-pend-i-ture
ex-pense
  ex-pen-sive
  ex-pen-sive-ly
  ex-pen-sive-ness
ex-pe-ri-ence
  ex-pe-ri-enced
  ex-pe-ri-enc-ing
ex-pe-ri-en-tial
  ex-pe-ri-en-tial-ly
ex-per-i-ment
  ex-per-i-men-ta-tion
  ex-per-i-men-tal
  ex-per-i-men-tal-ism
  ex-per-i-men-tal-ist
  ex-per-i-men-tal-ly
ex-pert
  ex-pert-ly
  ex-pert-ness
ex-per-tise
ex-pi-ra-tion
  ex-pir-a-to-ry
ex-pire
  ex-pired
  ex-pir-ing
ex-plain
  ex-plain-a-ble
  ex-plain-er
ex-pla-na-tion
  ex-plan-a-to-ry
  ex-plan-a-to-ri-ly
ex-ple-tive
ex-pli-ca-ble
ex-pli-cate
  ex-pli-cat-ed
  ex-pli-cat-ing
  ex-pli-ca-tion
  ex-pli-ca-tive
  ex-pli-ca-tor
ex-plic-it
  ex-plic-it-ly
  ex-plic-it-ness
ex-plode
  ex-plod-ed
  ex-plod-ing
  ex-plod-er
ex-ploit
  ex-ploit-a-ble
  ex-ploi-ta-tion
  ex-ploit-er
  ex-ploit-ive
ex-plore
  ex-plo-ra-tion

ex-plor-a-to-ry
ex-plor-er
ex-plo-sion
ex-plo-sive
ex-plo-sive-ly
ex-plo-sive-ness
ex-po-nent
ex-po-nen-tial
ex-po-nen-tial-ly
ex-port
ex-port-a-ble
ex-por-ta-tion
ex-port-er
ex-pose
ex-posed
ex-pos-ing
ex-pos-er
ex-po-si-tion
ex-pos-i-tor
ex-pos-i-to-ry
ex post fac-to
ex-pos-tu-late
ex-po-sure
ex-pound
ex-pound-er
ex-press
ex-press-er
ex-press-i-ble
ex-pres-sion
ex-pres-sive
ex-pres-sive-ly
ex-pres-sive-ness
ex-press-ly
ex-press-way
ex-pro-pri-ate
ex-pro-pri-at-ing
ex-pro-pri-a-tor
ex-pro-pri-a-tion
ex-pul-sion
ex-pul-sive
ex-punge
ex-pur-gate
ex-pur-ga-to-ry
ex-pur-ga-to-ri-al
ex-qui-site
ex-qui-site-ly
ex-qui-site-ness
ex-tant
ex-tem-po-ra-ne-ous
ex-tem-po-rize
ex-tem-po-rized
ex-tem-po-riz-ing
ex-tem-po-ri-za-tion
ex-tem-po-riz-er
ex-tend
ex-tend-i-bil-i-ty

ex-tend-i-ble
ex-tend-ed
ex-tend-ed-ly
ex-tend-ed-ness
ex-tend-er
ex-ten-si-ble
ex-ten-si-bil-i-ty
ex-ten-sion
ex-ten-sion-al
ex-ten-sive
ex-ten-sive-ly
ex-ten-sive-ness
ex-tent
ex-ten-u-ate
ex-te-ri-or
ex-te-ri-or-ly
ex-ter-mi-nate
ex-ter-mi-nat-ed
ex-ter-mi-nat-ing
ex-ter-mi-na-tion
ex-ter-mi-na-tor
ex-ter-nal
ex-ter-nal-ly
ex-tinct
ex-tinc-tion
ex-tin-guish
ex-tin-guish-a-ble
ex-tin-guish-er
ex-tin-guish-ment
ex-tir-pate
ex-tir-pat-ed
ex-tir-pat-ing
ex-tir-pa-tion
ex-tir-pa-tive
ex-tol
ex-tol-ler
ex-tol-lingly
ex-tol-ment
ex-tort
ex-tor-ter
ex-tor-tive
ex-tor-tion
ex-tra
ex-tract
ex-tract-a-ble
ex-trac-tive
ex-trac-tor
ex-trac-tion
ex-tra-cur-ric-u-lar
ex-tra-dite
ex-tra-ne-ous
ex-tra-ne-ous-ly
ex-tra-ne-ous-ness
ex-traor-di-nary
ex-traor-di-nar-i-ly
ex-trap-o-late

ex-trap-o-lat-ed
ex-trap-o-lat-ing
ex-trap-o-la-tion
ex-tra-sen-so-ry
ex-tra-ter-res-tri-al
ex-tra-ter-ri-to-ri-al
ex-trav-a-gance
ex-trav-a-gan-cy
ex-trav-a-gant
ex-trav-a-gant-ly
ex-trav-a-gan-za
ex-treme
ex-treme-ly
ex-treme-ness
ex-trem-ist
ex-trem-ism
ex-trem-i-ty
ex-trem-i-ties
ex-tri-cate
ex-tri-cat-ed
ex-tri-cat-ing
ex-tri-ca-ble
ex-tri-ca-tion
ex-trin-sic
ex-tro-vert
ex-tro-ver-sion
ex-trude
ex-u-ber-ance
ex-u-ber-ant
ex-u-ber-ant-ly
ex-ude
ex-ud-ed
ex-ud-ing
ex-u-da-tion
ex-ult
ex-ult-ant
ex-ult-ant-ly
ex-ul-at-tion
ex-ult-ing-ly
ex-ur-ban-ite
eye
eyed
eye-ing
eye-ball
eye-glass
eye-glass-es
eye-hole
eye-lash
eye-let
eye-lid
eye-o-pen-er
eye-o-pen-ing
eye-wit-ness
ey-rie
ey-ry
ey-ries

F

fa-ble
  fa-bled
fab-ric
fab-ri-cate
  fab-ri-cated
  fab-ri-cat-ing
  fab-ri-ca-tion
fab-u-lous
  fab-u-lous-ness
fa-cade
  fa-cades
face
  faced
  fac-ing
face card
face--lift
fac-et
fa-ce-tious
  fa-ce-tious-ly
fa-cial
  fa-cial-ly
fac-ile
  fac-ile-ly
  fac-ile-ness
fa-cil-i-tate
fa-cil-i-ty
fac-ing
fac-sim-i-le
fact
fac-tion
  fac-tion-al
  fac-tion-al-ly
fac-ti-tious
  fac-ti-tious-ly
fac-ti-tious-ness
fac-tor
fac-to-ry
  fac-to-ries
fac-to-tum
fac-tu-al
fac-ul-ty
fad
  fad-dish
  fad-dist
fade
  fad-ed
  fad-ing
fa-er-ie
  fa-ery
  fa-er-ies
fag
  faggged
  fag-ging
fag-got
fag-ot
Fahr-en-heit

fail-ing
  fail-ing-ly
fail-safe
fail-ure
faint
  faint-ly
  faint-ness
faint-heart-ed
fair
  fir-ness
fair-ground
fair-ly
fair-mind-ed
fair--trade
fair-y
  fair-ies
fair-y-like
fair-y tale
faith
faith-ful
faith-ful-less
fake
  faked
  fak-ing
  fak-er
fal-con
fal-con-ry
fall
  fall-en
  fall-ing
fal-la-cious
  fal-la-cious-ly
fal-la-cy
fall-guy
fal-li-ble
  fal-li-bly
fail-ing star
fall-out
fal-low
  fal-low-ness
false
  fals-er
  fals-est
false-hood
fal-si-fy
  fal-si-fied
  fal-si-fy-ing
  fal-si-fi-er
fal-si-ty
fal-ter
  fal-ter-er
  fal-ter-ing-ly
fame
famed
fa-mil-ial
fa-mil-iar

fa-mil-iar-ly
fa-mil-i-ar-i-ty
fa-mil-iar-ize
  fa-mil-iar-ized
  fa-mil-iar-iz-ing
fam-ily
  fam-i-lies
fam-ine
fam-ish
fam-ished
fa-mous
  fa-mous-ly
fan
  fan-like
  fan-ner
fa-nat-ic
  fa-nat-i-cal
  fa-nat-i-cism
  fa-nat-i-cize
  fa-nat-i-cized
fan-ci-er
fan-ci-ul
  fan-ci-ful-ly
fan-cy
  fan-cies
  fan-ci-ly
  fan-ci-ness
fan-cy-work
fan-fare
fang
fanged
fan-light
fan-tas-tic
  fan-tas-ti-cal
fan-ta-sy
  fan-ta-sies
far
  far-ther
  far-thest
far-a-way
farce
  farced
  farc-ing
far-ci-cal
  far-ci-cal-ly
fare
  fared
  far-ing
fare-well
far-fetched
far-flung
farm
farm-er
farm-hand
farm-house
farm-ing

farm-yard
far-off
far-reach-ing
  far-reach-ing-ly
far-see-ing
far-sight-ed
  far-sight-ed-ly
far-ther
far-ther-most
far-thest
fas-ci-a
  fas-ci-ae
fas-ci-cle
  fas-ci-cled
fas-ci-nate
  fas-ci-nat-ed
  fas-ci-nat-ing
fas-ci-na-tion
fas-cism
  fas-cist
  fa-scis-tic
fash-ion
fash-ion-ble
fast
fas-ten
  fas-ten-er
  fas-ten-ing
fas-tid-i-ous
  fas-ti-di-ous-ly
fat
  fat-ter
  fat-test
fa-tal
  fa-tal-ly
fa-tal-ism
  fa-tal-ist
fa-tal-i-ty
  fa-tal-i-ties
fate
  fat-ed
  fat-ing
fate-ful
  fate-ful-ly
  fate-ful-ness
fa-ther
fa-ther-hood
  fa-ther-ly
fa-ther-in-law
  fa-thers-in-law
fa-ther-land
fath-om
  fath-om-a-ble
  fath-om-less
fa-tique
  fa-tiqued
  fa-tiq-uing

fat-i-ga-ble
fat-ten
  fat-ten-er
fat-ty
  fat-ti-er
  fat-ti-est
  fat-ti-ness
  fat-tish
fa-tu-i-ty
  fa-tui-ties
fat-u-ous
  fat-u-ous-ly
  fat-u-ous-ness
fau-cet
fault
fault-find-er
  fault-find-ing
fault-less
fault-less-ly
fault-less-ness
fault-y
  fault-i-er
  fault-i-est
  fault-i-ly
fau-na
  fau-nas
  fau-nae
faux pas
fa-vor
  fa-vor-ing-ly
fa-vor-a-ble
  fa-vor-ably
fa-vored
  fa-vored-ly
  fa-vored-ness
fa-vor-ite
  fa-vor-it-ism
fawn
faze
  fazed
  faz-ing
fe-al-ty
fear
fear-ful
  fear-ful-ly
  fear-ful-ness
fear-less
  fear-less-ly
  fear-less-ness
fear-some
  fear-some-ly
  fear-some-ness
fea-si-ble
  fea-si-bil-i-ty
  fea-si-ble-ness
  fea-si-bly

feast
feat
feath-er
  fea-thered
feath-er-bed-ding
fea-ture
  fea-tured
  fea-tur-ing
fea-ture-ness
fe-brile
fe-ces
  fe-cal
feck-less
fe-cund
  fe-cun-di-ty
fe-cun-date
  fe-cun-dat-ed
  fe-cun-da-tion
fed-er-al
fed-er-al-ism
fed-er-li-ist
fed-er-al-ize
  fed-er-al-ized
  fed-er-al-iz-ing
  fed-er-al-i-za-tion
  fed-er-al-ly
fed-er-ate
  fed-er-at-ed
  fed-er-at-ing
fed-er-a-tion
fee
fee-ble
  fee-bler
  fee-blest
  fee-bly
fee-ble-mind-ed
  fee-ble-mind-ed-ness
feed
  fed
  feed-ing
  feed-er
feed-back
feel
  feel-ing
feel-er
feel-ing
  feel-ing-ly
  feel-ing-ness
feign
  feigned
  feign-ed-ly
  feign-er
  feign-ing-ly
feint
feist-y
  feist-i-er

feist-i-est
fe-lic-i-tate
  fe-lic-i-tat-ed
  fe-lic-i-tat-ing
  fe-lic-i-ta-tion
fe-lic-i-tous
  fe-lic-i-tous-ly
fe-lic-i-ty
  fe-lic-i-ties
fe-line
  fe-line-ly
  fe-line-i-ty
fell
fel-la-ti-o
fel-low
fel-low-ship
fe-lon
fel-o-ny
  fel-o-nies
  fe-lo-ni-ous
  fe-lo-ni-ous-ly
fe-male
fem-i-nine
  fem-i-nine-ly
  fem-i-nine-ness
  fem-i-nin-i-ty
fem-i-nism
  fem-i-nist
  fem-i-nis-tic
fem-i-nize
  fem-i-nized
  fem-i-niz-ing
fe-mur
  fe-murs
  fem-o-ra
  fem-o-ral
fen
  fen-ny
  fen-ni-er
  fen-ni-est
fence
  fecned
  fenc-ing
  fenc-er
fen-der
fe-ral
fer-ment
  fer-ment-a-ble
fer-men-ta-tion
fern
fern-er-y
  fern-er-ies
fe-ro-cious
  fe-ro-cious-ly
  fe-ro-ci-ty
fer-ret

fer-ret-er
fer-ro-con-crete
fer-ro-mag-net-ic
fer-ru-gi-nous
fer-rule
fer-ry
  fer-ries
  fer-ry-boat
  fer-ry-man
fer-tile
  fer-tile-ly
  fer-tile-ness
fer-til-i-ty
fer-ti-li-za-tion
fer-ti-li-za-tion-al
fer-ti-lize
  fer-ti-lized
  fer-ti-liz-ing
  fer-ti-liz-a-ble
  fer-ti-liz-er
fer-vent
  fer-ven-cy
fer-vid
  fer-vid-ly
  fer-vid-ness
fer-vor
fes-ter
fes-ti-val
fes-tive
  fes-tive-ly
  fes-tive-ness
fes-tiv-i-ty
fes-toon
  fes-toon-ery
  fes-toon-er-ies
fe-tal
fetch
fetch-er
fetch-ing
  fetch-ing-ly
fete
fet-id
  fet-id-ly
  fet-id-ness
fet-ish
fet-ish-ism
  fet-ish-ist
  fet-ish-is-tic
fet-lock
fet-ter
fet-tle
fe-tus
  fe-tus-es
feud
  feud-ist
feu-dal

feu-dal-ism
feu-dal-ist
  feu-dal-is-tic
feu-dal-i-za-tion
feu-dal-ize
  feu-dal-ized
  feu-dal-iz-ing
fe-ver
fe-ver blis-ter
fe-ver-ish
  fe-ver-ish-ly
  fe-ver-ish-ness
fe-ver-ous
  fe-ver-ous-ly
few
few-ness
fez-zes
fi-as-co
  fi-as-cos
  fi-as-coes
fi-at
fib
fi-ber
  fi-bered
fi-ber-board
fi-ber-glass
fi-bril
fi-bril-la-tion
fi-broid
fi-brous
fib-u-la
  fib-u-las
  fib-u-lae
fick-le
  fick-le-ness
fic-tion
  fic-tion-al
  fic-tion-al-ly
fic-ti-tious
fid-dle
  fid-dler
  fid-dled
fi-del-i-ty
fidg-et
  fidg-ety
field-er
field-glass
fiend
  fiend-ish
  fiend-ish-ly
  fiend-ish-ness
fierce
  fierce-ly
  fierce-ness
fier-y
  fier-i-er

fier-i-est
fier-i-ly
fier-i-ness
fif-teen
fif-teenth
fifth
fif-ti-eth
fif-ty
  fif-ties
fight
fight-er
fig-ment
fig-u-ra-tion
fig-u-ra-tive
  fig-u-ra-tive-ly
  fid-u-ra-tive-ness
fig-ure
  fig-ured
  fig-ur-ing
  fig-ur-er
fig-ure-head
fig-ur-ine
fil-a-ment
  fil-a-men-ta-ry
  fil-a-ment-ed
  fil-a-men-tous
filch
file
  filed
  fil-ing
fi-let
fi-let mi-gnon
fil-i-al
  fil-i-al-ly
fil-i-bus-ter
fil-i-gree
  fil-i-greed
  fil-i-gree-ing
  fil-lings
fill-er
fil-let
fill-ing
fil-lip
fil-ly
  fil-lies
film-strip
film-y
  film-i-er
  film-i-est
  film-i-ness
fil-ter
filth
  filth-i-ness
  filthy
  filth-i-er
  filth-i-est

fin
  finned
  fin-ning
  fin-less
  fin-like
fi-na-gled
  fi-na-gling
  fi-na-gler
fi-nal
fi-na-le
fi-nal-ist
fi-nal-i-ty
  fi-nal-i-ties
fi-nal-ize
  fi-nal-ized
  fi-nal-iz-ing
  fi-nal-ly
fi-nance
  fi-nanced
  fi-nanc-ing
  fi-nan-cial
  fi-nan-cial-ly
fin-an-cier
finch
find
  found
  find-ing
find-er
fine
  fin-er
  fin-est
  fine-ly
  fine-ness
fin-er-y
  fin-er-ies
fi-nesse
  fi-nessed
  fi-ness-ing
fin-ger
fin-ger-bowl
fin-ger-ing
fin-ger-nail
fin-ger-print
fin-i-al
fin-i-cal
  fin-i-cal-ly
fin-ick-y
  fin-ick-ing
fin-is
  fin-is-es
fin-ish
  fin-ished
  fin-ish-er
fi-nite
  fi-nite-ly
  fi-nite-ness

fire
  fired
  fir-ing
  fir-er
fire-arm
fire-ball
fire-brand
fire-bug
fire-crack-er
fire-fight-er
fire-fly
  fire-flies
fire-man
fire-place
fire-plug
fire-pow-er
fire-proof
fire-side
fire-trap
fire-wa-ter
fire-wood
fire-works
fir-ing-squad
firm
  firm-ly
  firm-ness
fir-ma-ment
first-born
first-hand
first-ling
first-ly
first-rate
first-string
fis-cal
  fis-cal-ly
fish-er
fish-er-man
  fish-er-men
fish-er-y
  fish-er-ies
fish-hook
fish-ing
fish-wife
  fish-wived
fish-y
  fish-i-er
  fish-i-est
fis-sle
fis-sion
fis-sure
  fis-sured
  fis-sur-ing
fist-ic
fist-i-cuff
fit
  fit-ter

78

fit-test
fit-ted
fit-ting
fit-ly
fit-ness
fit-ful
fit-ful-ly
fit-ful-ness
fit-ting
fit-ting-ly
fit-ting-ness
five-fold
five-and-ten
fix
fix-a-ble
fixed
fix-ed-ly
fix-er
fix-a-tion
fix-a-tive
fix-ings
fix-i-ty
fix-i-ties
fix-ture
fiz-zle
fiz-zled
fiz-zling
fiz-zy
fiz-zi-er
fiz-zi-est
flab-ber-gast
flab-by
flab-bi-er
flab-bi-est
flab-bi-ly
flab-bi-ness
flac-cid
flag
flagged
flag-ging
flag-el-lant
flag-el-lat-ed
flag-el-lat-ing
flag-el-la-tion
fla-gi-tious
flag-on
flag-pole
flag-rank
fla-grant
fla-grant-ly
flag-ship
flag-stone
flail
flair
flake
flaked

flak-ing
flak-y
flak-i-er
flak-i-est
flak-i-ness
flam-boy-ant
flam-boy-ance
flam-boy-an-cy
flam-boy-ant-ly
flame
flamed
falm-ing
flam-ing-ly
flam-ma-ble
flange
flank
flank-er
flan-nel-ette
flap
flapped
flap-ping
flap-per
flap-jack
flare
flared
flar-ing
flare-up
flash-back
flash-light
flash-i-er
flash-i-est
flash-i-ly
flash-i-ness
flask
flat
flat-ly
flat-ted
flat-ting
flat-ness
flat-car
flat-foot
flat-foot-ed
flat-foot-ed-ly
falt-ten
flat-ten-er
flat-ter
flat-ter-er
flat-ter-ing-ly
flat-ter-y
flat-ter-ies
flat-u-lent
flat-u-lence
flat-u-len-cy
flat-u-lent-ly
flat-ware
flaunt

flaunt-er
flaunt-ing-ly
flanty
flaunt-i-er
flaunt-i-est
flau-tist
fla-vor
fla-vored
fla-vor-less
fla-vor-ing
flaw-less
fla-zen
flax-seed
flay-er
flea-bite
flea-bit-ten
fleck
flec-tion
fledge
fledged
fledg-ing
fledg-ling
flee
fled
flee-ing
fleece
fleeced
fleec-ing
fleec-y
fleec-i-er
fleec-i-est
fleec-i-ness
fleet
fleet-ly
fleet-ness
fleet-ing
fleet-ing-ly
fleet-ing-ness
flesh-ly
flesh-li-er
flesh-li-est
flesh-pots
flesh-y
flesh-i-ert
flesh-i-est
flesh-i-ness
flex-i-ble
flex-i-bil-i-ty
flex-i-bly
flex-ion
flex-or
flex-ure
fib-ber-ti-gib-bet
flick-er
flick-er-ing
fli-er

flight
flight-less
flight-y
flight-i-er
flight-i-est
flight-i-ly
flight-i-ness
flim-flam
flim-flammed
flim-flam-ming
firm-sy
firm-si-er
firm-si-est
firm-si-ly
firm-si-ness
flinch
flinch-er
flinch-ing-ly
fin-ders
fling
flung
fling-ing
flint-y
flint-i-er
flint-i-est
flint-i-ness
flip
flipped
flip-ping
flip-flop
flip-pant
flip-pan-cy
flip-pant-ly
flip-per
flirt-er
flir-ta-tion
flir-ta-tious
flit
flit-ted
flit-ting
flit-ter
float-a-ble
float-a-tion
float-er
float-ing
floc-cu-lent
floc-cu-lence
flocked
flood-gate
flood-light
flood-lit
floor-ing
floor-walk-er
floo-zy
floo-zies
flop

flopped
flop-ping
flop-per
flop-house
flop-py
flop-pi-er
flop-pi-est
flop-pi-ly
flo-ra
flo-ras
flo-rae
flo-ral
flo-res-cence
flo-res-cent
flo-ret
flo-ri-cul-ture
flo-ri-cul-tur-al
flo-ri-cul-tur-ist
flor-id
flo-rid-i-ty
flor-id-ly
flor-id-ness
flo-rist
floss
flossy
floss-i-er
floss-i-est
flo-ta-tion
flo-til-la
flot-sam
flounce
flounced
flounc-ing
floun-der
flour-y
flour-i-er
flour-i-est
flour-ish
flou-rish-ing
flow-er
flow-ered
flow-er-ing
flow-ery
flow-er-i-ness
flub
flubbed
flub-bing
fluc-tu-ate
fluc-tu-at-ed
fluc-tu-at-ing
fluc-tu-a-tion
flue
flu-ent
flu-ency
flu-ent-ly
fluff

fluff-i-ness
fluff-y
fluff-i-er
fluff-i-est
flu-id
flu-id-ly
flu-id-ness
fluke
fluky
fluk-i-er
fluk-i-est
flum-mer-y
flum-mer-ies
flun-ky
flunk-ies
flu-o-resce
flu-o-resced
flu-o-resc-ing
flu-o-res-cence
flu-o-res-sent
flur-ry
flur-ries
flur-ried
flur-ry-ing
flus-ter
flute
flut-ed
flut-ing
flut-ist
flut-ter
flut-ter-er
flut-ter-ing-ly
flut-tery
flut-ter-i-er
flut-ter-i-est
flux-ion
fly-brown
fly-by-night
fly-er
fly-ing
fly-leaf
fly-leaves
fly-pa-per
fly-speck
fly-wheel
foal
foam
foam-i-ness
foam-y
foam-i-er
foam-i-est
fob
fobbed
fob-bing
fo-cal
fo-cal-lize

fo-cal-lized
fo-cal-iz-ing
fo-cus
fo-cus-es
fo-cus-ing
fo-cus-er
fod-der
foe-tus
foe-tal
fog
fogged
fog-ging
fog-gy
fog-gi-er
fog-gi-est
fog-gi-ly
fog-gi-ness
fog-horn
fo-gy
fo-gies
fo-gy-ish
foi-ble
fold-er
fol-de-rol
fo-li-a-ceous
fo-li-age
fo-li-ate
fo-li-at-ed
fo-li-at-ing
fol-li-a-tion
fo-li-o
fo-li-os
fol-li-oed
fo-li-o-ing
folk-lore
folk-lor-ist
flok-sy
flok-si-er
flok-si-est
flok-si-ness
folk-ways
fol-li-cle
fol-lic-u-lar
fol-low
fol-low-er
fol-low-ing
fol-ly
fol-lies
fo-ment
fo-men-ta-tion
fo-ment-er
fon-dant
fon-dle
fond-led
fon-dling
fon-dler

fond-ly
fond-ness
fon-due
food-stuff
fool-er-y
fool-er-ies
fool-har-dy
fool-har-di-ness
fool-proof
fools-cap
foot-age
foot-ball
foot-board
foot-can-dle
foot-ed
foot-fall
foot-hill
foot-hold
foot-ing
foot-lights
foot-loose
foot-note
foot-not-ed
foot-not-ing
foot-path
foot-print
foot-sore
foot-step
foot-stool
foot-wear
foot-work
foo-zle
foo-zled
foo-zling
fop
fop-pery
fop-per-ies
fop-pish
fop-pish-ly
fop-pish-ness
for-age
for-aged
for-ag-ing
for-ay
for-bear
for-bore
for-borned
for-bear-ing
for-bear-ance
for-bear-ing-ly
for-bid
for-bade
for-bid-den
for-bid-ding
for-bid-ding-ness
force

forced
forc-ing
forc-a-ble
force-less
forc-er
force-ful
force-ful-ly
force-ful-ness
for-ceps
for-ci-ble
for-ci-bly
ford-a-ble
fore-arm
fore-bear
fore-bode
fore-bod-ed
fore-bod-ing
fore-bod-er
fore-brain
fore-cast
fore-cast-ed
fore-cast-ing
fore-cast-er
fore-close
fore-closed
fore-clos-ing
fore-clo-sure
fore-fa-ther
fore-fin-ger
fore-foot
fore-feet
fore-front
fore-gath-er
fore-go
fore-went
fore-gone
fore-go-ing
fore-ground
fore-hand
fore-hand-ed
fore-hand-ed-ness
fore-head
for-eign
for-eign-er
for-eign-ness
fore-know
fore-knew
fore-known
fore-know-ing
fore-knowl-edge
fore-leg
fore-lock
fore-man
fore-men
fore-most
fore-noon

fo-ren-sic
fore-or-dain
fore-quar-ter
fore-run
  fore-ran
  fore-run-ning
fore-run-ner
fore-see
  fore-saw
  fore-seen
  fore-see-ing
  fore-see-a-ble
  fore-se-er
fore-shad-ow
  fore-shad-ow-er
fore-sight
  fore-sight-ed
  fore-sight-ed-ness
fore-skin
for-est
fore-stall
-for-est-a-tion
for-es-ter
for-es-try
fore-taste
  fore-tast-ed
  fore-tast-ing
fore-tell
  fore-told
  fore-tell-ing
  fore-tell-er
fore-thought
for-ev-er
for-ev-er-more
fore-warn
fore-word
for-feit
  for-feit-er
for-fei-ture
for-gath-er
forge
  forged
  forg-ing
  forg-er
for-ger-y
  fog-er-ies
for-get
  for-got
  for-got-ten
  for-get-ting
  for-get-ta-ble
  for-get-ter
for-get-ful
  for-get-ful-ly
  for-get-ful-ness
for-give

for-gave
for-giv-en
for-giv-ing
for-giv-a-ble
for-give-ness
for-giv-er
for-go
  for-went
  for-gone
  for-go-ing
  for-go-er
fork-loft
for-lorn
  for-lorn-ly
  for-lorn-ness
for-mal
  for-mal-ly
for-mal-ism
for-mal-i-ty
  for-mal-i-ties
for-mal-ize
  for-mal-ized
  for-mal-iz-ing
  for-mal-i-za-tion
for-mat
for-ma-tion
form-a-tive
for-mer
  for-mer-ly
for-mi-da-ble
  for-mi-da-ble-ness
  for-mi-da-bly
form-less
  form-less-ly
  form-less-ness
for-mu-la
  for-mu-las
  for-mu-lae
for-mu-lar-y
  for-mu-lar-ies
for-mu-late
  for-mu-lat-ed
  for-mu-lat-ing
  for-mu-la-tion
  for-mu-la-tor
for-ni-cate
  for-ni-cat-ed
  for-ni-cat-ing
  for-ni-cat-or
  for-ni-ca-tion
for-sake
  for-soke
  for-sak-en
  for-sak-ing
  for-sak-en-ly
for-swear

for-swore
for-sworn
for-swear-ing
for-swear-er
fort
forte
forth-com-ing
forth-right
  forth-right-ness
forth-with
for-ti-fi-ca-tion
for-ti-fy
  for-ti-fied
  for-ti-fy-ing
  for-ti-fi-er
for-tis-si-mo
for-ti-tude
fort-night
for-night-ly
  for-night-lies
for-tress
for-tu-i-tous
  for-tu-i-tous-ly
  for-tu-i-tous-ness
for-tu-nate
  for-tu-nate-ly
for-tune
for-tune-tell-er
  for-tune-tell-ing
for-ty
  for-ties
for-ty-nin-er
fo-rum
  fo-rums
  fo-ra
for-ward
  for-ward-er
  for-ward-ly
  for-ward-ness
fos-sil
fos-sil-ize
  fos-sil-ized
  fos-sil-iz-ing
  fos-sil-i-za-tion
fos-ter
  fos-tered
  fos-ter-ing
fought
fou-lard
found
foun-da-tion
  foun-da-tion-al
found-er
found-ling
found-ry
  found-ries

foun-tain
foun-tain-head
four-flush-er
four-square
four-teen
　four-teenth
fourth
　fourth-ly
fowl
　fowl-er
fox-hole
　fox-i-er
　fox-i-est
　fox-i-ly
　fox-i-ness
foy-er
fra-cas
　fra-cas-es
frac-tion
　frac-tion-al
frac-tious
　frac-tious-ly
frac-ture
　frac-tured
　frac-tur-ing
frag-ile
　fra-gil-i-ty
frag-ment
　frag-ment-al
　frag-men-ter-i-ness
　frag-men-tary
frag-men-ta-tion
frag-ment-ize
　frag-ment-ized
　frag-ment-iz-ing
fra-grance
　fra-grant
　fra-grant-ly
frail
　frail-ty
　frail-ness
frame
　framed
　fram-ing
　fram-er
frame-up
frame-work
franc
fran-chise
　fran-chised
frank
　frank-er
　frank-ly
　frank-ness
frank-furt-er
frank-in-cense

fran-tic
　fran-ti-cal-ly
fra-ter-nal
　fra-ter-nal-ly
fra-ter-ni-ty
　fra-ter-ni-ties
frat-er-nize
frat-ri-cide
　frat-ri-cid-al
fraud-u-lent
　fraud-u-lence
fraught
fraz-zle
　fraz-zled
　fraz-zling
freak
　freak-ish
freck-le
　freck-led
　freck-li-er
free
　fre-er
　free-ly
free-bie
free-boot-er
free-dom
free-lance
　free-lanced
　free-lanc-ing
free-spoken
　free-spo-ken-ness
free-stone
　free-think-ing
free-way
free-wheel
freeze
　froze
　fro-zen
　freez-ing
freeze-dry
　freeze-dried
　freeze-dry-ing
freez-er
fre-net-ic
　fre-net-i-cal-ly
fren-zy
　fren-zies
　fren-zied
　fren-zy-ing
fre-quen-cy
　fre-quen-cies
fre-quent
　fre-quent-er
　fre-quent-ly
fre-quen-ta-tive
fres-co

fres-coes
fres-cos
fres-coed
fres-co-ing
fresh
　fresh-ly
　fresh-ness
fresh-en
　fresh-en-er
fresh-et
fresh-man
　fresh-men
fret
　fret-ted
fret-work
fri-ary
　fri-ar-ies
fric-as-see
　fric-as-seed
fric-tion
　fric-tion-al
friend
　friend-less
friend-ly
　friend-li-er
　friend-li-est
frieze
fright-ful
　fright-ful-ly
frig-id
　fri-gid-i-ty
　frig-id-ly
　frig-id-ness
frilly
　frill-i-er
　frill-i-est
fringe
　fringed
　fring-ing
frip-pery
　frip-per-ies
frisky
　frisk-i-er
fit-ter
friv-o-lous
　fri-vol-i-ty
frizz
　friz-zi-ness
　friz-zi-er
friz-zle
　friz-zled
　friz-zling
frol-ic
　frol-ick-ed
　frol-ick-ing
frol-ic-some

front-age
  fron-tal-ly
fron-tier
frost
  frost-ed
frost-bite
  frost-bit
  frost-bit-ten
  frost-bit-ting
frost-ing
frost-y
  frost-i-er
froth
  froth-i-ness
  frothy
  froth-i-er
  froth-i-est
frou-frou
fro-ward
frown
  frown-ing-ly
frow-zy
  frow-zi-er
fro-zen
  fro-zen-ly
  fro-zen-ness
fruc-ti-fy
  fruc-ti-fied
  fruc-ti-fy-ing
  fruc-ti-fi-ca-tion
fru-gal
  fru-gal-i-ty
  fru-gal-i-ties
  fru-gal-ly
fruit-ful
  fruit-ful-ly
fru-i-tion
  fruit-less-ly
fruity
frump
  frump-ish
  frump-i-est
frus-trate
  frus-trat-ed
  frus-trat-ing
  frus-tra-tion
fry
  fried
  fry-ing
fry-er
fud-dle
  fud-dled
  fud-dling
fudge
  fudged
  fudg-ing

fu-el
  fu-eled
  fu-el-ing
fu-gi-tive
  fu-gi-tive-ly
ful-crum
  ful-crums
  ful-cra
ful-fill
  ful-filled
  ful-fil-ling
  ful-fil-ment
full
  full-ness
  ful-ly
full-back
ful-mi-nate
  ful-mi-nat-ed
  ful-mi-nat-ing
  ful-mi-na-tion
ful-some
  ful-some-ly
fum-ble
  fum-bled
  fum-bling
  fum-bler
fume
  fumed
  fum-ing
  fum-ing-ly
fu-mi-gate
  fu-mi-gat-ed
  fu-mi-gat-ing
func-tion
  func-tion-less
func-tion-al
  func-tion-al-ly
func-tion-ary
  func-tion-ar-ies
fun-da-men-tal
  fun-da-men-tal-ly
fun-da-men-tal-ism
  fun-da-men-tal-ist
fu-ner-al
fu-ner-re-al
fun-gi-cide
  fun-gi-cid-al
  fun-gi-cid-al-ly
fun-gous
fun-gus
  fun-gi
  fun-gus-es
funic-u-lar
funk-y
  funk-i-er
  funk-i-est

fun-nel
  fun-neled
  fun-nel-ing
fun-ny
  fun-ni-er
  fun-ni-est
fur
  furred
  fur-ring
fur-bish
fu-ri-ous
  fu-ri-ous-ly
fur-long
fur-lough
fur-nace
fur-nish
fur-nish-ings
fur-ni-ture
for-row
fur-ry
  fur-ri-er
  fur-ri-est
fur-ther
fur-ther-more
fur-ther-most
fur-thest
fur-tive
  fur-tive-ly
fu-ry
  fu-ries
fuse
  fused
  fus-ing
fu-see
fu-se-lage
fu-si-bil-i-ty
fu-si-ble
fu-si-form
fu-si-lade
  fu-si-lad-ed
  fu-si-lad-ing
fu-sion
fussy
  fuss-i-er
  fuss-i-est
  fuss-i-ly
fus-tian
fus-ty
fu-tile
fu-til-i-ty
  fu-til-i-ties
fu-ture
fu-tur-ism
fu-tur-is-tic
fu-tu-ri-ty
fuzz-y

G

gab
gabbed
gab-ber
gab-ar-dine
gab-ble
gab-bled
gab-bler
gab-by
gab-bi-er
gab-bi-est
ga-ble
ga-bled
ga-bling
gad
gad-ded
gad-ding
gad-a-bout
gad-fly
gad-flies
gad-get
gad-get-ry
gaffe
gaf-fer
gag
ga-ga
gai-e-ty
gai-e-ties
gai-ly
gain-ful
gain-say
gain-said
gain-say-ing
gait
ga-la
ga-lac-tic
gal-ax-y
gal-a-xies
gal-lant
gal-lant-ry
gal-lant-ries
gal-ler-y
gal-ler-ies
gal-ley
gal-li-cism
gal-li-mau-fry
gal-li-mau-fries
gall-ing
gal-li-vant
gal-lon
gal-lop
gal-lows
gal-lows-es
gall-stone
ga-loot
ga-lore
gal-van-ic

gal-va-nism
gal-va-nize
gal-va-nized
gal-va-nom-e-ter
gam-bit
gam-ble
gam-bled
gam-bling
gam-bol
gam-brel
game
gam-er
gam-est
gamed
gam-ing
game-keep-er
game-some
game-ster
gam-ete
ga-met-ic
gam-in
gam-ma
gam-mon
gam-ut
gam-y
gam-i-er
gam-i-est
gam-i-ly
gam-i-ness
gan-der
gang-land
gan-gling
gan-gli-on
gan-glia
gan-gli-ons
gan-gly
gan-gli-er
gan-gli-est
gang-plank
gan-grene
gan-grened
gan-gren-ing
gan-gre-nous
gang-ster
gang-way
gant-let
gan-try
gan-tries
gap
gapped
gap-ping
ga-rage
ga-raged
ga-rag-ing
gar-bage
gar-ble

gar-bled
gar-bling
gar-den
gar-gan-tu-an
gar-gle
gar-gled
gar-gling
gar-goyle
gar-ish
gar-land
gar-ment
gar-ner
gar-net
gar-nish
gar-nish-ee
gar-nish-ee-ing
gar-nish-ment
gar-ni-ture
gar-ret
gar-ri-son
gar-rote
gar-rot-ed
gar-rot-ing
gar-rot-er
gar-ru-lous
gar-ter
gas
gassed
gas-sing
gas-e-ous
gas-i-fy
gas-i-fied
gas-i-fy-ing
gas-i-fi-ca-tion
gas-i-fi-er
gas-ket
gas-light
gas-lit
gas-o-line
gas-ser
gas-sy
gas-si-er
gas-si-est
gas-si-ness
gas-tric
gas-ti-tis
gas-tro-in-tes-ti-nal
gas-tron-o-my
gas-tro-nom-ic
gas-tro-nom-i-cal
gas-tro-nom-i-cal-ly
gas-works
gate-crash-er
gate-crash-ing
gate-house
gate-keep-er

gate-post
gate-way
gath-er
  gath-er-ing
gauche
gau-cho
gaud-y
  gaud-i-er
  gaud-i-est
  gaud-i-ly
  gaud-i-ness
gauge
  gauged
  gaug-ing
gaunt-let
gauze
  gauz-i-er
  gauz-i-est
  gauz-i-ness
  gauzy
gay-e-ty
gaze
  gazed
  gaz-er
  gaz-ing
ga-ze-bo
  ga-ze-bos
  ga-ze-boes
ga-zelle
ga-zette
gaz-et-teer
gear-box
gear-ing
gear-shift
gear-wheel
gee
  geed
  gee-ing
gee-zer
gei-sha
gel
  gelled
  gel-ling
gel-a-tin
gel-lat-i-nous
ge-la-tion
geld
  geld-ed
  geld-ing
  gelt
gel-id
gem
  gemmed
  gem-ming
gem-i-nate
  gem-i-nat-ed

gem-i-nat-ing
gem-i-nate-ly
gem-i-na-tion
gem-ol-o-gy
  gem-o-log-i-cal
  gem-ol-o-gist
gem-stone
gen-darme
gen-der
gene
ge-ne-al-o-gy
  ge-ne-a-log-i-cal
  ge-ne-a-l-o-gist
gen-er-al
gen-er-al-is-si-mo
  gen-er-al-is-si-mos
gen-er-al-ist
gen-er-al-i-ty
  gen-er-al-i-ties
gen-er-al-ize
  gen-er-al-ized
  gen-er-al-iz-ing
  gen-er-al-i-za-tion
  gen-er-al-iz-er
gen-er-ate
  gen-er-at-ed
  gen-er-at-ing
  gen-er-a-tive
  gen-er-a-tive-ly
gen-er-a-tion
gen-er-a-tor
ge-ner-ic
  ge-ner-i-cal
  ge-ner-i-cal-ly
gen-er-ous
  gen-er-os-i-ty
  gen-er-os-i-ties
gen-e-sis
ge-net-ic
  ge-net-i-cal-ly
ge-net-ics
  ge-net-i-cist
gen-ial
  ge-ni-al-i-ty
ge-nie
  ge-nies
  ge-nii
gen-i-tal
gen-i-ta-lia
gen-i-tals
gen-ius
  gen-ius-es
gen-o-cide
  gen-o-ci-dal
gen-re
gen-teel

gen-tian
gen-tile
gen-til-i-ty
  gen-til-i-ties
gen-tle
  gen-tler
  gen-tlest
  gen-tly
gen-tle-folk
gen-tle-man
  gen-tle-men
gen-tle-wom-an
  gen-tle-wom-en
gen-try
gen-u-flect
  gen-u-flec-tion
  gen-u-flec-tor
gen-u-ine
ge-nus
  gen-e-ra
  ge-nus-es
ge-o-cen-tric
  ge-o-cen-tri-cal-ly
ge-o-chem-is-try
  ge-o-chem-i-cal
  ge-o-chem-ist
ge-ode
ge-o-des-ic
ge-o-gra-phy
  ge-o-gra-phies
  ge-o-gra-pher
  ge-o-gra-phic
  ge-o-graph-i-cal
ge-ol-o-gy
  ge-ol-o-gies
  ge-o-log-ic
  ge-o-log-i-cal
  ge-o-log-i-cal-ly
  ge-ol-o-gist
ge-o-met-ric
ge-om-e-try
  ge-om-e-tries
ge-o-phys-ics
  ge-o-phys-i-cal
  ge-o-phys-i-cist
ge-o-pol-i-tic
  ge-o-pol-i-tics
  ge-o-pol-o-tic
  ge-o-po-lit-i-cal
  ge-o-po-lit-i-cal-ly
ge-o-ther-mal
ger-bil
ger-i-at-ric
  ger-i-at-rics
  ger-i-a-tri-cian
  ger-i-at-rist

ger-mane
ger-mi-cide
  ger-mi-cid-al
ger-mi-nate
  ger-mi-nat-ed
  ger-mi-nat-ing
  ger-mi-na-tion
ger-on-tol-o-gy
  ger-on-tol-o-gist
ger-ry-man-der
ger-und
ges-so
ges-tate
  ges-tat-ed
  ges-tat-ing
  ges-ta-tion
ges-tic-u-late
  ges-tic-u-lat-ed
  ges-tic-u-lat-ing
  ges-tic-u-la-tion
  ges-tic-u-la-tive
  ges-tic-u-la-to-ry
  ges-tic-u-la-tor
ges-ture
  ges-tured
  ges-tur-ing
  ges-tur-er
ge-sund-heit
get-a-way
gew-gaw
gey-ser
ghast-ly
  ghast-li-er
  ghast-li-est
  ghast-li-ness
gher-kin
ghet-to
  ghe-tos
  ghet-toes
ghost-ly
  ghost-li-er
  ghost-li-est
  ghost-li-ness
ghost-write
  ghost-wrote
  ghost-writ-ten
  ghost-writ-ting
ghoul
gi-ant
gib-ber-ish
gib-bon
gibe
  gib-er
  gib-ing-ly
gib-let
gid-dy

gid-di-er
gid-di-est
gid-di-ly
gid-di-ness
gi-gan-tic
gi-gan-tism
gig-gle
  gig-gled
  gig-gling
  gig-gler
  gig-gly
  gig-gli-er
  gig-gli-est
gig-o-lo
gild-ed
gilt-edged
gim-crack
gim-let
gim-mick
gin-ger
gin-ger-bread
gin-ger-ly
  gin-ger-li-ness
gin-ger-snap
gin-ger-y
ging-ham
gird-er
gir-dle
  gir-dled
  gir-dling
girl-hood
girl-ish
girth
gist
give
  gave
  giv-en
  giv-ing
give-and-take
give-a-way
giz-zard
gla-cial
gla-cier
glad
  glad-der
  glad-dest
  glad-ly
  glad-ness
glad-den
glad-i-a-tor
  glad-i-a-to-ri-al
glad-i-o-lus
  glad-i-o-lus-es
  glad-i-o-la
glad-some
glam-or-ize

glam-or-ized
glam-or-iz-ing
glam-or-i-za-tion
glam-or-i-zer
glam-or-ous
  glam-or-ous-ly
  glam-or-ous-ness
glam-our
glance
  glanced
  glanc-ing
glan-du-lar
glare
  glared
  glar-ing
  glar-i-ness
  glar-y
  glar-i-er
  glar-i-est
glass-blow-ing
  glass-blow-er
glass-ful
glass-ware
glass-y
  glass-i-er
  glass-i-est
  glass-i-ly
  glass-i-ness
glau-co-ma
glaze
  glazed
  glaz-ing
gla-zier
gleam
  gleam-ing
  gleam-y
glean
  glean-er
  glean-ing
glee
  glee-ful
  glee-ful-ly
  glee-ful-ness
glen-gar-ry
glib
  glib-ber
  glib-best
  glib-ly
  glib-ness
glide
  glid-ed
  glid-ing
glim-mer
glimpse
  glimpsed
glis-san-do

glis-san-di
glis-san-dos
glis-ten
glit-ter
gloam-ing
gloat
gloat-er
gloat-ing
glob
glo-bal
glob-al-ly
globe-trot-ter
globe-trot-ting
glob-u-lar
glob-ule
glock-en-spiel
gloom-y
gloom-i-er
gloom-i-est
gloom-i-ly
gloom-i-ness
glo-ri-fy
glo-ri-fied
glo-ri-fy-ing
glo-ri-fi-ca-tion
glo-ri-fi-er
glo-ri-ous
glo-ri-ous-ly
glo-ri-ou-ness
glo-ry
glo-ries
glo-ried
glo-ry-ing
glos-sa-ry
glos-sa-ries
glossy
gloss-i-er
gloss-i-est
gloss-i-ly
gloss-i-ness
glot-tis
glot-tis-es
glot-ti-des
glove
gloved
glov-ing
glow
glow-er
glow-ing
glow-worm
glu-cose
glue
glued
glu-ing
glum
glum-mer

glum-mest
glut
glut-ted
glut-ting
glu-ten
glu-ti-nous
glut-ton
glut-ton-ous
glut-tony
glyc-er-in
glyc-er-ine
glyc-er-ol
gnarl
gnarled
gnarly
gnarl-i-er
gnarl-i-est
gnash
gnat
gnaw
gnawed
gnaw-ing
gneiss
gnome
gnu
gnus
goad-ed
go-a-head
goal-keep-er
goat-ee
goat-herd
goat-skin
gob-ble
gob-bled
gob-bling
gob-ble-dy-ween
gob-let
gob-lin
go-cart
god-child
god-chil-dren
god-daugh-ter
god-son
god-dess
good-fa-ther
god-head
god-less
god-less-ness
god-like
god-ly
god-li-er
god-li-est
god-li-ness
god-mo-ther
god-par-ent
god-send

go-get-ter
gog-gle
gog-gled
gog-gling
gog-gle-eyed
gog-gles
go-ing
goi-ter
gold-brick
gold-en
gold-smith
go-nad
gon-do-la
gon-do-lier
gon-er
gon-or-rhea
goo-ber
good-by
good-bye
good-for-noth-ing
good-heart-ed
good-ish
good-look-ing
good-ly
good-li-er
good-li-est
good-na-tured
good-ness
good-tem-pered
good-y
good-ies
goof-off
goof-y
goof-i-er
goof-i-est
goof-i-ness
goose-ber-ry
goose-ber-ries
gore
gored
gor-ing
gorge
gorged
gorg-ing
gor-geous
gor-geous-ly
gor-geous-ness
gor-y
gor-i-er
gor-i-est
gos-ling
gos-pel
gos-sa-mer
gos-sa-mery
gos-sa-mer-i-er
gos-sa-mer-i-est

gos-sip
  gos-sip-ing
  gos-sipy
gouge
  gouged
  goug-ing
  goug-er
gou-lash
gourd
gour-met
  gour-mets
gout
  gouty
  gout-i-er
  gout-i-est
gov-ern
  gov-ern-a-ble
  gov-ern-ess
  gov-ern-ment
  gov-ern-men-tal
gov-er-nor
  gov-er-nor-ship
gow-and
gowned
grab
  grabbed
  grab-bing
  grab-ber
grace
  graced
  grac-ing
grace-ful
  grace-ful-ly
  grace-ful-ness
grace-less
gra-cious
gra-da-tion
grade
  grad-ed
  grad-ing
grad-er
gra-di-ent
grad-u-al
  grad-u-al-ly
  grad-u-al-ness
grad-u-ate
  grad-u-at-ed
  grad-u-at-ing
grad-u-ation
graf-fi-to
  graf-fi-ti
graft
  graft-age
  graft-er
  graft-ing
gra-ham

grain
grain-y
  grain-i-er
  grain-i-est
  grain-i-ness
gram
gram-mar
  gram-mar-i-an
gram-mat-i-cal
  gram-mat-i-cal-ly
gra-na-ry
  gra-na-ries
grand
  grand-ly
grand-child
  grand-daugh-ter
gran-dee
gran-deur
grand-fa-ther
gran-dil-o-quence
  gran-dil-o-quent
gran-di-ose
  gran-di-ose-ly
grand-moth-er
grand-par-ent
grand-son
grand-stand
grange
  grang-er
gran-ite
  gra-nat-ic
gran-ny
  gran-nies
gran-u-lar
  gran-u-lar-i-ty
gran-u-late
  gran-u-lat-ed
  gran-u-lat-ing
gran-u-la-tion
gran-ule
grape-fruit
grape-vine
graph-ic
  graph-i-cal
  graph-i-cal-ly
graph-ite
graph-ol-o-gy
  graph-ol-o-gist
grap-nel
grap-ple
  grap-pled
  grap-pling
  grap-pler
grass
  grass-y
  grass-i-er

  grass-i-est
grass-hop-per
grass-land
grate
  grat-ed
  grat-ing
grate-ful
  grate-ful-ly
  grate-ful-ness
grat-i-fy
  grat-i-fied
  grat-i-fy-ing
gra-tis
grat-i-tude
gra-tu-i-tous
gra-tu-i-ty
  gra-tu-i-ties
grave
  graved
  grav-en
  grav-ing
  grav-er
  grave-ly
  grave-ness
grav-el
  grav-eled
  grav-el-ing
  grav-el-ly
grave-stone
grave-yard
grav-i-tate
  grav-i-tat-ed
  grav-i-tat-ing
grav-i-ta-tion
  grav-i-ta-tion-al
grav-i-ty
  grav-i-ties
gra-vy
  grav-ies
gray
  gray-ly
  gray-ness
gray-ling
graze
  grazed
  graz-ing
grease
  greas-ed
  greas-ing
greas-y
  greas-i-er
  greas-i-ness
great
  great-ly
great-coat
great-heart-ed

89

greed-y
  greed-i-er
  greed-i-est
  greed-i-ly
  greed-i-ness
green-back
green-er-y
  green-er-ies
green-gro-cer
green-horn
green-house
  green-hous-es
green-ing
green-ish
  green-ish-ness
green-sward
greet
  greet-er
greet-ing
gre-gar-i-ous
  gre-gar-i-ous-ly
  gre-gar-i-ous-ness
grem-lin
gren-a-dier
gren-a-dine
grey
  grey-ly
  grey-ness
grid-dle
grid-dle-cake
grid-i-ron
grief
griev-ance
grieve
  grieved
  griev-ing
griev-ous
  griev-ous-ly
grif-fin
  grif-fon
grill
gril-lage
grille
grill-room
grim
  grim-mer
  grim-mest
  grim-ly
grim-ness
grim-ace
  grim-aced
  grim-ac-ing
grime
  grimed
  grim-ing
grim-y

grim-i-er
grim-i-est
grim-i-ly
  grim-i-ness
grin
  grin-ned
  grin-ning
  grin-ner
grind
  ground
  grind-ing
grind-er
grind-stone
grin-go
  grin-gos
grip
  gripped
  grip-ping
gripe
  griped
  grip-er
grippe
gris-ly
  gris-li-er
  gris-li-est
  gris-li-ness
gris-tle
  gris-tly
  gris-tli-er
  gris-tli-est
grit
  grit-ted
  grit-ting
grit-ty
  grit-ti-er
  grit-ti-est
  grit-ti-ly
  grit-ti-ness
griz-zled
griz-zly
  griz-zli-er
  griz-zli-est
  griz-zlies
groan
  groan-er
gro-cer
gro-cer-y
  gro-cer-ies
grog-gy
  grog-gi-er
groin
grom-met
groom
groove
  grooved
  groov-er

groov-y
  groov-i-er
  groov-i-est
grope
  groped
  grop-ing
gros-grain
gross
  gross-es
  gross-ness
gro-tesque
  gro-tesque-ly
  gro-tesque-ness
grot-to
  grot-toes
  grot-tos
grouch
  grouchy
  grouch-i-er
  grouch-i-est
ground-er
ground-less
  ground-less-ly
  ground-less-ness
ground-ling
ground-nut
ground-work
group-ie
grouse
  groused
  grous-ing
  grous-er
grov-el
  grov-eled
  grov-el-er
grow
  grow-ing
  grow-er
growl
  growl-er
grown-up
growth
grub
  grubbed
  grub-bing
  grub-ber
grub-by
  grub-bi-er
  grub-bi-est
grub-stake
  grub-staked
  grub-stak-ing
grudge
  grudged
  grudg-ing
  grudg-ing-ly

gru-el
gru-el-ing
grue-some
  grue-some-ly
gruff
  gruff-ly
  gruff-ness
grum-ble
  grum-bled
  grum-bling
  grum-bler
grump-y
  grump-i-er
  grump-i-ness
grunt
  grunt-er
  grunt-ing
gua-no
  gua-nos
guar-an-tee
  guar-an-teed
  guar-an-tee-ing
guar-an-tor
guar-an-ty
  guar-an-ties
  guar-an-ty-ing
guard-ed
  guard-ed-ly
guard-house
guard-i-an
guards-man
  guards-men
gua-va
gu-ber-na-to-ri-al
gudg-eon
guer-ril-la
  gue-ril-la
guess
  gues-ser
guess-work
guest
guf-faw
guid-ance
guide
  guid-ed
  guid-ing
guide-book
guide-post
gui-don
guid-hall
guile
  guile-ful
  guile-ful-ly
  guile-less
  guile-less-ly
guil-to-tine

guil-lo-tined
guil-lo-tin-ing
guilt
  guilt-less
  guilt-less-ly
guilt-y
  guilt-i-er
  guilt-i-ness
guin-ea
guise
gui-tar
  gui-tar-ist
gul-let
gul-li-ble
  gul-li-bil-i-ty
  gul-li-bly
gul-ly
  gul-lies
  gul-lied
  gul-ly-ing
gum
  gummed
  gum-ming
gum-bo
  gum-bos
gum-drop
gum-my
  gum-mi-er
  gum-mi-est
  gum-mi-ness
gump-tion
gum-shoe
  gum-shoed
gun
  gunned
  gun-ning
gun-boat
gun-fight
  gun-fight-er
gun-fire
gun-man
  gun-men
gun-ner
  gun-ner-y
gun-ny
  gun-nies
gun-ny-bag
gun-pow-der
gun-stock
gun-wale
gup-py
  gup-pies
gur-gle
  gur-gled
  gur-gling
gu-ru

gush-er
gush-ing
gush-y
  gush-i-er
  gush-i-est
  gush-i-ness
gus-set
gus-ta-to-ry
  gus-to
gust-y
  gust-i-er
  gust-i-est
gut
  gut-ted
  gut-ting
gut-ter
gut-tur-al
  gut-tur-al-ly
guz-zle
  guz-zled
  guz-zling
  guz-zler
gym-na-si-um
  gym-na-si-ums
  gym-na-sia
gym-nast
gym-nas-tic
  gym-nas-tics
gy-ne-col-o-gy
  gy-ne-co-log-ic
  gy-ne-co-log-i-cal
  gy-ne-col-o-gist
gyp
  gypped
  gyp-ping
gyp-sum
gyp-sy
  gyp-sies
gy-ral
gy-rate
  gy-rat-ed
  gy-rat-ing
  gy-ra-tion
  gy-ra-tor
  gy-ra-to-ry
gyr-fal-con
gy-roi-dal
gy-rom-e-ter
gy-ro-plane
gy-ro-scope
  gy-ro-scop-ic
gy-rose
gy-rus
gyve
  gyved
  gyv-ing

hab-da-lah
ha-be-as cor-pus
hab-er-dash-er
  hab-er-dash-ery
  hab-er-dash-er-ies
ha-bil-i-ment
hab-it
hab-it-a-ble
ha-bi-tant
hab-i-ta-tion
ha-bit-u-al
  ha-bit-u-al-ly
  ha-bit-u-al-ness
ha-bit-u-ate
  ha-bit-u-at-ed
  ha-bit-u-at-ing
  ha-bit-u-a-tion
ha-ci-en-da
  ha-ci-en-das
hack-le
  hack-led
  hack-ling
hack-ney
  hack-neyed
hack-saw
hadn't
had-ron
hae-mo-glo-bin
hae-mo-phil-i-a
haft
ha-gar
hag-gard
  hag-gard-ly
hag-gle
  hag-gled
  hag-gling
  hag-gler
ha-gi-ol-o-gy
  hag-i-ol-o-gies
  hag-i-ol-o-gist
hag-rid-den
haik
hai-ku
hail-fel-low
hail-stone
hail-storm
hair-breadth
hair-brush
hair-cut
hair-do
hair-dress-er
hair-dress-ing
hair-line
hair-pin
hair-split-ter
  hair-split-ting

hair-spring
hair-y
  hair-i-er
  hair-i-est
ha-la-tion
hal-cy-on
hale
  haled
  hal-ing
half-back
half-baked
half-breed
half-caste
half-heart-ed
  half-heart-ed-ly
half hour
half--life
  half-lives
half--mast
half--moon
half note
half step
half-tone
half-track
half-truth
half-way
half--wit
  half--wit-ted
hal-i-but
hal-i-to-sis
hall-mark
hal-lo
hal-low
  hal-lowed
hal-lu-ci-nate
  hal-lu-ci-nat-ed
  hal-lu-ci-nat-ing
hal-lu-ci-na-tion
  hal-lu-ci-na-to-ry
hal-lu-cin-o-gen
  hal-lu-cin-o-gen-ic
hal-lux
hall-way
ha-lo
  ha-los
  ha-loes
halo-phile
halt
  halt-ing
  halt-ing-ly
hal-ter
hal-ter-break
halve
  halved
  halv-ing
  halv-ers

halves
hal-yard
ham-burg-er
ham-let
ham-mer
ham-mer-head
ham-mer-less
ham-mock
ham-my
  ham-mi-er
  ham-mi-est
hamp-er
ham-ster
ham-string
  ham-strung
  ham-string-ing
hand-bag
hand-ball
hand-bill
hand-book
hand-cuff
hand-ed
hand-ful
  hand-fuls
hand-i-cap
  hand-i-capped
  hand-i-cap-ping
  hand-i-cap-per
hand-i-craft
hand-i-ly
  handi-ness
hand-i-work
han-ker-chief
han-dle
  han-dled
  han-dling
  han-dler
han-dle-bar
hand-made
hand-maid-en
hand--me--down
hand-out
hand-pick
  hand-picked
hand-rail
hand-shake
hand-some
  hand-som-er
  hand-som-est
  hand-some-ly
  hand-some-ness
hand-spike
hand-spring
hand-to-hand
hand--to--mouth
hand-work

hand-writ-ing
handy
  hand-i-er
  hand-i-est
handy-man
  handy-men
hang
  hung
  hanged
  hang-ing
hang-ar
hang-dog
hang-er
hang-er--on
hang-man
  hanf-men
hang-nail
hang-out
hang-o-ver
hang--up
hank-er
han-som
hap-haz-ard
  hap-haz-ard-ly
  hap-haz-ard-ness
hap-less
  hap-less-ly
hap-ly
hap-pen
hap-pen-ing
hap-pen-stance
hap-pi-ness
hap-py
  hap-pi-er
  hap-pi-est
  hap-pi-ly
hap-py--go--lucky
hara-kiri
ha-rangue
  ha-rangued
  ha-rangu-ing
ha-rass
  ha-rass-ment
har-bin-ger
har-bor
hard--bit-ten
hard--boiled
hard--core
hard-cov-er
hard-en
  hard-en-er
hard hat
hard-head-ed
hard-heart-ed
har-di-hood
har-di-ness

hard-ly
har-di-er
har-di-est
har-di-ly
hare-brained
hare-lip
har-em
har-le-quin
har-lot
  har-lot-ry
harm-ful
  harm-ful-ly
  harm-ful-ness
harm-less
  harm-less-ly
  harm-less-ness
har-mon-ic
  har-mon-i-cal-ly
har-mon-i-ca
har-mon-ics
har-mo-ni-ous
  har-mo-ni-ous-ly
har-mo-nize
  har-mo-nized
  har-mo-niz-ing
har-mo-ny
  har-mo-nies
har-ness
harp-ist
har-poon
harp-si-chord
har-py
  har-pies
har-que-bus
har-ri-dan
har-row
  har-row-ing
har-ry
  har-ried
  har-ry-ing
harsh
  harsh-ly
  harsh-ness
har-um-scar-um
har-vest
har-ves-ter
has--been
hash-ish
  hash-eesh
hasn't
has-sle
  has-sled
  has-sling
has-sock
has-ten
hasty

hast-i-er
hast-i-est
hast-i-ness
hatch-ery
  hatch-er-ies
hatch-et
hatch-way
hate
  hat-ed
  hat-ing
  hat-er
hate-ful
  hate-ful-ly
  hate-ful-ness
ha-tred
hat-ter
haugh-ty
  haugh-ti-er
  haugh-ti-est
  haugh-ti-ly
  haught-ti-ness
haul
  haul-age
haunch
  haunch-es
haunt-ed
  haunt-ing
hau-teur
ha-ven
have--not
haven't
hav-er-sack
havers
hav-oc
hawk
  hawk-ish
haw-ser
hay-loft
hay-mak-er
hay-mow
hay-seed
hay-stack
hay-wire
haz-ard
  haz-ard-ous
  haz-ard-ous-ly
  haz-ard-ou-ness
haze
  hazed
  haz-ing
ha-zel
ha-zel-nut
hazy
  ha-zi-er
  ha-zi-est
  ha-zi-ly

ha-zi-ness
head-ache
head-band
head-dress
head-er
head-first
 head-fore-most
head-gear
head-hunt-er
head-ing
head-land
head-less
head-light
head-line
 head-lined
 head-lin-ing
head-long
head-mas-ter
head-mis-tress
head-most
head--on
head-piece
head-quar-ters
head-set
head-stone
head-strong
head-wait-er
head-wa-ter
head-way
head-wind
heady
 head-i-er
 head-i-est
 head-i-ly
 head-i-ness
heal-er
health-ful
 health-ful-ly
healthy
 health-i-er
 health-i-est
 health-i-ness
heaped
hear
 heared
 hear-ing
 hear-er
hear-ken
hear-say
hearse
heart-ache
heart-break
 heart-break-ing
heart-brok-en
heart-burn
heart-en

heart-felt
hearth-stone
heart-less
 heart-less-ly
 heart-less-ness
heart-rend-ing
heart-sick
heart-strings
heart--to--heart
hearty
 heart-i-er
 heart-i-est
 heart-i-ly
 heart-i-ness
heat-ed
heat-er
heath
hea-then
heave
 heaved
 heav-ing
heav-en
heav-en-ly
heav-en-ward
 heav-en-wards
heavy
 heav-i-er
 heav-i-est
 heav-i-ly
 heav-i-ness
heavy--du-ty
heavy--hand-ed
heavy-weight
heck-le
 heck-led
 heck-ling
 heck-ler
hect-are
hec-tic
 hec-ti-cal-ly
hec-to-gram
hec-to-li-ter
hec-to-me-ter
hedge
 hedged
 hedg-ing
 hedg-er
he-do-nism
 he-do-nist
 he-do-nis-tic
hee-haw
hefty
 heft-i-er
 heft-i-est
he-ge-mo-ny
 he-ge-mo-nies

heg-e-mon-ic
he-gi-ra
heif-er
height-en
 height-en-er
hei-nous
 hei-nous-ly
 hei-nous-ness
heir-ess
heir-loom
heist
he-li-cop-ter
he-li-um
he-lix
 he-li-ces
 he-lix-es
hell--bent
hell-cat
hel-lion
hell-ish
 hell-ish-ly
 hell-ish-ness
hel-lo
 hel-los
helm
 helm-less
hel-met
 hel-met-ed
helms-man
 helms-men
help-er
help-ful
 help-ful-ly
 help-ful-ness
help-ing
help-less
 help-less-ly
 help-less-ness
help-mate
hel-er--skel-ter
hem
 hemmed
 hem-ming
he--man
 he--men
hemi-sphere
 hemi-spher-ic
 hemi-sper-i-cal
hem-lock
he-mo-glo-bin
he-mo-phil-ia
hem-or-rhage
 hem-or-rhag-ing
 hem-or-rhag-ic
hem-or-rhoid
 hem-or-rhoid-al

hemp-en
hem-stitch
hence-forth
hench-man
hench-men
  hench-man-ship
hen-na
hen-peck
hep-a-ti-tis
her-ald
  he-ral-dic
her-ald-ry
  her-ald-ries
herb-age
her-biv-o-rous
Her-cu-le-an
herd-er
herds-man
  herds-men
here-af-ter
he-red-i-tary
  he-red-i-tar-i-ly
  he-red-i-tar-i-ness
he-red-i-ty
  he-red-i-ties
here-in
here-of
her-e-sy
  her-e-sies
her-e-tic
  he-ret-i-cal
  he-ret-i-cal-ly
here-to
here-to-fore
here-upon
here-with
her-i-ta-ble
  her-i-ta-bil-i-ty
  her-i-ta-bly
her-i-tage
her-maph-ro-dite
  her-maph-ro-dit-ic
  her-maph-ro-dit-ism
her-met-ic
  her-met-i-cal
  her-met-i-cal-ly
her-mit
  her-mit-age
her-nia
  her-ni-al
  her-ni-a-tion
he-ro
  he-roes
he-ro-ic
  he-ro-ical
  he-ro-ical-ly

her-o-in
her-o-ine
her-o-ism
her-on
her-ring-bone
  her-ring-boned
  her-ring-bon-ing
her-self
hes-i-tant
  hes-i-tan-cy
  hes-i-tan-cies
  hes-i-tant-ly
hes-i-tate
  hes-i-tat-ed
  hes-i-tat-ing
  hes-i-tat-er
  hes-i-ta-tor
  hes-i-tat-ing-ly
hes-i-ta-tion
het-ero-dox
  het-ero-doxy
het-er-o-ge-neous
  het-er-o-ge-ne-ity
  het-er-o-ge-neous-ly
het-ero-sex-u-al
  het-ero-sex-u-al-i-ty
hew
  hewed
  hewn
  hew-ing
  hew-er
hexa-gon
  hex-ag-o-nal
  hex-ag-o-nal-ly
hey-day
  hey-dey
hi-a-tus
  hi-a-tus-es
hi-ba-chi
hi-ber-nate
  hi-ber-nat-ed
  hi-ber-nat-ing
  hi-ber-na-tion
hi-bis-cus
hic-cup
  hic-cuped
  hic-cup-ing
hid-den
  hid-den-ness
hide
  hid
  hid-den
  hid-er
hide-bound
hid-eous
  hid-eous-ly

hid-eous-ness
hide-out
hi-er-ar-chy
hi-er-ar-chies
hi-er-ar-chal
hi-er-ar-chic
hi-er-ar-chi-cal
hi-er-ar-chi-cal-ly
hi-ero-glyph
  hi-ero-glyph-ic
  hi-ero-glyph-i-cal
  hi-ero-glyph-i-cal-ly
hi--fi
high-ball
high-born
high-boy
high-brow
  high-browed
  high-brow-ism
high-er--up
high-fa-lu-tin
  high-fa-lu-ting
high--flown
high--grade
high--hand-ed
  high--hand-ed-ly
  high--hand-ed-ness
high--hat
high-land
high-light
high--mind-ed
  high--mind-ed-ly
  high--mind-ed-ness
high-ness
high--pressure
  high--pressured
  high--pressur-ing
high school
high seas
high--spir-it-ed
  high--spir-it-ed-ly
  high--spir-it-ed-ness
high--strung
high-tail
high--tension
high--toned
high-way
high-way-man
  high-way-men
hi-jack
  hi-jack-er
  hi-jack-ing
hike
  hiked
  hik-ing
  hik-er

hi-lar-i-ous
  hi-lar-i-ous-ly
  hi-lar-i-ous-ness
  hi-lar-i-ty
hill-bil-ly
  hill-bil-lies
hill-ock
hill-side
hill-top
hilly
  hill-i-er
  hill-i-est
him-self
hin-der
  hin-der-er
hind-most
hind-quar-ter
hin-drance
hind-sight
hinge
  hinged
  hing-ing
hint-er
  hint-ing-ly
hin-ter-land
hipped
hip-pie
hip-po
  hip-pos
hip-po-drome
hip-po-pot-a-mus
  hip-po-pot-a-mus-es
  hip-po-pot-a-mi
hire-ling
hir-sute
  hir-sute-ness
hiss
  hiss-er
his-ta-mine
  his-ta-min-ic
his-to-ri-an
his-tor-ic
his-tor-i-cal
  his-tor-i-cal-ly
  his-tor-i-cal-ness
his-to-ry
  his-to-ries
his-tri-on-ic
  his-tri-on-i-cal
  his-tri-on-i-cal-ly
his-tri-on-ics
hit
  hit-ting
hit--and--run
hitch
hitch-er

hitch-hike
  hitch-hiked
  hitch-hik-ing
  hitch-hik-er
hith-er-to
hive
  hived
  hiv-ing
hoary
  hoar-i-er
  hoar-i-est
  hoar-i-ness
hoard
  hoard-er
  hoard-ing
hoar-frost
hoarse
  hoarse-ly
  hoars-en
  hoarse-ness
hoax
  hoax-er
hob-ble
  hob-bled
  hob-bling
hob-by
  hob-bies
hob-by-horse
hob-gob-lin
hob-nail
  hob-nail-ed
hob-nob
  hob-nobbed
  hob-nob-bing
ho-bo
  ho-boes
  ho-bos
  ho-bo-ism
hock-er
hock-ey
ho-cus-po-cus
hodge-podge
hoe
  hoed
  hoe-ing
hoe-down
hog
  hogged
  hog-ging
hog-gish
  hog-gish-ly
  hog-gish-ness
hogs-head
hog--tie
  hog--tied
  hog--ty-ing

hog-wash
hoi pol-loi
hoist-er
ho-kum
hold-er
hold-ing
hold-out
hold-over
hold-up
hole
  holed
  hol-ing
  holey
hol-i-day
ho-li-ness
Hol-land
hol-ler
hol-low
  hol-low-ly
  hol-low-ness
hol-ly
  hol-lies
hol-ly-hock
hol-mi-um
ho-lo-caust
ho-lo-gram
hol-o-graph
hol-ster
ho-ly
  ho-li-er
  ho-li-est
  ho-lies
hom-age
hom-bre
  hom-bres
home-com-ing
home-less
  home-less-ness
home-ly
  home-li-er
  home-li-est
  home-li-ness
home-made
hom-er
home-sick
  home-sick-ness
home-spun
home-stead
  home-stead-er
home-ward
  home-wards
home-work
homey
  hom-i-er
  hom-i-est
  hom-i-ness

hom-i-cide
hom-i-let-ics
hom-i-ly
  hom-i-lies
homing pigeon
hom-i-ny
ho-mo-ge-neous
  ho-mo-ge-ne-ity
  ho-mo-ge-neous-ness
ho-mog-e-nize
  ho-meg-e-nized
  ho-mog-e-niz-ing
ho-mo-graph
ho-mol-o-gous
  ho-mol-o-gy
  ho-mol-o-gies
hom-onym
  hom-onym-ic
ho-mo-phone
  ho-mo-pho-nic
ho-mo-sex-u-al
  ho-mo-sex-u-al-i-ty
hone
  honed
  hon-ing
hon-est
  hon-est-ly
hon-es-ty
  hon-es-ties
hon-ey
  hon-eys
  hon-eyed
  hon-ied
  hon-ey-ing
hon-ey-bee
hon-ey-comb
hon-ey-moon
  hon-ey-moon-er
hon-ey-suck-le
  hon-ey-suck-led
hon-ky--tonk
hon-or
hon-or-able
  hon-or-ably
hon-o-rar-i-um
  hon-o-rar-i-ums
  hon-o-rar-ia
hon-or-ary
hon-or-if-ic
hood-ed
hood-lum
hoo-doo
  hoo-doo-ism
hood-wink
  hood-wink-er
hoo-ey

hoof
  hoofs
  hooves
  hoofed
hooked
hook-er
hook-up
hoo-li-gan
  hoo-li-gan-ism
hoop
  hooped
  hoop-like
hoop-la
hoo-ray
hoose-gow
hoot
  hoot-er
  hoot-ing-ly
hop
  hopped
  hop-ping
  hop-er
hope-ful
  hope-ful-ly
  hope-ful-ness
hope-less
  hope-less-ly
  hope-less-ness
hop-head
hop-per
hop-scotch
horde
  hord-ed
  hord-ing
ho-ri-zon
hor-i-zon-tal
  hor-i-zon-tal-ly
hor-mone
  hor-mon-al
horn
  horned
  horn-like
  horny
  horn-i-er
  horn-i-est
hor-net
horn-swog-gle
  horn-swog-gled
  horn-swog-gling
hor-rol-o-gy
  ho-rol-o-ger
  ho-rol-o-gist
horo-scope
hor-ren-dous
  hor-ren-dous-ly
hor-ri-ble

hor-ri-bly
hor-rid
  hor-rid-ly
  hor-rid-ness
hor-ri-fy
  hor-ri-fied
  hor-ri-fy-ing
  hor-ri-fi-ca-tion
hor-ror
horse
  hors-es
  horsed
  hors-ing
horse-back
horse-fly
  horse-flies
horse-hair
horse-laugh
horse-men
  horse-man-ship
  horse-wom-an
  horse-wom-en
horse opera
horse-play
horse-pow-er
horse-rad-ish
horse-shoe
  horse-sho-er
horse-whip
  horse-whipped
  horse-whip-ping
hors-ey
  horsy
  hors-i-er
  hors-i-est
  hors-i-ly
  hors-i-ness
hor-ta-to-ry
hor-ti-cul-ture
  hor-ti-cul-tur-al
  hor-ti-cul-tur-ist
ho-san-na
hose
  hos-es
  hosed
  hos-ing
ho-siery
hos-pice
hos-pi-ta-ble
  hos-pi-ta-bly
hos-pi-tal
hos-pi-tal-i-ty
  hos-pi-tal-i-ties
hos-pi-tal-iza-tion
hos-pi-tal-ize
  hos-pi-tal-ized

hos-pi-tal-iz-ing
hos-tage
hos-tel
  hos-tel-ry
  hos-tel-ries
host-ess
hos-tile
  hos-tile-ly
hos-til-i-ty
  hos-til-i-ties
hos-tler
hot
  hot-ter
  hot-test
  hot-ly
hot-bed
hot--blood-ed
ho-tel
hot-head
  hot-head-ed
  hot-head-ed-ness
hot-house
hot-shot
hound
  hound-er
hour-glass
hour-ly
house
  hous-es
  housed
  hous-ing
house-boat
house-bro-ken
  house-break
  house-broke
  house-break-ing
house-fly
house-hold
house-keep-er
  house-keep-ing
house-maid
house-warm-ing
house-wife
  house-wives
  house-wife-ly
  house-wif-ery
house-work
hous-ing
hov-el
  hov-eled
  hov-el-ing
hov-er
  hov-er-er
  hov-er-ing
how-ev-er
how-it-zer

howl-er
how-so-ev-er
hoy-den
  hoy-den-ish
hob-bub
huck-le-ber-ry
  huck-le-ber-ries
huck-ster
hud-dle
  hud-dled
  hud-dling
  hud-dler
huffy
  huff-i-er
  huff-i-est
  huff-i-ly
  huff-i-ness
hug
  hugged
  hug-ging
  hug-ger
huge
  hug-er
  hug-est
  huge-ly
  huge-ness
hu-la
hulk-ing
hul-la-ba-loo
hum
  hummed
  hum-ming
  hum-mer
hu-man
  hu-man-ness
hu-mane
  hu-mane-ly
  hu-man-ness
hu-man-ism
  hu-man-ist
  hu-man-ist-ic
hu-man-i-tar-i-an-ism
hu-man-i-ty
  hu-man-i-ties
hu-man-ize
  hu-man-ized
  hu-man-iz-ing
  hu-man-i-za-tion
  hu-man-iz-er
hu-man-kind
hu-man-ly
hum-ble
  hum-bler
  hum-blest
  hum-bled
  hum-bling

  hum-ble-ness
  hum-bly
hum-bug
  hum-bugged
  hum-bug-ging
  hum-bug-ger
  hum-bug-gery
hum-ding-er
hum-drum
hu-mer-us
hu-mid
  hu-mid-ly
hu-mid-i-fy
  hu-mid-i-fied
  hu-mid-i-fy-ing
  hu-mid-i-fi-er
hu-mid-i-ty
hum-ming-bird
hum-mock
  hum-mocky
  hum-mock-i-er
  hum-mock-i-est
hu-mor
hu-mor-ist
  hu-mor-is-tic
hu-mor-ous
  hu-mor-ous-ly
  hu-mor-ous-ness
hump
  humped
  humpy
  hump-i-er
  hump-i-est
hump-back
hu-mus
hunch-back
  hunch-backed
hun-dred
hun-ger
hun-gry
  hun-gri-er
  hun-gri-est
  hun-gri-ly
  hun-gri-ness
hunt
  hunt-er
  hunt-ing
  hunt-ress
  hunts-man
  hunts-men
hur-dle
  hur-dled
  hur-dling
  hur-dler
hur-dy--gur-dy
  hur-dy--gur-dies

hurl-er
hurl-y--burl-y
  hurl-y--burl-ies
hur-rah
hur-ri-cane
hur-ry
  hur-ried
  hur-ry-ing
  hur-ried-ly
  hur-ry-ing-ly
hurt-ful
  hurt-ful-ly
  hurt-ful-ness
hurt-ing
hur-tle
  hur-tled
  hur-tling
hurt-less
hus-band
  hus-band-er
  hus-band-less
  hus-band-ly
hus-band-man
hus-band-ry
hush
husk-er
husk-ing
husky
  husk-i-er
  husk-i-est
  husk-i-ly
  husk-i-ness
  husk-ies
hus-sar
hus-sy
  hussies
hus-tings
hus-tle
  hus-tled
  hus-tling
  hus-tler
hutch
hut-ment
huz-zah
  huz-za
hy-a-cinth
  hy-a-cin-thine
hy-a-line
hy-a-lite
hy-a-loid
hy-a-lo-plasm
hy-brid
  hy-brid-ism
  hy-brid-i-ty
hy-brid-ize
  hy-brid-ized

hy-brid-iz-er
hy-brid-iz-ing
hy-brid-i-za-tion
hy-da-thode
hy-da-tid
hy-dra
  hy-dras
  hy-dae
hy-dral-azine
hy-dran-gea
hy-drant
hy-dra-ted
hy-dra-ting
hy-dra-tion
hy-dra-tor
hy-drau-lic
  hy-drau-li-cal-ly
hy-drau-lics
hy-dro-car-bon
hy-dro-chlo-ric acid
hy-dro-dy-nam-ics
  hy-dro-dy-na-mic
hy-dro-elec-tric
hy-dro-gen
  hy-drog-e-nous
hy-dro-ly-sis
hy-drom-e-ter
  hy-dro-met-ric
  hy-dro-met-ri-cal
  hy-drom-e-try
hy-dro-pho-bia
hy-dro-plane
  hy-dro-plan-er
  hy-dro-plan-ing
hy-dro-pon-ics
hy-dro-ther-a-py
  hy-dro-ther-a-pist
hy-drous
hy-drox-ide
hy-drox-yl
hy-dro-zo-an
hy-e-na
hy-giene
  hy-gien-ic
  hy-gien-i-cal-ly
  hy-gien-ist
hy-men
hy-me-ne-al
  hy-me-ne-al-ly
hym-nal
hy-per-bo-la
hy-per-bo-le
  hy-per-bo-lize
  hy-per-bo-lized
  hy-per-bo-liz-ing
hy-per-bol-ic

hy-per-crit-i-cal
  hy-per-crit-i-cal-ly
hy-per-sen-si-tive
  hy-per-sen-si-tiv-i-ty
hy-per-sex-u-al
  hy-per-sex-u-al-ity
hy-per-ten-sion
hy-per-thy-roid-ism
hy-phen
hy-phen-ate
  hy-phen-at-ed
  hy-phen-at-ing
hyp-no-sis
hyp-not-ic
hyp-no-tism
  hyp-no-tist
hyp-no-tize
  hyp-no-tized
  hyp-no-tiz-ing
hy-po
hy-po-chon-dria
hy-po-chon-dri-ac
hy-poc-ri-sy
  hy-poc-ri-sies
  hyp-o-crite
hy-po-der-mic
hy-po-sen-si-tize
  hy-po-sen-si-tized
  hy-po-sen-si-tiz-ing
hy-po-ten-sion
hy-pot-e-nuse
hy-poth-e-cate
  hy-poth-e-cat-ed
  hy-poth-e-cat-ing
  hy-poth-e-ca-tion
  hy-poth-e-ca-tor
hy-poth-e-sis
  hy-poth-e-ses
  hy-poth-e-size
  hy-poth-e-siz-ing
hy-po-thet-i-cal
  hy-po-thet-i-cal-ly
hyp-ox-emia
hyp-ox-ia
hyp-sog-ra-phy
hy-son
hys-sop
hys-ter-ec-to-my
  hys-ter-ec-to-mies
hys-ter-e-sis
hys-te-ria
  hys-ter-ic
  hys-ter-i-cal
  hys-ter-i-cal-ly
hys-ter-ics

iamb
iat-ric
ibid
ibi-dem
ibis
  ibis-es
ice
  iced
  ic-ing
ice-boat
ice--cream
ice-man
  ice-men
ice--skate
icon
icon-o-clasm
  icon-o-clas-tic
icon-o-clast
ide-al-ize
  ide-al-ized
  ide-al-iz-ing
  ide-al-i-za-tion
ide-al-ly
idem
iden-ti-cal
  iden-ti-cal-ly
iden-ti-fi-a-ble
  iden-ti-fy-ing
  iden-ti-fi-a-bly
iden-ti-fi-ca-tion
iden-ti-fy
  iden-ti-fied
  iden-ti-fy-ing
  iden-ti-fi-er
iden-ti-ty
  iden-ti-ties
ides
id-i-o-cy
  id-i-o-cies
id-i-om
  id-i-o-mat-ic
  id-i-o-mat-i-cal-ly
id-i-o-syn-cra-sy
  id-i-o-syn-cra-sies
  id-i-o-syn-crat-ic
id-i-ot
  id-i-ot-ic
  id-i-ot-i-cal-ly
idle
idol
idol-ize
idyll
  idyl-lic
  idyl-lic-al-ly
ig-ne-ous
ig-nite

ig-ni-tion
ig-no-ble
  ig-no-bil-i-ty
  ig-no-bly
ig-no-mi-ny
  ig-no-min-ies
  ig-no-min-i-ous
  ig-no-min-i-ous-ly
ig-no-ra-mus
ig-no-rant
  ig-no-rance
  ig-no-rant-ly
ig-nore
  ig-nored
  ig-nor-ing
igua-na
ill--ad-vised
  ill--ad-vis-ed-ly
ill--bred
il-le-gal
  il-le-gal-i-ty
  il-le-gal-ly
il-leg-i-ble
  il-leg-i-bil-i-ty
  il-leg-i-bly
il-le-git-i-mate
  il-le-git-i-ma-cy
  il-le-git-i-ma-cies
  il-le-git-i-mate-ly
ill--fat-ed
ill--fa-vored
ill--got-ten
il-lib-er-al
il-lic-it
il-lim-it-able
il-lit-er-a-cy
  il-lit-er-a-cies
il-lit-er-ate
ill-ness
il-log-i-cal
ill-starred
ill-tem-pered
  ill-tem-pered-ly
ill-timed
il-lu-mi-nate
  il-lu-mi-nat-ed
  il-lu-mi-nat-ing
  il-lu-mi-na-tor
il-lu-mi-na-tion
il-lu-mine
  il-lu-mined
  il-lu-min-ing
ill-use
il-lu-sion
  il-lu-sive
  il-lu-sive-ly

il-lu-sive-ness
il-lus-trate
il-lus-trat-ed
il-lus-trat-ing
il-lus-tra-tion
il-lus-tra-tive
il-lus-tra-tive-ly
il-lus-tra-tor
il-lus-tri-ous
il-lus-tri-ous-ly
im-age
im-aged
im-ag-ing
  im-age-a-ble
  im-ag-er
im-ag-ery
  im-ag-eries
  im-ag-eri-al
imag-in-able
  imag-in-able-ness
  imag-in-ably
imag-i-nary
  imag-i-nar-ies
  imag-i-nar-i-ly
  imag-i-nar-i-ness
imag-i-na-tion
  imag-i-na-tion-al
imag-i-na-tive
  imag-i-na-tive-ly
imag-ine
  imag-ined
  imag-in-ing
im-bal-ance
im-be-cile
  im-be-cil-ic
  im-be-cile-ly
  im-be-cil-i-ty
imbed
  imbed-ded
  im-bed-ding
im-bibe
im-bro-glio
im-brue
  im-brued
  im-bru-ing
im-i-ta-ble
im-i-tate
  im-i-tat-ed
  im-i-tat-ing
  im-i-ta-tor
im-i-ta-tion
  im-i-ta-tive
im-mac-u-late
  im-mac-u-la-cy
  im-mac-u-late-ly
im-ma-nent

im-ma-nence
im-ma-ne-cy
im-ma-nent-ly
im-ma-te-ri-al
im-ma-te-ri-al-ness
im-ma-te-ri-al-i-ty
im-ma-te-ri-al-ize
im-ma-ture
im-ma-ture-ly
im-ma-ture-ness
im-ma-tu-ri-ty
im-meas-ur-a-ble
im-meas-ur-a-bly
im-me-di-a-cy
im-me-di-a-cies
im-me-di-ate
im-me-di-ate-ly
im-me-di-ate-ness
im-me-mo-ri-al
im-me-mo-ri-al-ly
im-mense
im-mese-ly
im-mese-ness
im-men-si-ty
im-merge
im-merged
im-merse
im-mersed
im-mers-ing
im-mer-sion
im-mi-grant
im-mi-grat-ed
im-mi-gra-tion
im-mi-gra-tor
im-mi-nent
im-mi-nence
im-mo-bile
im-mo-bil-i-ty
im-mo-bi-lize
im-mod-er-ate
im-mod-er-ate-ly
im-mod-er-ate-ness
im-mod-est
im-mod-est-ly
im-mod-es-ty
im-mo-late
im-mo-lat-ed
im-mo-lat-ing
im-mo-la-tion
im-mo-la-tor
im-mor-al
im-mo-ral-ist
im-mo-ral-i-ty
im-mor-al-ly
im-mor-tal
im-mov-a-ble

im-mov-a-bli-i-ty
im-mov-a-bly
im-mune
im-mu-ni-ty
im-mu-ni-ties
im-mu-nize
im-mu-nized
im-mu-niz-ing
im-mu-ni-za-tion
im-mu-nol-o-gy
im-mure
im-mured
im-mur-ing
im-mu-ta-ble
im-mu-ta-bil-i-ty
im-mu-ta-bly
im-pact
im-pac-tion
im-pact-ed
im-pair
im-pair-er
im-pair-ment
im-pa-la
im-pal-as
im-pal-ae
im-pale
im-paled
im-pal-ing
im-pale-ment
im-pal-er
im-pal-pa-ble
im-pal-pa-bil-i-ty
im-pal-pa-bly
im-pan-el
im-pan-eled
im-pan-el-ing
im-part
im-par-tial
im-par-ti-al-i-ty
im-par-tial-ly
im-pass-able
im-pass-abil-i-ty
im-pass-able-ness
im-pass-ably
im-passe
im-pas-si-ble
im-pas-si-bil-i-ty
im-pas-si-bly
im-pas-sion
im-pas-sioned
im-pas-sioned-ly
im-pas-sive
im-pas-sive-ly
im-pas-sive-ness
im-pas-siv-i-ty
im-pa-tience

im-pa-tient
im-pa-tient-ly
im-peach
im-peach-a-ble
im-peach-ment
im-pec-ca-ble
im-pec-ca-bil-i-ty
im-pec-ca-bly
im-pe-cu-nious
im-pe-cu-nious-ly
im-pe-cu-nious-ness
im-pede
im-ped-ed
im-ped-ing
im-ped-i-ment
im-pel
im-pelled
im-pel-ling
im-pend
im-pend-ing
im-pen-e-tra-bil-i-ty
im-pen-e-tra-ble
im-pen-e-tra-ble-ness
im-pen-e-tra-bly
im-pen-i-tent
im-pen-i-tence
im-pen-i-tent-ly
im-per-a-tive
im-per-a-tive-ly
im-per-a-tive-ness
im-per-cep-ti-ble
im-per-cep-ti-bil-i-ty
im-per-cep-tive
im-per-cep-tive-ness
im-per-fect
im-per-fect-ly
im-per-fect-ness
im-per-fec-tion
im-pe-ri-al
im-pe-ri-al-ly
im-pe-ri-al-ism
im-pe-ri-al-ist
im-pe-ri-al-is-tic
im-pe-ri-al-is-ti-cal-ly
im-per-il
im-per-iled
im-per-il-ing
im-per-il-ment
im-pe-ri-ous
im-pe-ri-ous-ly
im-pe-ri-ous-ness
im-per-ish-able
im-per-ish-abil-i-ty
im-per-ish-able-ness
im-per-ish-ably
im-per-ma-nence

im-per-ma-nen-cy
im-per-ma-nent
  im-per-ma-nent-ly
im-per-me-able
  im-per-me-abil-i-ty
  im-per-me-able-ness
  im-per-me-ably
im-per-son-al
  im-per-son-al-i-ty
  im-per-son-al-i-ties
  im-per-son-al-ly
im-per-son-ate
  im-per-son-at-ed
  im-per-son-at-ing
  im-per-son-a-tion
  im-per-son-ator
im-per-ti-nent
  im-per-ti-nence
  im-per-ti-nent-ly
im-per-turb-able
  im-per-turb-ably
im-per-vi-ous
  im-per-vi-ous-ly
  im-per-vi-ous-ness
im-pe-ti-go
im-pet-u-os-i-ty
im-pet-u-ous
  im-pet-u-ous-ly
  im-pet-u-ous-ness
im-pe-tus
  im-pe-tus-es
im-pi-ety
  im-pi-eties
im-pinge
  im-pinged
  im-ping-ing
  im-pinge-ment
  im-ping-er
im-pi-ous
  im-pi-ous-ly
  im-pi-ous-ness
im-pla-ca-ble
  im-pla-ca-bil-i-ty
  im-pla-ca-ble-ness
  im-pla-ca-bly
im-plant
  im-plan-ta-tion
  im-plant-er
im-plau-si-ble
  im-plau-si-bly
  im-plau-si-bil-i-ty
im-ple-ment
  im-ple-men-tal
  im-ple-men-ta-tion
im-pli-cate
  im-pli-cat-ed

im-pli-cat-ing
im-pli-ca-tion
im-plic-it
  im-plic-it-ly
  im-plic-it-ness
im-plode
  im-ploded
  im-plod-ing
im-plore
  im-plored
  im-plor-ing
  im-plo-ra-tion
im-plo-sion
  im-plo-sive
im-ply
  im-plied
  im-ply-ing
im-po-lite
  im-po-lite-ly
  im-po-lite-ness
im-pol-i-tic
  im-pol-i-tic-ly
im-pon-der-a-ble
  im-pon-der-a-bil-i-ty
  im-pon-der-a-bly
im-pone
  im-poned
im-port
  im-port-a-ble
  im-port-er
im-por-tance
  im-por-tant
  im-por-tant-ly
im-por-ta-tion
im-por-tu-nate
  im-por-tu-nate-ly
im-por-tune
  im-por-tuned
  im-por-tun-ing
im-pose
  im-posed
  im-pos-ing
  im-pos-ter
  im-po-si-tion
im-pos-si-bil-i-ty
  im-pos-si-bil-i-ties
im-pos-si-ble
  im-pos-si-bly
im-post
im-pos-tor
im-pos-ture
im-po-tence
im-po-ten-cy
im-po-tent
  im-po-tent-ly
im-pound

im-pound-age
im-pov-er-ish
  im-pov-er-ish-ment
im-prac-ti-ca-ble
  im-prac-ti-ca-bil-i-ty
  im-prac-ti-ca-ble-ness
  im-prac-ti-ca-bly
im-prac-ti-cal
im-pre-cate
  im-pre-cat-ed
  im-pre-cat-ing
  im-pre-ca-tion
im-preg-na-ble
  im-preg-na-bil-i-ty
  im-preg-na-ble-ness
  im-preg-na-bly
im-preg-nate
  im-preg-nat-ed
  im-preg-nat-ing
  im-preg-na-tion
  im-preg-n-tor
im-pre-sa-rio
  im-pre-sa-ri-os
im-press
  im-press-er
  im-press-i-ble
  im-press-ment
im-pres-sion
  im-pres-sion-ist
im-pres-sion-a-ble
  im-pres-sion-a-bly
im-pres-sion-ism
  im-pres-sion-ist
  im-pres-sion-is-tic
im-pres-sive
  im-pres-sive-ly
  im-pres-sive-ness
im-pri-ma-tur
im-print
  im-print-er
im-pris-on
  im-pris-on-ment
im-prob-a-bil-i-ty
im-prob-a-ble
  im-prob-a-ble-ness
  im-prob-a-bly
im-promp-tu
im-prop-er
  im-prop-er-ly
  im-prop-er-ness
im-pro-pri-ety
  im-pro-pri-eties
im-prove
  im-proved
  im-prov-ing
  im-prov-a-bil-i-ty

im-prov-a-ble
im-prove-ment
im-prov-i-dence
im-prov-i-dent
im-prov-i-dent-ly
im-pro-vi-sa-tion
im-pro-vi-sa-tion-al
im-pro-vise
im-pro-vised
im-pro-vis-ing
im-pro-vis-er
im-pru-dence
im-pru-dent
im-pru-dent-ly
im-pugn
im-pugn-er
im-pulse
im-pul-sion
im-pul-sive
im-pu-ni-ty
im-pure
im-pure-ly
im-pure-ness
im-pu-ri-ty
im-pu-ri-ties
im-pute
im-put-ed
im-put-ing
im-put-able
im-put-a-tion
im-put-a-tive
im-put-er
in-a-bil-i-ty
in-ac-ces-si-ble
in-ac-ces-si-bil-i-ties
in-ac-ces-si-ble-ness
in-ac-ces-si-bly
in-ac-cu-rate
in-ac-cu-rate-ly
in-ac-cu-ra-cy
in-ac-cu-ra-cies
in-ac-tion
in-ac-tive
in-ac-tive-ly
in-ac-tiv-i-ty
in-ad-e-quate
in-ad-e-qua-cies
in-ad-e-qua-cy
in-ad-e-quate-ly
in-ad-mis-si-ble
in-ad-mis-si-bly
in-ad-ver-tence
in-ad-ver-ten-cy
in-ad-ver-tent
in-ad-ver-tent-ly
in-alien-a-ble

in-alien-a-bly
in-am-o-ra-ta
in-am-o-ra-tas
inane
inane-ly
inane-ness
inan-i-ty
inan-i-ties
in-an-i-mate
in-ap-pro-pri-ate
in-ap-pro-pri-ate-ly
in-ap-pro-pri-ate-ness
in-apt
in-apt-ti-tude
in-apt-ly
in-apt-ness
in-ar-tic-u-late
in-ar-tic-u-late-ly
in-ar-tic-u-late-ness
in-as-much as
in-at-ten-tion
in-at-ten-tive
in-at-ten-tive-ly
in-au-gu-ral
in-au-gu-rate
in-au-gu-rat-ed
in-au-gu-rat-ing
in-au-gu-ra-tion
in-aus-pi-cious
in-aus-pi-cious-ly
in-board
in-born
in-bred
in-breed
in-breed-ing
in-cal-cu-la-ble
in-cal-cu-la-bly
in-can-des-cent
in-can-des-cence
in-can-des-cent-ly
in-can-ta-tion
in-ca-pa-ble
in-ca-pa-bly
in-ca-pac-i-tate
in-ca-pac-i-tat-ed
in-ca-pac-i-tat-ing
in-ca-pac-i-ty
in-ca-pac-i-ties
in-car-cer-ate
in-car-cer-at-ed
in-car-cer-at-ing
in-car-cer-a-tion
in-car-nate
in-car-nat-ed
in-car-nat-ing
in-car-na-tion

in-cen-di-ary
in-cen-di-aries
in-cense
in-censed
in-ceas-ing
in-cen-tive
in-cep-tion
in-ces-sant
in-ces-sant-ly
in-cest
in-ces-tu-ous
in-ces-tu-ous-ly
in-ces-tu-ous-ness
in-cho-ate
in-cho-ate-ly
in-cho-ate-ness
in-ci-dence
in-ci-dent
in-ci-den-tal
in-ci-den-tal-ly
in-cin-er-ate
in-cin-er-at-ed
in-cin-er-at-ing
in-cin-er-a-tion
in-cin-er-a-tor
in-cip-i-ent
in-cip-i-ent-ly
in-cise
in-cised
in-cis-ing
in-ci-sion
in-ci-sive
in-ci-sive-ly
in-ci-sive-ness
in-ci-sor
in-cite
in-cit-ed
in-cit-ing
in-cite-ment
in-cit-er
in-clem-en-cy
in-clem-ent
in-clem-ent-ly
in-cli-na-tion
in-cline
in-clined
in-clin-ing
in-clin-er
in-clude
in-clud-ed
in-clud-ing
in-clud-a-ble
in-clu-sion
in-clu-sive
in-clu-sive-ly
in-clu-sive-ness

in-cog-ni-to
  in-cog-ni-tos
in-co-her-ence
in-co-her-ent
  in-co-her-ent-ly
in-come
in-com-ing
in-com-men-su-ra-ble
  in-com-men-su-ra-bly
in-com-men-su-rate
in-com-mo-di-ous
in-com-pa-ra-ble
  in-com-pa-ra-bly
in-com-pat-i-bil-i-ty
in-com-pat-i-ble
  in-com-pat-i-bly
in-com-pe-tence
in-com-pe-ten-cy
in-com-pe-tent
  in-com-pe-tent-ly
in-com-plete
  in-com-plete-ly
  in-com-plete-ness
  in-com-ple-tion
in-com-pre-hen-si-ble
  in-com-pre-hen-si-bly
in-com-pre-hen-sion
in-con-ceiv-able
  in-con-ceiv-ably
in-con-clu-sive
  in-con-clu-sive-ly
  in-con-clu-sive-ness
in-con-gru-ity
in-con-gru-ous
  in-con-gru-ous-ly
  in-con-gru-ous-ness
  in-con-gru-i-ties
in-con-se-quen-tial
  in-con-se-quen-tial-ly
in-con-sid-er-able
  in-con-sid-er-ably
in-con-sid-er-ate
  in-con-sid-er-ate-ly
  in-con-sid-er-ate-ness
in-con-sis-tent
  in-con-sist-ent-ly
in-con-sol-able
  in-con-sol-able-ness
  in-con-sol-ably
in-con-spic-u-ous
  in-con-spic-u-ous-ly
in-con-stant
  in-con-stan-cy
  in-con-stan-cies
  in-con-stant-ly
in-con-test-able

in-con-test-abil-i-ty
in-con-ti-nence
in-con-ti-nen-cy
in-con-ti-nent
  in-con-ti-nent-ly
in-con-trol-la-ble
in-con-tro-vert-ible
in-con-ve-nience
in-con-ve-nien-cy
in-con-ve-nient
  in-con-ve-nient-ly
  in-con-ven-ienc-ing
in-con-vert-ible
  in-con-vert-ibly
in-cor-po-rate
  in-cor-po-rat-ed
  in-cor-po-rat-ing
  in-cor-po-ra-tion
  in-cor-po-ra-tor
in-cor-po-re-al
in-cor-rect
  in-cor-rect-ly
in-cor-ri-gi-ble
  in-cor-ri-gi-bil-i-ty
  in-cor-ri-gi-ble-ness
  in-cor-ri-gi-bly
in-cor-rupt-ible
  in-cor-rupt-ibil-i-ty
  in-cor-rupt-ible-ness
  in-cor-rupt-ibly
in-crease
  in-creased
  in-creas-ing
  in-creas-able
  in-creas-ing-ly
in-cred-i-ble
  in-cred-i-bil-i-ty
  in-cred-i-ble-ness
  in-cred-i-bly
in-cre-du-li-ty
in-cred-u-lous
  in-cred-u-lous-ness
  in-cred-u-lous-ly
in-cre-ment
  in-cre-men-tal
in-crim-i-nate
  in-crim-i-nat-ed
  in-crim-i-nat-ing
  in-crim-i-na-tion
  in-crim-i-na-tor
  in-crim-i-na-to-ry
in-crust
  in-crus-ta-tion
in-cu-bate
  in-cu-bat-ed
  in-cu-bat-ing

in-cu-ba-tion
  in-cu-ba-tor
in-cu-bus
  in-cu-bus-es
in-cul-cate
  in-cul-cat-ed
  in-cul-cat-ing
  in-cul-ca-tion
  in-cul-ca-tor
in-cul-pate
  in-cul-pat-ed
  in-cul-pat-ing
  in-cul-pa-tion
in-cum-ben-cy
  in-cum-ben-cies
in-cum-bent
  in-cum-bent-ly
in-cur
  in-curred
  in-cur-ring
in-cur-able
  in-cur-a-bil-i-ty
  in-cur-a-ble-ness
  in-cur-a-bly
in-cur-sion
  in-cur-sive
in-debt-ed
  in-debt-ed-ness
in-de-cen-cy
  in-den-cies
in-de-cent
  in-de-cent-ly
in-de-ci-sion
in-de-ci-sive
  in-de-ci-sive-ly
  in-de-ci-sive-ness
in-deed
in-de-fat-i-ga-ble
  in-de-fat-i-ga-bil-i-ty
  in-de-fat-i-ga-ble-ness
  in-de-fat-i-ga-bly
in-def-i-nite
  in-def-i-nite-ly
  in-def-i-nite-ness
in-del-i-ble
  in-del-i-bil-ity
  in-del-i-ble-ness
  in-del-i-bly
in-del-i-ca-cy
in-del-i-cate
  in-del-i-cate-ness
  in-del-i-cate-ly
in-dem-ni-fi-ca-tion
in-dem-ni-fy
  in-dem-ni-fied
  in-dem-ni-fy-ing

104

in-dem-ni-fi-er
in-dem-ni-ty
in-dem-ni-ties
in-dent
in-den-ta-tion
in-dent-ed
in-den-ture
in-den-tured
in-den-tur-ing
in-de-pen-dence
in-de-pen-den-cy
in-de-pen-dent
in-de-pen-dent-ly
in-de-scib-able
in-de-scrib-abil-ity
in-de-scrib-able-ness
in-de-scrib-ably
in-de-struc-ti-ble
in-de-struc-ti-bil-i-ty
in-de-struc-ti-ble-ness
in-de-struc-ti-bly
in-det-mi-na-cy
in-de-ter-mi-nate
in-de-ter-mi-nat-ly
in-de-ter-mi-na-tion
in-dex
in-dex-er
in-dex-es
in-di-ces
in-di-cate
in-di-cat-ed
in-di-cat-ing
in-di-ca-tion
in-dic-a-tive
in-dic-a-tive-ly
in-di-ca-tor
in-dic-a-tory
in-dict
in-dict-a-ble
in-dict-er
in-dict-or
in-dict-ment
in-dif-fer-ence
in-dif-fer-ent
in-dif-fer-ent-ist
in-dif-fer-ent-ly
in-dig-e-nous
in-dig-e-nous-ly
in-dig-e-nous-ness
in-di-gent
in-di-gent-ly
in-di-gest-ed
in-di-gest-ible
in-di-gest-ibil-i-ty
in-di-gest-ible-ness
in-di-ges-tion

in-di-ges-tive
in-dig-nant
in-dig-ant-ly
in-dig-na-tion
in-dig-ni-ty
in-dig-ni-ties
in-di-go
in-di-goes
in-di-gos
in-di-rect
in-di-rect-ly
in-di-rect-ness
in-dis-creet
in-dis-creet-ly
in-dis-creet-ness
in-dis-crete
in-dis-cre-tion
in-dis-crim-i-nate
in-dis-crim-i-nate-ly
in-dis-crim-i-nat-ing
in-dis-crim-i-na-tion
in-dis-pens-able
in-dis-pens-able-ness
in-dis-pens-abil-i-ty
in-dis-pens-ably
in-dis-pose
in-dis-posed
in-dis-pos-ing
in-dis-po-si-tion
in-dis-sol-u-ble
in-dis-sol-u-bil-i-ty
in-dis-sol-u-ble-ness
in-dis-sol-u-bly
in-di-um
in-di-vid-u-al
in-di-vid-u-al-ly
in-di-vid-u-al-ism
in-di-vid-u-al-ist
in-di-vid-u-al-is-tic
in-di-vid-u-al-i-ty
in-di-vid-u-al-i-ties
in-di-vid-u-al-ize
in-di-vid-u-al-ized
in-di-vid-u-al-iz-ing
in-doc-tri-nate
in-doc-tri-nat-ed
in-doc-tri-nat-ing
in-doc-tri-na-tion
in-doc-tri-na-tor
in-do-lence
in-do-lent
in-do-lent-ly
in-dom-i-ta-ble
in-dom-i-ta-bil-i-ty
in-dom-ita-ble-ness
in-dom-i-ta-bly

in-door
in-doors
in-du-bi-ta-ble
in-du-bi-ta-bil-i-ty
in-dubi-ta-ble-ness
in-du-bi-tab-ly
in-duce
in-duced
in-duce-ment
in-duc-er
in-duc-i-ble
in-duc-ing
in-duct
in-duct-ee
in-duc-tion
in-duc-tive
in-dulge
in-dulged
in-dulg-ing
in-dul-gence
in-dul-gent
in-dul-gent-ly
in-dus-tri-al
in-dus-tri-al-ly
in-dus-tri-al-ness
in-dus-tri-al-ism
in-dus-tri-al-ize
in-dus-tri-al-ist
in-dus-tri-al-i-za-tion
in-dus-tri-al-ized
in-dus-tri-al-iz-ing
in-dus-tri-ous
in-dus-tri-ous-ly
in-dus-try
in-dus-tries
ine-bri-ate
ine-bri-at-ed
ine-bri-at-ing
ine-bri-a-tion
inc-bri-ety
in-ed-u-ca-ble
in-ef-fa-ble
in-ef-fa-bil-i-ty
in-ef-fa-ble-ness
in-ef-fa-bly
in-ef-fec-tive
in-ef-fec-tive-ly
in-ef-fec-tive-ness
in-ef-fec-tu-al
in-ef-fec-tu-al-i-ty
in-ef-fec-tu-al-ly
in-ef-fec-tu-al-ness
in-ef-fi-cient
in-ef-fi-cien-cy
in-ef-fi-cien-cies
in-ef-ffi-cient-ly

in-el-i-gi-ble
  in-el-i-gi-bil-i-ty
  in-el-i-gi-bly
in-e-luc-ta-ble
in-ept
  in-ept-i-tude
  in-ept-ly
in-ept-ness
in-e-qual-i-ty
in-eq-ui-ta-ble
in-eq-ui-ty
  in-eq-ui-ties
in-ert
  in-ert-ly
  in-ert-ness
in-er-tia
  in-er-tial
in-es-cap-a-ble
in-es-cap-a-ble
in-es-ti-ma-ble
  in-es-ti-ma-bly
in-ev-i-ta-ble
  in-ev-i-ta-bil-i-ty
  in-ev-i-ta-ble-ness
  in-ev-i-ta-ble-ness
  in-ev-i-ta-bly
in-ex-haust-i-ble
  in-ex-haust-i-bil-i-ty
  in-ex-haust-i-ble-ness
  in-ex-haust-i-bly
in-ex-o-ra-ble
  in-ex-o-ra-bil-i-ty
  in-ex-o-ra-ble-ness
  in-ex-o-ra-bly
in-ex-pe-ri-ence
  in-ex-pe-ri-enced
in-ex-pert
  in-ex-per-ly
  in-ex-pert-ness
in-ex-pe-ri-ence
  in-ex-pe-ri-enced
in-ex-pert
  in-ex-pert-ly
  in-ex-pert-ness
in-ex-pi-a-ble
  in-ex-pi-a-ble-ness
  in-ex-pi-a-bly
in-ex-pli-ca-ble
  in-ex-pli-ca-bil-i-ty
  in-ex-pli-ca-ble-ness
  in-ex-pli-ca-bly
in-fal-li-ble
  in-fal-i-bil-i-ty
  in-fal-li-ble-ness
  in-fal-li-bly
in-fa-mous

in-fa-mous-ly
in-fa-mous-ness
in-fa-my
  in-fa-mies
in-fan-cy
  in-fan-cies
in-fant
  in-fant-hood
  in-fant-like
in-fan-tile
  in-fan-tine
  in-fan-til-i-ty
in-fan-try
  in-fan-tries
  in-fan-try-man
  in-fan-try-men
in-fat-u-ate
  in-fat-u-at-ed
  in-fat-u-at-ing
  in-fat-u-at-ed-ly
  in-fat-u-a-tion
in-fect
  in-fect-ed-ness
  in-fect-er
  in-fect-or
in-fec-tion
in-fec-tious
  in-fec-tious-ly
  in-fec-tious-ness
  in-fec-tive
in-fer
  inferred
  in-fer-ring
  in-fer-a-ble
  in-fer-a-bly
  in-fer-ence
  in-fer-er
in-fe-ri-or
  in-fe-ri-or-i-ty
  in-fe-ri-or-ly
in-fer-nal
in-fer-no
  in-fer-nos
in-fest
  in-fes-ta-tion
  in-fest-er
in-fi-del
in-fi-del-i-ty
  in-fi-del-i-ties
in-field
  in-field-er
in-fight-ing
  in-fight-er
in-fil-trate
  in-fil-trat-ed
  in-fil-trat-ing

in-fil-tra-tion
in-fil-tra-tive
in-fil-tra-tor
in-fi-nite
  in-fi-nite-ly
  in-fi-nite-ness
  in-fin-i-tude
in-fin-i-tes-i-mal
  in-fin-i-tes-i-mal-ty
in-fin-i-tive
  in-fin-i-tive-ly
in-fin-i-ty
  in-fin-i-ties
in-firm
  in-firm-lly
  in-firm-ness
in-fir-ma-ry
  in-fir-ma-ries
in-fir-mi-ty
  in-fir-mi-ties
in-flame
  in-flamed
  in-flam-ing
  in-flam-er
in-flam-ma-ble
  in-flam-ma-bil-i-ty
  in-flam-ma-ble-ness
  in-flam-ma-bly
in-flam-ma-tion
in-flam-ma-to-ry
in-flate
  in-flat-ed
  in-flat-ing
  in-flat-a-ble
  in-flat-ed-ness
  in-fla-tor
  in-flat-er
in-fla-tion
  in-fla-tion-ary
  in-fla-tion-ism
  in-fla-tion-ist
in-flect
  in-flec-tion
  in-flec-tion-al
  in-flec-tion-al-ly
  in-flec-tion-less
  in-flec-tive
  in-flec-tor
in-flex-i-ble
  in-flex-i-bil-i-ty
  in-flex-i-ble-ness
  in-flex-i-bly
in-flict
  in-flict-a-ble
  in-flict-er
  in-flict-or

in-flic-tion
in-flic-tive
in-flu-ence
in-flu-enced
in-flu-enc-ing
in-flu-ence-a-ble
in-flu-enc-er
in-flu-en-tial
in-flu-en-tial-ly
in-flu-en-za
in-flu-en-zal
in-flu-en-za-like
in-flux
in-form
in-formed
in-for-mer
in-for-mal
in-for-mal-i-ty
in-for-mal-ly
in-form-ant
in-for-ma-tion
in-for-ma-tion-al
in-for-ma-tive
in-for-ma-tive-ly
in-for-ma-tive-ness
in-for-ma-to-ry
in-frac-tion
in-fran-gi-ble
in-fran-gi-bil-i-ty
in-fran-gi-ble-ness
in-fran-gi-bly
in-fra-red
in-fra-struc-ture
in-fre-quent
in-fre-quen-cy
in-fre-quent-ly
in-fringe
in-fringed
in-fring-ing
in-fringe-ment
in-fring-er
in-fu-ri-ate
in-fu-ri-at-ed
in-fu-ri-at-ing
in-fu-ri-at-ing-ly
in-fu-ri-a-tion
in-fuse
in-fused
in-fus-ing
in-fus-er
in-fus-i-bil-i-ty
in-fus-i-ble
in-fu-sion
in-fu-sive
in-gen-ious
in-gen-ious-ly

in-gen-ious-ness
in-gest
in-ges-tion
in-ges-tive
in-glo-ri-ous
in-glo-ri-ous-ly
in-glo-ri-ous-ness
in-got
in-grain
in-grained
in-grate
in-gra-ti-ate
in-gra-ti-at-ed
in-gra-ti-at-ing
in-gra-ti-a-tion
in-grat-i-tude
in-gre-di-ent
in-group
in-grow-ing
in-grown
in-growth
in-gulf
in-hab-it
in-hab-it-a-ble
in-hab-i-ta-tion
in-hab-it-er
in-hab-it-ed
in-hab-it-ant
in-hal-ant
in-ha-la-tion
in-ha-la-tor
in-hale
in-haled
in-hal-ing
in-hal-er
in-here
in-hered
in-her-ing
in-her-ence
in-her-ent
in-her-ent-ly
in-he-sion
in-her-it
in-her-i-tor
in-her-i-tance
in-hib-it
in-hib-i-tive
in-hib-o-to-ry
in-hib-i-ter
in-hib-it-or
in-hi-bi-tion
in-hos-pi-ta-ble
in-hos-pi-tal-i-ty
in-hu-man
in-hu-man-i-ty
in-hu-mane

in-im-i-cal
in-im-i-ta-ble
in-iq-ui-ty
in-iq-ui-ties
in-iq-ui-tous
in-i-tial
in-i-tialed
in-i-tial-ing
in-i-tial-ly
in-i-ti-ate
in-i-ti-at-ed
in-i-ti-at-ing
in-i-ti-a-tion
in-i-ti-a-tor
in-i-ti-a-tive
in-ject
in-jec-tion
in-jec-tor
in-ju-di-cious
in-junc-tion
in-junc-tive
in-jur
in-jured
in-jur-ing
in-ju-ri-ous
in-ju-ry
in-ju-ries
in-jus-tice
ink-blot
ink-ling
inky
in-law
in-lay
in-laid
in-lay-ing
in-let
in-me-mo-ri-an
in-most
in-nards
in-nate
in-ner
in-ner-most
in-ner-sole
in-ner-vate
in-ner-vat-ed
in-ner-vat-ing
in-ner-va-tion
in-nerve
in-ning
inn-keep-er
in-no-cence
in-no-cent
in-no-cent-ly
in-noc-u-ous
in-no-vate
in-no-vat-ed

in-no-vat-ing
in-no-va-tion
in-no-va-tive
in-no-va-tor
in-nu-en-do
in-nu-en-dos
in-nu-en-does
in-nu-mer-a-ble
in-nu-mer-ous
in-nu-mer-a-bly
in-ob-serv-ance
in-ob-serv-ant
in-ob-serv-ant-ly
in-oc-u-lant
in-oc-u-late
in-oc-u-lat-ed
in-oc-u-lat-ing
in-oc-u-la-tion
in-oc-u-la-tor
in-oc-u-lum
in-of-fen-sive
in-op-er-a-ble
in-op-er-a-tive
in-op-por-tune
in-op-por-tun-i-ty
in-or-di-nate
in-pa-tient
in-pour
in-put
in-quest
in-qui-e-tude
in-quire
in-quiry
in-quir-ies
in-qui-si-tion
in-qui-si-tive
in-quis-i-tor
in-road
in-rush
in-sane
in-san-i-ty
in-san-i-ties
in-sa-tia-ble
in-sa-tia-bil-i-ty
in-sa-tia-bly
in-sa-ti-ate
in-scribe
in-scru-ta-ble
in-scru-ta-bil-i-ty
in-scru-ta-bly
in-seam
in-sect
in-sec-ti-cide
in-sec-ti-cid-al
in-se-cure
in-se-cu-ri-ty

in-sem-i-nate
in-sem-i-nat-ed
in-sem-i-nat-ing
in-sem-i-na-tion
in-sen-sate
in-sen-si-ble
in-sen-si-tive
in-sen-si-tiv-i-ty
in-sen-ti-ent
in-sep-a-ra-ble
in-sep-a-ra-bil-i-ty
in-sep-a-ra-bly
in-sert
in-sert-er
in-ser-tion
in-set
in-set-ting
in-shore
in-side
in-sid-er
in-sid-i-ous
in-sight
in-sight-ful
in-sig-nia
in-sig-nif-i-cant
in-sig-nif-i-cance
in-sin-cere
in-sin-cer-i-ty
in-sin-cer-i-ties
in-sin-u-ate
in-sin-u-at-ed
in-sin-u-at-ing
in-sin-u-a-tor
in-sin-u-a-tion
in-sip-id
in-si-pid-i-ty
in-sip-id-ness
in-sist
in-sist-ence
in-sist-ent
in-so-bri-e-ty
in-so-cia-ble
in-so-cia-bil-i-ty
in-so-cia-bly
in-so-far
in-sole
in-so-lent
in-so-lence
in-sol-u-ble
in-sol-u-bil-i-ty
in-sol-u-bly
in-solv-a-ble
in-sol-vent
in-sol-ven-cy
in-som-nia
in-som-ni-ac

in-so-much
in-spect
in-spec-tion
in-spec-tor
in-spi-ra-tion
in-spi-ra-tion-al
in-spire
in-spir-ing
in-spir-it
in-sta-ble
in-sta-bil-i-ty
in-stall
in-stan-ta-ne-ous
in-stant-ly
in-state
in-stat-ed
in-stat-ing
in-state-ment
in-stead
in-step
in-sti-gate
in-sti-gat-ed
in-sti-gat-ing
in-sti-ga-tion
in-sti-ga-tor
in-still
in-stinct
in-stinc-tive
in-stinc-tu-al
in-stinc-tive-ly
in-sti-tute
in-sti-tut-ed
in-sti-tut-ing
in-sti-tut-er
in-sti-tu-tor
in-sti-tu-tion
in-sti-tu-tion-al
in-sti-tu-tion-al-ism
in-sti-tu-tion-al-ize
in-sti-tu-tion-al-ized
in-struct
in-struc-tion
in-struc-tive
in-struc-tor
in-stru-ment
in-stru-men-tal
in-stru-men-ta-list
in-stru-men-ta-tion
in-sub-or-di-nate
in-sub-or-di-na-tion
in-sub-stan-tial
in-sub-stan-ti-al-i-ty
in-suf-fer-a-ble
in-suf-fer-a-bly
in-suf-fi-cient
in-suf-fi-cien-cy

in-su-lar
in-su-lar-i-ty
in-su-late
in-su-lat-ed
in-su-lat-ing
in-su-la-tion
in-su-la-tor
in-su-lin
in-sult
in-sop-port-a-ble
in-sup-press-i-ble
in-sur-ance
in-sure
in-sured
in-sur-ing
in-sur-er
in-sur-gent
in-sur-gence
in-sur-gen-cy
in-sur-mount-a-ble
in-sur-rec-tion
in-sur-rec-tion-ary
in-sus-cep-ti-ble
in-tact
in-take
in-tan-gi-ble
in-tan-gi-bil-i-ty
in-tan-gi-bly
in-te-ger
in-te-gral
in-te-gral-ly
in-te-grate
in-te-grat-ed
in-te-grat-ing
in-te-gra-tion
in-te-gra-tion-ist
in-teg-ri-ty
in-tel-lect
in-tel-lec-tu-al
in-tel-lec-tu-al-ism
in-tel-li-gence
in-tel-li-gent
in-tel-li-gent-ly
in-tel-li-gent-sia
in-tel-li-gi-ble
in-tel-li-gi-bil-i-ty
in-tel-li-gi-bly
in-tem-per-ance
in-tem-per-ate
in-tend
in-tend-er
in-tend-ed
in-tense
in-tense-ly
in-tense-ness
in-ten-si-fy

in-ten-si-fied
in-ten-si-fy-ing
in-ten-si-fi-ca-tion
in-ten-si-fi-er
in-ten-sion
in-ten-si-ty
in-ten-si-ties
in-ten-sive
in-ten-sive-ly
in-ten-sive-ness
in-tent
in-ten-tion
in-ten-tion-al
in-en-tion-al-ly
in-ten-tioned
in-ter
in-ter-act
in-ter-ac-tion
in-ter-breed
in-ter-bred
in-ter-bredd-ing
in-ter-cede
in-ter-ced-ed
in-ter-ced-ing
in-ter-ced-er
in-ter-cept
in-ter-cep-ter
in-ter-cept-or
in-ter-cep-tion
in-ter-cep-tive
in-ter-ces-sion
in-ter-change
in-ter-changed
in-ter-chang-ing
in-ter-chang-a-ble
in-ter-chng-a-bil-i-ty
in-ter-chang-a-bly
in-ter-col-le-gi-ate
in-ter-com
in-ter-com-mun-i-cate
in-ter-con-nect
in-ter-con-nec-tion
in-ter-con-ti-nen-tal
in-ter-course
in-ter-cul-tur-al
in-ter-cur-rent
in-ter-de-part-men-tal
in-ter-de-pend-ent
in-ter-de-pend
in-ter-de-pend-ence
in-ter-de-pend-en-cy
in-ter-dict
in-ter-dic-tion
in-ter-dis-ci-pli-nary
in-ter-est
in-ter-est-ed

in-ter-est-ed-ly
in-ter-est-ing
in-ter-face
in-ter-fa-cial
in-ter-faith
in-ter-fere
in-ter-ga-lac-tic
in-ter-im
in-te-ri-or
in-ter-ject
in-ter-jec-tion
in-ter-jec-to-ry
in-ter-ly-er
in-ter-leaf
in-ter-leaves
in-ter-leave
in-ter-leaved
in-ter-leav-ing
in-ter-line
in-ter-lined
in-ter-lin-ing
in-ter-link
in-ter-lock
in-ter-lo-cu-tion
in-ter-loc-u-tor
in-ter-loc-u-to-ry
in-ter-lope
in-ter-loped
in-ter-loped
in-ter-lop-ing
in-ter-lop-er
in-ter-lude
in-ter-nar
in-ter-na-ry
in-ter-mar-ry
in-ter-mar-ried
in-ter-mar-ry-ing
in-ter-mar-riage
in-ter-me-di-ary
in-ter-me-di-ar-ies
in-ter-me-di-ate
in-ter-me-di-at-ed
in-ter-me-di-at-ing
in-ter-me-di-a-tion
in-ter-me-di-a-tor
in-ter-mi-na-ble
in-ter-min-gle
in-ter-min-gledd
in-ter-min-gling
in-ter-mis-sion
in-ter-mis-sive
in-ter-mit
in-ter-mix
in-ter-mix-ture
in-tern
in-ter-ship

in-ter-nal
  in-ter-nal-ly
in-ter-nal-ize
  in-ter-nal-ized
  in-ter-nal-iz-ing
  in-ter-nal-i-za-tion
in-ter-na-tion-al
  in-ter-na-tion-al-i-ty
  in-ter-na-tion-al-ize
  in-ter-na-tion-al-ized
in-ter-na-tion-al-ism
in-tern-ee
in-tern-ist
in-tern-ment
in-ter-of-fice
in-ter-pen-e-trate
  in-ter-pen-e-tra-tion
in-ter-plan-e-tary
in-ter-play
in-ter-po-late
in-ter-pose
  in-ter-posed
  in-ter-pos-ing
  in-ter-pos-er
  in-ter-po-si-tion
in-ter-pret
  in-ter-pret-a-ble
  in-ter-pret-er
  in-ter-pre-tive
in-ter-pre-ta-tion
  in-ter-pre-ta-tion-al
  in-ter-pre-ta-tive
in-ter-re-late
  in-ter-re-lat-ed
  in-ter-re-alt-ing
in-ter-ro-gate
  in-ter-ro-gat-ed
  in-ter-ro-gat-ing
in-ter-ro-ga-tion
  in-ter-ro-ga-tion
  in-ter-ro-ga-tion-al
in-ter-rog-a-tive
in-ter-rog-a-tor
in-ter-rupt
  in-ter-rup-tion
  in-ter-rup-tive
in-ter-rupt-er
  in-ter-rupt-or
in-terr-scho-las-tic
in-ter-sect
in-ter-sec-tion
in-ter-space
  in-ter-spaced
  in-ter-spac-ing
in-ter-sperse
  in-ter-spersed

in-ter-spers-ing
in-ter-sper-sion
in-ter-state
  in-ter-stel-lar
in-ter-tid-al
in-ter-twine
  in-ter-twined
  in-ter-twin-ing
in-ter-ur-ban
in-ter-val
in-ter-vence
in-ter-view
  in-ter-view-er
in-ter-weave
  in-ter-wove
  in-ter-weav-ing
  in-ter-wo-ven
in-tes-tate
in-tes-tine
  in-tes-ti-nal
in-ti-mate
  in-ti-mat-ed
  in-ti-mat-ing
  in-ti-mate-ly
  in-ti-ma-tion
in-tim-i-date
  in-tim-i-dat-ed
  in-tim-i-dat-ing
  in-tim-i-da-tion
  in-tim-i-da-tor
in-ti-tled
  in-ti-ling
in-to
in-tol-er-a-ble
  in-tol-er-a-bly
in-tol-er-ant
  in-tol-er-ance
in-tomb
in-to-mate
  in-to-nat-ed
  in-to-nat-ing
in-to-na-tion
in-tone
  in-toned
  in-ton-ing
  in-ton-er
in-tox-i-cant
in-tox-i-cate
  in-tox-i-cat-ed
  in-tox-i-cat-ing
in-tox-i-ca-tion
in-trac-ta-ble
  in-trac-ta-bil-i-ty
in-tra-mu-ral
  in-tra-mu-ral-ly
in-tran-si-gent

in-tran-si-gence
in-tran-si-tive
in-tra-state
in-tra-ve-nous
in-trench
in-trep-id
  in-tre-pid-i-ty
in-tri-cate
  in-tri-ca-cy
  in-tri-ca-cies
  in-tri-cate-ness
in-trique
  in-tri-quing
in-trin-sic
  in-trin-si-cal
  in-trin-si-cal-ly
in-tro-duce
  in-tro-duced
  in-tro-duc-ing
  in-tro-duc-er
  in-tro-duc-tion
  in-tro-duc-to-ry
in-tro-spect
  in-tro-spec-tion
  in-tro-spec-tive
in-tro-ver-sion
  in-tro-ver-sive
in-tro-vert
  in-tro-vert-ed
in-trude
in-trust
in-tu-it
in-tu-i-tion
  in-tu-i-tion-al
in-tu-i-tive
in-un-date
  in-un-dat-ed
  in-un-dat-ing
  in-un-da-tion
  in-un-da-tor
in-ure
  in-ured
  in-ur-ing
in-vade
in-val-id
  in-va-lid-i-ty
in-val-i-date
  in-val-i-dat-ed
  in-val-i-dat-ing
  in-val-i-da-tion
  in-val-i-da-tor
in-va-lid-ism
in-val-u-a-ble
in-var-i-a-ble
  in-var-i-a-bil-i-ty
in-var-i-ant

in-var-i-ance
in-va-sion
in-va-sive
in-vec-tive
in-vent
in-vent-a-ble
in-ven-tor
in-ven-tion
in-ven-tive
in-ven-tive-ness
in-ven-to-ry
in-ven-to-ries
in-ven-to-ried
in-ven-to-ry-ing
in-verse
in-ver-sion
in-vert
in-ver-te-brate
in-vert-ed
in-vest
in-ves-tor
in-ves-ti-gate
in-ves-ti-gat-ed
in-ves-ti-gat-ing
in-ves-ti-ga-tion
in-ves-ti-ga-tor
in-ves-ti-ture
in-vest-ment
in-vet-er-ate
in-vid-i-ous
in-vig-or-ate
in-vig-or-at-ed
in-vig-or-at-ing
in-vig-or-ant
in-vig-or-a-tion
in-vig-or-a-tor
in-vin-ci-ble
in-vin-ci-bil-i-ty
in-vin-ci-bly
in-vi-o-la-ble
in-vi-o-la-bil-i-ty
in-vi-o-la-bly
in-vi-o-late
in-vis-i-ble
in-vis-i-bil-i-ty
in-vis-i-bly
in-vi-ta-tion
in-vi-ta-tion-al
in-vite
in-vit-ed
in-vit-ing
in-vit-er
in-vo-ca-tion
in-voice
in-voke
in-voked

in-vok-ing
in-vol-un-tary
in-vol-un-tar-i-ly
in-vo-lute
in-vo-lu-tion
in-volve
in-volved
in-volv-ing
in-volve-ment
in-volv-er
in-vul-ner-a-ble
in-ward
in-wards
in-ward-ly
in-ward-ness
in-waeve
in-wrought
io-dine
ion
ion-ic
ion-ize
ion-ized
ion-iz-ing
ion-i-za-tion
ion-iz-er
ion-o-sphere
iota
ip-so fac-to
iras-ci-ble
iras-ci-bil-i-ty
iras-ci-bly
irate
ir-i-des-cent
ir-i-des-cence
irid-i-um
iris
irk-some
iron
iron-er
iron-clad
iron-ic
iron-i-cal
iron-smith
iron-ware
iron-work
iron-work-er
iro-ny
iro-nies
ir-ra-di-ate
ir-ra-di-at-ed
ir-ra-di-at-ing
ir-ra-di-a-tion
ir-ra-di-a-ter
ir-rad-i-ca-ble
ir-ra-tion-al
ir-ra-tion-al-i-ty

ir-re-claim-a-ble
ir-rec-on-cil-a-ble
ir-rec-on-cil-a-bil-i-ty
ir-re-cov-er-a-ble
ir-re-duc-i-ble
ir-ref-u-ta-ble
ir-re-gard-less
ir-reg-u-lar
ir-reg-u-lar-i-ty
ir-rel-e-vant
ir-rel-e-vance
ir-rel-e-van-cy
ir-re-li-gion
ir-re-li-gious
ir-re-mis-si-ble
ir-re-mov-a-ble
ir-rep-a-ra-ble
ir-re-plac-a-ble
ir-re-press-i-ble
ir-re-press-i-bil-i-ty
ir-re-press-i-bly
ir-re-proach-a-ble
ir-re-sist-i-ble
ir-re-sist-i-bil-i-ty
ir-res-o-lute
ir-res-o-lu-tion
ir-re-spec-tive
ir-re-spon-si-ble
ir-re-spon-si-bil-i-ty
ir-re-spon-sive
ir-re-spon-sive-ness
ir-re-triev-a-ble
ir-re-triev-a-bil-i-ty
ir-re-trieev-a-bly
ir-rev-o-ca-ble
ir-rev-o-ca-bil-i-ty
ir-ri-gate
ir-ri-gat-ed
ir-ri-ta-ble
ir-ri-tant
ir-ri-tate
ir-rupt
is-land
isle
iso-bar
iso-gloss
iso-late
iso-lat-ed
iso-met-ric
ison-o-my
iso-ton-ic
is-su-ance
is-sue
item
it-er-ate
ivo-ry

jab
 jabbed
 jab-bing
jab-ber
 jab-ber-er
jac-a-mar
jac-a-ram-da
jack-al
jack-ass
jack-boot
jack-et
 jack-et-ed
jack-ham-mer
jack--in--the--box
 jack--in--the--box-es
jack-knife
 jack-kives
 jack-knifed
 jack-knif-ing
jack--of--all--trades
jack--o'--lan-tern
jack-pot
jack rab-bit
jac-o-net
jac-quard
jade
 jad-ed
 jad-ing
Jaf-fa
jag
 jag-ged
 jag-ging
jag-uar
jail-bird
jail-break
jail-er
ja-lopy
 ja-lop-ies
jal-ou-sie
jam
 jammed
 jam-ming
 jam-mer
jamb
jam-bo-ree
jan-gle
 jan-gled
 jan-gling
 jan-gler
 jan-gly
jan-i-tor
 jan-i-to-ri-al
jar
 jar-ful
 jarred
 jar-ring

jar-di-niere
jar-red
jar-gon
 jar-gon-ize
jas-mine
jas-sid
jaun-dice
 jaun-diced
 jaun-dic-ing
jaunt
 jaun-ty
 jaun-ti-er
 jaun-ti-est
 jaun-ti-ly
 jaun-ti-ness
jav-e-lin
jaw-bone
jaw-break-er
jay-gee
jay-walk
 jay-walk-er
jazz
 jazz-ist
 jazz-man
jazzy
 jazz-i-er
 jazz-i-est
 jazz-i-ly
 jazz-i-ness
jeal-ous
 jeal-ous-ies
jeep
jeer-er
je-hu
jel-li-fy
 jel-li-fies
 jel-li-fy-ing
jel-ly
 jel-lied
 jel-lies
 jel-ly-ing
 jel-ly-like
jel-ly bean
jel-ly-fish
jen-ny
 jen-nies
jeop-ar-dy
 jeop-ar-dize
 jeop-ar-dized
 jeop-ar-diz-ing
jerk
 jerk-er
 jerk-i-ly
 jerk-i-ness
 jerk-y
 jerk-i-er

jerk-i-est
jer-kin
jer-ry--build
 jer-ry--built
 jer-ry--build-ing
 jer-ry--build-er
jer-sey
jes-sa-mine
jest-er
 jest-ing
Je-sus
jet
 jet-ted
 jet-ting
jet-lin-er
jet-port
jet-pro-polled
jet-sam
jet-ti-son
jet-ty
 jet-ties
jew-el
 jew-eled
 jew-el-ing
 jew-el-er
 jew-el-ry
jibe
 jibed
 jib-ing
jif-fy
 jif-fies
jig
 jigged
 jig-ging
jig-ger
jig-gle
 jig-gled
 jig-gling
 jig-gly
jig-saw
jilt-er
jim-dan-dy
jim-my
 jim-mies
 jim-mied
 jim-my-ing
jin-gle
 jin-gled
 jin-gling
jinx
jit-ney
 jit-neys
jit-ter
 jit-ters
 jit-tery
jit-ter-bug

jit-ter-bugged
job
  jobbed
  job-bing
job-ber
job-hold-er
jock-ey
  jock-eys
  jock-eyed
  jock-ey-ing
jock-strap
jo-cose
  jo-cos-i-ty
jo-cund
  jo-cun-di-ty
jodh-pur
jog
  jogged
  jog-ging
  jog-ger
jog-gle
  jog-gled
  jog-gling
join-able
join-er
joint
  joint-ed
  joint-ly
joist
joke
  joked
  jok-ing
  joke-ster
  jok-ing-ly
jok-er
jol-ly
  jol-li-er
  jol-li-est
  jol-lied
  jol-ly-ing
jolt
  jolt-er
  jolt-ing-ly
  jolty
jon-quil
jos-tle
  jos-tled
  jos-tling
  jos-tler
jot
  jott-ed
joule
jour-nal
jour-nal-ism
jour-nal-ist
  jour-na-lis-tic

jour-nal-ize
jour-ney
  jour-ney-man
  jour-ney-men
joust
jo-vi-al
  jo-vi-al-i-ty
jowl
  jowled
  jowy
joy-ful
joy-less
joy-ous
joy-ride
ju-bi-lant
  ju-bi-lance
  ju-bi-lan-cy
ju-bi-lar-i-an
ju-bi-la-tion
  ju-bi-late
  ju-bi-lat-ed
  ju-bi-lat-ing
ju-bi-lee
judge
  judged
  judg-ing
judge-ment
  judge-men-tal
ju-di-ca-ture
ju-di-cial
ju-di-cia-ry
ju-di-cious
Ju-dith
ju-do
jug
  jugged
  jug-gin
  jug-ful
  jug-gler
ju-gate
jug-u-lar
jug-u-lum
ju-gum
juice
  juic-i-er
  juic-i-est
  juic-i-ly
  juic-i-ness
ju-jit-su
juke-box
ju-lep
ju-li-enne
Ju-lius
Ju-ly
jum-ble
  jum-bled

jum-bling
jum-bo
  jum-bos
jump
  jump-ing
  jump-i-ness
  jumpy
jump-er
jump-off
junc-tion
junc-ture
jun-gle
jun-ior
ju-ni-per
junk
  junk-man
  junky
jun-ket
junk-ie
jun-ta
Ju-pi-ter
ju-ris-dic-tion
  ju-ris-dic-tion-al
ju-ris-pru-dence
  ju-ris-pru-den-tial
ju-ris-pru-dent
ju-rist
ju-ris-tic
ju-ror
ju-ry
  ju-ries
  ju-ry-man
just
  just-ly
  just-ness
jus-tice
  jus-tice-less
  jus-tice-like
  jus-ti-fi-ca-tion
jus-ti-fy
  jus-ti-fied
  jus-ti-fy-ing
  jus-ti-fi-a-ble
  jus-tif-i-ca-tory
jut
  jut-ted
  jut-ting
jute
ju-ve-nes-cence
  ju-ve-nes-cent
ju-ve-nile
  ju-ve-nil-i-ty
jux-ta-pose
  jux-ta-posed
  jux-ta-pos-ing
  jux-ta-po-si-tion

ka-bob
kai-ser
ka-lei-do-scope
  ka-lei-do-scop-ic
ka-mi-ka-ze
kan-ga-roo
ka-olin
  ka-oline
ka-pok
ka-put
ka-ra-te
kar-ma
  kar-mic
ka-ty-did
kay-ak
kay-o
kedge
  kedged
  kedg-ing
keel-haul
keel-son
keen-ly
  keen-ness
keep-ing
keep-sake
keg-ler
kelp
ken-nel
  ken-neled
  ken-nel-ing
ke-no
ker-a-tin
ker-chief
ker-mis
ker-nel
ker-o-sene
kes-trel
ketch-up
ke-tone
ket-tle
ket-tle-drum
key
  keyed
key-board
key-hole
key-note
key-stone
kha-ki
  khak-is
kha-lif
khan
kib-butz
  kib-but-zim
ki-bitz-er
ki-bosh
kick-back

kick-off
kid
kid-nap
kid-ney
  kid-neys
kill-deer
kill-ing
kill-joy
kiln
kilo
  kil-os
kilo-cy-cle
ki-lo-gram
ki-lo-me-ter
ki-lo-ton
kil-o-watt
kilt
ki-mo-no
kin-der-gar-ten
kin-dle
  kin-dled
  kin-dling
kind-ly
  kind-li-er
  kind-li-est
kin-dred
kin-e-mat-ic
kin-e-scope
ki-net-ic
  ki-net-ics
kin-folk
king-bird
king-dom
king-fish
  king-fish-er
king-ly
king-pin
king--size
  king--sized
kink-y
  kink-i-er
  kink-i-est
kins-folk
kins-man
  kins-men
  kins-wom-an
ki-osk
kip-per
kir-mess
kis-met
kiss-a-ble
kiss-er
kitch-en
kitch-en-ette
kitch-en-ware
kite

kit-ed
  kit-ing
kitsch
kit-ten
kit-ten-ish
  kit-ten-ish-ly
kit-ty
  kit-ties
kit-ty--cor-ner
ki-wi
klatch
  klatsch
klep-to-ma-nia
  klep-to-ma-ni-ac
knack
knap-sack
knave
knav-ery
knav-ish
  knav-ish-ly
knead
knee
  kneed
  knee-ing
knee-cap
knee--deep
kneel
  knelt
  kneel-ing
  kneel-er
knee-pan
knell
knick-knack
knife
  knives
  knifed
  knif-ing
  knife-like
knight
  knight-hood
  knight-ly
knight-er-rant
  knights-er-rant
  knight-er-rant-ry
knit
  knit-ted
  knit-ting
  knit-ter
knob
  knobbed
  knob-by
  knob-bi-er
  knob-bi-est
knock
knock-a-bout
knock-down

knock-er
knock--knee
  knock--kneed
knock-out
knoll
knot
  knot-ted
  knot-ting
  knot-less
  knot-like
  knot-ty
knot-hole
knout
know
  knew
  known
  know-ing
  know-a-ble
  know-er
know--how
know-ing-ly
knowl-edge
knowl-edge-able
know--noth-ing
knuck-le
  knuck-led
  knuck-ling
knurl
  knurled
  knurly
ko-ala
ko-bold
ko-el
ko-gas-in
kohl-ra-bi
  kohl-ra-bies
ko-la
ko-lin-sky
  ko-lin-skies
kook
  kooky
  kook-i-er
  kook-i-est
kook-a-bur-ra
ko-peck
ko-ru-na
ko-sher
kou-mis
kow-tow
krim-mer
kro-na
kro-ne
kryp-ton
ku-dos
ku-miss
kum-quat

la-bel
  la-beled
  la-bel-ing
  la-bel-er
la-bi-al
  la-bi-al-ly
la-bi-ate
la-bi-o-den-tal
la-bi-um
  la-bia
la-bor
  la-bor-er
lab-o-ra-to-ry
la-bored
la-bo-ri-ous
  la-bo-ri-ous-ly
  la-bo-ri-ous-ness
la-bor-sav-ing
la-bur-num
lab-y-rinth
  lab-y-rin-thine
  lab-y-rin-thi-an
lace
lac-er-ate
  lac-er-at-ed
  lac-er-at-ing
  lac-er-a-tion
lace-wing
la-ches
lach-ry-mal
lach-ry-mose
  lach-ry-mose-ly
lac-ing
lack-a-dai-si-cal
  lack-a-dai-si-cal-ly
lack-ey
lack-lus-ter
la-ci-nia
la-con-ic
  la-con-i-cal-ly
lac-quer
  lac-quer-er
la-crosse
lac-tate
  lac-tat-ed
  lac-tat-ing
  lac-ta-tion
lac-te-al
lac-tic
lac-tose
la-cu-na
  la-cu-nas
  la-cu-nae
lad-der
lad-die
lade

lad-ed
lad-en
lad-ing
la-dle
  la-dled
  la-dling
la-dy
  la-dy-bug
la-dy-fin-ger
la-dy--in--wait-ing
la-dy-like
la-dy-love
lag
  lagged
  lag-ging
la-ger
lag-gard
la-gniappe
la-goon
la-ic
  la-i-cal
  la-i-cal-ly
lair
laird
la-i-ty
  la-i-ties
lake-side
lal-la-tion
la-lop-a-thy
lam
  lammed
  lam-ming
la-ma
la-ma-sery
  la-ma-ser-ies
lam-baste
  lam-bast-ed
  lam-bast-ing
lam-ben-cy
lam-bent
  lam-bent-ly
lam-bre-quin
lamb-skin
lame
la-ment
  lam-en-ta-ble
  lam-en-ta-bly
  lam-en-ta-tion
lam-i-na
  lam-i-nae
  lam-i-nas
lam-i-nate
  lam-i-nat-ed
  lam-i-nat-ing
  lam-i-na-tion
lam-poon

lam-prey
 lam-preys
lance
 lanced
 lanc-ing
lance-wood
lan-dau
land-ed
land-ing
land-la-dy
 land-la-dies
land-locked
land-lord
land-lub-ber
land-own-er
 land-own-ing
 land-own-er-ship
land-slide
land-ward
 land-wards
lang syne
lan-gauge
lan-quid
 lan-quid-ly
lan-quish
 lan-quish-ing
 lan-quish-ing-ly
lan-quor
 lan-guor-ous
 lan-guor-ous-ly
lank-ness
lanky
 lank-i-er
 lank-i-est
 lank-i-ness
lan-o-lin
lan-tern
lan-tha-num
lan-yard
lap
la-pel
lap-ful
 lap-fuls
 laps-ful
lap-i-dary
 lap-i-dar-ies
lap-in
lap-pet
lapse
 lapsed
 laps-ing
lar-board
lar-ce-ny
 lar-ce-nies
 lar-ce-nous
larch

lar-der
large
 larg-er
 larg-est
 large-ly
lar-gess
lar-ghet-to
 lar-ghet-tos
larg-ish
lar-go
 lar-gos
lar-i-at
lar-rup
lar-va
 lar-vae
 lar-val
lar-yn-gi-tis
lar-ynx
 lar-ynx-es
 lar-ynx-ges
 la-ryn-ge-al
las-civ-i-ous
 las-ci-v-i-ous-ly
la-ser
lash
 lash-ing
 lash-er
las-sie
las-si-tude
las-so
 las-sos
 las-soes
 las-so-er
last-ing
 last-ing-ly
last-ly
latch-key
late
 lat-er
 lat-est
 late-ness
late-ly
la-tent
 la-ten-cy
 la-tent-ly
lat-er-al
 lat-er-al-ly
la-tex
 la-tex-es
lathe
lath-er
 lath-er-er
 lath-ery
lath-ing
lat-i-tude
 lat-i-tu-di-nal

lat-i-tu-di-nar-i-an
la-trine
lat-ter
lat-tice
 lat-tied
 lat-tic-ing
lat-tice-work
laud-able
 laud-ably
lau-da-num
lau-da-to-ry
 lau-da-tive
laugh
laugh-ter
launch
 launch-er
laun-der
 laun-der-er
 laun-dress
 laun-der-ette
laun-dry
 laun-dries
lau-re-ate
lau-rel
la-va
la-a-liere
lav-a-to-ry
 lav-a-to-ries
lave
 laved
 lav-ing
lav-en-der
lav-ish
 lav-ish-ly
 la-vish-ness
law-abid-ing
law-break-er
 law-break-ing
law-ful
 law-ful-ly
 law-ful-ness
law-less
 law-less-ly
 law-less-ness
law-mak-er
 law-mak-ing
lawn
law-ren-ci-um
law-suit
law-yer
lax
 lax-i-ty
 lax-ly
 lax-ness
lax-a-tive
lay-er

lay-ette
lay-man
  lay-men
lay-off
lay-out
lay-over
laze
  lazed
  laz-ing
la-zy
  la-zi-er
  la-zi-est
  la-zi-ly
la-zy-bones
lea
leach
lead
  lead-ing
lead-en
  lead-en-ly
lead-er
  lead-er-less
  lead-er-ship
leaf-age
leafy
  leaf-i-er
  leaf-i-est
leaque
  leaqued
  leaqu-ing
leak
  leak-age
  leak-i-ness
  leaky
  leak-i-er
  leak-i-est
lean
  lean-ly
  lean-ness
lean-ing
lean--to
  lean--tos
leap
  leaped
  leapt
  leap-ing
  leap-er
leap-frog
learn
  learn-ed
  learnt
  learn-ing
  learn-er
learn-ed-ly
learn-ed-ness
lease

leased
  leas-ing
leash
least-wise
  least-ways
leath-er
  leath-er-neck
leath-ery
leave
  left
  leav-ing
  lev-er
leav-en
leaves
leave-talk-ing
lech-er
  lech-er-ous
  lech-er-ous-ly
  lech-ery
  lech-er-ies
lec-tern
lec-ture
  lec-tured
  lec-tur-ing
  lec-tur-er
ledge
  ledg-er
leech
leek
leer-ing-ly
leery
lee-ward
lee-way
left--hand-ed
  left--hand-ed-ly
  left--hand-ed-ness
left-ist
left-over
left--wing
  left--wing-er
leg
  legged
  leg-ging
leg-a-cy
  leg-a-cies
le-gal
  le-gal-ly
le-gal-ist
  le-gal-is-tic
le-gal-i-ty
  le-gal-i-ties
le-gal-ize
  le-gal-ized
  le-gal-iz-ing
  le-gal-i-za-tion
leg-ate

leg-a-tee
le-ga-tion
le-ga-to
leg-end
leg-end-ary
leg-er-de-main
leg-gy
  leg-gi-er
  leg-gi-est
leg-horn
leg-i-ble
  leg-i-bil-i-ty
  leg-i-bly
le-gion
  le-gion-ary
  le-gion-ar-ies
  le-gion-naire
leg-is-late
  leg-is-lat-ed
  leg-is-la-tive
  leg-is-la-tor
leg-is-la-tion
leg-is-la-ture
le-git
le-git-i-mate
  le-git-i-mat-ed
  le-git-i-mat-ing
  le-git-i-ma-cy
  le-git-i-mate-ly
le-git-i-mist
le-git-i-mize
  le-git-i-mized
  le-git-i-miz-ing
le-gume
le-gu-mi-nous
lei
  leis
lei-sure
  lei-sure-ly
  lei-sure-li-ness
leit-mo-tif
lem-ming
lem-on
lem-on-ade
le-mur
lend
  lent
  lend-ing
  lend-er
length
length-en
length-wise
lengthy
  length-i-er
  length-i-est
  length-i-ly

length-i-ness
le-nient
le-ni-ence
le-ni-en-cy
le-ni-ent-ly
len-i-tive
len-i-ty
lens
len-til
len-to
le-o-nine
leop-ard
leop-ard-ess
le-o-tard
lep-er
lep-i-dop-ter-ous
lep-re-chaun
lep-ro-sy
lep-rous
les-bi-an
les-bi-an-ism
le-sion
les-see
less-en
les-sor
least
let-down
le-thal
le-thal-ly
leth-ar-gy
leth-ar-gies
le-thar-gic
le-thar-gi-cal
let-ter
let-ter-ed
let-ter-head
let-ter-ing
let-ter--per-fect
let-ter-press
let-tuce
let-up
leu-ke-mia
leu-ko-cyte
lev-ee
lev-el
lev-eled
lev-el-ing
lev-el-er
lev-el-ly
lev-el-ness
lev-el-head-ed
lev-el-head-ed-ness
lev-er
lev-er-age
le-vi-a-than
lev-i-tate

lev-i-tat-ed
lev-i-tat-ing
lev-i-ta-tion
lev-i-ty
levy
lev-ies
lev-ied
lev-y-ing
lewd
lewd-ly
lewd-ness
lex-i-cog-ra-phy
lex-i-cog-ra-pher
lex-i-co-graph-ic
lex-i-co-graph-i-cal
lex-i-con
li-a-bil-i-ty
li-a-bil-i-ties
li-a-ble
li-ai-son
li-ar
li-ba-tion
li-bel
li-beled
li-bel-ing
li-bel-er
li-bel-ous
li-bel-ous-ly
lib-er-al
lib-er-al-ly
lib-er-al-ness
lib-er-al-ism
lib-er-al-i-ty
lib-er-al-i-ties
lib-er-al-ize
lib-er-al-ized
lib-er-al-iz-ing
lib-er-al-i-za-tion
lib-er-ate
lib-er-at-ed
lib-er-at-ing
lib-er-a-tion
lib-er-a-tor
lib-er-tar-i-an
lib-er-tine
lib-er-tin-ism
lib-er-ty
lib-er-ties
li-bid-i-nous
li-bid-i-nous-ly
li-bid-i-nous-ness
li-bi-do
li-bid-in-al
li-brar-i-an
li-brary
li-brar-ies

li-bret-to
li-bret-tos
li-bret-ist
li-cense
li-censed
li-cens-ing
li-cen-see
li-cens-er
li-cen-ti-ate
li-cen-tious
li-cen-tious-ly
li-cen-tious-ness
li-chee
li-chen
lic-it
lick-e-ty--split
lick-spit-tle
lic-o-rice
lid-ded
lief
liege
lien
lieu
lieu-ten-an-cy
lieu-ten-ant
life-blood
life-boat
life-guard
life-less
life-less-ly
life-less-ness
life-like
life-line
lif-er
life-sav-er
life--size
life--style
life-time
life-work
lift-off
lig-a-ment
lig-a-ture
lig-tured
lig-a-tur-ing
light-en
light-er
light-fin-gered
light-foot-ed
light-foot-ed-ly
light-head-ed
light-head-ed-ly
light-head-ed-ness
light-heart-ed
light-heart-ed-ly
light-heart-ed-ness
light-house

light-ing
light-ly
light--mind-ed
  light--mind-ed-ly
  light--mind-ed-ness
light-ning
light-weight
light--year
lig-nite
like
  liked
  lik-ing
  lik-a-ble
  lik-a-ble-ness
  lik-a-ble-ness
like-li-hood
like-ly
  like-li-er
  like-li-est
like--mind-ed
lik-en
like-ness
like-wise
lik-ing
li-lac
lilt-ing
lily
  lil-lies
lil-y--liv-ered
li-ma
limb
limb-er
  lim-ber-ness
lim-bo
lime
  limed
  lim-ing
  limy
  lim-i-er
  lim-i-est
  lime-like
lime-light
  lime-light-er
lim-er-ick
lime-stone
lim-it
lim-it-a-ble
lim-i-ta-tive
lim-i-ter
lim-it-less
lim-i-ta-tion
lim-it-ed
  lim-it-ed-ly
  lim-it-ed-ness
lim-ou-sine
limp

limp-er
limp-ing-ly
limp-ly
limp-ness
lim-pet
lim-pid
  lim-pid-i-ty
  lim-pid-ly
  lim-pid-ness
lin-age
lin-den
line
  lined
  lin-ing
lin-e-age
lin-eal
lin-ea-ment
lin-ear
  lin-ear-ly
line-back-er
  line-back-ing
line-man
  line-men
lin-en
lin-er
line-up
lin-ger
  lin-ger-er
  lin-ger-ing-ly
lin-ge-rie
lin-go
  lin-goes
lin-gua fran-ca
lin-qual
  lin-qual-ly
lin-quist
lin-quis-tic
  lin-quis-tics
  lin-quis-ti-cal
  lin-quis-ti-cal-ly
lin-i-ment
lin-ing
link
  linked
  link-er
link-age
lin-net
li-no-leum
lin-seed
lint
  linty
  lint-i-er
  lint-i-est
lin-tel
li-on
  li-on-ess

li-on-like
li-on-heart-ed
li-on-ize
  li-on-ized
  li-on-iz-ing
  li-on-i-za-tion
  li-on-iz-er
lip-py
  lip-pi-er
  lip-pi-est
lip-stick
liq-ue-fy
  liq-ue-fied
  liq-ue-fy-ing
  liq-ue-fac-tion
  liq-ue-fi-able
  liq-ue-fi-er
li-queur
liq-uid
  li-quid-i-ty
  li-quid-ness
  li-quid-ly
liq-ui-date
  liq-ui-dat-ed
  liq-ui-dat-ing
  liq-ui-da-tion
  liq-ui-da-tor
liq-uor
lisle
lisp
  lisp-ing-ly
lis-some
  lis-some-ly
  lis-some-ness
list
  list-ed
  list-er
  list-ing
lis-ten
  lis-ten-er
list-less
  list-less-ly
  list-less-ness
lit-a-ny
  lit-a-nies
li-tchi
  li-tchis
li-ter
lit-er-a-cy
lit-er-al
  lit-er-al-i-ty
  lit-er-al-ness
  lit-er-al-ly
lit-er-ary
  lit-er-ar-i-ly
  lit-er-ar-i-ness

lit-er-ate
  lit-er-ate-ly
lit-e-ra-ti
lit-er-a-ture
lithe
  lithe-some
  lithe-ly
  lithe-ness
lith-i-um
lith-o-graph
  lith-o-gra-pher
  lith-o-graph-ic
  lith-o-graph-i-cal-ly
li-thog-ra-phy
lit-i-gate
  lit-i-gat-ed
  lit-i-gat-ing
  lit-i-ga-tion
  lit-i-ga-tor
lit-ter
lit-ter-bug
lit-tle
  lit-tler
  lit-tlest
lit-to-ral
lit-ur-gy
  lit-ur-gies
  lit-ur-gist
  lit-ur-gic
  li-tur-gi-cal
liv-able
  live-able
  liv-able-ness
  live-able-ness
live-li-hood
live-long
live-ly
  live-li-er
  live-li-est
  live-li-ness
liv-en
  liv-en-er
liv-er
liv-er-wurst
liv-ery
  liv-er-ies
  liv-er-ied
  liv-er-y-man
  liv-er-y-men
live-stock
liv-id
  li-vid-i-ty
  liv-id-ness
  liv-id-ly
liv-ing
  liv-ing-ly

liv-ing-ness
liz-ard
lla-ma
lla-no
  lla-mos
load
  load-ed
  load-er
loaf
  loaves
  loaf-er
loamy
loath
  loath-ness
loathe
  loathed
  loath-ing
  loath-ing-ly
loath-some
  loath-some-ly
  loath-some-ness
lob
  lobbed
  lob-bing
lob-by
  lob-bies
  lob-by-ist
lobe
  lo-bar
  lo-bate
  lobed
lob-ster
lo-cal
  lo-cal-ly
lo-cale
lo-cal-i-ty
  lo-cal-i-ties
lo-cal-i-ties
lo-cal-ize
  lo-cal-ized
  lo-cal-iz-ing
  lo-cal-i-za-tion
lo-cate
  lo-cat-ed
  lo-cat-ing
  lo-ca-tor
lo-ca-tion
loch
lock-able
lock-er
lock-et
lock-jaw
lock-out
lock-smith
lock-up
lo-co

lo-co-mo-tion
lo-co-mo-tive
lo-co-weed
lo-cus
  lo-ci
lo-cust
lo-cu-tion
lode-stone
lodge
  lodged
  lodg-ing
  lodg-er
lofty
  loft-i-er
  loft-i-est
  loft-i-ly
lo-gan-ber-ry
  lo-gan-ber-ries
log-a-rithm
  log-a-rith-mic
  log-a-rith-mi-cal
  log-a-rith-mi-cal-ly
log-book
loge
log-ger
log-ger-hed
log-ic
  lo-gi-cian
log-i-cal
  log-i-cal-i-ty
  log-i-cal-ly
lo-gis-tic
  lo-gis-tics
  lo-gis-ti-cal
log-jam
lo-gy
  lo-gi-er
  lo-gi-est
loin-cloth
loi-ter
  loi-ter-er
lol-li-pop
lone-ly
  lone-li-er
  lone-li-est
  lone-li-ly
lon-er
lone-some
  lone-some-ly
  lone-some-ness
lon-gev-i-ty
long-ing
  long-ing-ly
lon-gi-tude
lon-gi-tu-di-nal
  lon-gi-tu-di-nal-ly

long-lived
long--play-ing
long-shore-man
　long-shore-men
long--suf-fer-ing
long--term
long--wind-ed
　long--wind-ed-ly
long-wise
look-out
loony
　loon-i-er
　loon-i-est
　loon-ies
loose
　loos-er
　loos-est
　loosed
　loos-ing
　loose-ly
　loose-ness
loos-en
loot-er
lop
　looped
　lop-ping
lope
　loped
　lop-ing
　lop-er
lop-sid-ed
lo-qua-cious
　lo-qua-cious-ly
　lo-quac-i-ty
　lo-quac-i-ties
lord-ly
　lord-li-er
　lord-li-est
lord-ship
lor-gnette
lor-ry
　lor-ries
lose
　lost
　los-ing
　los-a-ble
　los-er
lot
lo-tion
lot-tery
　lot-ter-ies
lot-to
lo-tus
　lo-tus-es
loud
　loud-ly

loud-ness
loud-mouthed
loud-speak-er
lounge
　lounged
　loung-ing
　loung-er
louse
　lice
lousy
　lous-i-er
　lous-i-est
　lous-i-ly
lou-ver
　lou-vered
love
　loved
　lov-ing
　lov-able
love-lorn
love-ly
　love-li-er
　love-li-est
lov-er
lov-ing
　loving-ly
low-er
low-er-case
low-er-ing
　low-er-ing-ly
low-ery
low--key
　low--keyed
low-land
　low-land-er
low-ly
　low-li-er
　low-li-est
loy-al
　loy-al-ist
　loy-al-ly
　loy-al-ties
loz-enge
lu-au
lub-ber
　lub-ber-li-ness
　lub-ber-ly
lu-beak
lu-bri-cate
　lu-bri-cat-ed
　lu-bri-cat-ing
　lu-bri-ca-tion
lu-cid
　lu-cid-i-ty
　lu-cid-ness
　lu-cid-ly

luck
　luck-i-er
　luck-i-est
lu-cra-tive
　lu-cra-tive-ly
　lu-cra-tive-ness
lu-cre
lu-cu-brate
　lu-cu-brat-ed
　lu-cu-brat-ing
　lu-cu-bra-tion
　lu-cu-bra-tor
lu-di-crous
　lu-di-crous-ly
　lu-di-crous-ness
lug
　lugged
　lug-ging
lug-gage
lug-ger
lug-sail
lu-gu-bri-ous
　lu-gu-bri-ous-ly
luke-warm
　luke-warm-ly
lull-a-by
　lull-a-bies
lum-ba-go
lum-bar
lum-ber
　lum-ber-ing-ly
　lum-ber-er
　lum-ber-ing
　lum-ber-jack
　lum-ber-man
　lum-ber-men
lu-men
lu-mi-nary
　lu-mi-nar-ies
　lu-mi-nes-cence
　lu-mi-nes-cent
lu-mi-nous
　lu-mi-nos-i-ty
　lu-mi-nous-ly
lum-mox
lumpy
lu-na-cy
　lu-na-cies
lu-nar
lu-nate
lu-na-tic
lunch
　lunch-er
lun-cheon
lunge
　lunged

lung-ing
lu-pine
lurch
lure
  lured
  lur-ing
lu-rid
  lu-rid-ly
  lu-rid-ness
lurk
  lurk-er
  lurk-ing-ly
lus-cious
  lus-cious-ly
lush
  lush-ly
lust
  lust-ful
  lust-ful-ly
lust-er
  lus-ter-less
lus-trous
  lus-trous-ly
  lus-trous-ness
lusty
lut-ist
lux-u-ri-ant
  lux-u-ri-ance
  lux-u-ri-an-cy
  lux-u-ri-ant-ly
lux-u-ri-ate
  lux-u-ri-at-ed
  lux-u-ri-at-ing
  lux-u-ri-a-tion
lux-u-ri-ous
  lux-u-ri-ous-ly
lux-u-ry
  lux-u-ries
ly-ce-um
ly-ing
ly-ing--in
lymph
  lym-phoid
lym-phat-ic
lynch
  lynch-er
  lynch-ing
lynx
  lynx-es
  lynx-eyed
lyre
ly-ric
  lyr-i-cal
  lyr-i-cal-ly
ly-ser-gic acid
ly-sine

ma-ca-bre
  ma-ca-bre-ly
mac-ad-am
mac-ad-am-ize
  mac-ad-am ised
  mac-ad-am-iz-ing
  mac-ad-am-i-za-tion
ma-caque
mac-a-ro-ni
ma-caw
mace
  maced
  mac-ing
mac-er-ate
  mac-er-at-ed
  mac-er-at-ing
  mac-er-a-tion
  mac-er-a-tor
ma-chete
mach-i-nate
ma-chine
ma-chin-ery
  ma-chin-er-ies
ma-chin-ist
mack-er-el
mack-i-naw
mack-in-tosh
  mac-in-tosh
mac-ro-cosm
  mac-ro-cos-mic
  mac-ro-cos-mi-cal-ly
ma-cron
mad
  mad-der
  mad-ly
  mad-ness
mad-am
  mes-dames
mad-cap
mad-den
  mad-den-ing
  mad-den-ing-ly
mad-e-moi-selle
  mes-de-moi-selles
made-up
mad-house
mad-man
  mad-men
ma-dras
mad-ri-gal
  mad-ri-gal-ist
mael-strom
mae-stro-so
mag-a-zine
ma-gen-ta
mag-got

mag-goty
mag-ic
  mag-i-cal
  mag-i-cal-ly
ma-gi-cian
mag-is-te-ri-al
  mag-is-te-ri-al-ly
  mag-is-te-ri-al-ness
mag-is-tra-cy
  mag-is-tra-cies
mag-is-trate
mag-ma
  mag-mas
  mag-ma-ta
  mag-mat-ic
mag-nan-i-mous
  mag-nan-i-mous-ly
  mag-na-nim-i-ty
  mag-na-nim-i-ties
mag-nate
mag-ne-sia
  mag-ne-sian
mag-ne-sium
mag-net
  mag-net-ic
  mag-net-i-cal-ly
mag-net-ism
mag-net-ize
  mag-net-ized
  mag-net-iz-ing
  mag-net-iz-a-ble
  mag-net-i-za-tion
  mag-net-iz-er
mag-ne-to
  mag-ne-tos
mag-ne-tom-e-ter
  mag-ne-to-met-ric
  mag-ne-tom-e-try
mag-nif-i-cent
  mag-nif-i-cence
  mag-nif-i-cent-ly
mag-ni-fy
  mag-ni-fied
  mag-ni-fy-ing
  maf-ni-fi-a-ble
  mag-ni-fi-ca-tion
  mag-ni-fi-er
mag-ni-tude
mag-no-lia
mag-num
mag-uey
ma-ha-ra-jah
ma-ha-ra-ni
ma-hat-ma
  ma-hat-ma-ism
ma-hoe

ma-hog-a-ny
  ma-hog-a-nies
ma-hout
maid-en
mail-a-ble
mail-box
mail-man
  mail-men
maim
  maim-er
main-land
  main-land-er
main-ly
main-mast
main-sail
main-tain
  main-tain-a-ble
main-te-nance
maize
maj-es-ty
  maj-es-ties
  ma-jes-tic
  ma-jes-ti-cal
ma-jol-i-ca
ma-jor
ma-jor-do-mo
  ma-jor-do-mos
ma-jor-i-ty
  ma-jor-i-ties
make
  mak-a-ble
  mak-er
  mak-ing
make-shift
make-up
mal-a-dapt-ed
mal-ad-just-ment
  mal-ad-just-ed
mal-ad-min-is-ter
mal-adroit
  mal-adroit-ly
  mal-adroit-ness
mal-a-dy
  mal-a-dies
mal-aise
mal-a-prop
mal-a-prop-ism
ma-lar-ia
  ma-lar-i-al
  ma-lar-i-an
  ma-lar-i-ous
ma-lar-key
mal-con-tent
male-dict
male-dic-tion
  male-dic-to-ry

male-frac-tion
male-frac-tor
ma-lev-o-lent
  ma-lev-o-lence
  ma-lev-o-lent-ly
mal-fea-sance
  mal-fea-sant
mal-for-ma-tion
  mal-formed
mal-func-tion
mal-ice
  ma-li-cious
  ma-li-cious-ly
ma-lign
  ma-lign-er
  ma-lign-ly
ma-lig-nant
  ma-lig-nan-cy
  ma-lig-nan-cies
  ma-lig-nant-ly
ma-lin-ger
  ma-lin-ger-er
mal-lard
mal-lea-ble
  mal-lea-bil-i-ty
mal-let
ma-low
mal-nour-ished
mal-nu-tri-tion
mal-oc-clu-sion
mal-odor
  mal-odor-ous
  mal-odor-ous-ly
mal-prac-tice
  mal-prac-ti-tion-er
malt
  malty
  malt-i-er
mal-treat
  mal-treat-ment
mam-ma
  ma-ma
mam-mal
  mam-ma-li-an
mam-mam-ries
mam-mon
mam-moth
mam-my
  mam-mies
man
  manned
  man-ning
man-a-cle
  man-a-cled
  man-a-cling
man-age

man-aged
man-a-ging
man-age-a-ble
man-age-a-bil-i-ty
man-age-a-bly
man-age-ment
man-ag-er
  man-ag-er-ship
man-a-ge-ri-al
  man-a-ge-ri-al-ly
man-a-tee
man-da-la
man-da-rin
man-date
  man-dat-ed
  man-dat-ing
man-da-to-ry
  man-da-to-ries
  man-da-to-ri-ty
man-di-ble
  man-dib-u-lar
  man-dib-u-lary
  man-dib-u-late
man-do-lin
  man-do-lin-ist
man-drakes
man-drill
man-eat-er
  man-eat-ing
ma-neu-ver
  ma-neu-ver-a-nil-i-ty
  ma-neu-ver-a-ble
  ma-neu-ver-er
man-ga-nese
mange
man-ger
man-gle
  man-gled
  man-gling
man-go
  man-goes
  man-gos
man-grove
man-gy
  man-gi-er
  man-gi-est
  man-gi-ly
man-han-dle
  man-han-dled
  man-han-dling
man-hole
man-hood
man--hour
man-hunt
  man-hunt-er
ma-nia

man-ic
ma-ni-ac
 ma-ni-a-cal
 ma-ni-a-cal-ly
man-ic-de-pres-sive
man-i-cure
 man-i-cur-eed
 man-i-cur-ing
 man-i-cur-ist
man-i-fest
 man-i-fest-er
 man-i-fest-ly
man-i-fes-ta-tion
man-i-fes-to
 man-i-fes-tos
 man-i-fes-toes
man-i-fold
man-i-kin
 man-a-kin
 man-ni-kin
ma-nila
 ma-nil-la
ma-nip-u-late
man-kind
man-ly
 man-li-er
 man-li-est
man--made
man-na
man-ne-quin
man-ner
man-nered
man-ner-ism
man-ner-ly
 man-ner-li-ness
man-nish
man--of--war
 men--of--war
ma-nom-e-ter
man-or
 ma-no-ri-al
man pow-er
man-sard
man-ser-vant
man-sion
man-sized
man-slaugh-ter
man-slay-er
man-til-la
man-tle
 man-tled
 man-tling
man-trap
man-u-al
 man-u-al-ly
man-u-fac-ture

man-u-fac-tured
man-u-fac-tur-ing
man-u-fac-tur-a-ble
man-u-fac-tur-al
man-u-fac-tur-er
ma-nure
manu-script
many
man-y-sid-ed
map
mapped
 map-ping
 map-per
ma-ple
mar
 marred
 mar-ring
ma-ra-ca
mar-a-schi-no
mar-a-thon
ma-raud
 ma-raud-er
mar-ble
 mar-bled
 mar-bling
 mar-ble-ize
 mar-ble-ized
 mar-ble-iz-ing
 mar-bly
mar-cel
 mar-celled
 mar-cel-ling
march-er
mar-chio-ness
mare's tail
mar-ga-rine
mar-gin
mar-gi-nal
 mar-gi-na-lia
 mar-gin-al-i-ty
 mar-gin-al-ly
mar-gin-ate
 mar-gin-ated
 mar-gin-at-ing
 mar-gin-a-tion
mar-gue-rite
mar-i-cul-ture
mari-gold
mar-i-jua-na
ma-rim-ba
ma-ri-na
mar-i-nade
 mar-i-nad-ed
 mar-i-nad-ing
 mar-i-na-tion
mar-i-nate

mar-i-nat-ed
mar-i-nat-ing
mar-i-na-tion
ma-rine
mar-i-ner
mar-i-o-nette
mar-i-tal
mar-i-time
mar-jo-ram
marked
 mark-ed-ly
mark-er
mar-ket
 mar-ket-er
mar-ket-able
 mar-ket-abil-i-ty
mar-ket-ing
mar-ket-place
mark-ing
marks-man
 marks-men
 marks-man-ship
mar-lin
mar-ma-lade
mar-mo-set
mar-mot
ma-roon
mar-quee
mar-quis
 mar-quis-es
mar-quess
mar-quise
 mar-quis-es
mar-riage
 mar-riage-able
 mar-riage-abil-i-ty
mar-ried
mar-row
 mar-rowy
mar-row-bone
mar-ry
 mar-ried
 mar-ry-ing
mar-shall
 mar-shaled
 mar-shal-ing
marsh-mal-low
marshy
 marsh-i-er
 marsh-i-est
 marsh-i-ness
mar-su-pi-al
mar-tial
mar-tin
mar-ti-ni
 mar-ti-nis

mar-tyr
  mar-tyr-ize
  mar-tyr-ized
  mar-tyr-iz-ing
  mar-tyr-dom
mar-vel
  mar-veled
  mar-vel-ing
mar-vel-ous
  mar-vel-ous-ly
mar-zi-pan
mas-cara
mas-cu-line
  mas-cu-line-ness
  mas-cu-lin-i-ty
mas-cu-lin-ize
  mas-cu-lin-ized
  mas-cu-lin-iz-ing
mash-er
mask
  mask-like
masked
mas-och-ism
  mas-och-ist
  mas-och-is-tic
ma-son
  ma-son-ic
ma-son-ary
  ma-son-ries
masque
mas-quer-ade
  mas-quer-ad-ed
  mas-quer-ad-ing
  mas-quer-ad-er
mas-sa-cre
  mas-sa-cred
  mas-sa-cring
  mas-sa-cre
mas-sage
  mas-saged
  mas-sag-ing
  mas-sag-er
  mas-sag-ist
mas-seur
mas-sause
  mas-seus-es
mas-sive
mass-pro-duce
  mass-pro-duced
  mass-pro-duc-ing
  mass-pro-duc-er
  mass-pro-duc-tion
massy
  masss-i-er
  mass-i-est
  mass-i-ness

mas-tec-to-my
  mas-tec-to-mies
mas-ter
mas-ter-ful
mas-ter-mind
mas-ter-piece
mas-tery
  mas-ter-ies
mast-head
mas-tic
mas-ti-cate
  mas-ti-ca-ted
  mas-ti-ca-ting
  mas-ti-ca-ble
  mas-ti-ca-tion
  mas-ti-ca-tor
mas-tiff
mast-odon
mas-toid
mas-tur-bate
  mas-tur-bat-ed
  mas-tur-bat-ing
  mas-tur-ba-tion
mat
  mat-ted
  mat-ting
mat-a-dor
match-book
match-mak-er
  match-mak-ing
mate
  mat-ed
  mat-ing
  mate-less
ma-te-ri-al
  ma-te-ri-al-ly
ma-te-ri-al-ism
  ma-te-ri-al-ist
  ma-te-ri-al-is-tic
  ma-te-ri-al-is-ti-cal-ly
ma-te-ri-al-ize
  ma-te-ri-al-ized
  ma-te-ri-al-iz-ing
ma-te-ri-el
ma-ter-nal
  ma-ter-nal-ism
  ma-ter-nal-is-tic
  ma-ter-nal-ly
ma-ter-ni-ty
  ma-ter-ni-ties
math-e-mat-i-cal
  math-e-mat-ic
  math-e-mat-i-cal-ly
math-e-ma-ti-cian
math-e-mat-ics
ma-tin

mat-in-al
mat-i-nee
ma-tri-arch
  ma-tri-ar-chal-ism
  ma-tri-ar-chy
  ma-tri-ar-chies
ma-tri-cide
ma-tric-u-lant
ma-tric-u-late
  ma-tric-u-lat-ed
  ma-tric-u-lat-ing
  ma-tric-u-la-tion
ma-tri-lin-eal
mat-ri-mo-ny
  mat-ri-mo-nies
  mat-ri-mo-ni-al
ma-trix
  ma-tri-ces
  ma-trix-es
ma-tron
ma-tron-ly
mat-ter
mat-ter-of-course
mat-ter--of--fact
  mat-ter--of--fact-ly
  mat-ter--of--fact-ness
mat-ting
mat-tress
mat-u-rate
  mat-u-rat-ed
  mat-u-rat-ing
  mat-u-ra-tion
ma-ture
ma-tur-i-ty
mat-zo
  mat-zoth
  mat-zos
maud-lin
mau-so-le-um
  mau-so-le-ums
  mau-so-lea
mauve
mav-er-ick
mawk-ish
max-im
max-i-mal
  max-i-mal-ly
max-i-mize
  max-i-mized
  max-i-miz-ing
max-i-mum
  max-i-mums
  max-i-ma
may-be
may-flow-er
may-fly

may-flies
may-hem
may-on-naise
may-or
may-or-al
may-or-al-ty
may-or-al-ties
maze
mazed
maz-ing
ma-zy
ma-zi-er
ma-zi-est
ma-zi-ly
ma-zi-ness
mead-ow
mead-ow-lark
mea-ger
mea-ger-ly
mea-ger-ness
meal-time
meal-worm
mealy
meal-i-er
meal-i-est
meal-i-ness
meal-y-mouthed
mean
mean-ing
mean-ly
mean-ness
me-an-der
mean-ing-ful
mean-ing-ful-ly
mean-ing-less
mean-ing-less-ly
mean-ing-less-ness
meant
mean-time
mean-while
mea-sles
mea-sly
mea-sli-er
mea-sli-est
meas-ur-a-ble
meas-ur-a-bil-i-ty
meas-ur-a-bly
meas-ure
meas-ur-er
mea-sured
mea-sure-ment
meaty
meat-i-er
meat-i-est
meat-i-ness
mec-ca

me-chan-ic
mech-a-nism
mech-a-nis-tic
mech-a-nis-ti-cal-ly
mech-a-nize
mech-a-nized
mech-a-niz-ing
mech-a-ni-za-tion
mech-a-niz-er
med-al
med-aled
med-al-ing
me-dal-ic
me-dal-lion
med-dle
med-dled
med-dling
med-dler
med-dle-some
me-dia
me-di-al
me-di-an
me-di-an-ly
me-di-ate
me-di-at-ed
me-di-at-ing
me-di-a-tion
me-di-a-tive
me-di-a-to-ry
me-di-a-tor
med-ic
med-i-ca-ble
med-i-ca-bly
med-i-cal
med-i-cal-ly
me-di-ca-ment
med-i-cate
med-i-cat-ed
med-i-cat-ing
med-i-ca-tion
me-dic-i-nal
me-dic-i-nal-ly
med-i-cine
med-i-cined
med-i-cin-ing
med-i-co
me-di-e-val
me-di-e-val-ism
me-di-o-cre
me-di-oc-ri-ty
me-di-oc-ri-ties
med-i-tate
med-i-tat-ed
med-i-tat-ing
med-i-tat-ing-ly
med-i-ta-tor

med-i-ta-tion
med-i-ta-tive
Med-i-ter-ra-ne-an
me-di-um
me-dia
me-di-ums
med-ley
med-leys
meet-ing
meet-ing-house
meg-a-city
meg-a-cit-ies
mega-cy-cle
meg-a-lo-ma-nia
meg-a-lo-ma-ni-ac
meg-a-lo-ma-ni-a-cal
meg-a-lop-o-lis
meg-a-lo-pol-i-tan
mega-phone
mega-phoned
mega-phon-ing
mega-ton
mega-watt
mei-o-sis
mei-ot-ic
mel-a-mine
mel-an-cho-lia
mel-an-cho-li-ac
mel-an-choly
mel-an-chol-ies
mel-an-chol-ic
mel-an-chol-i-cal-ly
mel-an-chol-i-ty
mel-an-chol-i-ness
mel-a-nin
mel-a-no-ma
mel-a-no-mas
mel-a-no-ma-ta
me-lee
me-lio-rate
me-lio-rat-ed
me-lio-rat-ing
me-lio-ra-ble
me-lio-ra-tion
me-lio-ra-tor
mel-lif-lu-ous
mel-lif-lu-nt
mel-lif-lu-ous-ly
mel-low
me-lo-de-on
melo-dra-ma
melo-dra-mat-ic
melo-dra-mat-i-cal-ly
melo-dra-mat-ics
mel-o-dy
mel-o-dies

me-lod-ic
me-lod-i-cal-ly
me-lo-di-ous
me-lo-di-ous-ness
mel-on
melt
 melt-ed
 melt-ing
 melt-a-bil-i-ty
 melt-a-ble
 melt-er
mem-ber
 mem-bered
 mem-ber-less
mem-ber-ship
mem-brane
 mem-bra-nous
me-men-to
 me-men-tos
 me-men-toes
memo
mem-oir
mem-o-ra-bil-ia
mem-o-ra-ble
 mem-o-ra-bly
mem-o-ran-dum
 mem-o-ran-dums
 mem-o-ran-da
me-mo-ri-al
 me-mo-ri-al-ly
me-mo-ri-al-ize
 me-mo-ri-al-ized
 me-mo-ri-al-iz-ing
 me-mo-ri-al-i-za-tion
 me-mo-ri-al-iz-er
 me-mo-ri-al-ly
mem-o-rize
 mem-o-rized
 mem-o-riz-ing
 mem-o-riz-a-ble
 mem-o-ri-za-tion
mem-o-ry
 mem-o-ries
men-ace
 men-aced
 men-ac-ing
me-nag-er-ie
mend
 mend-able
men-da-cious
 men-da-cious-ly
 men-da-cious-ness
men-dac-i-ty
men-de-le-vi-um
men-di-cant
me-ni-al

me-ni-al-ly
me-nin-ges
men-in-gi-tis
me-nis-cus
 me-nis-cus-es
 me-nis-ci
men-o-pause
 men-o-pau-sal
me-nor-ah
men-sal
men-ses
men-stru-al
men-stru-a-tion
 men-stru-ate
 men-stru-at-ed
 men-stru-at-ing
men-sur-a-ble
men-tal
 men-tal-ly
men-tal-i-ty
 men-tal-i-ties
men-thol
 men-tho-lat-ed
men-tion
 men-tion-a-ble
 men-tion-er
men-tor
menu
me-ow
mep-ro-bam-ate
mer-can-tile
mer-can-til-ism
 mer-can-til-ist
mer-ce-nary
 mer-ce-nar-ies
 mer-ce-nar-ily
mer-cer-ize
 mer-cer-ized
 mer-cer-iz-ing
mer-chan-dise
 mer-chan-dised
 mer-chan-dis-ing
 mer-chan-dis-er
mer-chant
mer-chant-man
 mer-chant-men
mer-cu-ri-al
mer-cu-ry
 mer-cu-ries
mer-cy
 mer-cies
 mer-ci-ful
 mer-ci-ful-ly
 mer-ci-less
mere-ly
mer-e-tri-cious

mer-e-tri-cious-ly
mer-e-tri-cious-ness
merge
 merged
 merg-ing
 mer-gence
merg-er
me-rid-i-an
me-rid-i-o-nal
me-ringue
mer-it
 mer-i-ted
 mer-it-ed-ly
 mer-it-less
mer-i-to-ri-ous
mer-maid
 mer-man
 mer-men
mer-ri-ment
mer-ry
 mer-ri-er
 mer-ri-est
 mer-ri-ness
mer-ry--go--round
mer-ry-mak-er
mer-ry-mak-ing
me-sa
mes-cal
mes-dames
mes-de-moi-selles
mesh-work
me-si-al
mes-mer-ism
 mes-mer-ic
 mes-mer-i-cal-ly
 mes-mer-ist
mes-mer-ize
 mes-mer-ized
 mes-mer-iz-ing
 mes-mer-i-za-tion
 mes-mer-iz-er
mes-o-morph
 mes-o-mor-phic
 mes-o-mor-phism
 mes-o-mor-phy
me-son
mes-o-sphere
mes-quite
mess
 mess-i-ly
 mess-i-ness
 messy
 mess-i-er
 mess-i-est
mes-sage
mes-sen-ger

mes-ti-zo
me-tab-o-lism
  met-a-bol-ic
  met-a-bol-i-cal
me-tab-o-lize
  me-tab-o-lized
  me-tab-o-liz-ing
met-al
  met-aled
  met-al-ing
met-al-ize
  met-al-ized
  met-al-iz-ing
me-tal-lic
  me-tal-li-cal-ly
met-al-loid
met-al-lur-gy
  met-al-lur-gic
  met-al-lur-gi-cal
  met-al-lur-gi-cal-ly
  met-al-lur-gist
met-al-work
  met-al-work-er
  met-al-work-ing
meta-mor-phism
  meta-mor-phic
meta-mor-phose
  meta-mor-phosed
  meta-mor-phos-ing
meta-mor-pho-sis
  meta-mor-pho-ses
met-a-phor
  met-a-phor-ic
  met-a-phor-i-cal
meta-phys-ic
meta-phys-ics
  meta-phys-i-cal
meta-tar-sus
  meta-tar-si
  meta-tar-sal
meta-zo-an
  meta-zo-al
  meta-zo-ic
mete
  met-ed
  met-ing
me-te-or
me-te-or-ic
me-te-or-ite
  me-te-or-it-ic
me-te-or-oid
me-te-o-rol-o-gy
  me-te-o-ro-log-i-cal
  me-te-o-rol-o-gist
me-ter
met-es-trus

meth-a-done
meth-ane
meth-a-nol
meth-od
me-thodi-cal
  me-thodi-cal-ly
meth-od-ize
  meth-od-ized
  meth-od-iz-ing
  meth-od-iz-er
meth-od-ol-o-gy
  meth-od-ol-o-gies
  meth-od-o-log-i-cal
  meth-od-ol-o-gist
me-tic-u-lous
  me-tic-u-los-i-ty
  me-tic-u-lous-ly
met-ric
met-ri-cal
  met-ri-cal-ly
met-ri-fi-ca-tion
met-ro
met-ro-nome
  met-ro-nom-ic
me-trop-o-lis
met-ro-pol-i-tan
  met-ro-pol-i-tan-ism
met-tle
met-tle-some
mez-za-nine
mez-zo
mi-as-ma
  mi-as-mas
  mi-as-ma-ta
  mi-as-mat-ic
  mi-as-mic
mi-ca
mi-crobe
  mi-cro-bi-al
  mi-cro-bi-an
  mi-cro-bic
mi-cro-bi-ol-o-gy
  mi-cro-bi-o-log-i-cal
  mi-cro-bi-ol-o-gist
mi-cro-copy
  mi-cro-cop-ies
mi-cro-cosm
  mi-cro-cos-mos
  mi-cro-cos-mic
  mi-cro-cos-mi-cal
mi-cro-film
mi-cro-gram
mi-cro-groove
mi-crom-e-ter
mi-crom-e-try
mi-cro-mi-cron

mi-cro-min-ia-ture
mi-cro-mil-li-me-ter
mi-cron
  mi-crons
  mi-cra
mi-cro-or-gan-ism
mi-cro-phone
  mi-cro-phon-ic
mi-cro-pho-to-graph
mi-cro-read-er
mi-cro-scope
  mi-cro-scop-i-cal
  mi-cro-scop-i-cal-ly
mi-cros-co-py
  mi-cros-co-pist
mi-cro-sec-ond
mi-cro-wave
mid-day
mid-dle
  mid-dles
  mid-dling
mid-dle--aged
mid-dle-man
  mid-dle-men
mid-dle-most
mid-dle-weight
mid-dy
  mid-dies
midg-et
mid-land
mid-night
mid-sec-tion
mid-ship
mid-ship-man
  mid-ship-men
midst
mid-sum-mer
mid-term
mid-way
mid-wife
  mid-wives
mid-wife-ry
mid-year
mien
mighty
  might-i-er
  might-i-est
  might-i-ly
  might-i-ness
mi-graine
mi-grant
mi-grate
  mi-grat-ed
  mi-grat-ing
  mi-gra-tion
  mi-gra-tor

mi-gra-to-ry
mi-la-dy
  mi-la-dies
mild
  mild-ly
  mild-ness
mil-dew
  mil-dewy
mile-age
mil-er
mile-stone
mi-lieu
  mi-lieus
mil-i-tant
  mil-i-tan-cy
  mil-i-tant-ness
mil-i-ta-rism
  mil-i-ta-ris-tic
  mil-i-ta-ris-ti-cal-ly
  mil-i-ta-rize
  mil-i-ta-rized
  mil-i-ta-riz-ing
  mil-i-ta-ri-za-tion
mil-i-tary
  mil-i-tar-i-ly
mi-li-tia
milk
  milk-er
  milky
  milk-i-er
  milk-i-est
milk-maid
milk-man
  milk-men
milk-weed
mill-board
mil-len-ni-um
  mil-len-nia
  mil-len-ni-al
mil-ler
mil-let
mil-li-am-pere
mil-li-bar
mil-li-gram
mil-li-li-ter
mil-li-me-ter
mil-li-mi-cron
mil-li-ner
mil-li-nery
mill-ing
mil-lion
  mil-lionth
mill-lion-aire
mil-li-sec-ond
mill-pond
mill-run

mill-stone
mill-stream
mi-lord
milt
mime
  mimed
  mim-ing
  mim-er
mim-e-o-graph
mim-ic
  mim-icked
  mim-ick-ing
  mim-i-cal
  mim-i-cal
  mim-ick-r
mim-ic-ry
  mim-ic-ries
min-able
  mine-able
min-e-ret
mince
  minced
  minc-ing
  minc-er
  minc-ing-ly
mince-meat
mind-ed
mind-less
  mind-less-ly
  mind-less-ness
min-er
mine-field
min-er-al
min-er-al-ize
  min-er-al-ized
  min-er-al-iz-ing
  min-er-al-i-za-tion
min-er-al-o-gy
  min-er-al-og-ical
  min-er-al-o-gist
min-e-stro-ne
mine-sweep-er
  mine-sweep-ing
min-gle
  min-gled
  min-gling
min-i-a-ture
  min-i-a-tur-ize
  min-i-a-tur-ized
  min-i-a-tur-iz-ing
  min-i-a-tur-i-za-tion
min-im
min-i-mal
  min-i-mal-ly
min-i-mize
  min-i-mized

min-i-miz-ing
min-i-mi-za-tion
min-i-miz-er
min-i-mum
  min-i-mums
  min-i-ma
min-ing
min-ion
min-is-ter
  min-is-te-ri-al
min-is-trant
min-is-tra-tion
min-is-tries
min-now
mi-nor
mi-nor-i-ty
  mi-nor-i-ties
min-strel
mint-age
  mint-er
min-u-end
mi-nus
mi-nus-cule
min-ute
  min-ut-ed
  min-ut-ing
mi-nut-er
  mi-nut-est
min-ute-man
  min-ute-men
mi-nu-tia
  mi-nu-ti-ae
minx
mir-a-cle
mi-rac-u-lous
mi-rage
mire
  mired
  mir-ing
mir-ror
mirth
  mirth-ful
  mirth-ful-ly
  mirth-ful-ness
  mirth-less
mis-ad-ven-tage
mis-ad-vise
  mis-ad-vised
  mis-ad-vis-ing
mis-al-li-ance
mis-an-thrope
mis-an-tho-pist
  mis-an-throp-ic
  mis-an-throp-i-cal
  mis-an-thro-py
mis-ap-ply

mis-ap-plied
mis-ap-ply-ing
mis-ap-pli-ca-tion
mis-ap-pre-hend
mis-ap-pre-hen-sion
mis-ap-pro-pri-ate
mis-ap-pro-pri-at-ed
mis-ap-pro-pri-at-ing
mis-ap-pro-pri-a-tion
mis-be-have
mis-be-haved
mis-be-hav-ing
mis-be-hav-er
mis-be-ha-vior
mis-cal-cu-late
mis-cal-cu-lat-ed
mis-cal-cu-lat-ing
mis-cal-cu-la-tion
mis-cal-cu-la-tor
mis-call
mis-car-riage
mis-car-ry
mis-car-ried
mis-car-ry-ing
mis-ce-ge-na-tion
mis-ce-ge-net-ic
mis-cel-la-neous
mis-cel-la-ny
mis-cel-la-nies
mis-chance
mis-chief
mis-chie-vous
mis-che-vous-ly
mis-che-vous-ness
mis-ci-ble
mis-ci-bil-i-ty
mis-con-ceive
mis-con-ceived
mis-con-ceiv-ing
mis-con-ceiv-er
mis-con-cep-tion
mis-con-duct
mis-con-strue
mis-con-strued
mis-con-stru-ing
mis-con-struc-tion
mis-count
mis-cre-ant
mis-cue
mis-cued
mis-cu-ing
mis-deal
mis-dealt
mis-deal-ing
mis-deed
mis-de-mean-or

mis-di-rect
mis-di-rec-tion
mis-do
mis-did
mis-done
mis-do-ing
mis-em-ploy
mis-em-ploy-ment
mi-ser
mi-ser-li-ness
mi-ser-ly
mis-er-a-ble
mis-er-a-ble-ness
mis-er-a-bly
mis-ery
mis-er-ies
mis-fea-sance
mis-fire
mis-fired
mis-fir-ing
mis-fit
mis-fit-ted
mis-fit-ting
mis-for-tune
mis-giv-ing
mis-gov-ern
mis-gov-ern-ment
mis-guide
mis-guid-ed
mis-guid-ing
mis-guid-ance
mis-han-dle
mis-han-dled
mis-han-dling
mis-hap
mish-mash
mis-in-form
mis-in-form-ant
mis-in-form-er
mis-in-for-ma-tion
mis-in-ter-pret
mis-in-ter-pre-ta-tion
mis-in-ter-pret-er
mis-judge
mis-judged
mis-judg-ing
mis-judg-ment
mis-lay
mis-laid
mis-lay-ing
mis-lead
mis-led
mis-lead-ing
mis-lead-er
mis-man-age
mis-man-aged

mis-man-ag-ing
mis-man-age-ment
mis-match
mis-mate
mis-mat-ed
mis-mat-ing
mis-name
mis-named
mis-nam-ing
mis-no-mer
mi-sog-a-my
mi-sog-y-ny
mi-sog-y-nist
mi-sog-y-nous
mis-place
mis-placed
mis-plac-ing
mis-place-ment
mis-play
mis-print
mis-pri-sion
mis-prize
mis-prized
mis-priz-ing
mis-pro-nounce
mis-pro-nounced
mis-pro-nouc-ing
mis-pro-nun-ci-a-tion
mis-quote
mis-quoted
mis-quot-ing
mis-quo-ta-tion
mis-read
mis-read-ing
mis-rep-re-sent
mis-rep-re-sen-ta-tion
mis-rep-re-sen-ta-tive
mis-rule
mis-ruled
mis-rul-ing
mis-sal
mis-shape
mis-shaped
mis-shap-ing
mis-shap-en
mis-sile
miss-ing
mis-sion
mis-sion-ary
mis-sion-ar-ies
mis-sive
mis-spell
mis-spelled
mis-spel-ling
mis-spend
mis-spent

mis-spend-ing
mis-state
  mis-stat-ed
  mis-stat-ing
  mis-state-ment
mis-step
mist
  mist-i-ly
  mist-i-ness
mis-ta-a-ble
mis-take
  mis-took
  mis-tak-en
  mis-tak-ing
  mis-tak-en-ly
  mis-tak-er
mis-tle-toe
mis-tral
mis-treat
  mis-treat-ment
mis-tress
mis-tri-al
mis-trust
  mis-trust-ful
  mis-trust-ful-ly
  mis-trust-ing-ly
misty
  mist-i-er
  mist-i-est
mis-un-der-stand
  mis-un-der-stood
  mis-un-der-stand-ing
mis-us-age
mis-use
  mis-used
  mis-us-ing
  mis-us-er
mis-val-ue
  mis-val-ued
  mis-val-u-ing
mi-ter
  mi-tre
mi-ti-cide
  mi-ti-cid-al
mit-i-gate
  mit-i-gat-ed
  mit-i-gat-ing
  mit-i-ga-tion
  mit-i-ga-tive
  mit-i-ga-tor
  mit-i-ga-to-ry
mi-to-sis
mi-tral
mit-ten
mix
  mixed

mix-ing
mix-er
mix-ture
mix-up
miz-pah
miz-zen
mne-mon-ic
mne-mon-ics
moa
mob
  mobbed
  mob-bing
  mob-bish
mo-bile
  mo-bil-i-ty
mo-bi-lize
  mo-bi-lized
  mo-bi-liz-ing
  mo-bi-li-za-tion
mob-ster
moc-ca-sin
mo-cha
mock
  mock-er
  mock-ing-ly
mock-ery
  mock-er-ies
mock-ing-bird
mock-up
mod-al
  mo-dal-i-ty
  mod-al-ly
mod-el
  mod-eled
  mod-el-ing
  mod-el-er
mod-er-ate
  mod-er-at-ed
  mod-er-at-ing
  mod-er-ate-ly
  mod-er-ate-ness
mod-er-a-tion
mod-er-a-tor
  mod-er-a-tor-ship
mod-ern
mod-ern-ism
  mod-er-ist
  mod-er-ist-ic
mod-ern-ize
  mod-ern-ized
  mod-ern-iz-ing
  mod-ern-iz-er
  mod-ern-i-za-tion
mod-est
  mod-est-ly
  mod-est-ty

mod-es-ties
mod-i-cum
mod-i-fi-ca-tion
mod-i-fy
  mod-i-fied
  mod-i-fy-ing
  mod-i-fi-a-ble
  mod-i-fi-er
mod-ish
  mod-ish-ly
  mod-ish-ness
mo-diste
mod-u-late
  mod-u-lat-ed
  mod-u-lat-ing
mod-u-la-tion
  mod-u-la-tor
  mod-u-la-to-ry
mod-ule
mod-u-lar
mo-gulmo-hair
moi-ety
  moi-eties
moil
  moil-er
  moil-ing-ly
mois-ten
  moist-en-er
mois-ture
  mois-tur-ize
  mois-tur-ized
  mois-tur-iz-ing
  mois-tur-iz-er
mo-lar
mo-las-ses
mold
  mold-able
  mold-er
mold-board
mold-ing
moldy
  mold-i-er
  mold-i-est
  mold-i-ness
mol-e-cule
mole-hill
mole-skin
mo-lest
  mo-les-ta-tion
  mo-lest-er
mol-li-fy
  mol-li-fied
  mol-li-fy-ing
  mol-i-fi-ca-tion
  mol-li-fi-er
  mol-li-fy-ing-ly

mol-lusk
mol-ly-cod-dle
  mol-ly-cod-dled
  mol-ly-cod-dling
molt
  moult
  molt-er
mol-ten
  mol-ten-ly
mo-lyb-de-num
mo-ment
me-men-tary
  mo-men-tar-i-ly
  mo-men-tar-i-ness
mo-men-tous
  mo-men-tous-ly
  mo-men-tous-ness
mo-men-tum
mo-nad
  mo-nad-ic
  mo-nad-i-cal
  mo-nad-al
  mo-nad-i-cal-ly
mon-arch
  mo-nar-chal
  mo-nar-chal-ly
mo-nar-chi-cal
  mo-nar-chic
  mo-nar-chi-cal-ly
mon-ar-chism
  mon-ar-chist
  mon-ar-chis-tic
mon-ar-chy
  mon-ar-chies
  mon-as-tery
  mon-as-ter-ies
  mon-as-te-ri-al
mo-nas-tic
mo-nas-ti-cal
  mo-nas-ti-cal-ly
mo-nas-ti-cism
mon-au-ral
  mon-au-ral-ly
mon-e-tary
  mon-e-tar-i-ly
mon-e-tize
  mon-e-tized
  mon-e-tiz-ing
  mon-e-ti-za-tion
mon-ey
mon-ey-chang-er
mon-eyed
  mon-ied
mon-ey--mak-er
  mon-ey--mak-ing
mon-ger

mon-goose
  mon-gooses
mon-grel
mon-i-ker
mon-ism
  mon-ist
  mo-nis-tic
  mo-nis-ti-cal
  mo-nis-ti-cal-ly
mo-ni-tion
mon-i-tor
  mon-i-to-ri-al
monk
  monk-ish
  monk-ish-ly
mon-key
  mon-keys
  mon-keyed
  mon-key-ing
mon-key-shine
mon-chro-mat-ic
mon-o-chrome
  mon-o-chro-mic
  mon-o-chro-mi-cal
  mon-o-chro-mi-cal-ly
  mon-o-chrom-ist
mon-o-cle
  mon-o-cled
mon-o-cli-nal
mon-o-cline
  mon-o-cli-nal-ly
mon-o-cli-nous
mon-o-dist
mon-o-dy
  mon-o-dies
  mo-nod-ic
mo-noe-cious
  mo-noe-cious-ly
mo-nog-a-my
  mo-nog-a-mist
  mo-nog-a-mous
mon-o-gram
  mon-o-grammed
  mon-o-gram-ming
  mon-o-gram-mat-ic
mon-o-graph
  mo-nog-ra-pher
  mon-o-graph-ic
mon-o-lith
mon-o-logue
  mon-o-log
  mon-o-logu-ist
  mon-o-log-ist
mon-o-ma-nia
  mon-o-ma-ni-ac
  mon-o-ma-ni-a-cal

mon-o-met-al-lism
  mon-o-me-tal-lic
mo-no-mi-al
mon-nu-cle-o-sis
mon-o-pho-nic
mono-plane
mo-nop-o-lize
  mo-nop-o-lized
  mo-nop-o-liz-ing
  mo-nop-o-li-za-tion
  mo-nop-o-liz-er
mo-nop-o-ly
  mo-nop-o-lies
mono-rail
mon-o-syl-lab-ic
  mon-o-syl-lab-i-cal-ly
mon-o-syl-la-ble
mon-o-the-ism
  mon-o-the-ist
  mon-o-the-is-tic
  mon-o-the-is-ti-cal-ly
mon-o-tone
mo-not-o-nous
  mo-not-o-nous-ly
  mo-not-o-nous-ness
mo-not-o-ny
mone-treme
mono-type
  mon-o-typ-er
  mon-o-typ-ic
mon-o-va-lent
  mon-o-va-lence
  mon-o-va-len-cy
mon-ox-ide
mon-sei-gneur
  mes-sei-gneurs
mon-sieur
mon-soon
mon-ster
mon-stros-i-ty
  mon-stro-i-ties
mon-strous
  mon-strous-i-ties
mon-tage
month-ly
  month-lies
mon-u-ment
mon-u-men-tal
  mon-u-men-tal-ly
mooch
  mooch-er
moody
  mood-i-er
  mood-i-est
  mood-i-ly
  mood-i-ness

moon-beam
moon-light
moon-light-er
  moon-light-ing
moon-scape
moon-shine
  moon-shiner
moon-stone
moon-struck
moony
  moon-i-er
  moon-i-est
moor-ing
moot-ness
mop
  mopped
  mop-ping
mope
  moped
  mop-ing
  mop-er
  mop-ish
mop-pet
mo-raine
  mo-rain-al
  mo-rain-ic
mor-al
  mor-al-ly
mo-rale
mor-al-ist
  mor-al-is-tic
mo-ral-i-ty
  mo-ral-i-ties
mor-al-ize
  mor-al-ized
  mor-al-iz-ing
  mor-al-i-za-tion
  mor-al-iz-er
mo-rass
mor-a-to-ri-um
  mor-a-to-ri-ums
  mor-a-to-ria
mo-ray
mor-bid
  mor-bid-ly
  mor-bid-i-ty
  mor-bid-ness
mor-dant
  mor-dan-cy
  mor-dant-ly
more-over
mo-res
mor-ga-nat-ic
  mor-ga-nat-i-cal-ly
morque
mor-i-bund

mo-ri-on
morn-ing
morn-ing glo-ry
  morn-ing glo-ries
mo-roc-co
mo-ron
  mo-ron-ic
  mo-ron-i-cal-ly
mo-rose
  mo-rose-ly
  mo-rose-ness
mor-pheme
mor-phine
mor-phol-o-gy
  mor-pho-log-ic
  mor-pho-log-i-cal
  mor-phol-o-gist
mor-row
mor-sel
mor-tal
  mor-tal-ly
mor-tal-i-ty
  mor-tal-i-ties
mor-tar
mort-gage
  mort-gaged
  mort-gag-ing
  mort-gag-ee
  mort-gag-er
mor-ti-cian
mor-ti-fy
  mor-ti-fied
  mor-ti-fy-ing
  mor-ti-fi-ca-tion
mor-tise
  mor-tised
  mor-tising
mort-main
mor-tu-ary
  mor-tu-ar-ies
mo-sa-ic
Mo-ses
mo-sey
  mo-seyd
  mo-sey-ing
mosque
mos-qui-to
  mos-qui-toes
  mos-qui-tos
moss
most-ly
mo-tel
mo-tet
moth-ball
moth-eat-en
moth-er

moth-er-hood
moth-er-in-law
moth-er-ly
mo-tif
mo-tile
  mo-til-i-ty
mo-tion
  mo-tion-less
mo-ti-vate
  mo-ti-vat-ed
  mo-ti-vat-ing
  mo-ti-va-tion
mo-tive
mot-ley
mo-tor
mo-tor-bike
mo-tor-boat
mo-tor-bus
mo-tor-cade
mo-tor-cy-cle
  mo-tor-cy-cling
  mo-tor-cy-clist
mo-tor-ist
mo-tor-ize
  mo-tor-ized
  mo-tor-iz-ing
  mo-tor-i-za-tion
mo-tor-man
  mo-tor-men
mot-tle
  mot-tled
  mot-tling
  mot-tler
mound
mount
  mount-able
  mount-er
moun-tain
  moun-tain-eer
  moun-tain-ous
  moun-te-bank
mount-ing
mourn
  mourn-er
mourn-ful
  mourn-ful-ly
  mourn-ful-ness
mourn-ing
  mourn-ing-ly
mouse
  moused
  mous-ing
mous-er
mous-tache
mousy
  mous-i-er

mous-i-est
mouth
  mouthed
  mouth-er
mouth-ful
  mouth-fuls
mouth-piece
mouthy
  mouth-i-er
  mouth-i-est
mou-ton
mov-able
  mov-a-bil-i-ty
  mov-a-bly
move
  moved
  mov-ing
move-ment
mov-ie
mow
mox-ie
mu-ci-lage
  mu-ci-lag-i-nous
muck
  mucky
mu-cous
  mu-cos-i-ty
mu-cus
mud
  mud-ded
  mud-ding
mud-dle
  mud-dled
  mud-dling
  mud-dler
mud-dy
  mud-di-er
  mud-di-est
mu-ez-zin
muf-fin
muf-ti
mug
  mugged
  mug-ging
  mug-ger
mug-gy
  mug-gi-er
  mug-gi-est
mu-lat-to
  mu-lat-toes
mul-ber-ry
  mul-ber-ries
mulch
mu-le-teer
mul-ish
  mul-ish-ly

mul-let
mul-li-gan
mul-li-ga-taw-ny
mul-lion
  mul-lioned
mul-ti-far-i-ous
  mul-ti-far-i-ous-ly
mul-ti-lat-er-al
mul-ti-mil-lion-aire
mul-ti-ple
mul-ti-ple scle-ro-sis
mul-ti-i-cand
mul-ti-pli-ca-tion
mul-ti-plic-i-ty
mul-ti-pli-er
mul-ti-ply
  mul-ti-plied
  mul-ti-ply-ing
  mul-ti-pli-a-ble
mul-ti-tude
mul-ti-tu-di-nous
  mul-ti-tu-di-nous-ly
mum-ble
mum-mer
mum-mery
mum-mi-fy
  mum-mi-fied
  mum-mi-fy-ing
  mum-mi-fi-ca-tion
mum-my
  mum-mies
  mum-mied
  mum-my-ing
munch
  munch-er
mun-dane
  mun-dane-ly
mu-nic-i-pal
  mu-nic-i-pal-ly
mu-nic-i-pal-i-ty
mu-nif-i-cent
  mu-nif-i-cence
  mu-nif-i-cent-ly
mu-ni-tion
mu-ral
  mu-ral-ist
mur-der
  mur-der-er
  mur-der-ess
mur-der-ous
  mur-der-ous-ly
mu-ri-at-ic ac-id
murky
  murk-i-er
  murk-i-est
  murk-i-ly

mur-mur
mur-rain
mus-cat
  mus-ca-tel
mus-cle
  mus-cled
  mus-cling
mus-cle--bound
mus-cu-lar
  mus-cu-lar-i-ty
  mus-cu-lar-ly
  mus-cu-lar dys-tro-phy
mus-cu-la-ture
muse
  mused
  mus-ing
  mus-ing-ly
mu-se-um
mush
  mushy
  mush-i-er
  mush-i-est
mush-room
mu-sic
mu-si-cal
  mu-si-cal-ly
mu-si-cale
mu-si-cian
musk
  musky
  musk-i-er
  misk-i-est
mus-ket
  mus-ke-teer
  mus-ket-ry
musk-mel-on
musk-rat
mus-lin
muss
  mussy
  muss-i-er
mus-sel
mus-tache
mus-tang
mus-tard
mus-ter
mus-ty
  mus-ti-er
  mus-ti-est
  mus-ti-ly
mu-ta-ble
  mu-ta-bil-i-ty
  mu-ta-bly
mu-tant
mu-ta-tion
mu-tate

mu-tat-ed
mu-tat-ing
mu-ta-tion-al
mute
mut-ed
mut-ing
mute-ly
mute-ness
mu-ti-late
mu-ti-neer
mu-ti-ny
mu-ti-nies
mu-ti-nied
mu-ti-ny-ing
mu-ti-nous
mut-ter
mut-ter-er
mut-ton
mu-tu-al
mu-tu-al-i-ty
mu-tu-al-ly
muz-zle
my-col-o-gy
my-col-o-gist
my-na
my-nah
my-o-pia
my-op-ic
myr-i-ad
myr-mi-don
myrrh
myr-tle
mys-te-ri-ous
mys-te-ri-ous-ly
mys-tery
mys-ter-ies
mys-tic
mys-ti-cal
mys-ti-cal-ly
mys-ti-cism
mys-ti-fy
mys-ti-fied
mys-ti-fy-ing
mys-ti-fi-ca-tion
mys-tique
myth
myth-ic
myth-i-cal
myth-i-cal-ly
myth-i-cist
myth-i-cize
my-thol-o-gy
my-thol-o-gies
myth-o-log-ic
myth-o-log-i-cal
my-thol-o-gist

nab
nabbed
nab-bing
na-bob
na-cre
na-cre-ous
na-dir
nag
nagged
nag-ging
nag-ger
nail-er
na-ive
na-ive-ly
na-ive-te
na-ked
na-ked-ly
na-ked-ness
nam-by-pam-by
name
named
nam-ing
name-less
name-ly
name-sake
nan-keen
nan-kin
nan-ny
nan-nies
nap
napped
nap-ping
nap-per
na-palm
nape
naph-tha
naph-tha-lene
nap-kin
nar-cis-sism
nar-cism
nar-cis-sist
nar-co-sis
nar-cot-ic
nar-co-tize
nar-co-tized
nar-is
nar-es
nar-rate
nar-ra-ted
nar-ra-ting
nar-ra-tor
nar-ra-tion
nar-ra-tive
nar-ra-tive-ly
nar-row
nar-row-ly

nar-row--mind-ed
nary
na-sal
na-scent
na-scence
na-scen-cy
na-stur-tium
nas-ty
nas-ti-er
nas-ti-est
na-tal
na-tion
na-tion-hood
na-tion-al
na-tion-al-ly
na-tion-al-ism
na-tion-al-ist
na-tion-al-is-tic
na-tion-al-i-ty
na-tion-al-i-ties
na-tion-al-ize
na-tion-al-ized
na-tion-al-iz-ing
na-tion-al-i-za-tion
na-tion-wide
na-tive
na-tive-ly
na-tiv-i-ty
na-tiv-i-ties
nat-ty
nat-ti-er
nat-u-ral
nat-u-ral-ly
nat-u-ral-ness
nat-u-ral-ism
nat-u-ral-ist
nat-u-ral-is-tic
nat-u-ral-ized
nat-u-ral-iz-ing
nat-u-ral-i-za-tion
na-ture
naught
naugh-ty
naugh-ti-er
naugh-ti-est
nau-sea
nau-se-ate
nau-se-at-ed
nau-se-at-ing
nau-seous
nau-seous-ly
nau-ti-cal
nau-ti-cal-ly
nau-ti-lus
nau-ti-lus-es
nau-ti-li

na-val
na-vel
nav-i-ga-ble
nav-i-gate
  nav-i-gat-ed
  nav-i-gat-ing
nav-i-ga-tion
  nav-i-ga-tion-al
nav-i-ga-tor
na-vy
  na-vies
near
  near-ly
  near-ness
near-by
neat
  neat-ly
  neat-ness
neb-bish
neb-u-la
nec-es-sary
  nec-es-sar-ies
  nec-es-sar-i-ly
  ne-ces-si-tate
  ne-ces-si-ta-ting
ne-ces-si-ty
  ne-ces-si-ties
neck-er-chief
neck-ing
neck-lace
neck-tie
ne-crol-o-gy
  ne-crol-o-gies
nec-ro-man-cy
  nec-ro-man-cer
ne-cro-sis
  ne-crot-ic
nec-tar
  nec-tar-ine
need-ful
  need-ful-ly
  need-ful-ness
nee-dle
  nee-dled
  nee-dling
  nee-dle-like
  nee-dler
nee-dle-point
need-less
  need-less-ly
nee-dle-work
  nee-dle-work-er
needy
  need-i-er
  need-i-est
  need-i-ness

ne'er--do--well
ne-far-i-ous
  ne-far-i-ous-ly
  ne-far-i-ous-ness
ne-gate
  ne-ga-ted
  ne-ta-ting
ne-ga-tion
neg-a-tive
  neg-a-tive-ly
  neg-a-tive-ness
  neg-a-tive-i-ty
  neg-a-tiv-ism
ne-glect
  ne-glec-ter
  ne-glec-tor
  ne-glect-ful-ness
  ne-glect-ful
  ne-glect-ful-ly
neg-li-gee
neg-li-gent
  neg-li-gence
  neg-li-gent-ly
neg-li-gi-ble
  neg-li-gi-bly
  neg-li-gi-bil-i-ty
ne-go-tia-ble
  ne-go-tia-bil-i-ty
ne-go-ti-ate
  ne-go-ti-at-ed
  ne-go-ti-at-ing
  ne-go-ti-a-tion
  ne-go-ti-a-tor
neigh-bor
  neigh-bor-ing
  neigh-bor-ly
  neigh-bor-li-ness
  neigh-bor-hood
nei-ther
nem-e-sis
  nem-e-ses
neo-clas-sic
  neo-clas-si-cism
neo-lith-ic
ne-ol-o-gism
ne-ol-o-gy
ne-on
ne-o-phyte
ne-pen-the
  ne-pen-the-an
neph-ew
ne-phri-tis
  ne-phrit-ic
nep-o-tism
  nep-o-tist
nep-tu-ni-um

nerve
  nerved
  nerv-ing
  nerve-less
nerve--rack-ing
  nerve--wrack-ing
ner-vous
  ner-vous-ly
  ner-vous-ness
nervy
  nerv-i-er
  nerv-i-est
  nerv-i-ness
nes-tle
  nes-tled
  nes-tling
  nes-tler
net
  net-ted
  net-ting
neth-er
neth-er-most
net-tle
  net-tled
  net-tling
net-work
neu-ral
  neu-ral-ly
  neu-ral-gia
  neu-ral-gic
neu-ras-the-nia
  neu-ra-then-ic
neu-ri-tis
  neu-rit-ic
neu-rol-o-gy
  neu-ro-log-i-cal
  neu-rol-o-gist
neu-ron
  neu-ron-ic
neu-ro-sis
  neu-ro-ses
neu-rot-ic
  neu-rot-i-cal-ly
neu-ter
neu-tral
  neu-tral-i-ty
  neu-tral-ly
  neu-tral-ism
  neu-tral-ist
neu-tral-ize
  neu-tral-ized
  neu-tral-iz-ing
neu-tral-i-za-tion
neu-tral-iz-er
neu-tri-no
neu-tron

nev-er
nev-er-more
nev-er-the-less
new
  new-ish
  new-ness
new-born
new-com-er
new-el
new-fan-gled
new-ly
new-ly-wed
news-boy
news-cast
  news-cast-er
news-pa-per
  news-pa-per-man
news-print
news-reel
news-stand
newsy
  news-i-er
  news-i-est
newt
nex-us
ni-a-cin
nib-ble
  nib-bled
  nib-bling
  nib-bler
nib-lick
nice
  nic-er
  nic-est
  nice-ly
  nice-ness
nice-ty
  nice-ties
niche
nick-el
nick-el-ode-on
nick-name
nick-named
  nick-nam-ing
nic-o-tine
  nic-o-tin-ic
niece
nif-ty
  nif-ti-er
  nif-ti-est
nig-gard
  nig-gard-li-ness
  nig-gard-ly
nigh
  nigh-er
  nigh-est

night-cap
night-dress
night-fall
night-gown
night-hawk
night-in-gale
night-ly
night-mare
  night-mar-ish
night-shade
night-shirt
night-time
ni-hil-ism
  ni-hil-ist
  ni-hil-is-tic
nim-ble
  nim-bler
  nim-blest
  nim-ble-ness
  nim-bly
nim-bus
nin-com-poop
nine-pin
nine-teen
  nine-teenth
nine-ty
  nine-ties
  nine-ti-eth
nin-ny
  nin-nines
ninth
nip
  nipped
  nip-ping
  nip-per
nip-ple
nip-py
  nip-pi-er
  nip-pi-est
nir-va-na
nit
  nit-ty
  nit-ti-er
  nit-ti-est
ni-ter
nit-pick
ni-trate
  ni-trat-ed
  ni-trat-ing
  ni-tra-tion
  ni-tra-tor
ni-tric
ni-tro-gen
  ni-trog-e-nous
  ni-tro-glyc-er-in
  ni-trous ox-ide

nit-ty-grit-ty
nit-wit
no-be-li-um
no-bil-i-ty
  no-bil-i-ties
no-ble
no-body
noc-tur-nal
noc-turne
nod
  nod-ded
  nod-ding
  nod-der
node
  nod-al
nod-ule
  nod-u-lar
no-el
nog-gin
noise
  noised
  nois-ing
  noise-less
noi-some
  noi-some-ly
noisy
  nois-i-er
  nois-i-est
  nois-i-ly
no-mad
  no-mad-ic
  no-mad-i-cal-ly
  no-mad-ism
nom de plume
  noms de plume
no-men-cla-ture
nom-i-nal
  nom-i-nal-ly
nom-i-nate
  nom-i-nat-ed
  nom-i-nat-ing
  nom-i-na-tion
  nom-i-na-tor
  nom-i-na-tive
nom-i-nee
non-age
nonce
non-cha-lant
  non-cha-lance
  non-cha-lant-ly
non-com
  non-com-bat-ant
  non-com-mit-tal
  non-com-mit-tal-ly
non-con-duc-tor
  non-con-duc-ing

non-con-form-ist
  non-con-form-i-ty
non-de-script
non-en-ti-ty
  non-en-ti-ties
none-the-less
non-in-ter-ven-tion
non-met-al
  non-me-tal-lic
non-pa-reil
non-par-ti-san
  non-par-ti-san-ship
non-plus
  non-plused
  non-plus-ing
non-prof-it
non-res-i-dent
  non-res-i-dence
  non-res-i-den-cy
  non-res-i-den-cies
non-re-stric-tive
non-sec-tar-i-an
non-sense
  non-sen-si-cal
  non-sen-si-cal-ly
non se-qui-tur
non-stop
non-union
  non-union-ism
  non-union-ist
non-vi-o-lence
  non-vi-o-lent
  non-vi-o-lent-ly
noo-dle
noon
  noon-day
  noon-time
noose
  noosed
  noos-ing
nor-mal
  nor-mal-cy
  nor-mal-i-ty
  nor-mal-ly
nor-mal-ize
  nor-mal-ized
  nor-mal-iz-ing
  nor-mal-i-za-tion
north-east
  north-east-ern
north-east-er
north-er
north-ern
  north-ern-most
  north-ern-er
north-ward

north-wards
north-ward-ly
north-west
nose
  nosed
  nos-ing
nose-gay
nos-tal-gia
  nos-tal-gic
nos-tril
nos-trum
nosy
  nos-i-er
  nos-i-est
  nos-i-ly
  nos-i-ness
no-ta-ble
no-ta-rize
  no-ta-rized
  no-ta-riz-ing
  no-ta-ri-za-tion
no-ta-ry
  no-ta-ries
no-ta-tion
  no-ta-tion-al
notch
  notched
note
  not-ed
not-ed
  not-ed-ly
note-wor-thy
  note-wor-thi-ness
noth-ing
  noth-ing-ness
no-tice
  no-ticed
  no-tic-ing
  no-tice-a-ble
  no-tice-a-bly
no-ti-fy
  no-ti-fied
  no-ti-fy-ing
  no-ti-fi-ca-tion
  no-ti-fi-er
no-tion
no-to-ri-ous
  no-to-ri-ous-ly
  no-to-ri-e-ty
no-trump
nought
nour-ish
  nour-ish-er
  nour-ish-ing
  nour-ish-ment
no-va

no-vas
nov-el
  nov-el-ist
  nov-el-is-tic
  nov-el-ette
nov-el-ty
  nov-el-ties
no-ve-na
  no-ve-nae
nov-ice
no-vi-tiate
no-where
no-wise
nox-ious
  nox-ious-ly
noz-zle
nu-ance
nub-bin
nu-bile
nu-cle-ar
nu-cle-us
  nu-cle-us-es
  nu-clei
nude
  nude-ly
  nude-ness
  nu-di-ty
nudge
  nudged
  nudg-ing
  nudg-er
nud-ism
  nud-ist
nug-get
nui-sance
null
  nul-li-ty
  nul-li-ties
nul-li-fy
  nul-li-fied
  nul-li-fy-ing
  nul-li-fi-ca-tion
  nul-li-fi-er
numb
  numb-ly
  numb-ness
  numb-ing
num-ber
  num-ber-er
  num-ber-less
numb-skull
nu-mer-al
  num-er-al-ly
nu-mer-ate
  nu-mer-at-ed
  nu-mer-at-ing

nu-mer-a-tion
nu-mer-a-tor
nu-mer-i-cal
  nu-mer-i-cal-ly
nu-mer-ous
  nu-mer-ous-ly
nu-mis-mat-ics
  nu-mis-mat-ic
  nu-mis-mat-i-cal
  nu-mis-ma-tist
num-skull
nun-cio
  nun-ci-os
nun-nery
  nun-ner-ies
nup-tial
  nup-tial-ly
nurse
  nursed
  nurs-ing
  nurs-er
nurse-maid
nurs-ery
  nurs-er-ies
nur-ture
  nur-tured
  nur-tur-ing
  nur-tur-er
nut
  nut-ted
  nut-ting
nut-crack-er
nut-hatch
nut-meg
nu-tri-ent
  nu-tri-ment
nu-tri-tion
  nu-tri-tion-al
  nu-tri-tion-al-ly
  nu-tri-tion-ist
nu-tri-tious
  nu-tri-tious-ly
nu-tri-tive
  nu-tri-tive-ly
nut-shell
nut-ty
  nut-ti-er
  nut-ti-est
nuz-zle
  nuz-zled
  nuz-zling
ny-lon
nymph
  nym-phal
nym-pho-ma-nia
  nym-pho-ma-ni-ac

oaf
  oaf-ish
  oaf-ish-ly
oak-en
oa-kum
oar
  oared
  oars-man
  oars-men
oar-lock
oa-sis
  oa-ses
oat-en
oath
oat-meal
ob-bli-ga-to
  ob-bli-ga-tos
ob-du-rate
  ob-du-ra-cy
  ob-du-rate-ly
obe-di-ence
  obe-di-ent
  obe-di-ent-ly
obei-sance
  obei-sant
obe-lisk
obese
  obese-ness
  obes-i-ty
obey
  obey-er
ob-fus-cate
  ob-fus-ca-ted
  ob-fus-ca-ting
  ob-fus-ca-tion
obit
obit-u-ary
  obit-u-ar-ies
ob-ject
  ob-ject-less
  ob-ject-or
ob-jec-tion
  ob-jec-tion-a-ble
  ob-jec-tion-a-bly
ob-jec-tive
  ob-jec-tive-ly
  ob-jec-tive-ness
  ob-jec-tiv-i-ty
ob-jur-gate
  ob-jur-gat-ed
  ob-jur-gat-ing
  ob-jur-ga-tion
  ob-jur-ga-to-ry
ob-late
  ob-late-ly
  ob-late-ness

ob-li-gate
  ob-li-gat-ed
  ob-li-gat-ing
  ob-li-ga-tion
  ob-lig-a-to-ry
oblige
  obliged
  oblig-ing
  oblig-er
ob-lique
  ob-liqued
  ob-liqu-ing
  ob-lique-ly
oblit-er-ate
  oblit-er-at-ed
  oblit-er-at-ing
  oblit-er-a-tion
  oblit-er-a-tive
obliv-i-on
  obliv-i-ous
  obliv-i-ous-ly
ob-long
ob-lo-quy
  ob-lo-quies
ob-nox-ious
  ob-nox-ious-ly
oboe
obo-ist
ob-scene
  ob-scene-ly
  ob-scen-ity
  ob-scen-i-ties
ob-scure
  ob-scur-er
  ob-scur-est
  ob-scured
  ob-scur-ing
  ob-scure-ly
ob-se-qui-ous
  ob-se-qui-ous-ly
ob-se-quy
  ob-se-quies
ob-serv-able
  ob-serv-ably
ob-ser-vance
ob-ser-vant
  ob-ser-vant-ly
ob-ser-va-tion
  ob-ser-va-tion-al
ob-ser-va-to-ry
  ob-ser-va-to-ries
ob-serve
  ob-served
  ob-serv-ing
  ob-serv-ed-ly
  ob-serv-er

ob-serv-ing-ly
ob-sess
  ob-ses-sive
  ob-ses-sive-ly
ob-ses-sion
  ob-sid-i-an
ob-so-les-cent
  ob-so-les-cence
  ob-so-les-cent-ly
ob-so-lete
  ob-sta-cle
ob-ste-tri-cian
  ob-stet-rics
  ob-stet-ric
  ob-stet-ri-cal
ob-sti-nate
  ob-sti-na-cy
  ob-sti-na-cies
  ob-sti-nat-ly
ob-strep-er-ous
  ob-strep-er-ous-ly
ob-struct
  ob-struc-tive
  ob-struc-tor
ob-struc-tion
  ob-struc-tion-ism
  ob-struc-tion-ist
ob-tain
  ob-tain-a-ble
  ob-tain-er
  ob-tain-ment
ob-trude
  ob-trud-ed
  ob-trud-ing
  ob-trud-er
  ob-tru-sion
  ob-tru-sive
ob-tuse
  ob-tuse-ly
ob-verse
  ob-verse-ly
ob-vi-ate
  ob-vi-ated
  ob-vi-at-ing
  ob-vi-a-tion
  ob-vi-a-tor
ob-vi-ous
  ob-vi-ous-ly
oc-ca-sion
  oc-ca-sion-al
  oc-ca-sion-al-ly
oc-ci-dent
  oc-ci-den-tal
oc-clude
  oc-clud-ed
  oc-clud-ing

oc-clu-sive
oc-clu-sion
oc-cult
oc-cult-ism
  oc-cult-ist
oc-cu-pan-cy
  oc-cu-pan-cies
  oc-cu-pant
oc-cu-pa-tion
  oc-cu-pa-tion-al
  oc-cu-pa-tion-al-ly
oc-cu-py
  oc-cu-pied
  oc-cu-py-ing
  oc-cu-pi-er
oc-cur
  oc-curred
  oc-cur-ring
  oc-cur-rence
  oc-cur-rent
ocean
  oce-an-ic
ocean-og-ra-phy
  ocean-og-ra-pher
  ocean-o-graph-ic
oce-lot
ocher
  ocher-ous
  ochery
o'clock
oc-ta-gon
  oc-tag-o-nal
  oc-tag-o-nal-ly
oc-ta-he-dron
  oc-ta-he-drons
  oc-ta-he-dra
  oc-ta-he-dral
oc-tane
oc-tave
oc-ta-vo
oc-tet
oc-to-ge-nar-i-an
  oc-tog-e-nary
oc-to-pus
oc-u-lar
  oc-u-lar-ly
oc-u-list
odd
  odd-ly
  odd-ness
odd-ball
odd-i-ty
  odd-i-ties
od-ic
odi-ous
  odi-ous-ly

odi-um
odom-e-ter
odor
  odored
  odor-less
  odor-ous
  odor-ous-ly
odor-if-er-ous
  odor-if-er-ous-ly
od-ys-sey
oe-di-pal
of-fal
off-beat
off--col-or
of-fend
  of-fend-er
of-fense
  of-fense-less
of-fen-sive
  of-fen-sive-ly
  of-fen-sive-ness
of-fer
  of-fer-er
  of-fer-ing
of-fer-to-ry
  of-fer-to-ri-al
  of-fer-to-ries
off-hand
  off-hand-ed-ly
  off-hand-ed-ness
of-fice
  of-fice-hold-er
of-fi-cer
of-fi-cial
  of-fi-cial-dom
  of-fi-cial-ism
  of-fi-cial-ly
of-fi-ci-ate
  of-fi-ci-at-ed
  of-fi-ci-at-ing
  of-fi-ci-a-tion
  of-fi-ci-a-tor
of-fi-cious
  of-fi-cious-ly
  of-fi-cious-ness
off-ing
off-set
  off-set-ting
off-shoot
off-shore
off-side
off-spring
off-stage
off--the--cuff
of-ten
of-ten-times

ogle
 ogled
 ogler
 ogling
ogre
 ogre-ish
ohm
 ohm-ic
ohm-age
ohm-me-ter
oil-cloth
oil-er
oil-skin
oily
 oil-i-er
 oil-i-est
 oil-i-ness
oint-ment
okra
old
 old-en
 old-er
 old-est
 old-ish
 old-ness
old--fash-ioned
old-ster
old--time
 old--tim-er
old--world
ole-ag-i-nous
 ole-ag-i-nous-ly
 ole-ag-i-nous-ness
oleo
oleo-mar-ga-rine
ol-fac-tion
ol-fac-to-ry
 ol-fac-to-ries
oli-garch
oli-gar-chic
 oli-gar-chi-cal
oli-gar-chy
 oli-gar-chies
oli-gop-oly
ol-ive
om-buds-man
 om-buds-men
om-elet
omen
om-i-nous
 om-i-nous-ly
 om-i-nous-ness
omis-sion
omit
 omit-ted
 omit-ting

om-ni-bus
 om-ni-bus-es
om-nip-o-tence
 om-nip-o-tent-ly
om-ni-pres-ence
om-ni-pres-ent
 om-ni-pres-ent-ly
om-ni-science
 om-ni-scient
 om-ni-scient-ly
om-ni-vore
om-niv-o-rous
 om-niv-o-rous-ly
 om-niv-o-rous-ness
onan-ism
 onan-ist
 onan-is-tic
once--over
on-com-ing
oner-ous
 oner-ous-ly
 oner-ous-ness
one-self
one--sid-ed
 one--sid-ed-ly
 one--sid-ed-ness
one-time
one--track
one--way
on-go-ing
on-ion
 on-ion-like
 on-iony
on-ion-skin
on--line
on-look-er
 on-look-ing
on-ly
on-o-mato-poe-ia
 on-o-mato-poe-ic
 on-o-mato-po-et-ic
on-rush
 on-rush-ing
on-set
on-shore
on-slaught
onto-
onus
on-ward
on-yx
oo-dles
ooze
 oozed
 oo-zi-er
 oo-zi-est
 oo-zi-ness

 ooz-ing
 oo-zy
opac-i-ty
 opac-i-ties
opal
opal-es-cence
 opal-es-cent
opaque
 opaque-ly
 opaque-ness
open
 open-er
 open-ly
 open-ness
open--air
open door
open--end
open--eyed
open-hand-ed
 open-hand-ed-ly
open house
open-ing
open--mind-ed
 open--mind-ed-ly
open-mouthed
open ses-a-me
open-work
opera
 op-er-at-ic
 op-er-at-i-cal-ly
op-er-a-ble
 op-er-a-bil-i-ty
 op-er-a-bly
opera glass
opera house
op-er-ate
 op-er-at-ed
 op-er-at-ing
op-er-a-tion
 op-er-a-tive
 op-er-a-tive-ly
op-er-a-tor
op-er-et-ta
oph-thal-mic
 oph-thal-mo-log-ic
 oph-thal-mol-o-gist
 oph-thal-mol-o-gy
opi-ate
opine
 opined
 opin-ing
opin-ion
 opin-ion-at-ed
 opin-ion-at-ed-ly
opi-um
opos-sum

op-po-nent
op-por-tune
 op-por-tune-ly
 op-por-tune-ness
op-por-tun-ism
 op-por-tun-ist
 op-por-tun-is-tic
op-por-tu-ni-ty
 op-por-tu-ni-ties
op-pos-able
 op-pos-a-bil-i-ty
op-pose
 op-posed
 op-pos-er
 op-pos-ing
 op-pos-ing-ly
op-po-site
 op-po-site-ly
op-po-si-tion
 op-po-si-tion-al
op-press
 op-pres-si-ble
 op-pres-sor
op-pres-sion
op-pres-sive
 op-pres-sive-ly
 op-pres-sive-ness
op-pro-bri-ous
 op-pro-bri-ous-ly
op-pro-bri-um
op-tic
 op-ti-cal
 op-ti-cal-ly
op-ti-cian
op-tics
op-ti-mal
op-ti-mism
 op-ti-mist
 op-ti-mis-tic
 op-ti-mis-ti-cal-ly
op-ti-mize
 op-ti-mi-za-tion
 op-ti-mized
 op-ti-miz-ing
op-ti-mum
 op-ti-ma
op-tion
 op-tion-al
 op-tion-al-ly
op-tom-e-trist
op-tom-e-try
 op-to-met-ric
 op-to-met-ri-cal
op-u-lence
op-u-lent
 op-u-lent-ly

opus
 opus-es
or-a-cle
 orac-u-lar
 orac-u-lar-i-ty
 orac-u-lar-ly
oral
 oral-ly
or-ange
or-ange-ade
orang-utan
orate
 orat-ed
 orat-ing
ora-tion
or-a-tor
 or-a-tor-i-cal
 or-a-tor-i-cal-ly
or-a-to-rio
 or-a-to-ri-os
or-a-to-ry
or-bic-u-lar
 or-bic-u-lar-i-ty
 or-bic-u-lar-ly
or-bic-u-late
or-bit
 or-bit-al
 or-bit-er
or-chard
or-ches-tra
 or-ches-tral
 or-ches-tral-ly
or-ches-trate
 or-ches-trat-ed
 or-ches-trat-ing
 or-ches-tra-tion
or-chid
or-dain
 or-dain-er
 or-dain-ment
or-deal
or-der
 or-dered
 or-der-li-ness
 or-der-ly
or-di-nal
or-di-nance
or-di-nari-ly
or-di-nary
 or-di-nari-ness
or-di-na-tion
ord-nance
or-dure
oreg-a-no
or-gan
or-gan-dy

or-gan-ic
 or-gan-i-cal-ly
or-gan-ism
 or-gan-is-mal
 or-gan-is-mic
or-gan-ist
or-ga-ni-za-tion
 or-gan-i-za-tion-al
or-ga-nize
 or-ga-niz-able
 or-ga-nized
 or-ga-niz-er
 or-ga-niz-ing
 or-ga-niz-a-ble
or-gasm
 or-gas-mic
or-gi-as-tic
 or-gi-as-ti-cal-ly
or-gy
 or-gies
ori-ent
Ori-en-tal
ori-en-tal-ism
 ori-en-tal-ist
 ori-en-tal-ly
ori-en-tate
 ori-en-tat-ed
 ori-en-tat-ing
ori-en-ta-tion
or-i-fice
ori-ga-mi
orig-i-nal
 orig-i-nal-i-ty
 orig-i-nal-ly
orig-i-nate
 orig-i-nat-ed
 orig-i-nat-ing
 orig-i-na-tion
 orig-i-na-tive
 orig-i-na-tive-ly
 orig-i-na-tor
or-i-son
or-na-ment
 or-na-men-tal
 or-na-men-ta-tion
or-nate
 or-nate-ly
 or-nate-ness
or-nery
 or-ner-i-ness
or-ni-thol-o-gy
 or-ni-tho-log-ic
 or-ni-tho-log-i-cal
 or-ni-tho-log-i-cal-ly
 or-ni-thol-o-gist
oro-tund

oro-tun-di-ty
or-phan
  or-phan-hood
or-phan-age
orth-odon-tics
  orth-odon-tic
  orth-odon-tist
or-tho-dox
  or-tho-dox-ly
  or-tho-dox-ness
or-tho-doxy
  or-tho-dox-ies
or-tho-gen-ic
or-thog-o-nal
  or-thog-o-nal-ly
or-thog-ra-phy
  or-tho-graph-ic
  or-tho-graph-i-cal
  or-tho-graph-i-cal-ly
  or-thog-ra-phies
  or-thog-ra-pher
or-tho-pe-dic
  or-tho-pe-dics
  or-tho-pe-dist
os-cil-late
  os-cil-lat-ed
  os-cil-lat-ing
  os-cil-la-tion
  os-cil-la-tor
  os-cil-la-to-ry
os-cil-lo-scope
os-cu-late
  os-cu-lat-ed
  os-cu-lat-ing
  os-cu-la-tion
  os-cu-la-to-ry
os-mi-um
os-mose
  os-mosed
  os-mos-ing
os-mo-sis
  os-mot-ic
  os-mot-i-cal-ly
os-prey
os-si-fy
  os-si-fied
  os-si-fi-er
  os-si-fy-ing
os-ten-si-ble
  os-ten-si-bly
os-ten-sive
  os-ten-sive-ly
os-ten-ta-tion
os-ten-ta-tious
  os-ten-ta-tious-ly
os-te-op-a-thy

os-teo-path
  os-teo-path-ic
  os-teo-path-i-cal-ly
os-tra-cism
os-tra-cize
  os-tra-cized
  os-tra-ciz-ing
os-trich
oth-er
  oth-er-ness
oth-er-wise
oth-er-world
  oth-er-world-ly
oti-ose
  oti-ose-ly
  oti-os-i-ty
ot-ter
ot-to-man
ought
ounce
our-self
our-selves
oust-er
out-bid
  out-bid-den
  out-bid-ding
  out-bid-der
out-board
out-bound
out-brave
  out-braved
  out-brav-ing
out-break
out-build-ing
out-burst
out-cast
out-come
out-cry
  out-cries
out-dat-ed
out-dis-tance
  out-dis-tanced
  out-dis-tanc-ing
out-do
  out-did
  out-do-ing
  out-done
out-door
out-er
out-er-most
outer space
out-face
  out-faced
  out-fac-ing
out-field
  out-field-er

out-fit
  out-fit-ted
  out-fit-ter
  out-fit-ting
out-flank
out-fox
out-grow
  out-grew
  out-grow-ing
  out-grown
out-growth
out-guess
out-ing
out-land-ish
  out-land-ish-ly
out-last
out-law
  out-law-ry
out-lay
  out-laid
  out-lay-ing
out-let
out-line
  out-lined
  out-lin-ing
out-live
  out-lived
  out-liv-ing
out-look
out-ly-ing
out-mod-ed
out-num-ber
out--of--date
out-post
out-put
out-rage
  out-raged
  out-rag-ing
out-ra-geous
  out-ra-geous-ly
out-range
  out-ranged
  out-rang-ing
out-rank
out-rig-ger
out-right
out-run
  out-ran
  out-run-ning
out-sell
  out-sell-ing
  out-sold
out-set
out-shine
  out-shin-ing
  out-shone

out-side
out-sid-er
out-smart
out-spo-ken
  out-spo-ken-ly
out-stand-ing
  out-stand-ing-ly
out-strip
  out-stripped
  out-strip-ping
out-ward
  out-ward-ly
  out-wards
out-wear
  out-wear-ing
  out-wore
  out-worn
out-weigh
out-wit
  out-wit-ted
  out-wit-ting
ova
oval
  oval-ly
ova-ry
  ovar-i-an
  ova-ries
ovate
ova-tion
ov-en
over
over-act
over-age
over-all
over-awe
  over-awed
  over-aw-ing
over-bear-ing
  over-bear-ing-ly
over-blown
over-board
over-build
  over-build-ing
  over-built
over-cast
over-charge
  over-charged
  over-charg-ing
over-coat
over-come
  over-came
over-com-pen-sa-tion
  over-com-pen-sate
  over-com-pen-sat-ed
  over-com-pen-sat-ing
over-con-fi-dence

over-con-fi-dent
over-do
  over-did
  over-do-ing
  over-done
over-dose
  over-dos-age
over-draft
over-draw
  over-draw-ing
  over-drawn
  over-drew
over-drive
over-due
over-em-pha-sis
  over-em-pha-size
  over-em-pha-sized
  over-em-pha-sizing
over-es-ti-mate
  over-es-ti-mat-ed
  over-es-ti-mat-ing
  over-es-ti-ma-tion
over-flow
  over-flowed
  over-flowing
  over-flown
over-gen-er-ous
over-grow
  over-grew
  over-grow-ing
  over-grown
over-growth
over-hand
  over-hand-ed
over-hang
  over-hang-ing
  over-hung
over-haul
  over-haul-ing
over-head
over-hear
  over-heard
  over-hear-ing
over-joy
  over-joyed
over-kill
over-land
over-lap
  over-lapped
  over-lap-ping
over-lay
  over-laid
  over-lay-ing
over-look
over-lord
over-ly

over-much
over-night
over-pass
over-play
over-pow-er
  over-pow-er-ing
over-rate
  over-rat-ed
  over-rat-ing
over-reach
over-ride
  over-rid-den
  over-rid-ing
  over-rode
over-rule
  over-ruled
  over-rul-ing
over-run
over-seas
over-see
  over-saw
  over-see-ing
  over-seen
over-seer
over-shad-ow
over-shoe
over-shoot
  over-shoot-ing
  over-shot
over-sight
over-sim-pli-fy
  over-sim-pli-fi-ca-tion
  over-sim-pli-fied
  over-sim-pli-fy-ing
over-size
over-sleep
  over-sleep-ing
  over-slept
over-spread
  over-spread-ing
over-state
  over-stat-ed
  over-state-ment
  over-stat-ing
over-stay
over-step
  over-stepped
  over-step-ping
over-strung
over-stuff
overt
  overt-ly
over-take
  over-tak-en
  over-tak-ing
  over-took

over-tax
over--the--coun-ter
over-throw
  over-threw
  over-thrown
  over-throw-ing
over-time
over-tone
over-ture
over-turn
over-view
over-ween-ing
  over-ween-ing-ly
over-weight
over-whelm
  over-whelm-ing
over-work
  over-worked
  over-work-ing
over-wrought
ovi-duct
ovip-a-rous
  ovip-ar-ous-ly
ovoid
  ovoi-dal
ovu-late
  ovu-lat-ed
  ovu-lat-ing
  ovu-la-tion
ovule
  ovu-lar
ovum
ova
owe
  owed
  ow-ing
owl-ish
own-er
ox-al-ic ac-id
ox-bow
ox-en
ox-ford
ox-i-da-tion
  ox-i-da-tive
  ox-i-dant
ox-ide
ox-i-dize
  ox-i-dized
  ox-i-diz-ing
ox-y-a-cet-y-lene
ox-y-gen
ox-y-gen-ate
  ox-y-gen-at-ed
  ox-y-gen-at-ing
  ox-y-gen-a-tion
oys-ter

pab-u-lum
pace
  paced
  pac-ing
  pac-er
pace-mak-er
pa-cif-ic
pa-cif-i-ca-tion
  pa-cif-i-ca-tor
  pa-cif-i-ca-to-ry
pac-i-fi-er
pac-i-fism
  pac-i-fist
pac-i-fy
  pac-i-fied
  pac-i-fy-ing
pack-age
  pack-ag-er
pack-er
pack-et
pack-ing
pad
  pad-ded
  pad-ding
pad-dle
pad-dock
pad-dy
  pad-dies
pad-lock
pae-an
  pe-an
pe-gan
  pe-gan-ism
page
  paged
  pag-ing
pag-eant
  pag-ent-ry
pag-i-nate
  pag-i-nat-ed
  pag-i-nat-ing
pa-go-da
pain
  pain-ful
  pain-less
pain-kil-ler
pains-tak-ing
  pains-tak-ing-ly
paint-er
pais-ley
pa-ja-mas
pal-ace
pal-at-a-ble
  pal-at-a-bil-i-ty
  pal-at-a-bly
pal-ate

pa-la-tial
  pa-la-tial-ly
pal-a-tiner
  pa-lat-i-nate
pa-lav-er
pale
pa-le-on-tol-o-gy
  pa-le-on-to-log-ic
  pa-le-on-to-log-i-cal
pal-ette
pal-imp-sest
pal-in-drome
pal-ing
pal-i-sade
  pal-i-sad-ed
  pal-i-sad-ing
pal-la-di-um
pall-bear-er
pal-let
pal-li-ate
  pal-li-at-ed
  pal-li-at-ing
  pal-li-a-tion
pal-lid
pal-lor
palm
  pal-ma-ceous
pal-mate
  pal-mate-ly
palm-er
palm-is-try
  palm-ist
palmy
  palm-i-er
  palm-i-est
pal-o-mi-no
  pal-o-mi-nos
pal-pa-ble
  pal-pa-bil-i-ty
  pal-pa-bly
pal-pate
  pal-pat-ed
  pal-pat-ing
pal-sy
  pal-sied
  pal-sy-ing
pal-ter
  pal-ter-er
pal-try
  pal-tri-er
  pal-tri-est
pam-pas
  pam-pe-an
pam-per
  pam-per-er
pam-phlet

pan
  panned
  pan-ning
pan-a-ce-a
  pan-a-ce-an
pa-nache
pan-cake
pan-cre-as
  pan-cre-at-ic
pan-dem-ic
pan-de-mo-ni-um
pan-der
pan-el
  pan-eled
  pan-el-ing
pan-el-ist
pang
pan-ic
  pan-icked
  pan-ick-ing
pan-nier
  pan-ier
pan-o-ply
  pan-o-plies
  pan-o-plied
pan-ora-ma
  pan-oram-ic
  pan-oram-i-cal-ly
pan-sy
  pan-sies
pan-ta-loon
pan-the-ism
  pan-the-is-tic
pan-the-on
pan-ther
pan-ties
pan-to-mime
  pan-to-mimed
pan-try
  pan-tries
pant-suit
pant-y-hose
pa-pa
pa-pa-cy
  pa-pa-cies
pa-pal
pa-per
  pa-per-er
  pa-pery
pa-per-back
pa-pil-la
  pa-pil-pae
pa-poose
pap-ri-ka
pa-py-rus
par-a-ble

para-chute
  para-chut-ed
  para-chut-ing
  para-chut-ist
pa-rade
  pa-rad-ed
  pa-rad-ing
par-a-digm
  par-a-dig-mat-ic
par-a-dise
  par-a-di-si-a-cal
par-a-dox
  par-a-dox-i-cal
par-af-fin
par-a-gon
par-a-graph
  par-a-graph-er
par-a-keet
par-al-lax
  par-al-al-lac-tic
par-al-lel
  par-al-leled
  par-al-lel-ing
par-al-lel-o-gram
pa-ral-y-sis
  pa-ral-y-ses
  par-a-lyt-ic
par-a-lyze
  par-a-lyzed
  par-a-lyz-ing
par-a-me-cium
par-a-med-ic
pa-ram-e-ter
par-a-mount
  par-a-mount-cy
  par-a-mount-ly
par-amour
para-noia
  para-noid
par-a-pet
par-a-pher-nal-ia
para-phrase
  para-phrased
  para-phras-ing
para-ple-gia
  para-ple-gic
para-psy-chol-o-gy
par-a-site
  par-a-sit-ic
para-sol
par-a-sym-pa-thet-ic
para-thi-on
para-troop-er
para-ty-phoid
par-boil
par-cel

par-celed
par-cel-ing
parch-ment
par-don
  par-don-a-ble
  par-don-a-bly
pare
  pared
  par-ing
par-e-gor-ic
par-ent
  pa-ren-tal
par-ent-age
pa-ren-the-sis
pa-re-sis
  pa-ret-ic
par-fait
pa-ri-ah
par-i-mu-tu-el
par-ish
  pa-rish-ion-er
par-i-ty
par-ka
par-lance
par-lay
  par-lay-ed
  par-lay-ing
par-ley
  par-leyed
  par-ley-ing
par-lia-ment
par-lia-men-tar-ian
par-lia-men-ta-ry
par-lor
pa-ro-chi-al
par-o-dy
  par-o-dies
  par-o-died
pa-role
  pa-roled
par-ot-id
par-ox-ysm
  par-ox-ys-mal
par-quet
  par-queted
  par-quet-ing
  par-quet-ry
par-rot
  par-rot-like
  par-roty
par-ry
  par-ried
  par-ry-ing
parse
par-si-mo-ny
  par-si-mo-ni-ous

par-si-mo-ni-ous-ly
pars-ley
pars-nip
par-son-age
par-take
  par-took
  par-tak-en
part-ed
par-the-no-gen-e-sis
par-tial
  par-tial-ly
par-tial-i-ty
  par-tial-i-ties
par-tic-i-pant
par-tic-i-pate
  par-tic-i-pat-ed
  par-tic-i-pat-ing
par-ti-cip-i-al
par-ti-ci-ple
par-ti-cle
par-ti--col-ored
par-tic-u-lar
  par-tic-u-lar-ly
par-tic-u-lar-i-ties
par-tic-u-lar-ize
  par-tic-u-lar-ized
  par-tic-u-lar-iz-ing
par-tic-u-late
part-ing
par-ti-san
  par-ti-san-ship
par-tite
par-ti-tion
par-ti-tive
part-ly
part-ner
  part-ner-ship
par-tridge
  par-tridg-es
part--time
par-tu-ri-ent
par-tu-ri-tion
par-ty
  par-ties
par-ve-nu
pas-chal
pa-sha
pass-able
pass-ably
pas-sen-ger
pass-er-by
  pass-ers-by
pass-ing
pas-sion
  pas-sion-ies
pas-sion-ate

pas-sion-ate-ly
pas-sive
pas-ta
paste
  pas-ted
  pas-ting
paste-board
pas-tel
pas-teur-ize
  pas-teur-ized
  pas-teur-iz-ing
  pas-teur-i-za-tion
pas-tille
pas-time
pas-tor
pas-to-ral
pas-to-ral-ly
pas-tor-ate
pas-tra-mi
past-ry
  pas-tries
pas-ture
pas-ty
  past-i-er
  past-i-est
patch-work
patchy
  patch-i-er
  patch-i-est
pat-ent
  pa-ten-cy
  pat-ent-ly
pat-en-tee
pat-er-nal
  pat-ter-nal-ly
pa-ter-nal-ism
pa-ter-ni-ty
pa-thet-ic
path-find-er
pa-thol-o-gy
pa-thos
pa-tience
pa-tient
  pa-tient-ly
pat-i-na
pa-tio
  pa-tios
pa-tri-arch
pa-tri-ar-chy
  pa-tri-ar-chies
pa-tri-cian
pat-ri-mo-ny
  pat-ri-mo-nies
pa-tri-ot
  pa-tri-ot-ic
  pa-tri-ot-ism

pa-trol
  pa-trolled
  pa-trol-ling
pa-trol-man
  pa-trol-men
pa-tron
  pa-tron-ess
pa-tron-age
pa-tron-ize
  pa-tron-ized
  pa-tron-iz-ing
  pa-tron-iz-ing-ly
pat-ro-nym-ic
pat-sy
  pat-sies
pat-ter
pat-tern
  pat-terned
pat-ty
  pat-ties
pau-ci-ty
paunch
pau-per
  pau-per-ism
pause
  paused
  paus-ing
pa-vil-ion
pawn
  pawn-er
pawn-bro-ker
pay-a-ble
pay-ment
pay-off
peace
peace-able
  peace-ably
peace-ful
  peace-ful-ly
peach
pea-cock
peak-ed
pea-nut
pearl
  pear-ly
peas-ant
  peas-ant-ly
peaty
peb-ble
pe-can
pec-ca-dil-lo
  pec-ca-dil-loes
pec-ca-dil-los
peck-er
pec-tin
pec-to-ral

pec-u-late
  pec-u-lat-ed
  pec-u-lat-ing
pe-cu-liar
  pe-cu-liar-ly
  pe-cu-li-ar-i-ty
  pe-cu-li-ar-i-ties
pe-cu-ni-ary
ped-a-go-gue
ped-a-go-gy
ped-al
  ped-aled
  ped-al-ing
ped-ant
  pe-dan-tic
  pe-dan-ti-cal-ly
  ped-ant-ry
ped-dle
ped-es-tal
pe-des-tri-an
  pe-des-tri-an-ism
pe-di-at-ric
  pe-di-at-rics
pe-di-a-tri-cian
  pe-di-at-rist
ped-i-cure
  ped-i-cur-ist
ped-i-gree
  ped-i-greed
ped-i-ment
  ped-i-men-tal
  ped-i-ment-ed
pe-dom-e-ter
peep-hole
peer
peer-less
  peer-less-ly
peeve
  peeved
peev-ing
pee-vish
  pee-vish-ly
pee-wee
pe-jo-ra-tive
  pe-jo-ra-tive-ly
pe-koe
pel-let
pell--mell
pel-lu-cid
  pel-lu-cid-i-ty
  pel-lu-cid-ly
pelt-er
  pelt-ry
pel-vis
  pel-vis-es
  pel-ves

pel-vic
pem-mi-can
  pem-i-can
pe-nal
pe-nal-ize
  pe-nal-ized
  pe-nal-iz-ing
pen-al-ty
  pen-al-ties
pen-ance
pen-chant
pen-cil
pend-ant
pend-ent
  pend-en-cy
  pend-ent-ly
pend-ing
pen-du-lous
  pen-du-lous-ly
pen-du-lum
pen-a-tra-ble
  pen-a-tra-bil-i-ty
  pen-a-tra-bly
pen-e-trate
  pen-e-trat-ed
  pen-e-trat-ing
pen-e-tra-tion
pen-i-cil-lin
pen-in-su-la
  pen-in-su-lar
pe-nis
pen-i-tent
  pen-i-tence
  pen-i-ten-tial
pen-i-ten-tia-ry
  pen-i-ten-tia-ries
pen-knife
  pen-knives
pen-man-ship
pen-nant
pen-ni-less
pen-non
pen-ny
  pen-nies
pen-ny an-te
pe-nol-o-gy
  pe-no-log-i-cal
  pe-nol-o-gist
pen-sion
pen-sive
  pen-sive-ly
pen-ta-gon
  pen-tag-o-nal
  pen-tag-o-nal-ly
pen-tam-e-ter
pen-tath-lon

pent-up
pe-nult
  pe-nul-ti-ma
  pe-nul-ti-mate
pe-num-bra
  pe-num-bras
  pe-num-brae
  pe-num-bral
pe-nu-ri-ous
  pe-nu-ri-ous-ly
pen-u-ry
pe-on
  pe-on-age
pe-o-ny
  pe-on-ies
peo-ple
pep
  pepped
  pep-ping
pep-per
pep-pery
pep-py
  pep-pi-er
  pep-pi-est
pep-sin
pep-tic
per-am-bu-late
per-am-bu-la-tor
per an-num
per-cale
per cap-i-ta
per-ceive
  per-ceived
  per-ceiv-ing
  per-ceiv-a-ble
per-cent
  per-cent-age
per-cen-tile
per-cep-ti-ble
  per-cep-ti-bil-i-ty
  per-cep-ti-bly
per-cep-tion
  per-cep-tion-al
  per-cep-tu-al
  per-cep-tu-al-ly
perch
per-co-late
  per-co-lat-ed
  per-co-lat-ing
  per-co-la-tion
per-co-la-tor
per-cus-sion
  per-cus-sion-ist
per di-em
per-di-tion
per-e-gri-nate

148

pe-remp-to-ry
 pe-remp-to-ri-ly
pe-ren-ni-al
 pe-ren-ni-al-ly
per-fec-tion
 per-fec-tion-ist
per-fect-ly
per-fi-dy
 per-fid-i-ous
 per-fid-i-ous-ly
per-fo-rate
 per-fo-rat-ed
per-force
per-form
 per-form-a-ble
 per-form-er
per-for-mance
per-fume
 per-fumed
per-func-to-ry
 per-func-to-ri-ly
per-haps
per-i-gee
 per-i-ge-al
 per-i-ge-an
peri-he-li-on
 peri-he-lia
per-il
 per-il-ous
 per-il-ous-ly
pe-rim-e-ter
 per-i-met-ic
 per-i-met-ri-cal
pe-ri-od
pe-ri-od-ic
 pe-ri-o-dic-i-ty
pe-ri-od-i-cal
 pe-ri-od-i-cal-ly
pe-riph-ery
 pe-riph-er-ies
 pe-riph-er-al
 pe-riph-er-al-ly
per-i-phrase
peri-scope
 peri-scopic
 peri-scop-i-cal
per-ish
per-ish-able
 per-ish-abil-i-ty
 per-ish-ably
peri-stal-sis
 peri-stal-ses
 peri-style
peri-to-ne-um
 peri-to-ne-ums
 peri-to-nea

 peri-to-ne-al
peri-to-ni-tis
peri-wig
peri-win-kle
per-jure
 per-jured
 per-jur-ing
 per-jur-er
per-ju-ry
 per-ju-ries
perky
 perk-i-er
 perk-i-est
per-ma-nent
per-me-able
 per-me-abil-i-ty
 per-me-ably
per-me-ate
 per-me-at-ed
 per-me-at-ing
 per-me-a-tion
 per-me-a-tive
per-mis-si-ble
 per-mis-si-bil-i-ty
 per-mis-si-bly
per-mis-sion
per-mis-sive
 per-mis-sive-ly
per-mit
 per-mit-ted
 per-mit-ting
 per-mit-ter
per-mu-ta-tion
per-ni-cious
 per-ni-cious-ly
per-ora-tion
per-ox-ide
 per-ox-id-ed
 per-ox-id-ing
per-pen-dic-u-lar
 per-pen-dic-u-lar-i-ty
 per-pen-dic-u-lar-ly
per-pe-trate
 per-pe-trat-ed
 per-pe-trat-ing
 per-pe-tra-tion
 per-pe-tra-tor
per-pet-u-al
 per-pet-u-al-ly
per-pet-u-ate
 per-pet-u-at-ed
 per-pet-u-at-ing
 per-pet-u-a-tion
 per-pet-ua-tor
per-pe-tu-ity
 per-pe-tu-ities

per-plex
 per-plexed
 per-plex-ing
 per-plex-ing-ly
 per-plex-ed-ly
 per-plex-i-ty
 per-plex-i-ties
per-qui-site
per-se-cute
 per-se-cut-ed
 per-se-cut-ing
 per-se-cu-tive
 per-se-cu-tor
 per-se-cu-tion
per-se-vere
 per-se-vered
 per-se-ver-ing
 per-sse-ver-ance
 per-se-ver-ing-ly
per-si-flage
per-sim-mon
per-sist
 per-sist-ence
 per-sis-ten-cy
per-sist-ent
 per-sist-ent-ly
per-snick-e-ty
per-son
per-son-able
per-son-age
per-son-al-i-ty
 per-son-al-i-ties
per-son-al-ize
 per-son-al-ized
 per-son-al-iz-ing
per-son-al-ly
per-so-na non gra-ta
per-son-ate
 per-son-at-ed
 per-son-at-ing
 per-son-a-tion
 per-son-a-tor
per-son-i-fy
 per-son-i-fied
 per-son-i-fy-ing
 per-son-i-fi-ca-tion
 per-son-i-fi-er
per-son-nel
per-spec-tive
 per-spec-tive-ly
per-spi-ca-cious
 per-spi-ca-cious-ly
 per-spi-cac-i-ty
per-spi-cu-i-ty
 per-spic-u-ous
 per-spic-u-ous-ly

per-spi-ra-tion
per-spire
  per-spired
  per-spiring
per-suade
  per-suad-ed
  per-suad-ing
  per-suad-a-ble
  per-suad-er
per-sua-sion
per-sua-sive
  per-sua-sive-ly
  per-sua-sive-ness
pert
  pert-ly
  pert-ness
per-tain
per-ti-na-cious
  per-ti-na-cious-ly
  per-ti-nac-i-ty
per-ti-nent
  per-ti-nence
  per-ti-nen-cy
  per-ti-nent-ly
per-turb
  per-turb-a-ble
  per-tur-ba-tion
pe-ruke
pe-ruse
  pe-rused
  pe-rus-ing
  pe-rus-al
  pe-rus-er
per-vade
  per-vad-ed
  per-vad-ing
  per-vad-er
  per-va-sion
  per-va-sive
  per-va-sive-ly
per-verse
  per-verse-ly
  per-verse-ness
  per-ver-si-ty
per-ver-sion
per-vert
  per-vert-ed
  per-vert-ed-ly
  per-vert-er
  per-vert-i-ble
per-vi-ous
  per-vi-ous-ness
pes-ky
  pes-ki-er
  pes-ki-est
  pesk-i-ly

pes-si-mism
  pes-si-mist
  pes-si-mist
  pes-si-mis-tic
  pes-si-mis-ti-cal-ly
pes-ter
pest-hole
pest-i-cide
pes-tif-er-ous
  pes-tif-er-ous-ly
per-ti-lence
  pes-ti-len-tial
pes-ti-lent
  pes-ti-lent-ly
pes-tle
  pes-tled
  pes-tling
pet
  pet-ted
  pet-ting
  pet-ter
pet-al
  pet-aled
  pet-cock
pe-ter
pet-i-ole
pe-tite
  pe-tite-ness
pet-it four
pe-ti-tion
  pe-ti-tion-ary
  pe-ti-tion-er
pe-trel
pet-ri-fy
  pet-ri-fied
  pet-ri-fy-ing
  pe-tri-fac-tion
pe-tro-chem-is-try
  pe-tro-chem-i-cal
pet-rol
pet-ro-la-tum
pe-trol-leum
pet-ti-coat
pet-ti-fog
  pet-ti-fogged
  pet-ti-fog-ging
  pet-ti-fog-ger
  pet-ti-fog-gery
pet-tish
  pet-tish-ly
  pet-tish-ness
pet-ty
pet-ti-er
  pet-ti-est
  pet-ti-ly
  pet-ti-ness

pet-u-lant
  pet-u-lance
  pet-u-lan-cy
  pet-u-lant-ly
pe-tu-nia
pew-ter
pey-o-te
  pey-o-tes
pha-lanx
  pha-lanx-es
  pha-lang-es
pal-lus
  pal-li
  pahl-lus-es
  phal-lic
phan-tasm
  phan-tas-ma
  phan-tas-mal
  phan-tas-mic
phan-tas-ma-go-ria
  phan-tas-ma-go-ri-al
  phan-tas-ma-gor-ic
phan-ta-sy
  phan-ta-sies
phan-tom
phar-aoh
phar-ma-ceu-ti-cal
  phar-ma-cue-tic
  phar-ma-ceu-ti-cal-ly
phar-ma-cue-tics
phar-ma-cist
phar-ma-col-o-gy
  phar-ma-co-log-ic
  phar-ma-co-log-i-ca
  phar-ma-col-o-gist
phar-ma-co-poe-ia
  phar-ma-co-poe-ial
phar-ma-cy
  phar-ma-cies
phar-ynx
  pha-ryn-ges
  pha-ryn-ge-al
  pha-ryn-gal
phase
  phased
  phas-ing
  pha-sic
pheas-ant
phe-no-bar-bi-tal
phe-nol
  phe-nol-ic
phe-nom-e-non
  phe-nom-e-na
  phe-nom-e-nons
  phe-nom-e-nal
  phe-nom-e-nal-ly

phi-al
phi-lan-der
  phi-lan-der-er
phi-lan-thro-py
  phi-lan-thro-pies
  phil-an-throp-ic
  phil-an-throp-i-cal
  phi-lan-thro-pist
phi-late-ly
  phil-a-tel-ic
  phil-a-tel-i-cal
  phil-lat-e-list
phil-har-mon-ic
phil-o-den-dron
  phil-o-den-drons
  phil-o-den-dra
phi-log-o-gy
  phi-lol-o-gist
  phi-lol-o-ger
  phil-o-lo-gi-an
  phil-o-log-i-cal
  phil-o-log-ic
  phil-o-log-i-cal-ly
phi-los-o-pher
phil-o-soph-i-cal
  phil-o-soph-ic
  phil-o-soph-i-cal-ly
phi-los-o-phize
  phi-los-o-phized
  phi-los-o-phiz-ing
  phi-los-o-phiz-er
phi-los-o-phy
  phi-los-o-phies
phil-ter
  phil-tered
  phil-ter-ing
phle-bi-tis
  phle-bit-ic
phle-bot-o-my
  phle-bot-o-mist
phlegm
phleg-mat-ic
  phleg-mat-i-cal
  phleg-mat-i-cal-ly
phlox
pho-bia
  pho-bic
phoe-be
phoe-nix
phone
  phoned
  phon-ing
pho-neme
  pho-ne-mic
pho-net-ic
  pho-net-ics

pho-net-i-cal
  pho-net-i-cal-ly
phon-ic
phon-ics
pho-no-graph
  pho-no-graph-ic
  pho-no-graph-i-cal-ly
pho-nol-o-gy
  pho-nol-o-gies
  pho-no-log-ic
  pho-no-log-i-cal
  pho-no-log-i-cal-ly
  pho-nol-o-gist
pho-ny
  pho-ni-er
  pho-ni-est
  pho-nies
  pho-ni-ness
phos-phate
phos-pho-res-cence
  phos-pho-resce
  phos-pho-resced
  phos-pho-resc-ing
  phos-pho-res-cent
  phos-pho-res-cent-ly
phos-pho-rus
pho-to
  pho-tos
pho-to-copy
  pho-to-cop-ies
  pho-to-cop-ied
  pho-to-cop-y-ing
pho-to-e-lec-tric
pho-to-en-grav-ing
  pho-to-en-grave
  pho-to-en-graved
  pho-to-en-grav-er
pho-to-flash
pho-to-gen-ic
pho-to-graph
  pho-to-graph-er
pho-tog-ra-phy
  pho-to-graph-ic
  pho-to-graph-i-cal
  pho-to-graph-i-cal-ly
pho-to-gra-vure
pho-to--off-set
pho-to-stat
  pho-to-stat-ed
  pho-to-stat-ing
  pho-to-stat-ic
pho-to-syn-the-sis
phrase
  phrased
  phras-ing
  phras-al

phrase-ol-o-gy
phre-net-ic
phre-nol-o-gy
  phre-nol-o-gist
phy-lac-tery
  phy-lac-ter-ies
phy-log-e-ny
  phy-lo-gen-e-sis
  phy-lo-ge-net-ic
  phy-log-en-ic
  phy-log-e-nist
phy-lu
phys-ic
  phys-icked
  phys-ick-ing
phys-i-cal
  phys-i-cal-ly
phy-si-cian
phys-ics
  phys-i-cist
phys-i-og-no-my
  phys-i-og-no-mies
  phys-i-og-nom-ic
  phys-i-og-nom-i-cal
  phys-i-og-no-mist
phys-i-og-ra-phy
  phys-i-o-graph-ic
  phys-i-o-graph-i-cal
phys-i-ol-o-gy
  phys-i-o-log-ic
  phys-i-o-log-i-cal
  phys-i-o-log-i-cal-ly
  phys-i-ol-o-gist
phys-i-o-ther-a-py
phy-sique
pi-a-nis-si-mo
pi-an-ist
pi-ano
  pia-nos
pi-ano-forte
pi-az-za
pi-ca
pic-a-dor
pic-a-resque
pic-a-yune
  pic-a-yun-ish
pic-ca-lil-li
pic-co-lo
  pic-co-los
  pic-co-lo-list
pick-ax
picked
pick-er-el
pick-et
  pick-et-er
pick-ing

pick-le
  pick-led
  pick-ling
pick-pock-et
pick-up
picky
  pick-i-er
  pick-i-est
pic-nic
  pic-nicked
  pic-nick-ing
  pic-nick-er
pic-to-ri-al
  pic-to-ri-al-ly
pic-ture
  pic-tured
  pic-tur-ing
pic-tur-esque
  pic-tur-esque-ly
pid-dle
  pid-dled
  pid-dling
pid-gin
pie-bald
piece
  piec-er
piece-meal
piece-work
  piece-worker
pied
pier
pierce
  pierc-ed
  pierc-ing
pierc-ing-ly
pi-etism
  pi-etis-tic
  pi-etis-ti-cal
pi-ety
  pi-eties
pif-fle
pig
  pigged
  pig-ging
pi-geon
pe-geon-hole
  pi-geon-holed
  pi-geon-hol-ing
pi-geon--toed
pig-gish
  pig-ish-ly
  pig-gis-ness
pig-head-ed
  pig-head-ed-ly
  pig-head-ed-ness
pig-ment

pig-men-tary
pig-men-ta-tion
pig-pen
pig-skin
pig-sty
  pig-sties
pig-tail
pike
  piked
  pik-ing
pik-er
pi-las-ter
pil-chard
pile
  piled
  pil-ing
pil-fer
  pil-fer-age
  pil-fer-er
pil-grim
pil-grim-age
  pil-grim-aged
  pil-grim-ag-ing
pil-lage
  pil-laged
  pil-lag-ing
  pil-lag-er
pil-lar
pill-box
pil-lion
pil-lo-ry
  pil-lo-ries
  pil-lo-ry-ing
pil-low
pil-low-case
pi-lot
  pi-lot-age
  pi-lot-less
pi-lot-house
pi-men-to
  pi-men-tos
pim-ple
  pim-pled
  pim-p/y
pin
  pinned
  pin-ning
pin-afore
pince-nez
pin-cers
pinch
  pinch-er
pinch-beck
pin-cush-ion
pin-dling
pine

pine-like
piney
  pin-ing
pi-ne-al
pine-ap-ple
pin-feath-er
  pin-feath-ered
  pin-feath-ery
pin-fold
pin-head
  pin-head-ed
pin-hole
pin-ion
pink-eye
pink-ie
pinko
  pink-os
  pink-oes
pin-na
  pin-nas
  pin-nae
  pin-nal
pin-na-cle
  pin-na-cled
  pin-na-cling
pi-nate
  pin-nate-ly
  pin-na-tion
pi-noch-le
  pi-noc-le
pin-point
pin-prick
pin-set-ter
pin-tail
  pin-tailed
pin-tle
pin-to
  pin-tos
pin-up
pin-wheel
pin-worm
pi-o-neer
pi-ous
  pi-ous-ly
  pi-ous-ness
pip
  pipped
  pip-ping
pipe-line
  pipe-lined
  pipe-lin-ing
pip-er
pip-ing
pip-it
pip-pin
pip-squek

pi-quant
pi-quan-cy
pi-quant-ly
pique
piqued
pi-quing
pi-ra-cy
pi-ra-cies
pi-ra-nha
pi-rate
pi-rat-ed
pi-rat-ing
pi-rat-i-cal
pi-rat-i-cal-ly
pi-roque
pir-ou-ette
pir-ou-et-ted
pir-ou-et-ting
pi-sci-cul-ture
pis-ta-chio
pis-ta-chi-os
pis-til
pis-til-late
pis-tol
pis-toled
pis-tol-ing
pis-ton
pit
pit-ted
pit-ting
pitch--blake
pitch-blend
pitch-er
pitch-fork
pitchy
pitch-i-er
pitch-i-est
pit-e-ous
pit-e-ous-ly
pit-fall
pith
pith-i-er
pith-i-est
pith-i-ly
piti-a-ble
piti-anle-ness
piti-a-bly
piti-ful
piti-ful-ly
piti-ful-ness
piti-less
piti-less-ly
pit-man
pit-men
pit-tance
pi-tu--tar-ies

pity
pit-ies
pit-ied
pit-y-ing
pit-y-ing-ly
piv-ot
piv-ot-al
piv-ot-al-ly
pix-i-lat-ed
pixy
pix-ie
pix-ies
piz-za
piz-ze-ria
piz-zi-ca-to
place-a-ble
plac-a-bil-i-ty
plac-a-bly
plac-ard
pla-cate
pla-cat-ed
pla-cat-ing
pla-ca-tion
pla-ca-tive
pla-ca-to-ry
place
placed
plac-ing
pla-ce-bo
pla-ce-bos
pla-ce-boes
place-ment
pla-cen-ta
pla-cen-tas
pla-cen-tae
pla-cen-tal
plac-er
plac-id
pla-cid-i-ty
plac-id-ness
pla-gal
pla-gia-rism
pla-gia-rized
pla-gia-riz-ing
pla-gia-riz-er
pla-gia-ry
pla-gia-ries
plaque
plaqued
pla-quing
pla-quer
pla-guy
pla-guey
pla-gui-ly
plaid
plain

plain-ly
plain-ness
plain-song
plain-spo-ken
plain-tiff
plain-tive
plain-tive-ly
plait
plait-ing
plan
planned
plan-ning
plan-less
plan-ner
plane
planed
plan-ing
plan-er
plan-et
plan-e-tar-i-um
plan-e-tar-i-ums
plan-e-tar-ia
plan-e-tary
plan-e-toid
plan-ish
plan-ish-er
plank-ing
plank-ton
plank-ton-ic
plant
plant-able
plant-like
plan-tain
plan-ta-tion
plant-er
plaque
plasm
plas-ma
plas-mic
plas-mat-ic
plas-ter
plas-ter-er
plas-ter-ing
plas-ter-work
plas-ter-board
plas-tered
plas-tic
plas-ti-cal-ly
plas-tic-i-ty
plas-ti-ciz-er
plat
plat-ted
plat-ting
plate
plat-ed
plat-ing

plat-er
pla-teau
  pla-teaus
  pla-teaux
plate-ful
  plate-fuls
plate-let
plat-form
plat-i-num
plat-i-tude
  plat-i-tu-di-nal
  plat-i-tu-di-nous
plat-i-tu-di-nize
  plat-i-tu-di-nized
  plat-i-tu-di-niz-ing
pla-ton-ic
  pla-ton-i-cal-ly
pla-toon
plat-ter
platy-pus
  platy-pus-es
  platy-pi
plau-dut
plau-si-ble
  plau-si-bil-i-ty
  plau-si-bly
play-act
  play-act-ing
play-back
play-bill
play-boy
play-er
play-ful
  play-ful-ly
  play-ful-ness
play-go-er
play-ground
play-house
  play-hous-es
play-let
play-mate
play--off
play-pen
play-thing
play-time
play-wright
pla-za
plea
plead
  plead-ed
  plead-ing
  plead-a-ble
  plead-er
pleas-ant
  pleas-ant-ly
  pleas-ant-ness

pleas-ant-ry
  pleas-an-trioes
please
  pleased
  pleas-ing
  pleas-ing-ly
  pleas-ing-ness
plea-sur-a-ble
  plea-sur-able-ness
  plea-sur-ably
pleas-ure
pleat
  pleat-ed
  pleat-er
plebe
ple-be-ian
pleb-i-scite
pledge
  pledged
  pledg-ing
  pledg-ee
  pledg-er
ple-na-ry
pleni-po-ten-tia-ry
  pleni-po-ten-tia-ries
plen-i-tude
plen-te-ous
  plen-te-ous-ly
plen-ti-ful
  plen-ti-ful-ly
plen-ty
pleth-o-ra
  ple-thor-ic
pleu-ra
  pleu-rae
  pleu-ral
pleu-ri-sy
  pleu-rit-ic
plex-us
  plex-us-es
pli-able
  pli-a-bil-i-ty
  pli-a-ble-ness
  pli-a-bly
pli-ant
  pli-an-cy
  pli-ant-ness
  pli-ant-ly
pli-ca-tion
pli-ers
plight
plink
plod
  plod-ded
  plod-ding
  plod-der

plop
  plopped
  plop-ping
plot
  plot-ted
  plot-ting
  plot-ter
plow
  plow-a-ble
  plow-er
  plow-man
plow-share
pluck
  pluck-er
plucky
  pluck-i-er
  pluck-i-est
  pluck-i-ly
  pluck-i-ness
plug
  plugged
  plug-ging
  plug-ger
plum-age
plumb-er
plumb-ing
plume
  plumed
  plum-ing
  plume-like
  plumy
  plum-i-er
  plum-i-est
plum-met
plump
  plump-er
  plump-ly
  plump-ness
plun-der
  plun-der-er
  plun-der-ous
plunge
  plunged
  plung-ing
plung-er
plunk-er
plu-ral
  plu-ral-ly
  plu-ral-ize
  plu-ral-ized
  plu-ral-iz-ing
plu-ral-ism
  plu-ral-ist
  plu-ral-is-tic
plu-ral-i-ty
  plu-ral-i-ties

plush
  plush-i-ness
  plushy
  plush-i-er
  plush-i-est
plu-toc-ra-cy
  plu-tac-ra-cies
  plu-ta-crat
  plu-to-cart-ic
plu-to-ni-um
plu-vi-al
ply
  plied
  ply-ing
ply-wood
pneu-mat-ic
  pneu-mat-i-cal-ly
pneu-mat-ics
pneu-mo-nia
pneu-mon-is
poach
  poach-er
pock-et
pock-et-book
pock-et-ful
pock-et-knife
  pock-et-knives
pock-mark
  pock-marked
pod
  pod-ded
  pod-ding
  pod-like
podgy
  podg-i-er
  podg-i-est
po-di-trist
  po-di-a-try
po-di-um
  po-dia
  po-di-ums
po-esy
  po-esies
po-et
  po-et-ess
po-et-ize
  po-et-ized
  po-et-iz-ing
  po-et-iz-er
po-et lau-re-ate
  po-ets lau-re-ate
po-et-ry
po-go
po-grom
poi-gnant
  poi-gnan-cy

poi-gnant-ly
poin-set-tia
point--blank
point-ed
  point-ed-ly
  point-ed-ness
point-er
poin-til-lism
  poin-til-list
point-less
poise
  poised
  pois-ing
poi-son
  poi-son-er
  poi-son-ing
  poi-son-ous
poi-son--pen
poke
  poked
  pok-ing
pok-er
poky
  pok-i-er
  pok-i-est
  pok-i-ly
  pok-i-ness
po-lar
po-lar-i-ty
  po-lar-i-ties
  po-lar-i-za-tion
po-lar-ize
  po-lar-ized
  po-lar-iz-ing
  po-lar-iz-a-ble
  po-lar-iz-er
pole
  poled
  pol-ing
  pole-less
pole-cat
po-lem-ic
  po-lem-i-cal
  po-lem-i-cal-ly
  po-lem-i-cist
po-lem-ics
pole-star
po-lice
  po-liced
  po-lic-ing
pol-i-cy
  pol-i-cies
pol-i-o-my-e-li-tis
pol-ish
  pol-ish-er
po-lite

po-lite-ly
po-lite-ness
pol-i-tic
po-lit-i-cal
  po-lit-i-cal-ly
pol-i-ti-cian
po-lit-i-cize
  po-lit-i-cized
  po-lit-i-ciz-ing
pol-i-tick
  pol-i-tick-er
pol-i-tics
pol-i-ty
  pol-i-ties
pol-ka
  pol-kaed
  pol-ka-ing
poll
  poll-ee
  poll-er
pol-len
pol-li-nate
  pol-li-nat-ed
  pol-li-nat-ing
  pol-li-na-tion
  pol-li-na-tor
pol-li-wog
poll-ster
pol-lu-tant
pol-lute
  pol-lut-ed
  pol-lut-ing
  pol-lu-ter
  pol-lu-tion
po-lo
  po-lo-ist
pol-o-naise
po-lo-ni-um
pol-ter-geist
poly-an-dry
  poly-an-drous
poly-chro-mat-ic
poly-chrome
poly-es-ter
poly-eth-yl-ene
polyg-a-mist
polyg-a-my
  polyg-a-mous
poly-glot
poly-gon
  polyg-o-nal
  polyg-o-nal-ly
poly-graph
  poly-graph-ic
po-lyg-y-ny
  po-lyg-y-nous

155

poly-he-dron
  poly-he-drons
  poly-he-dra
  poly-he-dral
poly-mer
po-ly-mer-ize
  po-ly-mer-ized
  po-ly-mer-iz-ing
  po-lym-er-ism
  po-lym-er-i-za-tion
pol-y-mor-phism
  pol-y-mor-phic
  pol-y-mor-phous
poly-no-mi-al
pol-yp
poly-phon-ic
  po-lyph-ony
poly-sty-rene
poly-syl-lab-ic
  poly-syl-lab-i-cal-ly
poly-syl-la-ble
poly-tech-nic
poly-the-ism
  poly-the-ist
  poly-the-is-tic
  poly-the-is-ti-cal
poly-un-sat-u-rat-ed
pom-ace
po-made
  po-mad-ed
  po-mad-ing
pome-gran-ate
pom-mel
  pom-meled
  pom-mel-ing
pom-pa-dour
pom-pon
pomp-ous
  pom-pos-i-ty
  pom-pous-ly
pon-cho
pon-der
  pon-der-a-ble
  pon-der-er
pon-der-ous
  pon-der-ous-ly
  pon-der-ou-ness
pon-iard
pon-tiff
pon-tif-i-cal
  pon-tif-i-cal-ly
pon-tif-i-cate
  pon-tif-i-cat-ed
  pon-tif-i-cat-ing
pon-toon
po-ny

po-nies
po-nied
po-ny-ing
po-ny-tail
poo-dle
pool-room
poor
  poor-ish
  poor-ly
pop-corn
pop-ery
  pop-ish
pop-eyed
pop-gun
pop-in-jay
pop-lar
pop-lin
pop-per
pop-py
  pop-pies
  pop-pied
pop-py-cock
pop-u-lace
pop-u-lar
  pop-u-lar-ly
  pop-u-lar-i-ty
  pop-u-lar-ize
  pop-u-lar-ized
  pop-u-lar-iz-ing
  pop-u-lar-i-za-tion
  pop-u-lar-iz-er
pop-u-late
  pop-u-lat-ed
  pop-u-lat-ing
pop-u-la-tion
pop-u-lism
  pop-u-list
pop-u-lous
  pop-u-lous-ly
por-ce-lain
por-cine
por-cu-pine
pore
  pored
  por-ing
pork-er
por-nog-ra-phy
  por-nog-ra-pher
  por-no-graph-ic
  por-no-graph-i-cal-ly
po-rous
  po-rous-i-ty
  po-rous-ly
  po-rous-ness
por-poise
  por-pios-es

por-ridge
port-a-ble
  port-a-bil-i-ty
  port-a-bly
por-tage
  por-taged
  por-tag-ing
por-tal
por-tend
por-tent
  por-ten-tous
por-ter
por-ter-house
port-fo-lio
  port-fo-lios
port-hole
por-ti-co
  por-ti-coes
  por-ti-cos
por-tion
  por-tion-less
port-ly
  port-li-er
  port-li-est
por-trait
  por-trat-ist
por-trai-ture
por-tray
  por-tray-er
  por-tray-al
pose
  posed
  pos-ing
pos-er
po-suer
pos-it
po-si-tion
  po-si-tion-al
  po-si-tion-er
pos-i-tive
  pos-i-tive-ly
  pos-i-tive-ness
pos-i-tiv-ism
pos-i-tron
pos-se
pos-sess
  pos-ses-sor
pos-sessed
pos-ses-sion
pos-ses-sive
  pos-ses-sive-ly
  pos-ses-sive-ness
pos-si-bil-i-ty
pos-si-ble
pos-si-bly
pos-sum

post-age
post-box
post-date
 post-dat-ed
 post-dat-ing
post-er
pos-te-ri-or
 pos-te-ri-or-i-ty
pos-ter-i-ty
post-grad-u-ate
post-haste
post-hu-mous
 post-hu-mous-ly
post-lude
post-man
 post-men
post-mark
post-mas-ter
 post-mis-tress
post me-ri-di-em
post-mor-tem
post-na-sal
post-na-tal
 post-na-tal-ly
post-paid
post-par-tum
post-pone
 post-poned
 post-pon-ing
 post-pon-a-ble
 post-pone-ment
 post-pon-er
post-scipt
pos-tu-lant
pos-tu-late
 pos-tu-lat-ed
 pos-tu-lat-ing
 pos-tu-la-tion
 pos-tu-la-tor
pos-ture
 pos-tured
 pos-tur-ing
 pos-tur-al
 pos-tur-er
post-war
po-sy
 po-sies
pot
 pot-ted
 pot-ting
po-ta-ble
pot-ash
po-tas-si-um
po-ta-to
 po-ta-toes
pot-bel-ly

pot-bel-lied
pot-boil-er
po-tent
 po-ten-cy
 po-tent-ly
po-ten-tate
po-ten-tial
 po-ten-ti-al-i-ty
 po-ten-tial-ly
pot-hole
po-tion
pot-luck
pot-pour-ri
pot-sherd
pot-tage
pot-ter
pot-tery
 pot-ter-ies
pot-ty
 pot-ties
pot-ty--chair
pouch
 pouched
 pouchy
 pouch-i-er
 pouch-i-est
poul-tice
 poul-ticed
 poul-tic-ing
poul-try
pounce
 pounced
 pounc-ing
pound-age
pound--fool-ish
pour
 pour-a-ble
 pour-er
pout
pov-er-ty
pov-er-ty--strick-en
pow-der
 pow-dery
pow-er
pow-er-boat
pow-er-ful
 pow-er-ful-ly
 pow-er-ful-ness
pow-er-house
pow-er-less
Pow-ha-tan
pow-wow
prac-ti-ca-ble
 prac-ti-ca-bil-i-ty
 prac-ti-ca-bly
prac-ti-cal

prac-ti-cal-i-ty
prac-ti-cal-ly
prac-tice
prac-ti-tio-ner
prae-di-al
 pre-di-al
prag-mat-ic
 prag-mat-i-cal
 prag-mat-i-cal-ly
prag-ma-tism
 prag-ma-tist
 prag-ma-tis-tic
prai-rie
praise
 praised
 prais-ing
 prais-er
praise-wor-thy
 praise-wor-thi-ly
 praise-wor-thi-ness
pra-line
prance
 pranced
 pranc-ing
 pranc-er
prank
 prank-ish
 prank-ster
prate
 prat-ed
 prat-ing
 prat-er
 prat-ing-ly
prat-fall
prat-tle
 prat-tled
 prat-tling
 prat-tler
 prat-tling-ly
prawn
 prawn-er
pray-er
 pray-er-ful
preach
 prach-er
preach-ify
 preach-ified
 preach-ify-ing
preach-ment
preachy
 preach-i-er
 preach-i-est
pre-ad-o-les-cence
 pre-ad-o-les-cent
pre-am-ble
pre-ar-range

pre-ar-ranged
pre-ar-rang-ing
pre-ar-range-ment
pre-as-signed
pre-can-cel
pre-can-celed
pre-can-cel-ing
pre-can-cel-la-tion
pre-car-i-ous
pre-car-i-ous-ly
pre-car-i-ous-ness
pre-cau-tion
pre-cau-tion-ary
pre-cede
pre-ced-ed
pre-ced-ing
prec-e-dence
prec-e-dent
pre-cept
pre-cep-tive
pre-cep-tor
pre-cep-to-ri-al
pre-ces-sion
pre-ces-sion-al
pre-cinct
pre-cious
pre-ci-os-i-ty
pre-cious-ness
prec-i-pice
pre-cip-i-tous
pre-cip-i-tant
pre-cip-i-tant-ly
pre-cip-i-tate
pre-cip-i-tat-ed
pre-cip-i-tat-ing
pre-cip-i-ta-tive
pre-cip-i-ta-tor
pre-cip-i-ta-tion
pre-cip-i-tous
pre-cip-i-tous-ly
pre-cise
pre-cise-ness
pre-ci-sion
pre-ci-sion-ist
pre-clude
pre-clud-ed
pre-clud-ing
pre-clu-sion
pre-clu-sive
pre-co-cious
pre-coc-cious-ly
pre-coc-cious-ness
pre-coc-i-ty
pre-cog-ni-tion
pre-cog-ni-tive
pre-con-ceive

pre-con-ciev-ed
pre-con-ceiv-ing
pre-con-cep-tion
pre-cook
pre-cur-sor
pre-cur-so-ry
pre-date
pred-a-tor
pred-a-to-ry
pred-a-to-ri-ly
pre-dawn
pre-de-ces-sor
pre-des-ti-nate
pre-des-ti-nat-ed
pre-des-ti-nat-ing
pre-des-ti-na-tion
pre-des-tine
pre-des-tined
pre-des-tin-ing
pre-de-ter-mine
pre-de-ter-mined
pre-de-ter-min-ing
pre-de-ter-mi-na-tion
pred-i-ca-ble
pred-i-ca-bil-i-ty
pre-dic-a-ment
pred-i-cate
pred-i-cat-ed
pred-i-cat-ing
pred-i-ca-tion
pred-i-ca-tive
pre-dict
pre-dict-a-ble
pre-dict-a-bly
pre-dict-a-bil-i-ty
pre-dic-tion
pre-dic-tive
pre-di-lec-tion
pre-dis-po-si-tion
pre-dis-pose
pre-dis-posed
pre-dis-pos-ing
pre-dom-i-nant
pre-dom-i-nance
pre-dom-i-nan-cy
pre-dom-i-nate
pre-dom-i-nat-ed
pre-dom-i-nat-ing
pre-dom-i-na-tion
pre-em-i-nent
pre-em-i-nence
pre-empt
pre-emp-tor
pre-emp-tion
pre-emp-tive
preen-er

pre-ex-ist
pre-ex-ist-ence
pre-ex-ist-ent
pre-fab-ri-cate
pre-fab-ri-cat-ed
pre-fab-ri-cat-ing
pre-fab-ri-a-tion
pref-ace
pref-aced
pref-ac-ing
pref-a-to-ry
pre-fer
pre-ferred
pre-fer-ring
pre-fer-rer
pref-er-a-ble
pre-fer-a-bil-i-ty
pref-er-a-bly
pref-er-ence
pref-er-en-tial
pref-er-en-tial-ly
pre-fer-ment
pre-fix
pre-flight
pre-form
preg-n-able
preg-na-bil-i-ty
preg-nan-cy
preg-nan-cies
preg-nant
pre-heat
pre-hen-sile
pre-hen-sil-i-ty
pre-his-tor-ic
pre-his-to-ry
pre-judge
pre-judged
pre-judg-ing
pre-judg-er
pre-judge-ment
prej-u-dice
prej-u-diced
prej-u-dic-ing
prej-u-di-cial
prej-u-di-cial-ly
prel-ate
prel-ate-ship
prel-a-ture
pre-lim-i-nar-y
pre-lim-i-nar-ies
pre-lim-i-nar-i-ly
prel-ude
prel-uded
prel-ud-ing
pre-ma-ture
pre-na-tu-ri-ty

pre-med-i-cal
pre-med-i-tate
pre-med-i-tat-ed
pre-med-i-tat-ing
pre-med-i-ta-tor
pre-med-i-tat-ed-ly
pre-med-i-ta-tive
pre-med-i-ta-tion
pre-men-stru-al
pre-mier
pre-mier-ship
pre-miere
prem-ise
prem-ised
prem-is-ing
pre-mi-um
pre-mo-ni-tion
pre-mon-i-to-ry
pre-mon-i-to-ri-ly
pre-na-tal
pre-na-tal-ly
pre-oc-cu-pa-tion
pre-oc-cu-py
pre-oc-cu-pied
pre-oc-cu-py-ing
prep-a-ra-tion
pre-par-a-to-ry
pre-par-a-to-ri-ly
pre-pare
pre-pared
pre-par-ing
pre-par-er
pre-par-ed-ness
pre-pay
pre-paid
pre-pay-ing
pre-pay-ment
pre-plan
pre-planned
pre-plan-ning
pre-pon-der-ant
pre-pon-der-ance
pre-pon-der-an-cy
pre-pon-der-ant-ly
pre-pon-der-ate
pre-pon-der-at-ed
pre-pon-der-at-ing
pre-pon-der-at-ing-ly
pre-pon-der-a-tion
prep-o-si-tion
prep-o-si-tion-al
pre-pos-sess
pre-pos-sess-ing
pre-pos-sess-ing-ly
pre-pos-ter-ous
pre-puce

pre-pu-tial
pre-re-cord
pre-re-ui-site
pre-rog-a-tive
pres-age
pres-aged
pres-ag-ing
pres-ag-er
pres-by-ter-y
pres-by-ter-ies
pre-school
pre-scribe
pre-scribed
pre-scrib-ing
pre-scrib-er
pre-script
pre-scrip-tion
pre-scrip-tive
pre-sea-son
pres-ence
pre-sent
pre-sent-er
pres-ent
pre-sent-a-ble
pre-sent-a-bil-i-ty
pre-sent-a-ble-ness
pre-sent-a-bly
pres-en-ta-tion
pres-ent-day
pres-ent-ly
pre-serv-a-tive
per-serve
pre-served
pre-serv-ing
pre-serv-a-ble
pres-er-va-tion
pre-serv-er
pre-side
pre-sid-ed
pre-sid-ing
pre-sid-er
pres-i-den-cy
pres-i-den-cies
pres-i-dent
pres-i-den-tial
press-board
press-ing
pres-sure
pres-sured
pres-sur-ing
pre-su-rize
pres-su-rized
pres-su-riz-ing
pres-su-riz-er
pres-sur-i-za-tion
press-work

pres-ti-dig-i-ta-tion
pres-ti-dig-i-ta-tor
pres-tige
pres-tig-ious
pres-to
pe-sum-a-ble
pre-sum-a-bly
pre-sume
pre-sumed
pre-sum-ing
pre-sum-er
pre-sump-tion
pre-sump-tive
pre-sump-tu-ous
pre-sup-pose
pre-sup-posed
pre-sup-pos-ing
pre-sup-po-si-tion
pre-tend
pre-tend-ed
pre-tend-er
pre-tense
pre-ten-sion
pre-ten-tious
pre-ten-tious-ness
pre-test
pre-text
pret-ti-fy
pret-ti-fied
pret-ti-fy-ing
pret-ti-fi-ca-tion
pret-ty
pret-ties
pret-tied
pret-ty-ing
pret-ti-ly
pret-ti-ness
pret-ty-ish
pret-zel
pre-vail
pre-vail-ing
prev-a-lent
prev-a-lence
pre-vent
pre-vent-a-ble
pre-vent-a-bil-i-ty
pre-vent-er
pre-ven-tion
pre-view
pre-vi-ous
pre-war
prey
prey-er
price-less
prick-er
prick-le

prick-ly
  prick-li-er
  prick-li-est
  prick-li-ness
pride
  prid-ed
  prid-ing
pride-ful
pri-er
priest
  priest-ess
  priest-hood
priest-ly
  priest-li-er
  priest-li-est
priest-li-ness
prig
  prig-gish
prim
  prim-mer
  prim-mest
  primmed
  prim-ming
  prim-ness
pri-ma-cy
  pri-ma-cies
pri-ma don-na
  pri-ma don-nas
pri-mal
pri-ma-ri-ly
pri-ma-ry
  pri-mar-ies
pri-mate
prime
  primed
  prim-ing
prime me-rid-i-an
prim-er
pr-me-val
prim-i-tive
pri-mo-gen-i-tor
pri-mo-gen-i-ture
pri-mor-di-al
  pri-mor-di-al-ly
primp
prim-rose
prince-ly
  prince-li-er
  prince-li-est
prin-cess
prin-ci-pal
  prin-ci-pal-ly
prin-ci-pal-i-ty
  prin-ci-pal-i-ties
prin-ci-ple
prin-ci-pled

print-a-ble
print-ing
print-out
pri-or
  pri-or-ate
pri-or-ess
pri-or-i-ty
  pri-or-i-ties
pri-or-y
  pri-or-ies
prism
  pris-mat-ic
  pris-mat-i-cal-ly
pris-on
pris-on-er
pris-sy
  pris-si-er
  pris-si-est
  pris-si-ly
pris-tine
pri-va-cy
pri-vate
pri-va-tion
priv-et
priv-i-ledge
  priv-i-ledged
  priv-i-leg-ing
priv-y
  priv-ies
  priv-i-ly
prize
  prized
prize-fight
prob-a-bil-i-ty
  prob-a-bil-i-ties
prob-a-ble
  prob-a-bly
pro-bate
  pro-bat-ed
  pro-bat-ing
pro-ba-tion
  pro-ba-tion-al
  pro-ba-tion-ary
pro-na-tion-er
pro-ba-tive
probe
  probed
  prob-ing
  prob-er
prob-lem
prob-lem-at-ic
  pro-lem-at-i-cal
pro-bos-cis
  pro-bos-cis-es
  pro-bos-ci-des
pro-ce-dure

pro-ce-dur-al
  pro-ce-dur-al-ly
pro-ceed
pro-ceed-ing
pro-ceeds
pro-ces-sion
pro-ces-sion-al
pro-claim
  pro-claim-er
proc-la-ma-tion
pro-cliv-i-ty
  pro-cliv-i-ties
pro-cras-ti-nate
  pro-cras-ti-nat-ed
  pro-cras-ti-nat-ing
  pro-cras-ti-na-tion
  pro-cras-ti-na-tor
pro-cre-ate
  pro-cre-at-ed
  pro-cre-at-ing
  pro-cre-a-tion
proc-tor
  proc-to-ri-al
proc-u-ra-tor
  proc-u-ra-to-ri-al
  proc-u-ra-tor-ship
pro-cure
  pro-cured
  pro-cur-ing
  pro-cure-ment
prod
  prod-ded
  prod-ding
  prod-dler
prod-i-gal
  prod-i-gal-i-ty
  prod-i-gal-ly
pro-di-gious
  pro-di-gious-ness
prod-i-gy
  prod-i-gies
pro-duce
  pro-duced
  pro-duc-ing
pro-duc-er
prod-uct
pro-duc-tion
pro-duc-tive
  pro-duc-tive-ness
  pro-duc-tiv-i-ty
pro-fane
  pro-faned
pro-fan-i-ty
pro-fess
  pro-fessed
  pro-fess-ed-ly

pro-fes-sion
pro-fes-sion-al
  pro-fes-sion-al-ism
pro-fes-sion-al-ize
  pro-fes-sion-al-ized
  pro-fes-sion-al-iz-ing
pro-fes-sor
  pro-fes-so-ri-al
  pro-fes-sor-ship
prof-fer
  prof-fer-er
pro-fi-cien-cy
pro-fi-cient
pro-file
  pro-filed
  pro-fil-ing
prof-it
  prof-it-less
prof-it-able
  prof-it-a-bil-i-ty
  prof-it-ably
prof-i-teer
prof-li-gate
  prof-li-ga-cy
pro-found
pro-fun-di-ty
  pro-fun-di-ties
pro-fuse
pro-fu-sion
pro-gen-i-tor
prog-e-ny
  prog-e-nies
pro-ges-ter-one
prog-no-sis
  prog-no-ses
  prog-nos-tic
prog-nos-ti-cate
  prog-nos-ti-cat-ed
  prog-nos-ti-cat-ing
  prog-nos-ti-ca-tion
  prog-nos-ti-ca-tive
  prog-nos-ti-ca-tor
pro-gram
prog-ress
pro-gres-sion
pro-gres-sive
  pro-gres-siv-ism
pro-hib-it
pro-hi-bi-tion
pro-hi-bi-tion-ist
pro-hib-i-tive
pro-ject
pro-jec-tile
pro-jec-tion
pro-jec-tion-ist
pro-jec-tive

pro-jec-tive-ly
pro-jec-tiv-i-ty
pro-jec-tor
pro-le-tar-i-at
  pro-le-tar-i-an
pro-lif-er-ate
  pro-lif-er-at-ed
pro-lif-ic
  pro-lif-i-ca-cy
pro-lix
  pro-lix-i-ty
pro-logue
  pro-logued
  pro-logu-ing
pro-long
  pro-lon-ga-tion
  pro-long-er
prom-e-nade
  prom-e-nad-ed
  prom-e-nad-ing
  prom-e-nad-er
prom-i-nence
prom-i-nent
  prom-i-nent-ly
pro-mis-cu-ity
  pro-mis-cu-i-ties
pro-mis-cu-ous
  pro-mis-cu-ous-ly
prom-ise
  prom-ised
  prom-is-ing
prom-is-so-ry
prom-on-to-ry
  prom-on-to-ries
pro-mote
  pro-mot-ed
  pro-mot-ing
  pro-mot-a-ble
pro-mot-er
pro-mo-tion
  pro-mo-tive
prompt
  prompt-er
  prompt-ly
pro-mul-gate
  pro-mul-gat-ed
  pro-mul-ga-tion
prone
prong
pro-noun
pro-nounce
  pro-nounced
  pro-nounce-ment
pron-to
pro-nun-ci-a-tion
proof

proof-read
prop
pro-pa-gan-da
pro-pa-gate
pro-pa-ga-tion
  pro-pa-ga-tion-al
pro-pane
pro-pel
  pro-pelled
  pro-pel-ling
pro-pel-lant
pro-pel-ler
pro-pen-si-ty
  pro-pen-si-ties
prop-er
proph-e-cy
  proph-e-cies
proph-e-sy
  proph-e-sied
  proph-e-sy-ing
proph-et
pro-phet-ic
  pro-phet-i-cal-ly
pro-phy-lax-is
pro-pin-qui-ty
pro-pi-ti-ate
  pro-pi-ti-at-ed
  pro-pi-ti-a-tion
pro-pi-tious
  pro-pi-tious-ly
pro-po-nent
pro-por-tion
  pro-por-tion-a-ble
  pro-por-tion-a-bly
pro-por-tion-al
  pro-por-tion-al-i-ty
pro-por-tion-ate
  pro-por-tion-at-ed
  pro-por-tion-at-ing
pro-pos-al
pro-pose
  pro-posed
prop-o-si-tion
  prop-o-si-tion-al
pro-pound
  pro-pound-er
pro-pri-e-tary
  pro-pri-e-tar-ies
pro-pri-etor
  pro-pri-e-tor-ship
pro-pri-ety
pro-pul-sion
pro-pul-sive
pro-rate
  pro-rat-ed
pro-sa-ic

pro-sa-i-cal-ly
pro-scribe
  pro-scribed
  pro-scrib-ing
  pro-scrib-er
pro-scrip-tion
  pro-srip-tive
prose
pros-e-cute
  pros-e-cute-a-ble
pros-e-cu-tion
pros-e-cu-tor
pros-pect
  pros-pec-tor
pro-spec-tive
pro-spec-tus
pros-per-i-ty
pros-per-ous
pros-tate
pros-the-sis
  pros-the-ses
  pros-thet-ic
pros-thet-ics
  pros-the-tis
prosth-odon-tics
  prosth-odon-tist
pros-ti-tute
pros-trate
  pros-trat-ing
  pros-tra-tor
  pros-tra-tive
prosy
  pros-i-er
  pros-i-est
pro-tag-o-nist
pro-te-an
pro-tect
  pro-tect-ing
  pro-tec-tive
  pro-tec-tor
pro-tec-tion
pro-tec-tion-ism
  pro-tec-tion-ist
pro-tec-tor-ate
pro-tein
pro-test
prot-es-ta-tion
pro-tist
  pro-tis-tan
  pro-to-col
pro-ton
pro-to-plasm
  pro-to-plas-mic
pro-to-type
pro-to-typ-i-cal
pro-to-typ-ic

pro-to-typ-i-cal-ly
pro-to-zo-an
  pro-to-zo-ic
pro-tract
  pro-trac-tion
  pro-trac-tive
pro-trac-tile
pro-trac-tor
pro-trude
  pro-trud-ed
  pro-trud-ing
pro-tru-sion
pro-tru-sive
pro-tu-ber-ance
pro-tu-ber-ant
proud
  proud-ly
prov-erb
pro-ver-bi-al
  pro-ver-bi-al-ly
pro-vide
  pro-vid-ed
  pro-vid-ing
prov-i-dence
  prov-i-den-tial
prov-i-dent
prov-ince
pro-vin-cial
pro-vin-cial-ism
pro-vi-sion
  pro-vi-sion-er
pro-vi-sion-al
  pro-vi-sion-ary
prov-o-ca-tion
pro-voc-a-tive
  pro-voc-a-tive-ly
  pro-voc-a-tive-ness
pro-voke
  pro-voked
  pro-vok-ing
pro-vost
prow-ess
prowl
  prowl-er
prox-i-mal
prox-i-mate
  prox-i-mate-ly
prox-im-i-ty
proxy
  prox-ies
prude
pru-dence
  pru-dent
  pru-den-tial
prud-ery
  prud-er-ies

prud-ish
prune
  pruned
  prun-ing
pru-ri-ent
  pru-ri-ence
  pru-ri-en-cy
psalm-book
psalm-ist
pseu-do
pseud-onym
  pseud-on-y-mous
pseu-do-preg-nan-cy
  pseu-do-preg-nant
pseu-do-sci-ence
  pseu-do-sci-en-tif-ic
pshaw
psil-o-cy-bin
pso-ri-a-sis
  pso-ri-at-ic
psych
  psyched
  psych-ing
psy-che-del-ic
psy-chi-a-trist
psy-chi-a-try
  psy-chi-at-ric
  psy-chi-at-ri-cal-ly
psy-chic
  psy-chi-cal
  psy-chi-cal-ly
psy-cho
psy-cho-anal-y-sis
  psy-cho-an-a-lyt-ic
  psy-cho-an-a-lyt-i-cal
psy-cho-an-a-lyst
  psy-cho-an-a-lyze
  psy-cho-an-a-lyzed
  psy-cho-an-a-lyz-ing
psy-cho-bi-ol-o-gy
  psy-cho-bi-o-log-ic
  psy-cho-bi-o-log-i-cal
psy-cho-dra-ma
psy-cho-dy-nam-ic
  psy-cho-dy-nam-ics
psy-cho-gen-e-sis
  psy-cho-ge-net-ic
psy-cho-gen-ic
  psy-cho-gen-i-cal-ly
psy-cho-log-i-cal
  psy-cho-log-ic
  psy-cho-log-i-cal-ly
psy-chol-o-gist
psy-chol-o-gy
psy-cho-mo-tor
psy-cho-neu-ro-sis

psy-cho-neu-rot-ic
psy-cho-path
psy-cho-pa-thol-o-gy
  psy-cho-path-o-log-ic
psy-chop-a-thy
  psy-cho-path-ic
  psy-cho-path-i-cal-ly
psy-cho-sis
  psy-cho-ses
  psy-chot-ic
  psy-chot-i-cal-ly
psy-cho-ther-a-py
  psy-cho-ther-a-pist
pto-maine
pu-ber-ty
pu-bes-cence
  pu-bes-cen-cy
  pu-bes-cent
pu-bic
pub-lic
  pub-lic-ly
pub-li-ca-tion
pub-li-cist
pub-li-ci-ty
pub-li-cize
  pub-li-cized
  pub-li-ciz-jng
pub-lish
  pub-lish-a-ble
pub-lish-er
puce
puck-er
pud-ding
pud-dle
  pud-dled
  pud-dling
pudgy
  pudg-i-er
  pudg-i-est
pueb-lo
  pueb-los
pu-er-ile
  pu-er-il-i-ty
puff
  puffy
puff-er
pu-gi-lism
  pu-gi-list
  pu-gi-lis-tic
pug-na-cious
  pug-nac-i-ty
pulke
  puked
  puk-ing
pull-back
pul-let

pul-ley
pul-mo-nary
pulp
pul-pit
pulp-wood
pul-sate
  pul-sat-ed
  pul-sat-ing
pul-sa-tion
pul-sa-tor
  pul-sa-to-ry
pulse
  pulsed
  puls-ing
pul-ver-ize
pu-ma
  pu-mas
pum-ice
  pu-mi-ceous
pum-mel
pump
  pump-a-ble
  pump-er
pum-per-nick-el
pump-kin
pun
  punned
  pun-ning
punch
  punch-er
punch--drunk
punchy
  punch-i-er
  punch-i-est
punc-tu-al
punc-tu-ate
  punc-tu-at-ed
  punc-tu-at-ing
  punc-tu-a-tor
punc-tu-a-tion
punc-ture
  punc-tured
  punc-tur-ing
pun-dit
pun-gent
  pun-gen-cy
  pun-gent-ly
pun-ish
  pun-ish-able
pun-ish-ment
pu-ni-tive
pun-ster
punt-er
pu-ny
  pu-ni-er
  pu-ni-est

pup
  pupped
  pup-ping
pu-pa
  pu-pae
  pu-pas
  pu-pal
pu-pate
  pu-pat-ed
  pu-pat-ing
  pu-pa-tion
pu-pil
pup-pet
pup-pe-teer
pep-pet-ry
  pup-pet-ries
pup-py
  pup-pies
  pup-py-ish
pur-chase
  pur-chased
  pur-chas-ing
pure
  pure-ly
pur-ga-tive
pur-ga-to-ry
  pur-ga-to-ries
  pur-ga-to-ri-al
purge
  purged
pu-ri-fy
pur-ism
  pur-ist
  pu-ris-tic
pu-ri-tan
  pu-ri-tan-i-cal
  pu-ri-tan-i-cal-ly
pu-ri-ty
purl
pur-loin
  pur-loin-er
pur-port
  pur-port-ed
  pur-port-ed-ly
pur-pose
  pur-posed
  pur-pos-ing
pur-pose-ly
pur-pos-ive
purse
  pursed
  purs-ing
purs-er
pur-su-ant
pur-sue
  pur-sued

pur-su-ing
pur-suit
pur-sy
pu-ru-lent
  pu-ru-lence
  pu-ru-len-cy
pur-vey
  pur-vey-or
pur-vey-ance
pur-view
pushy
pu-sil-lan-i-mous
  pu-sil-la-nim-i-ty
  pu-sal-lan-i-mous-ly
pus-sy
pussy-foot
pussy-wil-low
pus-tule
  pus-tu-lar
  pus-tu-late
put
  put-ing
pu-ta-tive
  pu-ta-tive-ly
put--on
pu-tre-fac-tion
pu-tre-fy
  pu-tre-fied
  pu-tre-fy-ing
pu-trid
  pu-trid-i-try
putt
  putt-ed
  putt-ing
putt-er
  put-ter-er
put-ty
  put-tied
  put-ty-ing
put--up
puz-zle
puz-zle-ment
py-lon
pyr-a-mid
  py-ra-mi-dal
pyre
py-ric
py-ro-ma-nia
  py-ro-ma-ni-ac
  py-ro-ma-ni-a-cal
py-rom-e-ter
  py-rom-e-try
py-ro-tech-nics
  py-ro-tech-nic
  py-ro-tech-ni-cal
py-thon

quack-ery
  quack-er-ies
quad-ran-gle
  quad-ran-gu-lar
quad-rant
  quad-ran-tal
quad-ra-phon-ic
quad-rate
  quad-rat-ed
  quad-rat-ing
qua-drat-ic
  qua-drat-i-cal-ly
qua-drat-ics
quad-ra-ture
quad-ri-lat-er-al
qua-drille
qua-dril-lion
  qua-dril-lionth
qua-droon
quad-ru-ped
  quad-ru-pe-dal
qua-dru-ple
  qua-dru-pled
  qua-dru-pling
qua-dru-plet
qua-dru-pli-cate
  qua-dru-pli-cat-ed
  qua-dru-pli-cat-ing
quaff
  quaff-er
quag-mire
  quag-mired
  quag-miry
quail
quaint
quake
qual-i-fi-ca-tion
qual-i-fied
  qual-i-fied-ly
qual-i-fy
  qual-i-fy-ing
  qual-i-fi-a-ble
  qual-i-fier
qual-i-ta-tive
qual-i-ty
  qual-i-ties
qualm
  qualm-ish
quan-da-ry
  quan-dar-ies
quan-ti-fy
  quan-ti-fy-ing
  quan-ti-fi-ca-tion
quan-ti-ta-tive
quan-ti-ty
  quan-ti-ties

quan-tum
  quan-ta
quar-an-tine
  quar-an-tin-able
quar-rel
  quar-reled
  quar-rel-ing
  quar-rel-er
quar-rel-some
quar-ri-er
quar-ry
  quar-ries
  quar-ried
  quar-ry-ing
quart
quar-ter
quar-ter-back
  quar-ter-ing
quar-ter-ly
  quar-ter-lies
quar-ter-mas-ter
quar-tet
quartz
quash
qua-si
qua-ter-na-ry
qua-train
qua-ver
  quav-er-ing-ly
  qua-very
quay
quea-sy
  quea-si-er
  quea-si-est
  quea-si-ly
queen
  queen-ly
queer
quell
  quell-er
quench
  quench-able
  quench-er
que-ry
  que-ries
  que-ried
  que-ry-ing
quest
ques-tion
  ques-tion-er
ques-tion-able
  ques-tion-ably
ques-tion-naire
queue
  queued
  queu-ing

quib-ble
quick
quick-en
  quick-en-er
quick--freeze
quick-sand
quick-sil-ver
quick-tem-pered
quick--wit-ted
  quick--wit-ted-ly
  quick--wit-ted-ness
qui-es-cent
  qui-es-cence
qui-et
  qui-et-ly
  qui-et-ter
qui-e-tude
quill
quilt
quilt-er
quilt-ing
quince
quin-til-lion
quin-tu-ple
  quin-tu-pled
  quin-tu-pling
quin-tu-plet
quip
  quipped
  quip-ping
quirk
  quirky
quis-ling
quit
  quit-ed
  quit-ing
quit-claim
quite
quits
quit-er
quiv-er
quix-ot-ic
quiz
quiz-zi-cal
  quiz-zi-cal-ly
quoin
quoit
quon-dam
quo-rum
quo-ta
quot-able
  quot-a-bil-i-ty
quo-ta-tion
quote
quo-tid-i-an
quo-tient

rab-bet
  rab-bet-ted
  rab-bet-ting
rab-bi
  rab-bis
ra-bin-ate
rab-bin-i-cal
  rab-bin-i-al-ly
rab-bit
rab-ble
  rab-bled
  rab-bling
ra-bid
  ra-bid-ly
ra-bies
rac-coon
race
  raced
  rac-er
  rac-ing
race-course
race-horse
ra-ceme
rac-er
ra-ce-ric
ra-ce-ri-za-tion
race-track
ra-chis
  ra-chis-es
  rach-i-des
ra-cial
  ra-cial-ism
  ra-cial-ly
rac-ism
  ra-cial-ism
  rac-ist
rack-et
rack-e-teer
ra-con-teur
racy
  rac-i-ly
  rac-i-ness
ra-dar
ra-di-al
  ra-di-al-ly
ra-di-ance
  ra-di-an-cy
ra-di-ant
ra-di-ate
  ra-di-at-ed
  ra-di-at-ing
ra-di-a-tion
ra-di-a-tor
rad-i-cal
  rad-i-cal-ly
  rad-i-cal-ism

ra-dio
ra-dio-ac-tive
ra-dio-ac-tive-i-ty
ra-di-o fre-quen-cy
ra-dio-gram
ra-dio-graph
  ra-diog-ra-phy
ra-di-ol-o-gy
  ra-di-ol-o-gist
rad-ish
ra-di-um
ra-di-us
  ra-dii
  ra-di-us-es
ra-don
raf-fia
raf-fi-nose
raff-ish
raf-fle
  raf-fled
  raf-fling
raft
raft-er
rag
rag-ged
rag-gle
rag-man
rag-time
rag-weed
raid-er
rail-ing
rail-lery
  rail-ler-ies
rail-road
  rail-road-er
  rail-road-ing
rail-way
rai-ment
rain-bow
rain-fall
rainy
raise
  raised
rai-sin
rake
  raked
  rak-ing
rake--off
rak-ish
  rak-ish-ly
ral-li-form
ral-ly
  ral-lied
ram
  rammed
ram-ble

ram-bled
ram-bling
ram-bler
ram-bunc-tious
ram-bu-tan
ram-i-fi-ca-tion
ram-i-fy
ram-i-fied
ram-i-fy-ing
ram-page
ram-paged
ram-pag-ing
ram-pan-cy
ram-pant
ram-pant-ly
ram-part
ram-rod
ram-shack-le
ranch-er
ran-cid
ran-cid-i-ty
ran-cor
ran-cor-ous
ran-dom
ran-dom-ly
range
ranged
rang-ing
rang-er
rangy
rang-i-er
rang-i-est
ran-kle
ran-kling
ran-sack
rant-er
ran-u-la
rap
rapped
rap-ping
ra-pa-cious
ra-pa-cious-ly
ra-pac-i-ty
rape
rap-ist
ra-phe
raph-ide
rap-id
ra-pi-er
rap-ine
rap-pel
rap-port
rap-proche-ment
rap-scal-lion
rap-to-ri-al
rap-ture

rap-tur-ous
rare
rar-er
rar-est
rare-bit
rar-efy
rar-efied
rar-efy-ing
rare-ly
rar-i-ty
rar-i-ties
ras-cal
ras-cal-i-ty
ras-cal-ly
rash
ra-so-ri-al
rasp
rasp-ber-ry
rat
rat-ted
rat-ting
rat-able
ratch-et
rate
rat-ed
rat-ing
rath-er
rat-icide
rat-i-fy
rat-i-fi-ca-tion
ra-tio
ra-tios
ra-ti-o-ci-na-tion
ra-tion
ra-tio-nal
ra-tio-nal-i-ty
ra-tio-nal-ly
ra-tion-able
ra-tio-nal-ism
ra-tio-nal-ize
ra-tio-nal-iz-ing
ra-tio-nal-i-za-tion
rat-line
rat-tan
rat-tle
rat-tled
rat-tling
rat-tle-snake
rat-ty
rat-ti-er
rat-ti-est
rau-cous
rau-cous-ly
raun-chy
raun-chi-er
raun-chi-est

rav-age
rav-aged
rave
rav-el
ra-ven
rav-en-ous
rav-en-ous-ly
ra-vine
rav-i-o-li
rav-ish
rav-ish-ment
rav-ish-ing
raw
raw-hide
ray-on
raze
razed
raz-ing
ra-zor
raz-zle--daz-zle
re-act
re-ac-tive
re-ac-tion
re-ac-tion-ary
re-ac-tion-ar-ies
re-ac-ti-vate
re-ac-ti-vat-ed
re-ac-ti-vat-ing
re-ac-tor
read-able
read-er
read-ing
re-ad-just
re-ad-just-ment
ready
read-i-er
read-i-est
read-ied
read-y-ing
read-i-ly
read-i-ness
ready--made
re-agent
re-al
re-al-ism
re-al-ist
re-al-is-tic
re-al-is-ti-cal-ly
re-al-ize
re-al-ized
re-al-iz-ing
re-al-iz-a-ble
re-al-i-za-tion
re-al-ly
realm
Re-al-tor

re-al-ty
ream-er
re-an-i-mate
  re-an-i-mat-ed
  re-an-i-mat-ing
  re-an-i-ma-tion
reap-er
re-ap-pear
  re-ap-pear-ance
re-ap-por-tion
re-ap-por-tion-ment
rear ad-mir-ral
re-arm
  re-ar-ma-ment
re-ar-range
  re-ar-ranged
  re-ar-rang-ing
  re-ar-range-ment
rear-ward
rea-son
  rea-son-er
rea-son-able
  rea-son-abil-i-ty
  rea-son-able-ness
  rea-son-ably
rea-son-ing
re-as-sem-ble
  re-as-sem-bled
  re-as-sem-bling
  re-as-sem-bly
re-as-sume
  re-as-sump-tion
re-as-sure
  re-as-sured
  re-as-sur-ing
  re-as-sur-ance
  re-as-sur-ing-ly
re-bate
  re-bat-ed
  re-bat-ing
  re-bat-er
reb-el
re-bel
  re-belled
  re-bel-ling
re-bel-lion
re-bel-lious
  re-bel-lious-ly
re-birth
re-born
re-bound
re-buff
re-build
  re-built
  re-build-ing
re-buke

re-bus
  re-bus-es
re-but
re-but-tal
re-cal-ci-trant
  re-cal-ci-trance
  re-cal-ci-tran-cy
re-call
re-cant
  re-can-ta-tion
re-ca-pit-u-late
re-cap-ture
  re-cap-tured
re-cede
  re-ced-ed
  re-ced-ing
re-ceipt
re-ceiv-able
re-ceive
  re-ceiv-ed
  re-ceiv-ing
re-ceiv-er
  re-ceiv-er-ship
re-cent
  re-cent-ly
  re-cen-cy
re-cep-ta-cle
re-cep-tion
re-cep-tion-ist
re-cep-tive
re-cess
re-ces-sion
  re-ces-sion-ary
re-ces-sion-al
re-ces-sive
re-charge
  re-charg-ed
  re-charg-ing
rec-i-pe
re-cip-i-ent
  re-cip-i-ence
  re-cip-i-en-cy
re-cip-ro-cal
  re-cip-ro-cal-ly
re-cip-ro-cate
rec-i-proc-i-ty
re-cit-al
rec-i-ta-tion
rec-i-ta-tive
re-cite
  re-cited
  re-cit-ing
reck-less
  reck-less-ly
reck-on
re-claim

rec-la-ma-tion
re-cline
  re-clined
rec-luse
rec-og-ni-tion
re-cog-ni-zance
rec-og-nize
  rec-og-nized
  rec-og-niz-ing
  rec-og-niz-a-ble
re-coil
  re-coil-less
re-col-lect
re-col-lect
  re-col-lec-tion
rec-om-mend
  rec-om-mend-able
  rec-om-mend-er
rec-om-men-da-tion
rec-om-pense
  rec-om-pensed
  rec-om-pens-ing
rec-on-cile
  rec-on-ciled
rec-con-dite
re-con-di-tion
re-con-firm
re-con-nais-sance
re-con-noi-ter
  re-con-noi-tered
  re-con-noi-ter-ing
re-con-sid-er
  re-con-sid-er-a-tion
re-con-struct
re-con-struc-tion
re-cord
re-cord-er
re-count
re-coup
re-course
re-cov-er
re-cov-ery
  re-cov-er-ies
rec-re-ant
re-cre-ate
  re-cre-at-ed
  re-cre-at-ing
  re-cre-a-tion
rec-re-ation
  rec-re-ation-al
re-crim-i-nate
  re-crim-i-nat-ed
  re-crim-i-nat-ing
re-cruit
  re-cruit-er
  re-cruit-ment

rec-tal
rect-an-gle
rect-an-gu-lar
rec-ti-fi-er
rec-ti-fy
  rec-ti-fied
  rec-ti-fy-ing
  rec-ti-fi-ca-tion
rec-ti-lin-ear
rec-ti-tude
rec-tor
rec-to-ry
  rec-to-ries
rec-tum
  rec-tums
  rec-ta
re-cum-bent
  re-cum-ben-cy
  re-cum-bent-ly
re-cu-per-ate
re-cur
  re-cur-ring
  re-cur-rence
re-cur-rent
red-bird
red--blood-ed
re-dec-o-rate
  re-dec-o-rat-ed
  re-dec-o-ra-tion
re-ded-i-cate
  re-ded-i-cat-ed
  re-ded-i-ca-tion
re-deem
  re-deem-able
re-deem-er
re-demp-tion
  re-demp-tive
red--hand-ed
red--hot
re-di-rect
  re-di-rec-tion
red--let-ter
red--neck
re-do
red-o-lence
red-o-len-cy
red-o-lent
re-dou-ble
  re-dou-bled
  re-dou-bling
re-doubt-able
  re-doubt-ably
re-dound
re-dress
red-start
re-duce

re-duc-tion
re-dun-dance
re-dun-dant
re-du-pli-cate
  re-du-pli-cat-ed
  re-du-pli-ca-tion
red-wood
re-echo
  re-ech-oed
reedy
  reed-i-er
reef-er
re-elect
  re-elec-tion
re-em-pha-sie
  re-em-pha-sized
  re-em-pha-siz-ing
re-en-force
  re-en-forced
  re-en-forc-ing
  re-en-force-ment
re-en-list
  re-en-list-ment
re-en-ter
  re-en-trance
re-en-try
  re-en-tries
re-es-tab-lish
  re-es-tab-lish-ment
re-ex-am-ine
  re-ex-am-i-na-tion
re-fec-to-ry
  re-fec-to-ries
re-fer
  re-fer-ral
ref-er-ee
ref-er-ence
  ref-er-enced
  ref-er-enc-ing
ref-er-en-dum
  ref-er-en-dums
  ref-er-en-da
ref-er-ent
re-fill
  re-fill-able
re-fine
  re-fined
  re-fin-ing
re-fine-ment
re-fin-ery
  re-fin-er-ies
re-fin-ish
re-fit
  re-fit-ted
  re-fit-ting
re-flect

re-flec-tion
re-flec-tive
  re-flec-tive-ly
  re-flec-tive-ness
re-flec-tor
re-flex
re-flex-ive
re-for-est
  re-for-est-a-tion
re-form
re-form-a-tory
re-fract
  re-frac-tive
re-frac-tion
re-frac-to-ry
  re-frac-to-ri-ly
re-frain
re-fresh
  re-fresh-ing
re-fresh-ment
re-frig-er-ant
  re-frig-er-ate
  re-frig-er-at-ed
  re-frig-er-a-tor
re-fu-el
ref-uge
ref-u-gee
re-ful-gence
re-ful-gent
re-fund
re-fur-bish
re-fus-al
re-fuse
  re-fused
  re-fus-ing
ref-use
re-fute
re-gain
re-gal
  re-gal-ly
re-gale
  re-galed
  re-gal-ing
re-ga-lia
re-gard
re-gard-ful
re-gard-ing
re-gard-less
  re-gard-less-ly
re-gat-ta
re-gen-cy
  re-gen-cies
re-gen-er-ate
  re-gen-er-at-ed
  re-gen-er-at-ing
  re-gen-er-a-vy

re-gen-er-a-tion
re-gen-er-a-tive
re-gent
re-grime
reg-i-men
reg-i-ment
  reg-i-men-tal
  reg-i-men-ta-tion
re-gion
re-gion-al
  re-gion-al-ly
reg-is-ter
  reg-is-tered
  reg-is-trant
reg-is-trar
reg-is-tra-tion
reg-is-try
  reg-is-tries
re-gress
  re-gres-sion
  re-gres-sor
re-gret
  re-gret-ted
  re-gret-ting
  re-gret-ta-ble
  re-gret-ta-bly
  re-gret-er
  re-gret-ful
  re-gret-ful-ly
reg-u-lar
  reg-u-lar-i-ty
reg-u-late
  reg-u-lat-ed
  reg-u-lat-ing
  reg-u-la-tive
  reg-u-la-tor
  reg-u-la-to-ry
reg-u-la-tion
re-gur-gi-tate
  re-gur-gi-tat-ed
  re-gur-gi-tat-ing
  re-gur-gi-ta-tion
re-ha-bil-i-tate
  re-ha-bil-i-tat-ed
  re-ha-bil-i-tat-ing
  re-ha-bil-i-ta-tion
  re-ha-bil-i-ta-tive
re-hash
re-hears-al
re-hearse
  re-hearsed
  re-hears-ing
  re-hears-er
reign
re-im-burse
  re-im-bursed

re-im-burs-ing
re-im-burse-meny
rein
re-in-car-na-tion
rein-deer
re-in-force
  re-in-forced
  re-in-forc-ing
re-in-force-ment
re-in-state
  re-in-stat-ed
  re-in-stat-ing
  re-in-state-ment
re-it-er-ate
  re-it-er-at-ed
  re-it-er-at-ing
  re-it-er-a-tion
re-ject
  re-jec-tion
re-joice
  re-joiced
  re-joic-ing
  re-joic-er
  re-joic-ing-ly
re-join
re-join-der
re-ju-ve-nate
  re-ju-ve-nat-ed
  re-ju-ve-nat-ing
  re-ju-ve-na-tion
  re-ju-ve-na-tor
re-kin-dle
  re-kin-dled
  re-kin-dling
re-lapse
  re-lapsed
  re-laps-ing
  re-laps-er
re-late
  re-lat-ed
  re-lat-ing
  re-lat-er
  re-lat-or
re-la-tion
  re-la-tion-al
re-la-tion-ship
rel-a-tive
  rel-a-tive-ly
rel-a-tiv-ism
  rel-a-tiv-ist
rel-a-tiv-is-tic
rel-a-tiv-i-ty
rel-a-tiv-ize
re-la-tor
re-lax
  re-lax-er

re-lax-ation
re-lay
  re-laid
  re-lay-ing
re-lay
  re-layed
  re-lay-ing
re-lease
  re-leas-ed
  re-leas-ing
  re-leas-a-ble
  re-leas-er
rel-e-gate
  rel-e-gat-ed
  rel-e-ga-tion
re-lent
re-lent-less
rel-e-vant
  rel-e-vance
  rel-e-van-cy
  rel-e-vant-ly
re-li-able
  re-li-abil-i-ty
  re-li-able-ness
  re-li-ably
re-li-ance
  re-li-ant
rel-ic
re-lief
re-leive
  re-liev-ed
  re-liev-ing
  re-liev-able
  re-liev-er
re-li-gion
re-li-gi-os-i-ty
re-li-gious
re-lin-quish
rel-ish
re-live
  re-lived
  re-liv-ing
re-lo-cate
  re-lo-ct-ed
  re-lo-cat-ing
  re-lo-ca-tion
re-luc-tance
  re-luc-tant
re-ly
  re-lied
  re-ly-ing
re-main
re-main-der
re-mand
re-mark
re-mark-able

re-mark-able-ness
re-mark-ably
re-me-di-a-ble
re-me-di-al
rem-e-dy
rem-e-dies
rem-e-died
rem-e-dy-ing
re-mem-ber
re-mem-brance
re-mind
re-mind-er
re-mind-ful
rem-i-nisce
rem-i-nisced
rem-i-nisc-ing
rem-i-nis-cence
rem-i-nis-cent
re-miss
re-mis-sion
re-mit
re-mit-ted
re-mit-ting
re-mit-tance
rem-nant
re-mod-el
re-mon-strance
re-mon-strate
re-mon-strat-ed
re-mon-strat-ing
re-morse
re-morse-ful
re-morse-ful-ly
re-morse-less
re-mote
re-mot-er
re-mot-est
re-mount
re-mov-able
re-mov-al
re-move
re-moved
re-mov-ing
re-mu-ner-ate
re-mu-ner-at-ed
re-mu-ner-at-ing
re-mu-ner-a-tion
re-nais-sance
re-na-scence
re-na-scent
rend
rend-er
ren-dez-vous
ren-dez-voused
ren-dez-vous-ing
ren-di-tion

ren-e-gade
re-nege
re-neged
re-neg-ing
re-new
re-new-al
ren-net
re-nounce
re-nounced
re-nounc-ing
ren-o-vate
ren-o-vat-ed
ren-o-vat-ing
ren-o-va-tion
re-nown
re-nowned
rent-al
re-nun-ci-a-tion
re-or-ga-ni-za-tion
re-or-ga-nize
re-or-ga-niz-ed
re-or-gan-iz-ing
re-pair
re-pair-man
re-pair-men
rep-a-ra-ble
rep-a-ra-tion
rep-ar-tee
re-pa-tri-ate
re-pa-tri-at-ed
re-pay
re-paid
re-pay-ing
re-pay-ment
re-peal
re-peat
re-peat-able
re-peat-ed
re-peat-er
re-pel
re-pelled
re-pel-ling
re-pel-lent
re-pent
re-pent-ance
re-pen-tant
re-per-cus-sion
rep-er-toire
rep-er-to-ry
rep-er-to-ries
rep-e-ti-tion
rep-e-ti-tious
re-pet-i-tive
re-place
re-placed
re-plac-ing

re-plac-able
re-place-ment
re-plen-ish
re-plete
re-ple-tion
rep-li-ca
re-ply
re-plied
re-ply-ing
re-plies
re-port
re-port-ed-ly
re-port-er
rep-or-to-ri-al
re-pose
re-posed
re-pos-ing
re-pose-ful
re-pos-i-to-ry
re-pos-i-tor-ies
re-pos-sess
re-pos-ses-sion
rep-re-hend
rep-re-hen-si-ble
rep-re-sent
rep-re-sen-ta-tion
rep-re-sen-ta-tive
re-press
re-pres-sion
re-prieve
re-prieved
re-priev-ing
rep-ri-mand
re-print
re-pris-al
re-proach
re-proach-ful
rep-ro-bate
rep-ro-ba-tion
re-pro-duce
re-pro-duced
re-pro-duc-ing
re-pro-duc-tion
re-pro-duc-tive
re-proof
re-prove
re-proved
re-prov-ing
rep-tile
rep-til-ian
re-pub-lic
re-pub-li-can
re-pub-li-can-ism
re-pu-di-ate
re-pu-di-at-ed
re-pu-di-at-ing

re-pu·di-a-tion
  re-pu-di-a-tion-ist
re-pugn
  re-pug-nan-cy
re-pug-nant
re-pulse
  re-pulsed
  re-puls-ing
re-pul-sion
re-pul-sive
rep-u-ta-ble
  rep-u-ta-bly
  rep-u-ta-bil-i-ty
rep-u-ta-tion
re-pute
  re-put-ed
  re-put-ing
  re-put-ed-ly
re-quest
re-qui-em
re-quire
  re-quired
  re-quir-ing
re-quire-ment
req-ui-site
re-quit-al
re-quite
  re-quit-ed
  re-quit-ing
re-run
  re-run-ning
re-sale
re-scind
res-cue
  res-cued
  res-cu-ing
  res-cu-er
re-search
  re-search-er
re-sem-blance
re-sem-ble
  re-sem-bled
  re-sem-bling
re-sent
re-sent-ful
re-sent-ment
re-ser-va-tion
re-serve
  re-served
  re-serv-ing
re-serv-ist
res-er-voir
re-set
  re-set-ting
re-side
  re-sid-ed

re-sid-ing
res-i-dence
res-i-den-cy
  res-i-den-cies
res-i-dent
res-i-den-tial
re-sid-u-al
res-i-due
re-sign
res-ig-na-tion
re-signed
re-sil-ient
  re-sil-ience
  re-sil-ien-cy
res-in
res-in-ous
re-sist
re-sist-er
  re-sist-ible
re-sist-ance
  re-sis-tant
re-sist-less
re-sis-tor
res-o-lute
  res-o-lu-tion
re-solve
  re-solved
  re-solv-ing
res-o-nance
res-o-nant
res-o-nate
  res-o-nat-ed
  res-o-nat-ing
res-o-na-tor
re-sort
re-sound
  re-sound-ing
re-source
  re-source-ful
re-spect
  re-spect-ful
  re-spect-ful-ly
re-spect-able
  re-spect-a-bil-i-ty
re-spect-ing
re-spec-tive
re-spec-tive-ly
res-pi-ra-tion
  res-pi-ra-to-ry
res-pi-ra-tor
re-spire
  re-spired
  re-spir-ing
re-spite
re-splend-ant
  re-splend-ence

re-spond
re-spon-dent
re-sponse
re-spon-si-bil-i-ty
  re-spon-si-bil-i-ties
re-spon-si-ble
re-spon-sive
res-tau-rant
rest-ful
res-ti-tu-tion
res-tive
rest-less
res-to-ra-tion
re-stor-a-tive
re-store
  re-stored
  re-stor-ing
re-strain
re-straint
re-strict
  re-strict-ed
  re-strict-ed-ly
re-stric-tion
re-stric-tive
re-sult
re-sul-tant
re-sume
  re-sumed
  re-sum-ing
re-sump-tion
re-sur-gence
re-sur-gent
res-ur-rect
res-ur-rec-tion
re-sus-ci-tate
  re-sus-ci-tat-ed
  re-sus-ci-tat-ing
  re-sus-ci-ta-tion
re-sus-ci-ta-tor
re-tail
  re-tail-er
re-tain
re-tainer
re-take
  re-took
  re-tak-en
  re-tak-ing
re-tal-i-ate
  re-tal-i-at-ed
  re-tal-i-at-ing
  re-tal-i-a-tion
re-tard
  re-tard-ant
re-tar-da-tion
re-tard-ed
re-ten-tion

re-ten-tive
ret-i-cence
ret-i-cent
ret-i-na
 ret-i-nas
 ret-i-nae
 ret-i-nal
ret-i-nue
re-tire
 re-tired
 re-tir-ing
re-tire-ment
re-tool
re-tort
re-touch
re-trace
 re-traced
 re-trac-ing
re-tract
 re-trac-tion
 re-trac-tor
re-trac-tile
re-tread
re-treat
re-trench
 re-trench-ment
re-tri-al
ret-ri-bu-tion
re-trieve
 re-trieved
 re-triev-ing
re-triev-er
ret-ro-ac-tive
ret-ro-grade
 ret-ro-grad-ed
 ret-ro-grad-ing
ret-ro-gress
 ret-ro-gees-sion
 ret-ro-ges-sive
ret-ro--rock-et
ret-ro-spect
 ret-ro-spec-tion
 ret-ro-spec-tive
re-turn
re-turn-able
re-turn-ee
re-union
re-unite
 re-unit-ed
 re-unit-ing
rev
 rev-ved
 rev-ving
re-vamp
re-veal
rev-eil-le

rev-el
 rev-el-er
 rev-e-la-tion
 rev-el-ry
 rev-el-ries
re-venge
 re-venged
 re-veng-ing
re-venge-ful
rev-e-nue
rev-e-nu-er
re-ver-ber-ate
 re-ver-ber-at-ed
 re-ver-ber-at-ing
 re-ver-ber-a-tion
re-vere
 re-vered
 re-ver-ing
rev-er-ence
 rev-er-enced
 rev-er-enc-ing
rev-er-end
rev-er-ent
rev-er-en-tial
rev-er-ie
re-ver-sal
re-verse
 re-versed
 re-vers-ing
re-vers-i-ble
re-ver-sion
re-vert
re-view
re-view-er
re-vile
 re-viled
 re-vil-ing
re-vise
 re-vised
 re-vis-ing
re-vi-sion
re-vi-sion-ist
 re-vi-sion-ism
re-viv-al
re-viv-al-ist
re-vive
 re-vived
 re-viv-ing
rev-o-ca-ble
rev-o-ca-tion
re-voke
 re-voked
 re-vok-ing
re-volt
rev-o-lu-tion
rev-o-lu-tion-ary

rev-o-lu-tion-ar-ies
rev-o-lu-tion-ist
rev-o-lu-tion-ize
 rev-o-lu-tion-ized
 rev-o-lu-tion-iz-ing
re-volve
 re-volved
 re-volv-ing
re-volv-er
re-vue
re-vul-sion
re-write
 re-wrote
 re-writ-ten
 re-writ-ting
rhap-sod-ic
 rhap-sod-i-cal
 rhap-sod-i-cal-ly
rhap-so-dize
 rhap-so-dized
 rhap-so-diz-ing
rhap-so-dy
 rhap-so-dies
 rhap-so-dist
rhea
rhe-ni-um
rheo-stat
rhe-tor
rhet-o-ric
rhe-tor-i-cal
rhet-o-ri-cian
rheum
rheu-mat-ic
 rheu-mat-i-cal-ly
rheu-ma-tism
rhine-stone
rhi-no
rhi-noc-er-os
 rhi-noc-er-os-es
rhi-zome
rho-di-um
rho-do-den-dron
rhom-bic
rhom-boid
 rhom-boi-dal
rhom-bus
 rhom-bus-es
 rhom-bi
rhu-barb
rhyme
 rhymed
 rhym-ing
rhyme-ster
rhythm
 rhyth-mic
 rhyth-mi-cal

rhyth-mi-cal-ly
rib
  ribbed
  rib-bing
rib-ald
  rib-ald-ry
  rib-ald-ries
rib-bon
ri-bo-fla-vin
rib-bo-nu-cle-ase
rice
  riced
  ric-ing
rich-es
rich-less
rick-ets
rick-ety
  rick-et-i-er
  rick-et-i-est
rick-shaw
ric-o-chet
rid
  rid-ded
  rid-ding
rid-dance
rid-dle
  rid-dled
  rid-dling
ride
  rid-den
  rid-ding
ride-er
ridge
  ridged
  ridg-ing
ridge-pole
rid-i-cule
  rid-i-culed
  rid-i-cul-ing
ri-dic-u-lous
rif-fle
  rif-fled
  rif-fling
riff-raff
rig
  rigged
  rig-ging
rig-ger
righ-teous
right-ful
right-hand
right--hand-ed
right-ism
rig-id
  ri-gid-i-ty
rig-ma-role

rig-or
rig-or-ous
rile
  riled
  ril-ing
rim
rime
ring-er
ring-lead-er
ring-let
ring-mas-ter
ring-worm
rinse
  rinsed
  rins-ing
ri-ot-ous
rip
  ripped
  rip-ping
  rip-per
ri-par-i-an
rip-en
rip--off
rip-ple
  rip-pled
  rip-pling
rip-saw
rip-tide
rise
  rose
  ris-en
  ris-ing
ris-er
ris-i-ble
  ris-i-bil-i-ty
risky
  risk-i-er
  risk-i-est
rit-u-al
rit-u-al-ism
  rit-u-al-ist
  rit-u-al-is-tic
  rit-u-al-is-ti-cal-ly
ritzy
  ritz-i-er
  ritz-i-est
ri-val
ri-val-ry
  ri-val-ries
riv-er
riv-er-side
riv-et
  riv-et-er
riv-i-era
riv-u-let
roach

road-runner
road-ster
road-way
roast-er
rob
  robbed
  rob-bing
  rob-ber
rob-bery
  rob-ber-ies
robe
  robed
  rob-ing
rob-in
ro-bot
ro-bust
rock-er
rock-et
rock-et-ry
rocky
  rock-i-er
  rock-i-est
ro-co-co
ro-dent
ro-deo
  ro-de-os
roe-buck
roent-gen
rog-er
roque
  ro-guish
  ro-guish-ly
roqu-ery
  roqu-er-ies
roist-er
roll-er
roll-er bear-ing
roll-er coast-er
roll-er skate
rol-lick
  rol-lick-ing
roll-ing pin
ro-ly--po-ly
  ro-ly--po-lies
ro-maine
ro-mance
  ro-manced
  ro-manc-ing
ro-man-tic
ro-man-ti-cism
ro-man-ti-cize
  ro-man-ti-ciz-ing
romp-er
roof-ing
rook-ery
  rook-er-ies

rook-ie
room-er
room-ful
room-mate
roomy
  room-i-er
  room-i-est
  room-i-ly
room-i-ness
roos-ter
root-stock
rope
  roped
  rop-ing
ropy
  rop-i-er
  rop-i-est
ro-sa-ry
  ro-sa-ries
ro-se-ate
rose-bud
rose--col-ored
rose-mary
  rose-mar-ies
ro-sette
ros-in
ros-ter
ros-trum
  ros-tra
  ros-trums
rosy
  ros-i-er
  ros-i-est
rot
  rot-ted
  rot-ting
ro-ta-ry
  ro-tar-ies
ro-tate
  ro-tat-ed
  ro-tat-ing
ro-ta-tion
ro-tis-ser-ie
ro-tor
rot-ten
ro-tund
  ro-tun-di-ty
  ro-tun-di-ties
ro-tun-da
rouge
  rouged
  roug-ing
rough-age
rough--and--tumble
rough-en
rough-house

rough-neck
rough-shod
rou-lette
round-ed
round-er
round-ish
round-up
rouse
  roused
  rous-ing
  rous-er
roust
roust-a-bout
rout
route
  rout-ed
  rout-ing
  rout-er
rou-tine
rou-tin-ize
  rou-tin-ized
  rou-tin-iz-ing
rove
  roved
  rov-ing
  rov-er
row-boat
row-dy
  row-dies
  row-di-er
  row-di-est
row-lock
roy-al
  roy-al-ly
  roy-al-ist
  roy-al-ty
  roy-al-ties
rub
  rubbed
  rub-bing
rub-ber
  rub-bery
rub-ber-ize
  rub-ber-ized
  rub-ber-iz-ing
rub-ber-neck
rub-bish
  rub-bish-ly
rub-ble
  rub-bly
  rub-bli-er
  rub-bli-est
rub-down
ru-bel-la
ru-be-o-la
ru-bi-cund

ru-bid-i-um
ru-bric
ru-by
  ru-bies
ruck-sack
ruck-us
rud-der
rud-dy
  rud-di-er
  rud-di-est
  rud-di-ly
rude
ru-di-ment
  ru-di-ment-al
  ru-di-men-ta-ry
rue
  rued
  ru-ing
rue-ful
  rue-ful-ly
ruff
  ruffed
ruf-fi-an
ruf-fle
  ruf-fled
  ruf-fling
rug-ged
  rug-ged-ly
  rug-ged-ness
ru-in
ru-in-ation
ru-in-ous
rule
  ruled
  rul-ing
rul-er
rum-ba
  rum-baed
  rum-ba-ing
rum-ble
  rum-bled
  rum-bling
  rum-bler
  rum-bly
ru-mi-nant
ru-mi-nate
  ru-mi-nat-ed
  ru-mi-nat-ing
  ru-mi-na-tion
  ru-mi-na-tor
rum-mage
  rum-maged
  rum-mag-ing
  rum-mag-er
rum-my
  rum-mies

ru-mor
ru-mor-mon-ger
rum-ple
  rum-pled
  rum-pling
rum-pus
run
  run-ning
run-about
run-around
run-away
run-ner
run-ner--up
run-ny
  run-ni-er
  run-ni-est
run-off
run--on
runt
  runty
  runt-i-er
  runt-i-est
run--through
run-way
rup-ture
  rup-tured
  rup-tur-ing
ru-ral
  ru-ral-ly
ru-ral-ize
  ru-ral-ized
  ru-ral-iz-ing
  ru-ral-i-za-tion
rus-set
rus-tic
rus-ti-cate
  rus-ti-cat-ed
  rus-ti-cat-ing
  rus-ti-ca-tion
rus-tle
  rus-tled
  rus-tling
rus-tler
rust-proof
rus-ty
  rust-i-er
  rust-i-est
rut
  rut-ted
  rut-ting
ru-ta-ba-ga
ru-the-ni-um
ruth-less
  ruth-less-ly
rut-ty

sa-ber
sa-ber-toothed ti-ger
sa-ble
sab-o-tage
  sab-o-taged
  sab-o-tag-ing
sab-o-teur
sa-bra
sac-cha-rin
sac-er-do-tal
sa-chet
sack-cloth
sack-ful
  sack-fuls
sack-ing
sac-ra-ment
  sac-ra-men-tal
sa-cred
  sa-cred-ly
  sa-cred-ness
sac-ri-fice
  sac-ri-ficed
  sac-ri-fic-ing
  sac-ri-fic-er
  sac-ri-fi-cial
sac-ri-lege
sac-ri-le-gious
sc-ro-il-li-ac
sac-ro-sanct
  sac-ro-sanc-i-ty
sac-rum
  sac-rums
  sac-ra
  sa-cral
sad
  sad-der
  sad-dest
  sad-ly
  sad-ness
sad-den
sad-dle
  sad-dled
  sad-dling
sad-dle-backed
sad-dle-bag
sad-ism
  sad-ist
  sa-dis-tic
sad-o-mas-o-chism
  sad-o-mas-o-chist
sa-fa-ri
  sa-fa-ris
safe
  saf-er
  saf-est
safe--con-duct

safe-crack-er
  safe-crack-ing
safe--de-pos-it
safe-guard
safe-keep-ing
safe-ty
  safe-ties
safe-ty match
safe-ty pin
safe-ty valve
safe-ty zone
saf-flow-er
sag
  sagged
  sag-ging
sa-ga
sa-ga-cious
  sa-gac-i-ty
sage
  sag-er
  sag-est
sage-brush
sail-boat
sail-cloth
sail-er
sail-fish
sail-ing
sail-or
saint
  saint-hood
saint-ed
saint-ly
  saint-li-er
  saint-li-est
sa-ke
sal-a-ble
  sal-a-ble
  sal-a-bil-i-ty
  sal-a-bly
sa-la-cious
sal-ad
sal-a-man-der
sa-la-mi
sal-a-ry
  sal-a-ries
sales-man
  sales-men
sales-man-ship
sales-per-son
  sales-peo-ple
sales-room
sa-li-ent
  sa-li-ence
  sa-li-en-cy
  sa-li-ent-ly
sa-line

sa-lin-i-ty
sa-li-va
sal-i-vary
sal-i-vate
sal-i-vat-ed
sal-i-vat-ing
sal-i-va-tion
sal-low
sal-low-ish
sal-ly
sal-lies
sal-lied
sal-ly-ing
salm-on
sa-lon
sa-loon
salt-cel-lar
salt-ed
sal-tine
salt-shak-er
salt-wa-ter
salt-wort
salt-y
salt-i-er
salt-i-est
salt-i-ness
sa-lu-bri-ous
sal-u-tar-y
sal-u-ta-tion
sa-lu-ta-to-ry
sa-lu-ta-to-ries
sa-lute
sa-luted
sa-lut-ing
sa-lut-er
sal-vage
sal-vaged
sal-vag-ing
sal-vage-a-ble
sal-vag-er
sal-va-tion
salve
salved
salv-ing
salv-or
sal-vo
sal-vos
sal-voes
sam-ba
sam-baed
sam-ba-ing
same-ness
sam-o-var
sam-ple
sam-pled
sam-pling

sam-pler
san-a-to-ri-um
sanc-ti-fy
sanc-ti-fied
sanc-ti-fy-ing
sanc-ti-fi-ca-tion
sanc-ti-fi-er
sanc-ti-mo-ny
sanc-ti-mo-ni-ous
sanc-tion
sanc-tion-a-ble
sanc-tion-er
sanc-ti-ty
sanc-ti-ties
sanc-tu-ary
sanc-tu-ar-ies
sanc-tum
sanc-ta
san-dal
san-dal-wood
sand-bag
sand-bagged
sand-bank
sand-blast
sand-box
sand-cast
sand-cast-ed
sand-cast-ing
sand-lot
sand-man
sand-men
sand-pa-per
sand-pi-per
sand-stone
sand-wich
sandy
sand-i-er
sand-i-est
sane
san-er
san-est
sane-ly
sang-froid
san-gui-nary
san-quine
san-quine-ly
san-i-tar-i-um
san-i-tar-i-ums
san-i-tar-ia
san-i-tary
san-i-tar-i-ly
san-i-ta-tion
san-i-tize
san-i-tized
san-i-tiz-ing
san-i-ty

sap
sapped
sap-ping
sap-head
sap-head-ed
sa-pi-ent
sa-pi-ence
sa-pi-en-cy
sap-less
sap-ling
sa-pon-i-fy
sa-pon-i-fied
sa-pon-i-fy-ing
sap-per
sap-phire
sap-phism
sap-py
sap-pi-er
sap-pi-est
sap-suck-er
sap-wood
sa-ran
sar-casm
sar-cas-tic
sar-cas-ti-cal-ly
sar-co-ma
sar-co-mas
sar-co-ma-ta
sar-coph-a-gus
sar-coph-a-gus-es
sar-dine
sar-don-ic
sar-don-i-cal-ly
sar-gas-sum
sa-ri
sa-ris
sa-rong
sar-sa-pa-ril-la
sar-to-ri-al
sa-shay
sas-sa-fras
sas-sy
sas-si-er
sas-si-est
sa-tan-ic
sa-tan-i-cal
sa-tan-ism
sa-tan-ist
satch-el
sate
sat-ed
sat-ing
sa-teen
sat-el-lite
sa-ti-a-ble
sa-ti-a-bly

sa-ti-a-bil-i-ty
sa-ti-ate
 sa-ti-at-ed
 sa-ti-at-ing
 sa-ti-a-tion
sa-ti-e-ty
sat-in
 sat-iny
sat-ire
sa-tir-i-cal
 sa-tir-i-cal-ly
sat-i-rist
sat-i-rize
 sat-i-rized
 sat-i-riz-ing
 sat-i-riz-er
sat-is-fac-tion
sat-is-fac-to-ry
 sat-is-fa-to-ri-ly
sat-is-fy
 sat-is-fied
 sat-is-fy-ing
 sat-is-fi-a-ble
 sat-is-fi-er
 sat-is-fy-ing-ly
sat-u-rate
 sat-u-rat-ed
 sat-u-rat-ing
 sat-u-ra-tion
sat-ur-na-li-a
sat-ur-nine
sa-tyr
 sa-tyr-ic
sauce
 sauced
 sauc-ing
sau-cer
sau-cy
sau-er-bra-ten
sau-er-kraut
sau-na
saun-ter
 saun-ter-er
sau-sage
 sau-sage-like
sav-age
 sav-age-ry
 sav-age-ries
sa-van-na
sa-vant
save
 saved
 sav-ing
 sav-er
sav-ior
sa-voir-faire

sa-vor
 sa-vor-er
sa-vory
 sa-vor-i-er
 sa-vor-i-est
sav-vy
saw-buck
saw-dust
sawed--off
saw-horse
saw-mill
saw-toothed
saw-yer
sax-o-phone
 sax-o-phon-ist
say
 said
 say-ing
 say-a-ble
 say-er
say-s-o
scab
 scabbed
 scab-bing
scab-bard
scab-by
 scab-bi-er
 scab-bi-est
sca-bies
scaf-fold
sac-fold-ing
sca-lar
scal-a-wag
scald
 scald-ing
scale
 scaled
 scal-ing
 scale-less
scamp
 scamp-er
scan
scan-dal
scan-dal-ize
 scan-dal-ized
 scan-dal-iz-ing
scan-dal-mon-ger
scan-dal-ous
scan-sion
scant
 scant-ness
scan-ties
scanty
 scant-i-er
 scant-i-est
scape-goat

scape-grace
scap-u-la
 scap-u-las
scap-u-lae
scar
 scarred
 scar-ring
scarce
 scar-ci-ty
scare
 scared
 scar-ing
 scar-er
scare-crow
scare-mon-ger
scarf
 scarfs
scarf-skin
scar-i-fy
 scar-i-fied
 scar-i-fy-ing
scar-let
scarp
scary
 scar-i-er
 scar-i-est
scat
 scat-ted
 scat-ting
scathe
scat-o-log-i-cal
scat-ter
 scat-ter-a-ble
 scat-ter-er
scav-enge
 scav-enged
 scav-eng-ing
scav-en-ger
sce-nar-i-o
 sce-nar-i-os
sce-nar-ist
scen-ery
 scen-er-ies
sce-nic
 sce-ni-cal
scent
 scent-ed
scep-ter
 scep-tered
 scep-ter-ing
sched-ule
 sched-ul-ed
 sched-ul-ing
sche-ma
 sche-ma-ta
 sche-mat-i-cal-ly

sche-ma-tize
 sche-ma-tized
 sche-ma-tiz-ing
scheme
 schem-er
 schem-ing
scher-zo
 scher-zos
 scher-zi
schism
schis-mat-ic
 schis-mat-i-cal
schist
schizo
 schiz-os
schiz-oid
schiz-o-phre-ni-a
 schiz-o-phren-ic
schle-miel
schmaltz
 schmaltzy
schmo
schnapps
schnau-zer
schnit-zel
schnook
schnor-kel
schnoz-zle
schol-ar
schol-ar-ly
 schol-ar-li-ness
schol-ar-ship
scho-las-tic
 scho-las-ti-cal
scho-las-ti-cism
school board
school bus
school-child
 school-chil-dern
school-ing
school-mas-ter
school-teach-er
 school-teach-ing
school-work
schoon-er
schuss
schwa
sci-at-ic
sci-ence
sci-en-tif-ic
 sci-en-tif-i-cal-ly
sci-en-tist
scim-i-tar
scin-tig-ra-phy
scin-til-la
scin-til-lant

scin-til-late
 scin-til-lat-ed
 scin-til-lat-ing
 scin-til-la-tion
sci-on
scis-sor
scis-sors
scle-ra
 scle-rot-i-ca
scle-ro-sis
 scle-ro-ses
scle-rot-ic
scle-rous
scoff
 scoff-er
 scoff-ing-ly
scold
 scold-er
 scold-ing
scol-lop
sconce
scone
scoop
scoot-er
scope
scorch
 scorched
 scorch-ing
 scorch-er
score
 scored
 scor-ing
 score-less
 scor-er
score-board
score-keep-er
scorn
 scorn-er
 scorn-ful
scot-free
scot-tie
scoun-drel
 scoun-drel-ly
scour
 scour-er
scourge
 scourged
 scourg-ing
 scourg-er
scour-ing
scout-ing
scout-mas-ter
scowl
 scowl-er
srab-ble
 scrab-bled

scrab-bling
scrab-bler
scrag
 scragged
 scrag-ging
scrag-gly
 scrag-gli-er
 scrag-gli-est
scrag-gy
 scrag-gi-er
 scrag-gi-est
scram
 scrammed
 scram-ming
scram-ble
 scram-bled
 scram-bling
 scram-bler
scrap
 scrapped
 scrap-ping
scrap-book
scrape
scrap-per
scrap-py
 scrap-pi-er
 scrap-pi-est
 scrap-pi-ly
scratch
 scratch-a-ble
 scratch-er
scratch-y
 scratch-i-er
 scratch-i-est
scratch-i-ly
 scratch-i-ness
scrawl
scrawn-y
 scrawn-i-er
 scrawn-i-est
screamer
scream-ing-ly
screech
 screech-er
screen
 scrren-a-ble
 screen-er
 screen-play
screw
 screw-driv-er
screw-y
 screw-i-er
 screw-i-est
scrib-ble
 scrib-bled
 scrib-bling

scrib-bler
scribe
 scribed
 scrib-ing
 scrib-al
scrim
 scrim-mage
 scrim-mag-ing
scrimp-y
 scrimp-i-er
 scrimp-i-est
script
scrip-tur-al
scrip-ture
script-writ-er
scroll-work
scrooge
scro-tum
 scro-ta
scrounge
 scroung-er
scrub
 scrubbed
 scrub-bing
 scrub-ber
scrub-by
 scrub-bi-er
 scrub-bi-est
scrub-wom-an
 scrub-wom-en
scruffy
 scruff-i-er
 scruff-i-est
scrump-tious
scru-ple
 scru-bled
 scru-bling
scru-pu-lous
 scru-pu-los-i-ty
 scru-pu-lous-ly
scru-ta-ble
scru-ti-nize
 scru-ti-nized
scru-ti-ny
 scru-ti-nies
scu-ba
scud
 scud-ded
 scud-ding
scuf-fle
 scuf-fled
 scuf-fling
scul-ler-y
 scul-ler-ies
sculp-tor
sculp-ture

sculp-tur-ed
sculp-tur-ing
sculp-tur-al
scum
 scummed
 scum-ming
scur-ri-lous
 scur-ril-i-ty
 scur-ril-i-ties
scur-ry
 scur-ri-ed
 scur-ry-ing
scur-vy
scut-tle
 scut-tled
 scut-tling
scut-tle-butt
scythe
 scythed
 scyth-ing
sea-bed
sea-coast
sea-drome
sea-far-ing
 sea-far-er
sea-food
sea gull
sea horse
seal
 seal-er
sea-lam-prey
sea legs
sea lev-el
seal-ing wax
sea li-on
seal-skin
seam
 seam-er
sea-maid
sea-man
 sea-men
sea-man-ship
seam-stree
seam-y
 seam-i-er
 seam-i-est
sea ot-ter
sea-plane
sea-port
search
 search-a-ble
 search-er
search-ing
search-light
search war-rant
sea-scape

sea ser-pent
sea-shell
sea-shore
sea-sick
 sea-sick-ness
sea-side
sea-son
 sea-son-er
sea-son-a-ble
sea-son-al
 sea-son-al-ly
sea-son-ing
seat-ing
sea ur-chin
sea-ward
sea-weed
sea-wor-thy
 sea-wor-thi-ness
se-ba-ceous
se-cant
se-cede
 se-ced-ed
 se-ced-ing
 se-ced-er
se-ces-sion
 se-ces-sion-ist
se-clude
 se-clud-ed
 se-clud-ing
se-clu-sion
 se-clu-sive
sec-ond
sec-ond-ar-y
 sec-ond-ar-i-ly
sec-ond--best
sec-ond--class
sec-ond-quess
sec-ond-hand
sec-ond-rate
sec-ond--sto-ry man
se-cre-cy
 se-cre-cies
se-cret
sec-re-tar-i-at
sec-re-tary
 sec-re-tar-ies
 sec-re-tar-i-al
se-crete
 se-cret-ed
 se-cret-ing
se-cre-tion
se-cre-tive
se-cre-to-ry
 se-cre-to-ries
sec-tar-i-an
 sec-tar-i-an-ism

sec-tion
sec-tion-al
sec-tor
 sec-to-ri-al
sec-u-lar
sec-u-lar-ism
sec-u-lar-ize
 sec-u-lar-ized
 sec-u-lar-iz-ing
se-cure
 se-cured
 se-cur-ing
se-cu-ri-ty
 se-cu-ri-ties
se-dan
se-date
 se-dat-ed
 se-dat-ing
se-da-tion
sed-a-tive
sed-en-tary
 sed-en-tar-i-ness
sedge
sed-i-ment
 sed-i-men-tal
 sed-i-men-ta-ry
 sed-i-men-ta-tion
se-di-tion
 se-di-tion-ary
se-di-tious
se-duce
 se-duced
 se-duc-ing
 se-duc-er
se-duc-tive
 se-duc-tive-ness
sed-u-lous
 se-du-li-ty
 sed-u-lous-ness
seed-bed
seed-case
seed-ing
seed-pod
seedy
 seed-i-er
 seed-i-est
see-ing
seek
 sought
 seek-ing
seem-ing
 seem-ing-ness
seem-ly
seep
 seepy
 seep-i-er

seep-i-est
seep-age
se-er
 seer-ess
seer-suck-er
see-saw
seethe
 seethed
 seeth-ing
seg-ment
 seg-men-tal
 seg-men-tary
seg-men-ta-tion
seg-re-gate
 seg-re-gat-ed
 seg-re-gat-ing
seg-re-ga-tion
seg-re-ga-tion-sit
sei-gneur
seine
 seined
 sein-ing
seis-mic
 seis-mal
 seis-mi-cal
 seis-mi-cal-ly
seis-mo-graph
 seis-mog-ra-pher
 seis-mo-graph-ic
 seis-mog-ra-phy
seis-mol-o-gy
 seis-mo-log-ic
 seis-mo-log-i-cal
 seis-mol-o-gist
seize
 seized
 seiz-ing
 seiz-er
sei-zure
sel-dom
se-lect
 se-lect-ed
 se-lec-tor
se-lec-tion
se-lec-tive
se-lec-tiv-i-ty
se-le-ni-um
self-a-base-ment
self-ab-ne-ga-tion
self-a-buse
self--ad-dressed
self-ag-gran-dize-ment
 self-ag-gran-diz-ing
self--as-sur-ance
 self--as-sured
self--cen-tered

self--cen-tered-ness
self--col-lect-ed
self--com-mand
self--com-posed
self--con-fessed
self--con-fi-dence
 self--con-fi-dent
self--con-scious
 self--con-scious-ness
self--con-tained
self--con-trol
 self--con-trolled
self--cor-rect-ing
self--crit-i-cal
self--crit-i-cism
self--de-cep-tion
 self--de-cep-tive
self--de-fense
self--de-ni-al
 self--de-ny-ing
self--de-ter-mi-na-tion
 self--de-ter-min-ing
self--dis-ci-pline
 self--dis-ci-plined
self--ed-u-cate-ed
 self--ed-u-ca-tion
self--ef-fac-ing
self--em-ployed
 self--em-ploy-ment
self--es-teem
self--ev-i-dent
 self--ev-i-dence
self--ex-plan-a-to-ry
self--ex-pres-sion
 self--ex-pres-sive
self--ful-fill-ing
self--ful-fill-ment
self--gov-ern-ment
 self--gov-erned
 self--gov-ern-ing
self--help
self--im-age
self--im-por-tance
self--im-por-tant
self--im-posed
self--im-prove-ment
self--in-duced
self--in-dul-gence
 self--in-dul-gent
self--in-flict-ed
self--in-ter-est
 self--in-ter-est-ed
self-ish
 self-ish-ness
self--kow-ledge
self-less

180

self-less-ness
self--love
  self--lov-ing
self--made
self--per-pet-u-at-ing
  self-per-pet-u-a-tion
self--pity
  self--pit-y-ing
self--pol-li-na-tion
self--pos-sessed
  self--pos-sess-ed-ly
  self--pos-ses-sion
self--pres-er-va-tion
self--pro-pelled
  self--pro-pel-ling
self--re-al-i-za-tion
self--re-li-ance
  self--re-li-ant
self--re-spect
  self--re-spect-ing
self--re-straint
  self--re-strain-ing
self--right-eous
  self--right-eous-ness
self--sac-ri-fice
  self--sac-ri-fic-ing
self--same
self--sat-is-fied
  self-sat-is-fac-tion
  self--sat-is-fy-ing
self--ser-vice
self--serv-ing
self--start-er
  self--start-ing
self--styled
self--suf-fi-cient
  self--suf-fic-ing
  self--suf-fi-cien-cy
self--sup-port
  self--sup-port-ing
self--taught
self--will
  self--willed
sell
  sell-ing
sell-er
sell-out
sel-vage
  sel-vaged
se-man-tics
  se-man-tic
  se-man-ti-cal
  se-man-ti-cal-ly
sem-a-phore
  sem-a-phor-ed
  sem-a-phor-ing

sem-blance
se-men
se-mes-ter
sem-i-an-nu-al
  sem-i-an-nu-al-ly
sem-i-ar-id
sem-i-au-to-mat-ic
sem-i-cir-cle
  sem-i-cir-cu-lar
sem-i-clas-si-cal
  sem-i-clas-sic
sem-i-co-lon
sem-i-con-duc-tor
  sem-i-con-duct-ing
sem-i-con-scious
  sem-i-con-sious-ness
sem-i-de-tached
sem-i-fi-nal
  sem-i-fi-nal-ist
sem-i-flu-id
sem-i-for-mal
sem-i-gloss
sem-i-liq-uid
sem-i-month-ly
sem-i-nal
  sem-i-nal-ly
sem-i-nar-y
  sem-i-nar-ies
  sem-i-nar-ian
sem-i-of-fi-cial
  sem-i-of-fi-cial-ly
sem-i-per-ma-nent
sem-i-per-me-a-ble
sem-i-pre-cious
sem-i-pri-vate
sem-i-pro-fes-sion-al
sem-i-pro
sem-i-pub-lic
sem-i-skilled
sem-i-sol-id
sem-i-trail-er
sem-i-trop-ic
  sem-i-trop-i-cal
  sem-i-trop-ics
sem-i-vow-el
sem-i-week-ly
  sem-i-week-lies
sem-i-year-ly
sen-a-ry
sen-ate
sen-a-tor
  sen-a-tor-ship
sen-a-to-ri-al
  sen-a-to-ri-al-ly
send--off
se-nile

se-nil-i-ty
sen-ior
sen-ior-i-ty
sen-na
sen-sate
san-sa-tion
sen-sa-tion-al
  sen-sa-tion-al-ly
  sen-sa-tion-al-ism
sense
  sensed
  sens-ing
sense-less
  sense-less-ness
sen-si-bil-i-ty
  sen-si-ble-ness
sen-si-ble
  sen-si-ble-ness
  sen-si-bly
sen-si-tive
  sen-si-tiv-i-ty
  sen-si-tiv-i-ties
sen-si-tize
  sen-si-tized
  sen-si-tiz-ing
  sen-si-ti-za-tion
  sen-si-tizer
sen-sor
sen-so-ry
  sen-so-ri-al
sen-su-al
  sen-su-al-i-ty
  sen-su-al-ly
  sen-su-al-ism
  sen-su-al-ist
  sen-su-al-ize
  sen-su-al-ized
  sen-su-al-iz-ing
  sen-su-al-i-za-tion
sen-su-ous
sen-tence
  sen-tenced
  sen-tenc-ing
sen-tient
sen-ti-ment
sen-ti-men-tal
  sen-ti-men-tal-ly
sen-ti-men-til-i-ty
  sen-ti-men-tal-i-ties
  sen-ti-men-tal-ist
sen-ti-men-tal-ize
  sen-ti-men-tal-ized
  sen-ti-men-tal-iz-ing
sen-ti-nel
  sen-ti-neled
  sen-ti-nel-ing

sen-try
  sen-tries
se-pal
  se-paled
  se-palled
sep-a-ra-ble
  sep-a-ra-bil-i-ty
  sep-e-ra-bly
sep-a-rate
  sep-a-rat-ed
  sep-a-rat-ing
sep-a-ra-tion
sep-a-ra-tist
  sep-a-ra-tism
sep-a-ra-tive
sep-a-ra-tor
se-pi-a
sep-sis
  sep-ses
sep-ten-ni-al
sep-tet
sep-tic
  sep-ti-cal-ly
  sep-tic-i-ty
sep-tu-a-ge-nar-i-an
sep-tum
  sep-ta
sep-tu-ple
  sep-tu-pled
  sep-tu-pling
sep-ul-cher
  sep-u-chered
  sep-u-cher-ing
  se-pul-chral
se-quel
se-quence
se-quent
se-quen-tial
  se-quen-tial-ly
se-ques-ter
  se-ques-tered
  se-ques-tra-ble
se-ques-tra-tion
se-quin
  se-quined
se-quoi-a
se-ra-pe
ser-aph
  ser-aphs
  ser-a-phim
  se-raph-ic
ser-e-nade
  ser-e-nad-ed
  ser-e-nad-ing
  ser-e-nad-er
ser-en-dip-i-ty

ser-en-dip-i-tous
se-rene
  se-rene-ness
se-ren-i-ty
  se-ren-i-ties
serf
serge
ser-geant
ser-geant at arms
ser-geant ma-jor
se-ri-al
  se-ri-al-ly
  se-ri-al-ist
  se-ri-al-i-za-tion
  se-ri-al-ize
  se-ri-al-ized
  se-ri-al-iz-ing
se-ries
se-ri-ous
  se-ri-ous-ly
  se-ri-ous-ness
se-ri-ous--mind-ed
  se-ri-us--mind-ed-ly
ser-mon
  ser-mon-ize
  ser-mon-ized
  ser-mon-iz-ing
se-rol-o-gy
  se-ro-log-ic
  se-ro-log-i-cal
  se-rol-o-gist
se-rous
ser-pent
ser-pen-tine
ser-rate
  ser-rat-ing
ser-ra-tion
se-rum
  se-rums
  se-ra
serv-ant
serve
  served
  serv-ing
serv-er
serv-ice
  serv-iced
  serv-ic-ing
serv-ice-a-ble
  serv-ice-a-bil-i-ty
  serv-ice-a-ble-ness
  serv-ice-a-bly
serv-ice-man
ser-vile
  ser-vil-i-ty
  ser-vile-ness

ser-vi-tude
ser-vo-mech-an-ism
ses-a-me
ses-qui-cen-ten-ni-al
ses-sion
set-back
set-in
set-off
set-ter
set-ting
set-tle
  set-tled
  set-tling
set-tle-ment
set-tler
set-to
set-up
sev-en
sev-enth
sev-en-teen
  sev-en-teenth
sev-en-ty
  sev-en-ti-eth
sev-er
  sev-er-a-bil-i-ty
  sev-er-a-ble
sev-er-al
  sev-er-al-ly
  sev-er-al-fold
sev-er-ance
se-vere
  se-ver-er
  se-ver-est
  se-vere-ness
se-ver-i-ty
  se-ver-i-ties
sew
sew-age
sew-ing
sew-ing ma-chine
sex-less
sex-ol-o-gy
  sex-o-log-i-cal
  sex-ol-o-gist
sex-tant
sex-tet
sex-ton
sex-tu-ple
  sex-tu-pled
  sex-tu-pling
sex-tu-plet
sex-u-al
  sex-u-al-ly
  sex-u-al-i-ty
sex-y
  sex-i-er

sex-i-est
shab-by
 shab-bi-er
 shab-bi-est
 shab-bi-ly
shack-le
 shack-led
 shack-ling
 shack-ler
shade
 shad-ed
 shad-ing
 shade-less
shad-ow
shad-ow-box
shad-owy
shad-y
 shad-i-er
 shad-i-est
 shad-i-ly
shaft-ing
shag
 shagged
 shag-ging
 shag-gi-ly
shake
 shak-en
 shak-ing
shake-down
shak-er
shake-up
shak-y
 shak-i-er
 shak-i-est
 shak-i-ly
shal-lot
shal-low
 shal-low-ness
sham
 shammed
 sham-ming
sha-man
 sha-man-ism
 sha-man-ist
sham-bles
shame
 shamed
 sham-ing
shame-faced
 shame-fac-ed-ly
shame-ful
 shame-ful-ly
 shame-ful-ness
sham-mer
sham-my
sham-poo

sham-pooed
sham-poo-ing
sham-poo-er
sham-rock
shan-tey
 shan-ties
shan-ty-town
shape
 shaped
 shap-ing
 shap-a-ble
 shap-er
shape-less
shape-ly
 shape-li-ier
 shape-li-est
share
 shared
 shar-ing
 shar-er
share-crop-per
share-crop
 share-cropped
 share-crop-ping
share-hold-er
shark-skin
sharp-en
 sharp-en-er
sharp-er
sharp-eyed
sharp-ie
sharp-shoot-er
 sharp-shoot-ing
sharp-tongued
sharp-wit-ted
 sharp-wit-ted-ly
 sharp-wit-ted-ness
shat-ter
shat-ter-proof
shave
 shaved
 shav-ing
shav-er
shawl
sheaf
 sheaves
shear
 sheared
 shear-ing
 shear-er
sheath
 sheath-less
sheathe
 sheathed
 sheath-ing
 sheath-er

shed
 shed-ding
sheen
 sheeny
 sheen-i-er
sheep-dog
sheep-herd-er
 sheep-herd-ing
sheep-ish
sheep-skin
sheer
 sheer-ly
sheet-ing
sheik
shelf
 shelves
shell
 shelled
shel-lac
 shel-lacked
 shel-lack-ing
shell-fire
shell-fish
shell shock
shel-ter
 shel-ter-er
shelve
 shelved
 shelv-ing
she-nan-i-gan
shep-herd
 shep-herd-ess
sher-bet
sher-iff
sher-ry
 sher-ries
shib-bo-leth
shield
 shield-er
shift
 shift-er
shift-less
shift-y
 shift-i-er
 shift-i-est
 shift-i-ly
shil-ly--shal-ly
 shil-ly-shal-lied
 shil-ly-shal-ly-ing
shim-mer
 shim-mery
 shim-mer-i-er
 shim-mer-i-est
shim-my
 shim-mies
 shim-mied

shim-my-ing
shin
  shinned
  shin-ning
shin-bone
shin-dig
shine
  shined
  shone
  shin-ing
shin-er
shin-gle
  shin-gled
  shin-gling
  shin-gler
shin-gles
shin-ing
  shin-ing-ly
shin-ny
  shin-nied
  shin-ny-ing
shin-y
  shin-i-er
  shin-i-est
ship
  shipped
  ship-ping
  ship-a-ble
ship-board
ship-build-er
  ship-build-ing
ship-mate
ship-ment
ship-per
ship-yard
shirk
  shirker
shirt-tail
shirt-waist
shish ke-bab
shiv-er
  shiv-ery
  shiv-er-i-er
  shiv-er-i-est
shoal
shock-er
shock-ing
shod-dy
  shod-di-er
  shod-di-ly
  shod-di-ness
shoe-horn
shoe-lace
shoe-mak-er
sho-er
shoe-string

shoo--in
shoot
  shot
  shoot-ing
  shoot-er
shop
  shopped
  shop-ping
shop-keep-er
shop-lift-er
  shop-lift-ing
shop-per
shop-talk
shop-worn
shore
  shore-line
short
  short-ly
  short-ness
short-age
short--change
  short--changed
  short--chang-ing
short-com-ing
short-cut
  short-cut-ting
short-en
  short-en-er
  short-en-ing
short-hand
  short--hand-ed
short--lived
short--sight-ed
  short--sight-ed-ly
  short--sight-ed-ness
short--tem-pered
short--term
short-wave
short--wind-ed
shot-gun
  shot-gunned
  shot-gun-ning
shoul-der
shoul-der blade
shout-er
shout-ing
shove
  shoved
  shov-ing
  shov-er
shov-el
  shov-eled
  shov-el-ing
shov-el-ful
show
  showed

  shown
  show-ing
show-bill
show-boat
show-case
  show-cased
  show-cas-ing
show-down
show-er
  show-ery
show-man
  show-men
  show-man-ship
show-off
show-piece
show-place
show-room
show-y
  show-i-er
  show-i-est
  show-i-ly
shrap-nel
shred
  shred-ded
  shred-ding
  shred-der
shrew
shrewd
  shrewd-ly
  shrewd-ness
shrew-ish
shriek
shrill
shirl-ly
shrimp
shrine
  shrined
  shrin-ing
shrink
  shrunk-ed
  shrink-a-ble
  shrink-er
shrink-age
shriv-el
  shriv-eled
  shriv-el-ing
shroud
shrub-bery
  shrub-ber-ies
shrub-by
  shrub-bi-er
  shrub-bi-est
shrug
  shrugged
  shrug-ging
shuck-er

shud-der
shud-dery
suf-fle
shuf-fled
shuf-fling
shuf-fler
shuf-fle-board
shun
shunned
shun-ning
shun-ner
shunt
shunt-er
shut-down
shut-eye
shut-in
shut-off
shut-out
shut-ter
shut-tle
shut-tled
shut-tling
shut-tle-like
shy
shi-er
shy-est
shy-ness
shy-ster
sib-i-lant
sib-i-lance
sib-ling
sick
sicked
sick-ing
sick-bed
sick-en
sick-en-ing
sick-ish
sick-le
sick-ly
sick-li-er
sick-li-est
sick-ness
sick-room
side-arm
side-board
sid-ed
side-kick
side-line
side-lined
side-lin-ing
side--long
side-show
side-split-ting
side-step
side-step-ped

side-step-ping
side-swipe
side-swiped
side-swip-ing
side-track
side-ways
sid-ing
si-dle
si-dled
si-dling
siege
si-en-na
si-er-ra
si-es-ta
sieve
sieved
siev-ing
sift-er
sift-ings
sigh-er
sight-ed
sight-less
sight-ly
sight-read
sight-read-ing
sight-see-ing
sight-see-er
sig-nal
sig-naled
sig-nal-ing
sig-nal-er
sig-nal-man
sig-nal-men
sig-na-to-ry
sig-na-to-ries
sig-na-ture
sign-board
sig-net
sig-nif-i-cance
sig-nif-i-cant
sig-ni-fi-ca-tion
sig-ni-fy
sig-ni-fied
sig-ni-fy-ing
sig-ni-fi-a-ble
sig-ni-fi-er
sign-post
si-lage
si-lence
si-lenced
si-lenc-ing
si-lenc-er
si-lent
si-lent part-ner
sil-hou-ette
sil-hou-et-ted

sil-hou-et-ting
sil-ic-a
sil-i-con
sil-i-cone
silk-en
silk-like
silk-weed
silk-worm
silk-y
silk-i-er
silk-i-est
silk-i-ly
sil-ly
sil-li-er
sil-li-est
sil-li-ness
si-lo
si-los
si-loed
si-lo-ing
silt
sil-ta-tion
silt-y
silt-i-er
silt-i-est
sil-ver
sil-ver-fish
sil-ver-fox
sil-ver-ware
sil-ver-y
sim-i-an
sim-i-lar
sim-i-lar-i-ty
sim-i-lar-i-ties
sim-i-le
si-mil-i-tude
sim-mer
si-mon-ize
si-mon-ized
si-mon-iz-ing
sim-pa-ti-co
sim-per
sim-per-er
sim-per-ing-ly
sim-ple
sim-pler
sim-plest
sim-ple-ness
sim-ple--mind-ed
sim-ple sen-tence
sim-ple-ton
sim-plex
sim-plic-i-ty
sim-plic-i-ties
sim-pli-fy
sim-pli-fied

sim-pli-fy-ing
sim-pli-fi-ca-tion
sim-pli-fi-èr
sim-plism
sim-plis-tic
sim-plis-ti-cal-ly
sim-ply
sim-u-late
sim-u-lat-ed
sim-u-lat-ing
sim-u-la-tion
sim-u-la-tive
sim-u-la-tor
si-mul-cast
si-mul-cast-ing
si-mul-ta-ne-ous
si-mul-ta-ne-ous-ly
si-mul-ta-ne-i-ty
sin
sinned
sin-ning
sin-cere
sin-cer-i-ty
si-ne-cure
si-ne qua non
sin-ew
sin-ew-y
sin-ful
sin-ful-ly
sin-ful-ness
sing
sing-ing
sing-a-ble
singe
singed
singe-ing
sing-er
sin-gle
sin-gled
sin-gling
sin-gle-ness
sin-gle-brest-ed
sin-gle--hand-ed
sin-gle-hand-ed-ly
sin-gle--mind-ed
sin-gle--mind-ed-ly
sin-gle--space
sin-gle--spaced
sin-gle--spac-ing
sin-gle-ton
sin-gle--track
sin-gly
sing-song
sin-gu-lar
sin-gu-lar-i-ty
sin-gu-lar-i-ties

sin-is-ter
sin-is-ter-ness
sink-a-ble
sink-er
sink-hole
sin-less
sin-ner
sin-u-ate
sin-u-at-ed
sin-u-at-ing
sin-u-ous
sin-u-os-i-ty
sin-u-ous-ness
si-nus
si-nus-i-tis
sip
sipped
sip-ping
sip-per
si-phon
sire
sired
sir-ing
si-ren
sir-loin
sis-sy
sis-sies
sis-si-fied
sis-sy-ish
sis-ter
sis-ter-li-ness
sis-ter-ly
sis-ter-in-law
sis-ters-in-law
si-tar
sit-in
sit-ter
sit-ting
sit-u-ate
sit-u-at-ed
sit-u-at-ing
sit-u-a-tion
six--pack
six--shoot-er
six-teen
six-teenth
sixth
six-ty
six-ti-eth
siz-a-ble
siz-a-ble-ness
siz-a-bly
size
sized
siz-ing
siz-zle

siz-zled
siz-zling
siz-zler
skate
skat-ed
skat-ing
skat-er
ske-dad-dle
ske-dad-dled
ske-dad-dling
skein
skel-e-ton
skel-e-tal
skep-tic
skep-ti-cal
skep-ti-cism
sketch
sketch-er
sketch-book
sketch-y
sketch-i-er
sketch-i-est
sketch-i-ly
skew-er
skew-ness
ski
skied
ski-ing
ski-er
skid
skid-ded
skid-ding
skid-der
skilled
skil-let
skill-ful
skill-ful-ly
skill-ful-ness
skim
skimmed
skim-ming
skim-mer
skimp
skimp-i-ly
skimp-y
skimp-i-er
skimp-i-est
skin
skinned
skin-ning
skin--deep
skin dive
skin div-ing
skin div-er
skin-flint
skin-less

skin-ner
skin-ny
  skin-ni-er
  skin-ni-est
skin-tight
skip-per
skir-mish
  skir-mish-er
skirt-er
  skirt-ing
skit-ter
skit-tish
skiv-vy
  skiv-vies
skoal
skul-dug-ger-y
skulk-er
skull-cap
skunk
sky
  skies
  skied
  sky-ing
sky-blue
sky-cap
sky-div-ing
sky-rock-et
sky-svap-er
sky-ward
sky-way
sky-writ-ing
  sky-writ-er
slab
  slabbed
  slab-bing
slack
  slack-ness
slack-en
slack-er
slack-jawed
slake
  slaked
  slak-ing
sla-lom
slam
  slammeed
  slam-ming
slam-bang
slan-der
  slan-der-er
  slan-der-ous
slang
  slang-i-er
  slang-i-est
slant
  slant-ways

slant-wise
slap
  slapp-ed
  slap-ping
  slap-per
slap-dash
slap-hap-py
  slap-hap-pi-er
  slap-hap-pi-est
slap-stick
slash-er
slash-ing
slat
  slat-ted
  slat-ting
slate
  slat-ed
  slat-ing
slath-er
slat-tern
  slat-tern-ly
slaugh-ter
  slaugh-ter-er
slaugh-ter-house
slave
  slaved
  slav-ing
slav-er
slav-er-y
slav-ish
  sla-vish-ly
slay
  slain
  slay-ing
  slay-er
slea-zy
  slea-zi-er
  slea-zi-est
sled
  sled-ded
  sled-ding
  sled-der
sledge
  sledged
  sledg-ing
sleek
  sleek-er
  sleek-ness
sleep-er
sleep-less
  sleep-less-ness
sleep-walk
  sleep-walk-er
  sleep-walk-ing
sleep-y
  sleep-i-er

sleep-i-est
sleep-i-ly
sleep-y-head
sleet
  sleet-y
  sleet-i-ness
sleeve
  sleeved
  sleev-ing
  sleeve-less
sleigh
  sleigh-er
sleight
slen-der
  slen-der-ness
slen-der-ize
  slen-der-ized
  slen-der-iz-ing
sleuth
slice
  sliced
  slic-ing
  slic-er
slick-er
slick-ness
slide
slid
  slid-ing
  slid-er
slight
  slight-er
  slight-ing
slim
  slim-mer
  slim-mest
  slimmed
  slim-ming
  slim-ness
slime
  slimed
  slim-ing
slimy
  slim-i-er
  slim-i-est
  slim-i-ly
sling-er
sling-shoot
slink-y
  slink-i-er
  slink-i-est
slip
  slipped
  slip-ping
slip-cov-er
slip-knot
slip--on

slip-o-ver
slip-page
slip-per
slip-per-y
  slip-per-i-er
  slip-per-i-est
slip-py
slip-shod
slip-stick
slip-up
slit
  slit-ting
  slit-ter
slith-er
  slith-ery
sliv-er
  sliv-er-er
  sliv-er-like
slob-ber
  slob-ber-er
  slob-ber-ing-ly
sloe--eyed
slo-gan
  slo-gan-eer
slop
  slopped
  slop-ping
slope
  sloped
  slop-ing
  slop-er
slop-py
  slop-pi-er
  slop-pi-est
  slo-pi-ly
  slop-pi-ness
slosh-y
  slosh-i-er
  slosh-i-est
slot
  slot-ted
  slot-ting
sloth
  sloth-ful
  sloth-ful-ly
slouch
  slouch-er
  slouch-i-ly
  slouch-i-ness
  slouch-y
  slouch-i-er
  slouch-i-est
slough
  slough-y
  slough-i-er
  slough-i-est

slov-en
slov-en-ly
  slov-en-li-ness
slow-down
slow--mo-tion
slow-poke
slow--wit-ted
sludge
  slug-y
  sludg-i-er
  sludg-i-est
slug
  slugged
  slug-ging
  slug-ger
slug-gard
  slug-gard-li-ness
slug-gish
  slug-gish-ness
sluice
  sluiced
  sluic-ing
slum
  slummed
  slum-ming
slum-ber
  slum-ber-er
slum-ber-ous
slur
  slurred
  slur-ring
slush
  slush-i-ness
  slush-y
  slush-i-er
  slush-i-est
slut
  slut-tish
sly
smack
smack-ing
small--mind-ed
  small--mind-ed-ness
small-pox
small--time
  small--tim-er
smart
  smart-ness
smart al-eck
  smart-al-eck-y
smart-en
smash
smash-ing
smash--up
smat-ter
  smat-ter-er

  smat-ter-ing
smear
  smear-er
smear-y
  smear-i-er
  smear-i-est
smell
  smelled
  smel-ling
  smell-er
  smell-y
  smell-i-er
  smell-i-est
smelt
  smelt-er
  smelt-ery
smid-gen
snile
  smil-er
  smil-ing-ly
smirch
smirk
  smirk-er
  smirk-ing-ly
smite
  smote
  smit-ten
  smit-ting
  smit-er
smith-er-eens
smit-ten
smock-ing
smog-gy
  smog-gi-er
  smog-gi-est
smoke
  smoked
  smok-ing
  smoke-less
smoke-house
  smok-er
smoke-stack
smok-ing jack-et
smok-y
  smok-i-er
  smok-i-est
  smok-i-ly
smol-der
smooth
  smooth-er
  smooth-ness
smooth-en
smooth-ie
smoth-er
  smoth-er-y
  smoth-er-i-er

smoth-er-i-est
smudge
  smudged
  smudg-ing
  smudg-i-ly
smug
  smug-ger
  smug-gest
  smug-ly
  smug-ness
smug-gle
  smug-gled
  smug-gling
  smug-gler
smut
  smut-ted
  smut-ting
smut-ty
  smut-ti-er
  smut-ti-est
  smut-ti-ly
sna-fu
  sna-fued
  sna-fu-ing
snag
  snagged
  snag-ging
  snag-gy
snag-gle-tooth
  snag-gle-teeth
  snag-gle-toothed
snail
  snail-like
  snail-paced
snake
snake-bite
snake-skin
snak-y
  snak-i-er
  snak-i-est
snap
  snapped
  snap-ping
snap-back
snap-drag-on
snap-per
snap-pish
  snap-pish-ness
snap-py
  snap-pi-er
  snap-pi-est
  snap-pi-ly
snap-shot
snare
  snared
  snar-ing

snar-er
snarl
  snarl-er
  snarl-y
  snarl-i-er
  snarl-i-est
snatch
  snatch-i-er
  snatch-i-est
  snatch-i-ly
snaz-zy
  snaz-zi-er
  snaz-zi-est
sneak-er
sneak-ing
sneak-y
  sneak-i-er
  sneak-i-est
  sneak-i-ly
sneer
  sneer-er
  sneer-ing-ly
sneeze
  sneezed
  sneez-ing
  sneez-er
  sneez-y
  sneez-i-er
  sneez-i-est
snick-er
snif-fle
  snif-fled
  snif-fling
  snif-fler
snif-fy
  snif-fi-er
  snif-fi-est
  snif-fi-ly
snif-ter
snip
  snipped
  snip-ping
  snip-per
snipe
  sniped
  snip-ing
  snip-er
snip-py
  snip-pi-er
  snip-pi-est
  snip-pi-ly
snitch-er
sniv-el
  sniv-eled
  sniv-el-ing
  sniv-el-er

snob
  snob-ber-y
  snob-bish
  snob-bish-ness
snoop
  snoop-y
  snoop-i-er
  snoop-i-est
  snoop-er
snoot-y
  snoot-i-er
  snoot-i-est
  snoot-i-ly
  snoot-i-ness
snooze
  snoozed
  snooz-ing
  snooz-er
snore
  snored
  snor-ing
  snor-er
snor-kel
snort
  snort-er
snot-ty
  snot-ti-er
  snot-ti-est
snout
  snout-ed
  snout-y
  snout-i-er
  snout-i-est
snow-ball
snow-blow-er
snow-bound
snow-cap
snow-drift
snow-fall
snow-flake
snow-man
  snow-men
snow-mo-bile
snow-plow
snow-shoe
  snow-shoed
  snow-shoe-ing
snow-suit
snow--white
snow-y
  snow-i-er
  snow-i-est
snub
  snubbed
  snub-bing
  snub-ber

snub-by
  snub-bi-er
  snub-bi-est
  snub-bi-ness
snub--nosed
snuf-fle
snuff-y
  snuff-i-er
  snuff-i-est
snug
snug-gle
  snug-gled
  snug-gling
soak
  soak-age
  soak-er
  soak-ing-ly
so--and--so
soap-box
soap-suds
soap-y
  soap-i-er
  soap-i-est
  soap-i-ly
  soap-i-ness
soar-er
sob
  sobbed
  sob-bing
  sob-ber
so-ber
  so-ber-ing-ly
  so-ber-ness
so-bri-e-ty
so-bri-quet
so--called
soc-cer
so-cia-ble
  so-cia-bil-i-ty
  so-cia-bly
so-cial
  so-ci-al-i-ty
  so-cial-ly
so-cial-ism
so-cial-ist
  so-cial-is-tic
  so-cial-is-ti-cal-ly
so-cial-ite
so-cial-ize
  so-cial-ized
  so-cial-iz-ing
  so-cial-i-za-tion
  so-cial-iz-er
so-ci-e-ty
  so-ci-e-ties
  so-ci-e-tal

so-ci-o-ec-o-nom-ic
so-ci-ol-o-gy
  so-ci-o-log-i-cal
  so-ci-ol-o-gist
so-ci-o-po-lit-i-cal
sock-et
sod
  sod-ded
  sod-ding
so-da
so-dal-i-ty
  so-dal-i-ties
sod-den
  sod-den-ness
so-di-um
sod-om-y
so-ev-er
so-fa
soft
  soft-ness
soft-ball
soft--boiled
sof-ten
  sof-ten-er
soft--head-ed
soft--heart-ed
  soft--heart-ed-ness
soft ped-al
  soft-ped-aled
  soft-ped-al-ing
soft--shell
soft--shoe
soft--spok-en
soft-ware
soft-wood
soft-y
  sof-ties
sog-gy
  sog-gi-er
  sog-gi-est
  sog-gi-ly
  sog-gi-ness
so-journ
  so-journ-er
sol-ace
  sol-aced
  sol-ac-ing
  sol-ac-er
so-lar
so-lar-i-um
  so-lar-i-ums
  so-lar-ia
so-lar-ize
  so-lar-ized
  so-lar-iz-ing
  so-lar-i-za-tion

sol-der
  sol-der-er
sol-dier
  sol-dier-y
sol-e-cism
sole-ly
sol-emn
  sol-emn-ly
  sol-emn-less
so-lem-ni-fy
  so-lem-ni-ties
sol-em-nize
  sol-em-nized
  sol-em-niz-ing
  sol-em-ni-za-tion
sole-ness
so-lic-it
  so-lic-i-ta-tion
so-lic-i-tor
so-lic-i-tous
  so-lic-i-tous-ness
so-lic-i-tude
sol-id
  so-lid-i-ty
  sol-id-ness
sol-i-dar-i-ty
  sol-i-dar-i-ties
so-lid-i-fy
  so-lid-i-fied
  so-lid-i-fy-ing
  so-lid-i-fi-ca-tion
so-lil-o-quize
  so-lil-o-quized
  so-lil-o-quiz-ing
  so-lil-o-quist
so-lil-o-quy
  so-lil-o-quies
sol-i-taire
sol-i-tar-y
  sol-i-tar-ies
  sol-i-tar-i-ly
  sol-i-tar-i-ness
sol-i-tude
so-lo
  so-loed
  so-lo-ing
  so-lo-ist
sol-stice
sol-u-ble
  sol-u-bil-i-ty
  sol-u-bly
sol-ute
so-lu-tion
solve
  solved
  solv-ing

190

solv-a-ble
solv-a-bil-i-ty
solv-er
sol-vent
sol-ven-cy
so-mat-ic
so-ma-to-type
som-ber
som-ber-ly
som-ber-ness
som-bre-ro
som-bre-ros
some-bod-y
some-bod-ies
some-day
some-how
some-place
som-er-sault
some-thing
some-time
some-times
some-way
some-what
some-where
sosm-nam-bu-late
som-no-lent
som-no-lence
som-no-len-cy
so-nar
so-na-ta
song-bird
song-fest
song-ster
song-stress
song-writ-er
son-ic
son--in--law
sons--in--law
son-net
son-ny
son-nies
so-no-rous
so-nor-i-ty
so-no-rous-ness
soon-er
soothe
soothed
sooth-ing
sooth-er
sooth-say-er
sooth-say-ing
soot-y
soot-i-er
soot-i-est
soot-i-ly
sop

sopped
sop-ping
soph-ist
soph-ism
so-phis-tic
so-phis-ti-cal
so-phis-ti-cate
so-phis-ti-cat-ed
so-phis-ti-cat-ing
so-phis-ti-ca-tion
so-phis-ti-ca-tor
soph-ist-ry
soph-ist-ries
soph-o-more
soph-o-mor-ic
soph-o-mor-i-cal
soph-o-mor-i-cal-ly
sop-o-rif-ic
sop-py
sop-pi-er
sop-pi-est
so-pran-o
so-pran-os
sor-cer-er
sor-cer-ess
sor-cer-y
sor-cer-ies
sor-cer-ous
sor-did
sor-did-ness
sore
sor-er
sor-est
sore-ly
sore-ness
sore-head
sore-head-ed
sor-ghum
so-ror-i-ty
so-ror-i-ties
sor-rel
sor-row
sor-row-er
sor-row-ful
sor-ry
sor-ri-er
sor-ri-est
sor-ri-ly
sort-a-ble
sort-er
sor-tie
so--so
sot
sot-ted
sot-tish
sot-tish-ness

sot-vo vo-ce
sought
soul-ful
soul-ful-ly
soul-ful-ness
soul-less
soul-searching
sound
sound-a-ble
sound-ly
sound-ness
sound-box
sound-er
sound-ing
sound-less
sound-less-ly
sound-proof
soup-y
soup-i-er
soup-i-est
sour
sour-ish
sour-ness
sour-ball
source
souse
soused
sous-ing
south-bound
south-east
south-east-er
south-east-er-ly
south-east-ern
south-east-ward
south-east-ward-ly
south-er
south-er-ly
south-ern
south-ern-most
south-ern-er
south-paw
south-ward
south-ward-ly
south-west
south-west-er
south-west-ern
south-west-ern-er
south-west-ward
south-west-ward-ly
sou-ve-nir
sov-er-eign
sov-er-eign-ty
sov-er-eign-ties
so-vi-et
sow-er
soy-bean

space
  spaced
  spac-ing
  space-less
  spac-er
space-craft
space-man
  space-men
space-ship
space-walk
spa-cious
  spa-cious-ness
spade
  spad-ed
  spad-ing
  spade-ful
  spad-er
spade-work
spa-ghet-ti
span
  spanned
  span-ning
span-gle
  span-gled
  span-gling
span-iel
spank-er
spank-ing
spar
  sparred
  spar-ring
spare
  spared
  spar-ing
  spar-er
  spar-est
  spar-a-ble
  spare-ness
spare-rib
spar-ing
  spar-ing-ness
spark-er
spar-kle
  spar-kled
  spar-kling
spar-kler
spar-row
spar-row-grass
sparse
  spars-er
  spars-est
spasm
spas-mod-ic
  spas-mod-i-cal
  spas-mod-i-cal-ly
spas-tic

spas-ti-cal-ly
spat
  spat-ted
  spat-ting
spa-tial
  spa-cial
  spa-ti-al-i-ty
  spa-tial-ly
spat-ter
spat-u-la
spawn
speak
  spok-en
  speak-ing
  speak-a-ble
speak-eas-y
  speak-eas-ies
speak-er
  speak-er-ship
spear-er
spear-head
spear-mint
spe-cial
  spe-cial-ly
  spe-cial-ist
spe-cial-ize
  spe-cial-ized
  spe-cial-iz-ing
  spe-cial-i-za-tion
spe-cial-ty
  spe-cial-ties
spe-cie
spe-cies
spec-i-fia-ble
spe-cif-ic
  spe-cif-i-cal-ly
  spec-i-fic-i-ty
spec-i-fi-ca-tion
spec-i-fy
  spec-i-fied
  spec-i-fy-ing
  spec-i-fi-er
spec-i-men
spe-cious
  spe-ci-os-i-ty
  spe-ci-os-i-ties
  spe-cious-ness
speck-le
  speck-led
  speck-ling
spec-ta-cle
  spec-ta-cled
spec-tac-u-lar
  spec-tac-u-lar-ly
spec-ta-tor
spec-ter

spec-tral
spce-tro-scope
  spec-tro-scop-ic
  spec-tro-scop-i-cal
  spec-tros-co-py
spec-trum
  spec-tra
  spec-trums
spec-u-late
  spec-u-lat-ed
  spec-u-lat-ing
  spec-u-la-tion
  spec-u-la-tive
  spec-u-la-tor
speech-i-fy
  speech-i-fie
  speech-i-fy-ing
speech-less
  speech-less-ness
speed
  speed-ed
  speed-ing
  speed-er
  speed-ster
speed-boat
  speed-boat-ing
speed-om-e-ter
speed--up
speed-way
speed-y
  speed-i-er
  speed-i-est
  speed-i-ly
  speed-i-ness
spe-le-ol-o-gy
  spe-le-ol-o-gist
spell
  spelled
  spell-ing
spell-bind
  spell-bouns
  spell-bind-ing
  spell-bind-er
spell-er
spe-lun-ker
spend
  spent
  spend-ing
  spend-a-ble
  spend-er
spend-thrift
sper-ma-cet-i
sper-mat-ic
sper-ma-to-zo-on
  sper-ma-to-zo-a
  sper-ma-tozo-ic

spew-er
sphag-num
sphere
  sphered
  spher-ing
  spher-ic
  sphe-ric-i-ty
sphe-roid
  sphe-roi-dal
sphinc-ter
  sphin-ter-al
  sphin-ter-ic
sphinx
  sphinxes
  sphin-ges
spice
  spiced
  spic-ing
spi-cule
  spic-u-lar
  spic-u-late
spic-y
  spic-i-er
  spic-i-esst
  spic-i-ly
spi-der
spi-der-y
spiel
  spiel-er
spi-er
spiff-y
  spiff-i-er
  spiff-i-est
spig-ot
spike
  spiked
  spik-ing
spik-y
  spik-i-er
  spik-i-est
spill
  spilled
  spill-ing
spil-lage
spill-way
spin
  spun
  spin-ning
spin-ach
spi-nal
  spi-nal-ly
spin-dle
  spin-dled
  spin-dling
spin-dle-legs
  spin-dle-leg-ged

spin-dly
  spin-dli-er
  spin-dli-est
spine-less
spin-et
spin-na-ker
spin-ner
spin-ning wheel
spin--off
spi-nose
spi-nous
spin-ster
spin-y
  spin-i-ness
spi-ra-cle
spi-ral
  spi-raled
  spi-ral-ing
  spi-ral-ly
spire
  spired
  spir-ing
spir-it
spir-it-ed
spir-it-ism
  spir-ir-ist
spir-it-less
  spir-it-les-ness
spir-i-tous
spir-it-u-al
  spir-it-u-al-ly
spir-it-u-al-ism
  spir-it-u-al-ist
  spir-it-u-al-is-tic
spir-it-u-al-i-ty
  spir-it-u-al-i-ties
spir-it-u-al-ize
  spir-it-u-al-ized
  spir-it-u-al-iz-ing
  spir-it-u-al-i-za-tion
spir-it-u-ous
  spir-it-u-os-i-ty
spi-ro-chete
spit
  spat
  spit-ting
  spit-ter
spite
  spit-ed
  spit-ing
spite-ful
spit-fire
spit-tle
spit-toon
splash
  splash-er

splashy
  splash-i-er
  splash-i-est
  splash-i-ly
splash-board
splash-down
splat-ter
splay-foot
  splay-feet
  splay-foot-ed
spleen
  spleen-ful
splen-did
splen-dif-er-ous
sple-net-ic
splice
  spliced
  splic-ing
  splic-er
splin-ter
  splin-tery
split
  split-ting
  split-a-ble
  split-ter
split--lev-el
split--sec-ond
splotch
  spotch-y
  splotch-i-er
  splotch-i-est
splurge
  splurged
  splurg-ing
splut-ter
  splut-ter-er
spoil
  spoil-ed
  spoil-ing
spoil-age
spoil-er
spoil-sport
spoke
  spoked
  spok-ing
spo-ken
spokes-man
  spokes-men
  spokes-wom-an
  spokes-wom-en
sponge
  sponged
  spong-ing
spong-er
spon-gy
  spon-gi-er

spon-gi-est
spon-gi-ness
spon-sor
  spon-sor-ship
spon-ta-ne-i-ty
  spon-ta-ne-i-ties
spon-ta-ne-ous
  spon-ta-ne-ous-ly
  spon-ta-ne-ous-ness
spook
  spook-ish
spook-y
  spook-i-er
  spook-i-est
  spook-i-ly
spoon-er-ism
  spoon-er-is-tic
spoon--fed
spoon--feed
  spoon--feed-ing
spoon-ful
  spoon-fuls
spo-rad-ic
  spo-rad-i-cal
  spo-rad-i-cal-ly
spo-ran-gi-um
  spo-ran-gia
spore
  spored
  spor-ing
sport
sport-ing
  sport-ing-ly
spor-tive
sports-cast
  sports-cast-er
sports-man
sports-wear
sports-writ-er
sport-y
  sport-i-er
  sport-i-est
  sport-i-ly
spot
  spot-ted
  spot-ting
  spot-less
  spot-less-ly
spot-light
spot-ted
spot-ted fe-ver
spot-ter
spot-ty
  spot-ti-er
  spot-ti-est
  spot-ti-ly

spouse
spout
spout-er
sprain
sprawl
spray
  spray-er
spread
  spread-ing
spread--ea-gle
  spread--ea-gled
  spread--ea-gling
spread-er
sprig
  sprigged
  sprig-ging
spright-ly
  spright-li-er
  spright-li-est
spring
  spring-ing
spring-board
spring--clean-ing
spring-time
spring-y
  spring-i-er
  spring-i-est
  spring-i-ly
sprin-kle
  sprin-kled
  sprin-kling
  sprink-ler
sprint
  sprint-er
sprock-et
spruce
  spruc-er
  spruc-est
  spruced
  spruc-ing
spry
  spry-er
  spry-est
  spry-ly
spue
  spued
  spu-ing
spume
  spumed
  spum-ing
  spum-ous
spunk-y
  spunk-i-er
  spunk-i-est
  spunk-i-ly
  spunk-i-ness

spur
  spurred
  spur-ring
spu-ri-ous
  spu-ri-ous-ness
spurner
spurt
  spurt-er
  spur-tive
sput-nik
sput-ter
  sput-ter-er
spu-tum
  spu-ta
spy
  spies
  spied
  spy-ing
spy-glass
squad-ron
squal-id
  squal-id-ly
  squal-id-ness
squall
  squally
  squall-i-er
  squall-i-est
squal-or
squan-der
  squan-der-er
square
  squared
  squar-ing
  square-ly
  square-ness
square-dance
  square-danced
  square-danc-ing
squar-ish
  squar-ish-ly
squash
  squash-er
  squash-es
squash-y
  squash-i-er
  squash-i-est
squat
  squat-ted
  squat-ting
  squat-ly
squat-ter
squat-ty
  squat-ti-er
  squat-ti-est
squawk
  squawk-er

sqauwk-y
squawk-i-er
squawk-i-est
squeak
squeak-er
squeak-ing-ly
squeak-y
squeak-i-er
squeak-i-est
squeal
squeal-er
squeam-ish
squeam-ish-ly
squeam-ish-ness
squee-gee
squeeze
squeez-ed
squeez-ing
squeez-er
squelch
squelch-er
squib
squid
squig-gle
squig-gled
squig-gling
squint
squint-er
squint-ing-ly
squinty
squint-i-er
squint-i-est
squint--eyed
squire
squired
squir-ing
squirm
squirmy
squirm-i-er
squirm-i-est
squir-rel
squirt
squirt-er
squish
squish-y
squish-i-er
squish-i-est
stab
stabbed
stab-bing
stab-ber
sta-bil-i-ty
sta-bil-i-ties
sta-bi-lize
sta-bi-lized
sta-bi-liz-ing

sta-bi-li-za-tion
sta-bi-liz-er
sta-ble
sta-bled
sta-bling
stac-ca-to
stack-er
sta-di-um
staff-er
stag
stagged
stag-ging
stage-coach
stage-hand
stage--struck
stag-ger
stag-ger-er
stag-ger-ing
stag-nant
stag-nan-cy
stag-nate
stag-nat-ed
stag-nat-ing
stag-na-tion
stag-y
stag-i-er
stag-i-est
stag-i-ly
stag-i-ness
stain
stain-a-ble
stained
stain-er
stained glass
stain-less
stair-case
stair-way
stair-well
stake
staked
stak-ing
stake-hold-er
sta-lac-tite
sta-lag-mite
stale
stal-er
stal-est
staled
stal-ing
stale-ness
stale-mate
stale-mat-ed
stale-mat-ing
stalk
stalled
stal-lion

stal-wart
stal-wart-ness
sta-men
sta-mens
stam-i-na
stam-mer
stam-mer-ing-ly
stam-pede
stam-ped-ed
stam-ped-ing
stam-ped-er
stam-ped-ing-ly
stamp-er
stance
stand
stand-ing
stand-er
stand-ard
stand-ard-ize
stand-ard-ized
stand-ard-iz-ing
stand-ard-i-za-tion
stand-by
stnad-ee
stand--in
stand--off-ish
stand--off-ish-ness
stand-out
stand-pipe
stand-point
stand-still
sta-nine
stan-za
stan-za-ic
sta-pes
sta-pes
sta-ped-es
sta-pe-di-al
staph-y-lo-coc-cus
sta-ple
sta-pled
sta-pling
sta-pler
star
star-board
star-dom
stare
stared
star-ing
star-er
star-fish
star-gaze
star-gazed
star-gaz-ing
star-let
star-light

star-ling
star-ry
  star-ri-er
  star-ri-est
  star-ri-ly
star-ry--eyed
star-span-gled
start-er
star-tle
  star-tled
  star-tling
  star-tling-ly
star-va-tion
starve
  starved
  starv-ing
sta-sis
state
  stat-ed
  stat-ing
  stat-a-ble
state-craft
state-hood
state-less
  state-less-ness
state-ly
  state-li-er
  state-li-est
state-ment
state-room
state-side
states-man
  states-men
  states-man-like
  states-man-ship
stat-ic
stat-ics
sta-tion
sta-tion-ar-y
ssta-tion-er
sta-tion-er-y
stat-ism
  stat-ist
sta-tic-tic
  sta-tis-ti-cal
  sta-tic-ti-cal-ly
stat-is-ti-cian
sta-tis-tics
sta-tor
stat-u-ar-y
  stat-u-ar-ies
stat-ue
stat-u-esque
stat-u-ette
stat-ure
sta-tus

stat-ute
staunch
stave
  staved
  stav-ing
stay
  stay-ed
  stay-ing
  stay-er
stead-fast
  stead-fast-ly
stead-y
steal
  stol-en
  steal-ing
  steal-er
stealth
  stealth-y
  stealth-i-er
  stealth-i-est
steam-boat
steam-er
steam-fit-ter
  steam-fit-ting
steam-roll-er
steam-ship
steam-y
  steam-i-er
  steam-i-est
  steam-i-ly
ste-a-tite
sted-fast
steel-head
steel-works
  steel-work-er
steel-y
  steel-i-er
steel-yard
steep
  steep-ly
steep-en
stee-ple
stee-ple-chase
  stee-ple-chas-er
stee-ple-jack
steer
  steer-a-ble
  steer-er
steer-age
stein
stel-lar
stem
  stemmed
stem-ware
stem-wind-er
  stem-wind-ing

stench
  stench-y
  stench-i-er
  stench-i-est
sten-cil
  sten-ciled
  sten-cil-ing
ste-nog-ra-pher
ste-nog-ra-phy
  sten-o-graph-ic
  sten-o-raph-i-cal-ly
sten-to-ri-an
step
  stepped
  step-ping
step-broth-er
step-child
  step-child-ren
step-daugh-ter
step-fa-ther
step-lad-der
step-moth-er
step-par-ent
stepped-up
step-sis-ter
step-son
ster-e-o
  ster-e-os
ster-e-o-phon-ic
  ster-e-o-phon-i-cal-ly
ster-e-o-scope
  ster-e-o-scop-ic
ster-e-o-type
  ster-e-o-typed
  ster-e-o-typ-ing
ster-ile
  ste-ril-i-ty
ster-i-lize
  ster-i-lized
  ster-i-liz-ing
  ster-i-li-za-tion
  ster-i-li-zer
ster-ling
stern
  stern-ly
  stern-ness
ster-num
  ster-na
  ster-nums
stern-wheel-er
ster-oid
steth-o-scope
  steth-o-scop-ic
ste-ve-dore
  ste-ve-dored
  ste-ve-dor-ing

ste-ward
stew-ard-ness
stick-er
stick-ing
stick-le-back
stick-ler
stick-pin
stick-up
stick-y
  stick-i-er
  stick-i-est
stiff
  stiff-ly
  stiff-ness
stiff-en
  stiff-en-er
stiff--necked
sti-fle
  sti-fled
  sti-fling
  sti-fler
  sti-fling-ly
stig-ma
  stig-mas
  stig-ma-ta
  stig-ma-tic
  stig-mat-i-cal-ly
stig-ma-tize
  stig-ma-tized
  stig-ma-tiz-ing
  stig-ma-ti-za-tion
sti-let-to
  sti-let-tos
  sti-let-toes
still-birth
  still-born
still life
still-ness
stilt-ed
  stilt-ed-ly
stim-u-lant
stim-u-late
  stim-u-lat-ed
  stim-u-lat-ing
  stim-u-la-tion
  stim-u-la-tive
stim-u-lus
  stim-u-li
sting
  sting-ing
  sting-er
  sting-ing-ly
stin-gy
  stin-gi-er
  stin-gi-est
  stin-gi-ly

stin-gi-ness
stink
  stink-ing
  stink-er
  stink-y
  stink-i-er
  stink-i-est
stint-er
sti-pend
stip-ple
  stip-pled
  stip-pling
stip-u-late
  stip-u-lat-ed
  stip-u-lat-ing
  stip-u-la-tion
  stip-u-la-to-ry
stir
  stirred
  stir-ring
  stri-ring-ly
stir-rup
stitch
  stitch-er
stock-ade
  stock-ad-ed
  stock-ad-ing
stock-brok-er
stock-hold-er
Stock-holm
stock-ing
stock-pile
  stock-piled
  stock-pil-ing
stock-y
  stock-i-er
  stock-i-est
  stock-i-ly
  stock-i-ness
stock-yard
stodg-y
  stodg-i-er
  stodg-i-est
  stodg-i-ly
sto-ic
sto-i-cal
stoke
  stoked
  stok-ing
  stok-er
stol-id
  sto-lid-i-ty
  stol-id-ly
sto-ma
  sto-ma-ta
  sto-mas

stom-ach
stom-ach-er
stone
  stoned
  ston-ing
stone-deaf
stone-ma-son
  stone-ma-son-ry
stone-wall
ston-y
  ston-i-er
  ston-i-est
  ston-i-ly
stop
  stopped
  stop-ping
stop-gap
stop-light
stop-o-ver
stop-page
stop-per
stop-watch
stor-age
store
  stored
  stor-ing
store-house
store-keep-er
store-room
sto-ried
storm-y
  storm-i-er
  storm-i-est
  storm-i-ly
  storm-i-ness
sto-ry
  sto-ries
  sto-ry-ing
sto-ry-book
sto-ry-tell-er
  stor-y-tell-ing
stout
  stout-ly
  stout-ness
stout--heart-ed
stove
  stoved
  stov-ing
stove-pipe
stow-age
stow-a-way
stra-bis-mus
strad-dle
  strad-dled
  strad-dling
  strad-dler

strafe
  strafed
  straf-ing
strag-gle
  strag-gled
  strag-gling
  strag-gler
strag-gly
  strag-gli-er
  strag-gli-est
straight-en
  straight-en-er
straight-for-ward
  straight-for-ward-ly
straight-way
strain-er
strait-en
strait-jack-et
strait-laced
strange
  strang-er
  strang-est
  strang-ly
  strange-ness
stran-ger
stran-gle
  stran-gled
  stran-gling
  stran-gler
stran-gu-la-tion
  strn-gu-late
  stran-gu-lat-ed
  stran-gu-lat-ing
strap
  srapped
  strap-ping
  strap-less
stra-te-gic
  str-te-gi-cal-ly
strat-e-gy
  strat-e-gies
  strat-e-gist
strat-i-fi-ca-tion
strat-i-fy
  strat-i-fied
  strat-i-fy-ing
stra-to-cu-mu-lus
strat-o-sphere
  strat-o-spher-ic
stra-tum
  stra-ta
  stra-tums
stra-tus
  stra-ti
straw-ber-ry
  straw-ber-ries

stray-er
stray-ing
streak
  streaky
  streak-i-er
  streak-i-est
stream-er
stream-line
  stream-lined
  stream-lin-ing
street-car
street-walk-er
  street-walk-ing
strength-en
  strength-en-er
stren-u-ous
  stren-u-os-i-ty
  stren-u-ous-ly
strep-to-coc-cus
  strep-to-coc-ci
  strep-to-coc-cal
  strep-to-coc-cic
strep-to-my-cin
stress
  stress-ful
  stress-ful-ly
  stress-ful-ness
stretch
  stretch-a-bil-i-ty
  stretch-a-ble
stretch-er
strew
  strewed
  strew-ing
stri-a
  stri-ae
stri-ate
  stri-at-ed
  stri-at-ing
strick-en
strict
  strict-ly
  strict-ness
stric-ture
stride
  strid-den
  strid-ding
stri-dent
strid-u-la-tion
strife
  strife-ful
  strife-less
strike
  strick-en
  strick-ing
string

strung
string-ing
strin-gent
  strin-gen-cy
  strin-gent-ly
string-y
  string-i-er
  string-i-est
strip
  stripped
  strip-ping
stripe
  striped
  strip-ing
strip-ling
strip-per
strip-tease
  strip-teas-er
strive
  strove
  striv-en
  striv-ing
stro-bo-scope
  stro-bo-scop-ic
  stro-bo-scop-i-cal-ly
stroke
  stroked
  strok-ing
stroll-er
strong
  strong-ish
  strong-ly
strong--arm
strong-box
strong-hold
strong-mind-ed
  strong-mind-ed-ly
  strong-mind-ed-ness
stron-ti-um
  stron-tic
strop
  stropped
  strop-ping
struc-tur-al
  struc-tur-al-ly
struc-ture
  struc-tured
  struc-tur-ing
  struc-ture-less
strug-gle
  strug-gled
  strug-gling
  strug-gler
strum
  strum-mer
  strum-pet

strut
strut-ted
strut-ting
strych-nine
strych-nia
strych-nic
stub
stubbed
stub-bing
stub-by
stub-bi-er
stub-bi-est
stub-ble
stub-bled
stub-bling
stub-by
stub-bi-er
stub-bi-est
stub-born
stub-born-ly
stub-born-ness
stuc-co
stuc-coes
stuc-cos
stuc-coed
stuc-co-ing
stuck--up
stud
stud-ded
stud-ding
stu-dent
stud-ied
stud-ied-ly
stud-ied-ness
stu-di-o
stu-di-os
stu-di-ous
stu-di-ous-ly
stu-di-ous-ness
stud-y
stud-ies
stud-ied
stud-y-ing
stuff-er
stuff-ing
stuff-y
stul-ti-fy
stul-ti-fied
stul-ti-fy-ing
stul-ti-fi-ca-tion
stul-ti-fi-er
stum-ble
stum-bled
stum-bling
stum-bler
stum-bling-ly

stump
stump-er
stumpy
stump-i-er
stump-i-est
stun-ning
stunt
stunt-ed
stunt-ed-ness
stu-pe-fy
stu-pe-fied
stu-pe-fy-ing
stu-pe-fac-tion
stu-pe-fi-er
stu-pe-fy-ing-ly
stu-pen-dous
stu-pen-dous-ly
stu-pen-dous-ness
stu-pid
stu-pid-i-ty
stu-pid-ly
stu-pid-ness
stu-por
stu-por-ous
stur-dy
stur-di-er
stur-di-est
stur-geon
stut-ter
stut-ter-er
stut-ter-ing-ly
style
styled
styl-ing
styl-er
styl-ish
styl-ish-ly
styl-ish-ness
styl-ist
sty-lis-tic
sty-lis-ti-cal
sty-lis-ti-cal-ly
styl-ize
styl-ized
styl-iz-ing
styl-i-za-tion
styl-iz-er
sty-lus
sty-lus-es
sty-li
sty-mie
sty-mies
sty-mied
sty-mie-ing
styp-tic
styp-ti-cal

styp-tic-i-ty
suave
suave-ly
suave-ness
suav-i-ty
sub
subbed
sub-bing
sub-al-tern
sub-arc-tic
sub-as-sem-bly
sub-as-sem-blies
sub-as-sem-bler
sub-base-ment
sub-chas-er
sub-class
sub-com-mit-tee
sub-con-scious
sub-con-scious-ly
sub-con-scious-ness
sub-con-ti-nent
sub-con-ti-nen-tal
sub-con-tract
sub-con-trac-tor
sub-cul-ture
sub-cul-tur-al
sub-cu-ta-ne-ous
sub-cu-ta-ne-ous-ly
sub-deb-u-tante
sub-di-vide
sub-di-vid-ed
sub-di-vid-ing
sub-di-vid-a-ble
sub-di-vid-er
sub-di-vi-sion
sub-di-vi-sion-al
sub-due
sub-dued
sub-du-ing
sub-du-a-ble
sub-du-al
sub-du-er
sub-en-try
sub-en-tries
sub-freez-ing
sub-group
sub-head
sub-hu-man
sub-ject
sub-jec-tion
sub-jec-tive
sub-jec-tive-ly
sub-jec-tive-ness
sub-jec-tiv-i-ty
sub-join
sub-ju-gate

199

sub-ju-gat-ed
sub-ju-gat-ing
sub-ju-ga-tion
sub-ju-ga-tor
sub-junc-tive
sub-lease
sub-leased
sub-leas-ing
sub-let
sub-let-ting
sub-li-mate
sub-li-mat-ed
sub-li-mat-ing
sub-li-ma-tion
sub-lime
sub-lim-i-nal
sub-lim-i-nal-ly
sub-lim-i-ty
sub-lim-i-ties
sub-ma-chine gun
sub-mar-gin-al
sub-ma-rine
sub-merge
sub-merged
sub-merg-ing
sub-mer-gence
sub-mer-gi-ble
sub-merse
sub-mersed
sub-mers-ing
sub-mer-sion
sub-mers-i-ble
sub-mi-cro-scop-ic
sub-mis-sion
sub-mis-sive
sub-mis-sive-ly
sub-mis-sive-ness
sub-mit
sub-mit-ted
sub-mit-ting
sub-nor-mal
sub-nor-mal-i-ty
sub-or-di-nate
sub-or-di-nat-ed
sub-or-di-nat-ing
sub-or-di-nate-ly
sub-or-di-nate-ness
sub-or-di-na-tion
sub-or-di-na-tive
sub-orn
sub-or-na-tion
sub-orn-er
sub-poe-na
sub-poe-naed
sub-poe-na-ing
sub-scribe

sub-scribed
sub-scrib-ing
sub-scrib-er
sub-scrip-tion
sub-se-quent
sub-se-quence
sub-se-quent-ly
sub-ser-vi-ent
sub-ser-vi-ence
sub-ser-vi-en-cy
sub-side
sub-sid-ed
sub-sid-ing
sub-sid-ence
sub-sid-i-ar-y
sub-sid-i-ar-ies
sub-si-dize
sub-si-dized
sub-si-diz-ing
sub-si-dy
sub-si-dies
sub-sist
sub-sist-ence
sub-soil
sub-son-ic
sub-stance
sub-stand-ard
sub-stan-tial
sub-stan-ti-al-i-ty
sub-stan-tial-ly
sub-stan-ti-ate
sub-stan-ti-at-ed
sub-stan-ti-at-ing
sub-stan-tive
sub-stan-ti-val
sub-stan-ti-val-ly
sub-stan-tive-ly
sub-sti-tute
sub-sti-tut-ed
sub-sti-tut-ing
sub-sti-tu-tion
sub-stra-tum
sub-stra-ta
sub-stra-tums
sub-struc-ture
sub-sume
sub-sumed
sub-sum-ing
sub-sum-a-ble
sub-sump-tive
sub-sump-tion
sub-teen
sub-tend
sub-ter-fuge
sub-ter-ra-ne-an
sub-ter-ra-ne-ous

sub-ter-ra-ne-an-ly
sub-ter-ra-ne-ous-ly
sub-ti-tle
sub-tle
sub-tle-ness
sub-tle-ty
sub-tle-ties
sub-tly
sub-tract
sub-tract-er
sub-trac-tion
sub-trac-tive
sub-tra-hend
sub-trop-i-cal
sub-trop-ic
sub-trop-ics
sub-urb
sub-ur-ban
sub-ur-ban-ite
sub-ur-bia
sub-ver-sion
sub-ver-sion-ary
sub-ver-sive
sub-ver-sive-ly
sub-ver-sive-ness
sub-vert
sub-vert-er
sub-way
suc-ceed
suc-ceed-er
suc-cess
suc-cess-ful-ly
suc-cess-ful-ness
suc-ces-sion
suc-ces-sion-al
suc-ces-sion-al-ly
suc-ces-sive
suc-ces-sive-ly
suc-ces-sive-ness
suc-ces-sor
suc-cinct
suc-cinct-ly
suc-cinct-ness
suc-cor
suc-cor-er
suc-co-tash
suc-co-bus
suc-cu-bi
suc-cu-lent
suc-cu-lence
suc-cu-len-cy
suc-cu-lent-ly
suc-cumb
suck-er
suck-le
suck-led

suck-ling
su-crose
suc-tion
sud-den-ly
  sud-den-less
suds-y
  suds-i-er
  suds-i-est
sue
  sued
  su-ing
  su-er
suede
su-et
  su-ety
suf-fer
  suf-fer-a-ble
  suf-fer-a-bly
  suf-fer-ing
suf-fer-ance
suf-fice
  suf-ficed
  suf-fic-ing
  suf-fic-er
suf-fi-cien-cy
  suf-fi-cien-cies
suf-fi-cient
  suf-fi-cient-ly
suf-fix
suf-fo-cate
  suf-fo-cat-ed
  suf-fo-cat-ing
suf-frage
suf-fra-gette
suf-fuse
  suf-fused
  suf-fus-ing
sug-ar
  sug-ary
  sug-ar-i-er
  sug-ar-i-est
sug-ar-coat
sug-gest
  sug-gest-er
  sug-gest-i-ble
sug-ges-tion
sug-ges-tive
  sug-ges-tive-ly
  sug-ges-tive-ness
su-i-cide
  su-i-cid-ed
  su-i-cid-ing
  su-i-cid-al
suit-a-ble
  suit-a-bil-i-ty
suit-case

suite
suit-ing
suit-or
sul-fa
sul-fa-nil-a-mide
sul-fate
sul-fide
sul-fur
sul-fu-ric
sul-fur-ous
  sul-fur-ous-ly
sulk-y
sul-ly
  sul-lied
  sul-ly-ing
sul-tan
  sul-tan-ic
sul-tan-a
  sul-tan-ess
  sul-tan-ate
sul-try
  sul-tri-er
  sul-tri-est
sum
su-mac
sum-ma-rize
  sum-ma-rized
  sum-ma-riz-ing
  sum-ma-ri-za-tion
sum-ma-ry
  sum-ma-ries
  sum-mar-i-ly
sum-ma-tion
  sum-ma-tion-al
sum-mer
  sum-mery
sum-mer-house
sum-mit
sum-mon
  sum-mon-er
sum-mons
  sum-mons-es
sump-tu-ar-y
sump-tu-ous
  sump-tu-ous-ly
sun
  sunned
  sun-ning
sun-bathe
sun-beam
sun-bon-net
sun-burn
  sun-burned
  sun-burnt
sun-dae
sun-der

sun-der-ance
sun-di-al
sun-down
sun-dries
sun-dry
sun-dries
sun-fish
sun-flow-er
sun-glass-es
sunk-en
sun-light
sun-lit
sun-ny
sun-rise
sun-set
sun-shine
  sun-shiny
sun-spot
sun-stroke
sun-up
sup
  supped
su-per
su-per-a-bun-dant
  su-per-a-bun-dance
su-per-an-nu-ate
su-perb
  su-perb-ly
su-per-car-go
  su-per-car-goes
su-per-charge
  su-per-charg-er
su-per-cil-i-ous
  su-per-cil-i-ous-ly
su-per-e-go
su-per-e-rog-a-to-ry
su-per-fi-cial
  su-per-fi-ci-al-i-ty
  su-per-fi-ci-al-i-ties
su-per-high-way
su-per-hu-man
  su-per-hu-man-i-ty
  su-per-hu-man-ly
su-per-im-pose
  su-per-im-posed
  su-per-im-pos-ing
su-per-in-tend
  su-per-in-tend-en-cy
su-per-in-tend-ent
su-pe-ri-or
  su-pe-ri-or-i-ty
  su-pe-ri-or-ly
su-per-la-tive
  su-per-la-tive-ly
su-per-man
su-per-mar-ket

su-per-nal
  su-per-nal-ly
su-per-nat-u-ral
su-per-nu-mer-ar-y
  su-per-nu-mer-ar-ies
su-per-pow-er
su-per-scribe
  su-per-scib-ing
  su-per-scrip-tion
su-per-script
su-per-sede
  su-per-sed-ed
  su-per-sed-ing
su-per-son-ic
  su-per-son-i-cal-ly
su-per-star
su-per-sti-tion
su-per-sti-tious
  su-per-sti-tious-ly
su-per-struc-ture
su-per-vene
  su-per-vened
  su-per-ven-ing
  su-per-ven-tion
su-per-vise
  su-per-vised
  su-per-vis-ing
  su-per-vi-sion
su-pine
  su-pine-ly
sup-per
sup-plant
  sup-plan-ta-tion
  sup-plant-er
sup-ple
  sup-pler
  sup-plest
sup-ple-ment
  sup-ple-men-tal
sup-pli-ant
  sup-pli-ant-ly
sup-pli-cant
sup-ply
sup-port
  sup-port-a-ble
  sup-port-er
  sup-por-tive
sup-pose
sup-po-si-tion
  sup-po-si-tion-al
sup-pos-i-to-ry
sup-press
  sup-pres-sion
  sup-pres-sor
sup-pu-rate
  sup-pu-rat-ed

sup-pu-ra-tion
  sup-pu-ra-tive
su-pra-re-nal gland
su-prem-a-cy
  su-prem-a-cies
  su-prem-a-cist
su-preme
  su-preme-ly
sur-cease
sur-charge
  sur-charged
  sur-charg-ing
sur-cin-gle
sure
  sur-er
  sur-est
  sure-ly
sure--fire
sure--foot-ed
  sure--foot-ed-ly
sure-ty
  sure-ties
  sure-ty-ship
surf
  surfy
  surf-i-er
sur-face
  sur-faced
  sur-fac-ing
surf-board
  surf-board-er
sur-feit
  sur-feit-er
surge
  surged
  surg-ing
sur-geon
sur-ger-y
  sur-ger-ies
  sur-gi-cal
sur-ly
sur-mise
  sur-mised
  sur-mis-ing
sur-mount
  sur-mount-a-ble
sur-name
sur-pass
  sur-pass-a-ble
  sur-pass-ing
sur-plice
sur-plus
  sur-plus-age
sur-prise
  sur-prised
  sur-pris-ing

sur-re-al-ism
  sur-re-al-ist
  sur-re-al-is-tic
sur-ren-der
sur-rep-ti-tious
  sur-rep-ti-tious-ly
sur-rey
  sur-reys
sur-ro-gate
  sur-ro-gat-ed
  sur-ro-gat-ing
sur-round
  sur-round-er
sur-round-ing
sur-tax
sur-veil-lance
  sur-veil-lant
sur-vey
  sur-vey-ing
  sur-vey-or
sur-viv-al
sur-vive
  sur-vived
  sur-viv-ing
  sur-vi-vor
sus-cep-ti-ble
  sus-cep-ti-bil-i-ty
  sus-cep-ti-bly
sus-pect
sus-pend
  sus-pend-er
sus-pense
  sus-pense-ful
sus-pen-sion
sus-pi-cious
  sus-pi-cious-ly
sus-tain
  sus-tain-a-ble
  sus-tain-er
  sus-tain-ment
sus-te-nance
su-ture
su-ze-rain
  su-ze-rain-ly
svelte
  svelte-ly
swab
  swabbed
  swab-bing
  swab-ber
swad-dle
  swad-dled
  swad-dling
swag-ger
  swag-ger-er
  swag-ger-ing

swain
 swain-ish
swal-low
 swal-low-er
swal-low-tail
swa-mi
 swa-mis
swamp
 swampy
swank
 swank-i-ly
swan's--down
swap
 swapped
 swap-ping
sward
swarth-y
 swarth-i-er
 swarth-i-est
swas-ti-ka
swat
swathe
 swathed
 swath-ing
swat
 sway-a-ble
 sway-er
sway-back
 sway-backed
swear
 swore
 swear-ing
 swear-er
swear-word
sweat
sweat-er
sweat-shop
sweep
 swept
 sweep-ing
 sweep-er
sweep-stakes
sweet
 sweet-ish
 sweet-ly
sweet-bread
 sweet-bri-er
sweet-en
 sweet-en-er
 sweet-en-ing
sweet-heart
sweet-meat
sweet-talk
swell
 swelled
 swoll-en

swell-ing
swell-head
swel-ter
 swel-ter-ing
swerve
 swerved
 swerv-ing
swift
 swift-ly
swim-ming
 swim-ming-ly
swin-dle
 swin-dled
 swin-dling
 swin-dler
swipe
 swiped
 swip-ing
swirl
swish
 swish-er
switch
 switch-er
switch-blade
switch-board
switch--hit-ter
swiv-el
 swiv-eled
 swiv-el-ing
swiz-zle
swoon
 swoon-er
 swoon-ing-ly
swoop-er
swop
 swopped
 swop-ping
sword
sword-fish
sword-play
 sword-play-er
swords-man
 swords-man
 swords-man-ship
syc-a-more
syc-o-phant
 syc-o-phan-cy
 syc-o-phan-tic
syl-lab-bic
syl-lab-i-cate
 syl-lab-i-cat-ed
 syl-lab-i-cat-ing
 syl-lab-i-ca-tion
syl-la-ble
 syl-la-bled
 syl-la-bling

syl-la-bus
 syl-la-bus-es
 syl-la-bi
syl-lo-gism
 sul-lo-gis-tic
sylph-like
syl-van
sym-bi-o-sis
 sym-bi-ot-ic
 sym-bi-ot-i-cal-ly
sym-bol
 sym-bol-ic
 sym-bol-i-cal
sym-bol-ism
 sym-bol-ist
sym-bol-ize
 sym-bol-ized
 sym-bol-iz-ing
 sym-bol-i-za-tion
 sym-bol-iz-er
sym-me-try
 sym-me-tries
sym-pa-thize
 sym-pa-thized
 sym-pa-thiz-ing
 sym-pa-thiz-er
sym-pa-thy
 sym-pa-thies
sym-pho-ny
 sym-pho-nies
 sym-phon-ic
sym-po-si-um
 sym-po-sia
 sym-po-si-ums
symp-tom
symp-to-mat-ic
 symp-to-mat-i-cal
 symp-to-mat-i-cal-ly
syn-a-gogue
 syn-gog-al
 syn-gog-i-cal
syn-apse
sync
 synced
 sync-ing
syn-chro-nism
 syn-chro-nis-tic
 syn-chro-nis-ti-cal
 syn-chro-nis-ti-cal-ly
syn-chro-nize
 syn-chro-nized
 syn-chro-niz-ing
 syn-chro-ni-za-tion
syn-chro-nous
 syn-chro-nous-ly
syn-co-pate

syn-co-pat-ed
syn-co-pat-ing
syn-co-pa-tion
syn-co-pa-tor
syn-di-cate
syn-di-cat-ed
syn-di-cat-ing
syn-drome
syn-drom-ic
syn-od
syn-od-al
syn-o-nym
syn-no-nym-ic
syn-no-nym-i-cal
syn-no-nym-i-ty
syn-on-y-mous
syn-on-y-mous-ly
syn-on-y-my
syn-on-y-mies
syn-op-sis
syn-op-ses
syn-op-ti-cal
syn-tac-tic
syn-tac-ti-cal
syn-tac-ti-cal-ly
syn-tax
syn-the-sis
syn-the-ses
syn-the-sist
syn-the-size
syn-the-sized
syn-the-siz-ing
syn-the-ic
syn-thet-i-cal
syn-thet-i-cal-ly
syph-i-lis
syph-i-lit-ic
sy-ringe
sy-ringed
sy-ring-ing
syr-up
syr-upy
syr-up-i-er
syr-up-i-est
sys-tem
sys-tem-at-ic
sys-tem-at-i-cal
sys-tem-a-tize
sys-tem-a-tized
sys-tem-a-tiz-ing
sys-tem-a-ti-za-tion
sys-tem-a-tiz-er
sys-tem-ic
sys-tem-i-cal-ly
sys-to-le
sys-tol-ic

tap
tab-er-na-cle
ta-ble
ta-ble-spoon
tab-leau
tab-let
tab-loid
ta-boo
tab-u-lar
tab-u-lar-ly
ta-chom-e-ter
tac-it
tac-it-ly
tack
tack-er
tack claw
tacki-ness
tack-le
ta-co
tact
tact-ful
tact-less
tac-tic
tac-tic-al
tac-tic-ian
tad
tad-pole
taf-fe-ta
taf-fet-ized
taff-rail
tag
tag-ger
tail
tail-gate
tai-lor
taint
take
talc
tale
tal-ent
tal-ent-ed
tal-ent scout
talk
talk-er
talk-a-tive
tall
tall-ish
tal-low
tal-low
tal-ly
tal-on
tal-on-ed
tam-bou-rine
tame
tame-ly
tam-per

tan
tan-dem
tang
tangy
tan-gent
tan-gen-cy
tan-gen-tial
tan-ger-ine
tan-gi-ble
tan-gi-bil-ity
tan-gle
tanglement
tan-go
tank
tank-ful
tan-kard
tan-ta-lize
tan-ta-lizer
tan-ta-liz-ingly
tan-ta-lum
tan-trum
tap
tape
ta-per
tap-es-try
tap-i-o-ca
taps
tar-dy
tar-di-ness
tar-get
tar-iff
tar-nish
tar-nish-able
tar-ot
tar-pau-lin
tar-ry
tart
tart-ly
tart-ness
tar-tan
tar-tar
tar-tar-ic
task
tas-sel
taste
taste-ful
taste-less
tat-ter
tat-tle
tat-tler
tattle-tale
tat-too
tat-too
tat-too-er
taught
taut

taut-ly
taut-ness
tau-tol-o-gy
tav-ern
  tav-ern-er
tax
  tax-able
  tax-a-tion
tax--ex-empt
tax shel-ter
tax-i
taxi-cab
tax-i-der-my
  tax-i-derm-ist
tea
teach
  teach-ing
  teach-able
teach-er
team
team-ster
tear
  teary
tease
  teaser
tech-ne-tium
tech-ni-cal
  tech-ni-cal-ly
tech-nique
tech-nol-o-gy
te-dious
  te-dious-ly
tee
teem
teens
teeth
tele-cast
tele-graph
  tele-graph-er
  tele-graph-ic
te-lep-a-thy
  te-lep-a-thic
  te-lep-a-thist
tele-phone
  tele-phoner
tele-pho-to
  tele-pho-to-graph
tele-scope
  tele-scopic
tele-thon
tele-vi-sion
tel-ex
tell
  tell-able
  tell-ing
  tell-er

tel-lu-ri-um
tem-per
  tem-per-able
tem-per-a-ment
  tem-per-a-ment-al
tem-per-ance
tem-per-ate
  tem-per-ate-ly
tem-per-a-ture
tem-pest
tem-ple
tem-po
tem-po-rary
tempt
  tempt-er
ten
te-na-cious
  te-na-cious-ly
ten-ant
tend
ten-den-cy
ten-der
  ten-der-ly
  ten-der-ness
ten-der-loin
ten-don
ten-dril
  ten-dril-ed
ten-nis
ten-or
tense
ten-sion
  ten-sion-al
tent
ten-ta-cle
ten-ta-tive
  ten-ta-tive-ly
ten-ure
te-pee
tep-id
  tep-id-ly
ter-bi-um
ter-cen-ten-a-ry
term
ter-mi-nal
ter-mi-nate
  ter-mi-nation
ter-mite
ter-race
ter-rain
ter-ra-pin
ter-res-tri-al
ter-ri-ble
  ter-ri-bly
ter-ri-er
ter-rif-ic

ter-rif-ical-ly
ter-ri-fy
  ter-ri-fied
  ter-ri-fying
ter-ri-to-ry
  ter-ri-to-rial
  ter-ri-to-rial-ly
ter-ror
ter-ror-ism
terse
test
  test-er
tes-ta-ment
  tes-ta-ment-ary
tes-tate
tes-ti-fy
  tes-ti-fier
tes-ti-mo-ni-al
tes-ti-mo-ny
tes-tis
test tube
test--tube baby
tet-a-nus
teth-er
text
text-book
tex-tile
tex-ture
  tex-tural
  tex-tural-ly
thal-li-um
than
thank
thank-ful
  thank-ful-ly
  thank-ful-ness
  thank-less
thanks
that
thatch
thaw
the
the-atre
the-at-ri-cal
  the-at-ri-cals
theft
their
the-ism
them
theme
  the-matic
them-selves
then
thence
  thence-forth
  thence-for-ward

the-oc-ra-cy
　the-oc-rat
the-ol-o-gy
　the-ol-o-gian
the-o-rize
　the-o-re-ti-cian
　the-o-ri-za-tion
　the-o-rist
the-o-ry
　ther-a-peu-tics
　ther-a-peu-tist
ther-a-py
　ther-a-pist
there
　there-abouts
　there-after
　there-by
　there-fore
　there-from
　there-in
ther-mal
ther-mom-e-ter
　ther-mom-e-tric
ther-mo-plas-tic
ther-mo-stat
　ther-mo-stat-ic
the-sau-rus
these
the-sis
they
they'd
they'll
they're
they've
thick
　thick-ly
　thick-ness
　thick-en
thief
thieve
thigh
thim-ble
　thim-ble-ful
thin
　thin-ly
　thin-ness
thing
think
　think-able
　think-er
third
thirst
　thirst-y
thir-teen
this
this-tle

thith-er
thong
tho-rax
　tho-racic
tho-ri-um
thorn
　thorn-y
thor-ough
　thor-ough-ness
　thor-ough-ly
thor-ough-bred
thor-ough-fare
those
though
thought
　thought-ful
　thought-less
thou-sand
thrash
　thrash-er
thread
　thread-y
thread-bare
threat
　threat-en
three
thresh
thresh-old
threw
thrice
thrift
　thrift-i-ly
　thrift-i-ness
　thrift-y
thrill
　thrill-ing
　thrill-ing-ly
thrive
throat
throb
throm-bo-sis
throng
throt-tle
through
through-out
throw
thru
thrush
thrust
thru-way
thud
thug
　thug-gish
thumb
thump
thun-der

thun-der-bolt
thun-der-cloud
thun-der-show-er
thus
thwack
thwart
thy
thyme
thy-roid
thy-rox-ine
ti-ara
tick
tick-et
tick-le
　tick-ler
tidal wave
tid-bit
tide
tid-ings
ti-dy
　ti-di-ly
　ti-di-ness
tie
tier
　tier-ed
ti-ger
tiger-eye
tight
tight-en
　tight-en-er
tight-rope
tights
tile
till
　till-er
tilt
tim-ber
time
time--shar-ing
time tri-al
tim-id
tin
tinc-ture
tin-der
tin-der-box
tine
tinge
tin-gle
　tin-gly
tink-er
tin-kle
tin-ny
tin-sel
tint
ti-ny
tip

tip-ple
tip-sy
  tip-si-ness
ti-rade
tire
tire-less
  tire-less-ly
tis-sue
ti-ta-ni-um
tithe
  tither
tit-il-late
  tit-il-lat-ing
  tit-il-la-tive
  tit-il-lat-ing-ly
  tit-il-lat-ion
ti-tle
to
toad
  toad-stool
toast
  toast-y
toast-er
to-bac-co
to-bog-gan
  to-bog-gan-ist
to-day
tod-dle
  tod-dler
tod-dy
toe
tof-fee
to-geth-er
  to-geth-er-ness
toil
  toil-some
toi-let
toi-lette
to-ken
tol-er-ate
  tol-er-a-tion
  tol-er-ance
  tol-er-ant
toll
tom-a-hawk
to-ma-to
tomb
tom-boy
  tom-boy-ish
tomb-stone
tom-cat
to-mor-row
ton
tone
tongs
tongue

ton-ic
to-night
ton-sil
ton-sil-lec-to-my
too
tool
tooth
  tooth-ed
  tooth-less
top
to-paz
top-coat
top-ic
top-most
to-pog-ra-phy
top-ple
top-sy--tur-vy
torch
tor-ment
  tor-ment-ing-ly
  tor-ment-or
tor-na-do
tor-pe-do
tor-pid
  tor-pid-ity
  tor-pid-ly
tor-rent
  tor-rent-ial
tor-rid
  tor-rid-ly
tor-sion
  tor-sion-al
tor-so
tort
tor-toise
tor-tu-ous
  tor-tu-ous-ness
toss
tot
to-tal
  to-tal-ly
to-tal-i-tar-i-an
  to-tal-i-tar-i-an
tote
to-tem
tot-ter
tou-can
touch
  touch-able
tough
  tough-ly
  tough-ness
tou-pee
tour
  tour-ism
  tour-ist

tour-na-ment
tour-ni-quet
tou-sle
tout
  tout-er
tow
to-ward
tow-el
tow-er
  tow-er-ing
town
town-ship
tox-e-mi-a
tox-ic
tox-in
toy
trace
  trace-able
  trace-ably
  trac-er
track
  track-able
  track-er
tract
trac-tion
trac-tor
trade
  trade-able
trade-mark
trade--off
tra-di-tion
  tra-di-tion-al
  tra-di-tion-al-ly
tra-duce
  tra-duce-ment
  tra-ducer
traf-fic
trag-e-dy
trail
trail-er
train
  train-able
  train-er
  train-ing
trait
trai-tor
tra-jec-to-ry
tram-mel
  tram-mel-er
tramp
tram-ple
  tram-pler
tram-po-line
  tram-po-lin-ist
trance
tran-quil

tran-quil-lity
tran-quil-ly
tran-quil-ize
trans-act
  trans-action
  trans-actor
tran-scend
  tran-scend-ent
  tran-scend-ence
tran-scribe
tran-script
tran-scrip-tion
trans-fer
  trans-fer-able
  trans-fer-ence
  trans-fer-er
trans-fig-ure
  trans-fig-ura-tion
trans-fix
  trans-fix-ion
trans-form
  trans-for-mable
  trans-for-ma-tion
  trans-for-mer
trans-fuse
  trans-fus-ion
  trans-fus-er
trans-gress
  trans-gress-ion
  trans-gress-or
  trans-gres-sive
tran-sient
  tran-sient-ly
tran-sit
trans-late
  trans-la-tion
  tran-sla-tor
trans-lu-cent
trans-mis-sion
trans-mit
  trans-miss-ible,
  trans-mitt-able
  trans-mitt-er
trans-mute
  trans-mu-ta-tion
tran-som
trans-par-ent
  trans-par-ency
  trans-par-ent-ly
tran-spire
trans-plant
  trans-plant-able
trans-port
  trans-port-able
  trans-por-ta-tion
  trans-port-er

trans-pose
trans-sex-u-al
trap
tra-peze
trap-shoot-ing
trau-ma
tra-vail
trav-el
  trav-el-er
tra-verse
  tra-vers-able
  tra-ver-sal
  tra-ver-ser
trawl
tray
treach-er-ous
  treach-er-ous-ly
  treach-ery
tread
trea-son
  trea-son-able
  trea-son-ous
treas-ure
treas-ur-er
treas-ur-y
treat
  treat-able
  treat-er
treat-ment
treb-le
tree
  tree-less
tre-foil
trek
trel-lis
trem-ble
  trem-bler
  trem-bly
tre-men-dous
trem-or
trench
  trench-er
trend
  trend-set-ter
tres-pass
tres-tle
tri-al
tri-an-gle
  tri-an-gu-lar-i-ty
tribe
trib-u-la-tion
trib-un-al
trib-ute
tri-ceps
trick
  trick-y

trick-er-y
trick-le
tri-col-or
  tri-col-or-ed
tri-cy-cle
tri-dent
tried
tri-en-ni-al
  tri-en-ni-al-ly
tri-fle
trig-ger
trill
tril-lion
trim
tri-ni-tro-tol-u-ene
trin-ket
tri-o
trip
tripe
trip-le
trip-let
trip-li-cate
tri-pod
trite
tri-umph
  tri-umph-ant
  tri-umph-ant-ly
triv-i-al
Tro-jan
troll
trol-ley
trom-bone
troop
  troop-er
tro-phy
trop-ic
trop-i-cal
  trop-i-cal-ly
tro-pism
tro-po-sphere
trot
troth
trou-ble
  trou-bler
  trou-bling-ly
trough
trounce
troupe
trou-sers
trous-seau
trout
trow-el
  trow-el-er
tru-ant
truce
truck

truck-er
trudge
true
  true-ness
trump
trum-pet
trunk
truss
trust
  trust-er
  trust-less
truth
  truth-ful
  truth-ful-ly
  truth-ful-ness
try
  try-ing
tryst
tsu-na-mi
tub
tu-ba
tube
tu-ber
tu-ber-cu-lo-sis
tuck
tuft
tug
tu-i-tion
tu-lip
tum-ble
  tum-bler
tum-ble-down
tum-brel
tu-mor
tu-mult
tu-mul-tu-ous
tu-na
tun-dra
tune
tune-ful
tung-sten
tu-nic
tun-nel
tur-ban
tur-bine
tur-bu-lent
  tur-bu-lent-ly
tu-reen
turf
tur-key
tur-moil
turn
  turn-er
turn-buck-le
turn-down
tur-nip

turn-key
turn-off
turn-over
tur-pen-tine
tur-quoise
tur-ret
tur-tle
tur-tle-neck
tusk
tus-sle
tu-tor
tut-ti--frut-ti
tu-tu
tux-e-do
twain
twang
tweak
tweed
twee-zers
twelve
twen-ty
twice
twid-dle
twig
twi-light
twill
twin
twine
twinge
  twing-ed
twin-kle
twirl
twist
  twist-er
twit
twitch
twit-ter
  twit-ter-y
two-fold
two--time
ty-coon
tyke
type
type-face
type-set-ter
type-writ-er
ty-phoid
ty-phoon
typ-i-cal
  typ-i-cal-ly
typ-i-fy
  typ-i-fy-ing
typ-ist
ty-po
ty-ran-no-sau-rus
tyr-an-ny

ubiq-ui-tous
  ubiq-ui-tary
  ubiq-ui-tous-ly
  ubiq-ui-ty
ud-der
ug-ly
  ug-li-er
  ug-li-est
ukase
uku-le-le
ul-cer
  ul-cer-ous
ul-cer-ate
  ul-cer-at-ed
  ul-cer-at-ing
  ul-cer-at-ion
ul-na
  ul-nae
ul-ster
ul-te-ri-or
  ul-te-ri-or-ly
ul-ti-mate
  ul-ti-mate-ly
ul-ti-ma-tum
  ul-ti-ma-tums
  ul-ti-ma-ta
ul-tra
ul-tra-con-serv-a-tive
ul-tra-high
ul-tra-ma-rine
ul-tra-son-ic
ul-tra-vi-o-let
ul-u-late
  ul-u-lat-ed
  ul-u-lat-ing
um-bel
  um-bel-lar
  um-bel-late
  um-bel-lat-ed
um-ber
um-bil-i-cal
um-bra
  um-bras
  um-brae
um-brage
  um-bra-geous
um-brel-la
umi-ak
um-laut
um-pire
  um-pired
  um-pir-ing
ump-teen
  ump-teenth
un-a-bashed
  un-a-bash-ed-ly

un-a-ble
un-a-bridged
un-ac-cep-t-able
un-ac-cept-ed
un-ac-com-pa-nied
un-ac-count-able
un-ac-count-a-bly
un-ac-cus-tomed
un-ac-quaint-ed
un-a-dorned
un-a-dul-ter-at-ed
un-a-dul-ter-at-ed-ly
un-ad-vised
un-ad-vis-ed-ly
un-af-fect-ed
un-af-fect-ed-ly
un-a-fraid
un--Amer-i-can
unan-i-mous
una-nim-i-ty
unan-i-mous-ly
un-an-swer-able
un-an-swered
un-ap-pe-tiz-ing
un-ap-pre-ci-at-ed
un-ap-pre-ci-a-tive
un-ap-proach-able
un-ap-proach-ably
un-ap-proached
un-armed
un-a-shamed
un-asked
un-a-spir-ing
un-as-sail-able
un-as-sail-ably
un-as-sailed
un-at-tached
un-at-tain-able
un-at-tained
un-at-tend-ed
un-au-thor-ized
un-a-vail-a-ble
un-a-vail-a-bil-i-ty
un-a-vail-a-bly
un-a-void-a-ble
un-a-void-a-bil-i-ty
un-a-void-ably
un-a-ware
un-a-ware-ness
un-a-wares
un-backed
un-bal-anced
un-bar
un-barred
un-bar-ring
un-bear-able

un-bear-ably
un-beat-en
un-beat-able
un-be-com-ing
un-be-com-ing-ly
un-be-lief
un-be-liev-able
un-be-liev-ably
un-be-liev-er
un-be-liev-ing
un-be-liev-ing-ly
un-bend
un-bend-ed
un-bend-ing
un-bi-ased
un-bi-ased-ly
un-bid-den
un-bind
un-bound
un-bind-ing
un-blem-ished
un-bolt
un-bolt-ed
un-born
un-bos-om
un-bound
un-bound-ed-ly
un-bowed
un-bread-able
un-bri-dle
un-bri-dled
un-bri-dling
un-bro-ken
un-bro-ken-ly
un-buck-le
un-buck-led
un-buck-ling
un-bur-den
un-but-ton
un-but-toned
un--called--for
un-can-ny
un-can-ni-er
un-can-ni-est
un-can-ni-ly
un-cap
un-capped
un-cap-ping
un-ceas-ing
un-ceas-ing-ly
un-cer-e-mo-ni-ous
un-cer-e-mo-ni-ous-ly
un-cer-tain
un-cer-tain-ly
un-cer-tain-ty
un-cer-tain-ties

un-chal-lenged
un-change-able
un-change-ably
un-changed
un-chang-ing
un-char-i-ta-ble
un-char-i-ta-bly
un-chart-ed
un-chris-tian
un-cir-cum-cised
un-civ-il
un-civ-il-ly
un-civ-i-lized
un-class-i-fi-able
un-clas-si-fied
un-cle
un-clean
un-clean-ly
un-clear
un-cloak
un-clothe
un-clut-tered
un-coil
un-com-fort-able
un-com-fort-ably
un-com-mit-ted
un-com-mon
un-com-mon-ly
un-com-mu-ni-ca-tive
un-com-pre-hend-ing
un-com-pro-mis-ing
un-com-pro-mised
un-con-cern
un-con-cerned
un-con-di-tion-al
un-con-di-tion-al-ly
un-con-firmed
un-con-nect-ed
un-con-nect-ed-ly
un-con-quer-a-ble
un-con-quered
un-con-scion-able
un-con-scion-ably
un-con-scious
un-con-scious-ly
un-con-scious-ness
un-con-sti-tui-tion-al
un-con-strained
un-con-test-ed
un-con-trol-la-ble
un-con-trol-la-bly
un-con-trolled
un-con-ven-tion-al
un-con-ven-tion-al-ly
un-count-ed
un-cou-ple

un-cou-pled
un-cou-pling
un-couth
un-couth-ly
un-couth-ness
un-cov-er
un-cov-ered
unc-tion
unc-tu-ous
unc-tu-os-i-ty
unc-tu-ous-ly
un-curl
un-cut
un-daunt-ed
un-daunt-ed-ly
un-de-ceive
un-de-ceived
un-de-ceiv-ing
un-de-ceiv-a-ble
un-de-cid-ed
un-de-cid-ed-ly
un-de-cid-ed-ness
un-de-fined
un-de-fin-a-ble
un-de-mon-stra-tive
un-de-ni-a-ble
un-de-ni-a-bly
un-de-nied
un-de-pend-able
un-de-pend-a-bil-i-ty
un-der
un-der-a-chiev-er
un-der-a-chiev-ment
un-der-act
un-der-age
un-der-arm
un-der-bel-ly
un-der-car-riage
un-der-charge
un-der-charged
un-der-charg-ing
un-der-class-man
un-der-class-men
un-der-clothes
un-der-coast
un-der-cov-er
un-der-cur-rent
un-der-cut
un-der-cut-ting
un-der-de-vel-oped
un-der-de-vel-op-ing
un-der-dog
un-der-done
un-der-es-ti-mate
un-der-es-ti-mat-ed
un-der-es-ti-mat-ing

un-der-es-ti-ma-tion
un-der-foot
un-der-gar-ment
un-der-go
un-der-went
un-der-gone
un-der-grad-u-ate
un-der-ground
un-der-growth
un-der-hand
un-der-lie
un-der-lay
un-der-lain
un-der-ly-ing
un-der-line
un-der-lined
un-der-lin-ing
un-der-ling
un-der-mine
un-der-mined
un-der-min-ing
un-der-min-er
un-der-most
un-der-neath
un-der-pants
un-der-pass
un-der-pin-ning
un-der-priv-i-leged
un-der-rate
un-der-rat-ed
un-der-rat-ing
un-der-score
un-der-scored
un-der-scor-ing
un-der-sea
un-der-sec-re-tary
un-der-sec-re-tar-ies
un-der-sell
un-der-sold
un-der-ell-ing
un-der-sell-er
un-der-shirt
un-der-shot
un-der-side
un-der-signed
un-der-stand
un-der-stood
un-der-stand-ing
un-der-stand-a-ble
un-der-stand-a-bly
un-der-stand-ing-ly
un-der-state
un-der-stat-ed
un-der-stat-ing
un-der-state-ment
un-der-stood

un-der-study
un-der-stud-ied
un-der-stud-y-ing
un-der-stud-ies
un-der-take
un-der-took
un-der-tak-en
un-der-tak-ing
un-der-tak-er
un-der-the-coun-ter
un-der-tone
un-der-tow
un-der-wa-ter
un-der-wear
un-der-weight
un-der-world
un-der-write
un-der-wrote
un-der-writ-ten
un-der-writ-ing
un-der-writ-er
un-de-sir-a-ble
un-de-sir-a-bil-i-ty
un-de-sir-a-bly
un-de-ter-mined
un-dies
un-dip-lo-mat-ic
un-dip-lo-mat-i-cal-ly
un-dis-ci-plined
un-dis-closed
un-dis-posed
un-dis-tin-guished
un-di-vid-ed
un-do
un-did
un-done
un-do-ing
un-do-er
un-doubt-ed
un-doubt-ed-ly
un-doubt-ing
un-dress
un-dress-ed
un-dress-ing
un-due
un-du-lant
un-du-late
un-du-lat-ed
un-du-lat-ing
un-du-la-tion
un-du-ly
un-dy-ing
un-earth
un-earth-ly
un-easy
un-eas-i-er

un-eas-i-est
un-ease
un-eas-i-ly
un-eas-i-ness
un-em-ployed
un-em-ploy-ment
un-e-qual
un-e-qual-ly
un-e-qual-ed
un-e-quiv-o-cal
un-e-quiv-o-cal-ly
un-err-ing
un-err-ing-ly
un-eth-i-cal
un-eth-i-cal-ly
un-e-ven
un-e-ven-ly
un-e-ven-ness
un-ex-cep-tion-able
un-ex-pect-ed
un-ex-pect-ed-ly
un-fail-ing
un-fail-ing-ly
un-faith-ful
un-faith-ful-ly
un-faith-ful-ness
un-fa-mil-iar
un-fa-mil-i-ar-i-ty
un-fa-mil-iar-ly
un-fast-en
un-fas-ten-a-ble
un-fas-ten-er
un-fath-om-a-ble
un-fa-vor-a-ble
un-fa-vor-a-bly
un-feel-ing
un-feel-ing-ly
un-feigned
un-feign-ed-ly
un-fet-ter
un-fet-tered
un-fin-ished
un-fit
un-fit-ly
un-fit-ness
un-fit-ting
un-flat-ter-ing
un-flinch-ing
un-flinch-ing-ly
un-fold
un-for-get-ta-ble
un-for-get-ta-bly
un-for-giv-a-ble
un-for-tu-nate
un-for-tu-nate-ly
un-found-ed

un-found-ed-ness
un-friend-ly
un-friend-li-er
un-friend-li-est
un-friend-li-ness
un-frock
un-furl
un-gain-ly
un-gain-li-ness
un-gird
un-gird-ed
un-gird-ing
un-glazed
un-god-ly
un-god-li-er
un-god-li-est
un-god-li-ness
un-gov-ern-able
un-gov-ern-ably
un-gra-cious
un-gra-cious-ly
un-gra-cious-ness
un-gram-mat-i-cal
un-gram-mat-i-cal-ly
un-grate-ful
un-grate-ful-ly
un-grate-ful-ness
un-guard-ed
un-guard-ed-ly
un-guent
un-gu-late
un-ham-pered
un-hand
un-handy
un-hand-i-er
un-hand-i-est
un-hap-py
un-hap-pi-er
un-hap-pi-est
un-hap-pi-ly
un-hap-pi-ness
un-harmed
un-healthy
un-health-i-er
un-health-i-ly
un-heard
un-heed-ed
un-heed-ful
un-heed-ing
un-hinge
un-hinged
un-hing-ing
un-hitch
un-ho-ly
un-ho-li-er
un-ho-li-est

un-hol-li-ly
un-ho-li-ness
un-hook
un-horse
un-horsed
un-hors-ing
un-hur-ried
un-hurt
uni-cam-er-al
uni-cam-er-al-ly
uni-cel-lu-lar
uni-corn
uni-fi-ca-tion
uni-form
uni-formed
uni-form-i-ty
uni-form-ly
uni-fy
uni-fied
uni-fy-ing
uni-fi-er
uni-lat-er-al
uni-lat-er-al-ism
uni-lat-er-al-ly
un-imag-in-able
un-im-pair-ed
un-im-peach-able
un-im-peach-a-bly
un-im-por-tance
un-im-por-tant
un-im-proved
un-in-hib-it-ed
un-in-hib-it-ed-ly
un-in-ter-est-ed
un-in-ter-est-ing
un-ion
un-ion-ism
un-ion-ist
un-ion-ize
un-ion-ized
un-ion-iz-ing
un-ion-i-za-tion
unique
unique-ly
unique-ness
uni-son
unit
unite
unit-ed
unit-ing
unit-er
uni-ty
uni-ties
uni-valve
uni-valved
uni-val-vu-lar

212

uni-ver-sal
  uni-ver-sal-i-ty
  uni-ver-sal-ly
  uni-ver-sal-ness
uni-ver-sal-ize
  uni-ver-sal-ized
  uni-ver-sal-iz-ing
uni-verse
uni-ver-si-ty
  uni-ver-si-ties
un-just
  un-just-ly
un-kempt
un-kind
  un-kind-ness
  un-kind-ly
un-known
un-law-ful
  un-law-ful-ly
  un-law-ful-ness
un-learn
  un-learned
  un-learn-ing
  un-learn-ed
  un-learn-ed-ly
un-leash
un-less
un-let-ter-ed
un-like
  un-like-ness
un-like-ly
  un-like-li-er
  un-like-li-est
  un-like-li-ness
un-lim-ber
un-lim-it-ed
un-load
  un-load-er
un-lock
un-looked--for
un-loose
  un-loosed
  un-loos-ing
  un-loos-en
un-lucky
  un-luck-i-er
  un-luck-i-est
  un-luck-i-ly
un-make
  un-made
  un-mak-ing
  un-mak-er
un-man
  un-manned
  un-man-ning
un-mask

un-mean-ing
  un-mean-ing-ly
un-men-tion-able
un-mer-ci-ful
  un-mer-ci-ful-ly
un-mis-tak-able
  un-mis-tak-a-bly
un-mit-i-gat-ed
  un-mit-i-gat-ed-ly
un-nat-u-ral
  un-nat-u-ral-ly
  un-nat-u-ral-ness
un-nec-es-sary
  un-nec-es-sar-i-ly
un-nerve
  un-nerved
  un-nerv-ing
un-num-bered
un-ob-jec-tion-able
un-or-gan-ized
un-pack
un-par-al-leled
un-par-don-able
un-pleas-ant
  un-pleas-ant-ly
  un-pleas-ant-ness
un-plumbed
un-pop-u-lar
  un-pop-u-lar-i-ty
  un-pop-u-lar-ly
un-prec-e-dent-ed
  un-prec-e-dent-ed-ly
un-prin-ci-pled
un-print-able
un-pro-fes-sion-al
  un-pro-fes-sion-al-ly
un-qual-i-fied
  un-qual-i-fied-ly
un-ques-tion-able
  un-ques-tion-ably
  un-ques-tioned
un-quote
  un-quot-ed
  un-quot-ing
un-rav-el
  un-rav-eled
  un-rav-el-ing
  un-rav-el-ment
un-read
un-re-al
un-rea-son-able
  un-rea-son-ably
  un-rea-son-ing
un-re-fined
un-re-gen-er-ate
un-re-lat-ed

un-re-lent-ing
  un-re-lent-ing-ly
un-remit-ting
un-re-serve
  un-re-served
  un-re-serv-ed-ly
un-rest
un-ri-valed
un-roll
un-ruf-fled
un-ru-ly
  un-ruy-li-er
  un-ru-li-est
un-sad-dle
  un-sad-dled
  un-sad-dling
un-said
un-sa-vory
un-say
  un-say-ing
un-scathed
un-schooled
un-scram-ble
  un-scram-bled
  un-scram-bling
un-screw
un-scru-pu-lous
  un-scru-pu-lous-ly
un-seal
un-sea-son-able
  un-sea-son-ably
un-seat
un-seem-ly
un-set-tle
  un-set-tled
  un-set-tling
un-sheathe
  un-sheathed
  un-sheath-ing
un-shod
un-sight-ly
  un-sight-li-er
  un-sight-li-est
un-skilled
  un-skill-ful
  un-skill-ful-ly
un-snap
  un-snapped
  un-snap-ping
un-snarl
un-so-phis-ti-cat-ed
  un-so-phis-ti-cat-ed-ly
  un-so-phis-ti-ca-tion
un-sound
  un-sound-ly
un-spar-ing

un-spar-ing-ly
un-speak-a-ble
  un-speak-a-bly
un-sta-ble
  un-sta-bly
un-steady
  un-stead-i-er
  un-stead-i-est
  un-stead-i-ly
un-stop
  un-stopped
  un-stop-ping
un-strung
un-stud-ied
un-sung
un-tan-gle
  un-tan-gled
  un-tan-gling
un-taught
un-think-able
  un-think-ing
  un-think-ing-ly
un-ti-dy
un-tie
  un-tied
  un-ty-ing
un-til
un-time-ly
  un-time-li-ness
un-to
un-told
  un-touch-a-ble
  un-touch-a-bly
un-to-ward
  un-to-ward-ly
un-truth
un-tu-tored
un-used
un-u-su-al
  un-u-su-al-ly
  un-u-su-al-ness
un-ut-ter-able
  un-ut-ter-ably
un-var-nished
un-veil
un-wary
  un-war-i-ly
un-well
un-whole-some
  un-whole-some-ly
un-wieldy
  un-wield-i-ness
un-will-ing
  un-will-ing-ly
  un-will-ing-ness
un-wind

un-wound
un-wind-ing
un-wise
  un-wise-ly
un-wit-ting
  un-wit-ting-ly
un-wont-ed
  un-wont-ed-ly
un-wor-thy
  un-wor-thi-ly
  un-wor-thi-ness
un-wrap
  un-wrapped
  un-wrap-ping
un-yield-ing
up-beat
up-braid
  up-braid-er
  up-braid-ing
up-com-ing
up-coun-try
up-date
  up-dat-ed
  up-dat-ing
up-end
up-grade
  up-grad-ed
  up-grad-ing
up-heav-al
up-heave
  up-heaved
  up-heav-ing
up-hill
up-hold
  up-held
  up-hold-ing
up-hol-ster
  up-hol-ster-er
  up-hol-stery
up-keep
up-land
up-lift
up-most
up-on
up-per
  up-per--class
up-per-cut
  up-per-cut-ting
  up-per-most
up-pish
  up-pish-ly
up-pi-ty
up-raise
  up-raised
  up-rais-ing
up-rear

up-right
  up-right-ly
  up-right-ness
up-ris-ing
up-roar
  up-roar-i-ous
up-root
  up-root-er
up-set
  up-set-ting
up-shot
up-side
up-stage
  up-staged
  up-stag-ing
up-stairs
up-stand-ing
up-start
up-state
up-stream
up-swing
up-take
up-to-date
up-town
up-trend
up-turn
up-ward
  up-ward-ly
  up-ward-ness
ura-ni-um
ur-ban
ur-bane
  ur-bane-ly
  ur-ban-i-ty
ur-ban-ize
  ur-ban-ized
  ur-ban-iz-ing
  ur-ban-i-za-tion
ur-chin
urea
  ure-al
ure-ter
ure-thra
  ure-thrae
  ure-thras
  ure-thral
uge
  urged
  urg-ing
  urg-er
  urg-ing-ly
ur-gent
  ur-gen-cy
  ur-gen-cies
  ur-gent-ly
uric

V

uri-nal
uri-nal-y-sis
  uri-nal-y-ses
uri-nary
  uri-nar-ies
uri-nate
urine
urol-o-gy
  uro-log-ic
  uro-log-i-cal
  urol-o-gist
us-able
  us-ably
  us-abil-i-ty
us-age
use
  used
  us-ing
  us-er
use-ful
  use-ful-ly
  use-ful-ness
use-less
  use-less-ly
  use-less-ness
ush-er
usu-al
  usu-al-ly
usurp
  usur-pa-tion
  usurp-er
usu-ry
  usu-ries
  usu-rer
  usu-ri-ous
uten-sil
uter-us
  ut-eri
util-i-tar-ian
util-i-ty
  util-i-ties
uti-lize
  uti-lized
  uti-liz-ing
  uti-li-za-tion
ut-most
ut-ter
  ut-ter-a-ble
  ut-ter-er
ut-ter-ance
ut-ter-most
uvu-la
  uvu-las
  uvu-lae
ux-o-ri-ous
  ux-o-ri-ous-ly

va-can-cy
  va-can-cies
va-cant
  va-cant-ly
va-cate
  va-cat-ed
  va-cat-ing
va-ca-tion
vac-ci-nate
  vac-ci-nat-ed
  vac-ci-nat-ing
  vac-ci-na-tion
vac-cine
vac-il-late
  vac-il-lat-ed
  vac-il-lat-ing
  vac-il-la-tion
  vac-il-la-tor
va-cu-i-ty
  va-cu-i-ties
vac-u-ous
  vac-u-ous-ly
vac-u-um
  vac-u-ums
  vac-ua
vac-u-um--packed
vag-a-bond
  vag-a-bond-age
  vag-a-bond-ish
  vag-a-bond-ism
va-gary
  va-gar-ies
  va-gar-i-ous
  va-gar-i-ous-ly
va-gi-na
  va-gi-nas
  va-gi-nae
  vag-i-nal
va-grant
  va-gran-cy
  va-gran-cies
  va-grant-ly
vague
  vague-ly
  vague-ness
vain
  vain-ly
  vain-ness
vain-glo-ry
  vain-glo-ries
  vain-glo-ri-ous
val-ance
  val-anced
val-e-dic-tion
  val-e-dic-to-ri-an
val-e-dic-to-ry

  val-e-dic-to-ries
va-lence
  va-len-cy
val-en-tine
va-let
val-iant
  val-iant-ly
val-id
  val-id-ly
  val-id-ness
val-i-date
  val-i-dat-ed
  val-i-dat-ig
  val-i-da-tion
va-lid-i-ty
  va-lid-i-ties
va-lise
val-ley
  val-leys
val-or
  val-or-ous
  val-or-ous-ly
val-u-able
  val-u-ably
val-u-a-tion
  val-u-a-tion-al
val-ue
  val-ued
  val-u-ing
  val-ue-less
valve
  valve-less
  val-vu-lar
va-moose
vam-pire
  vam-pir-ic
  vam-pir-ism
va-na-di-um
van-dal
  van-dal-ism
  van-dal-ize
  van-dal-ized
  van-dal-iz-ing
vane
  vaned
  vane-less
van-guard
va-nil-la
van-ish
  van-ish-er
van-i-ty
  van-i-ties
van-quish
  van-quish-a-ble
  van-quish-er
van-tage

vap-id
 va-pid-i-ty
 vap-id-ly
va-por
 va-por-er
 va-por-ish
va-por-ize
 va-por-ized
 va-por-iz-ing
 va-por-i-za-tion
 va-por-iz-er
va-por-ous
 va-por-opus-ly
va-que-ro
 va-que-ros
var-i-able
 var-i-abil-i-ty
 var-i-ably
var-i-ance
var-i-ant
var-i-a-tion
 var-i-a-tion-al
 var-i-a-tion-al-ly
var-i-col-ored
var-i-cose
var-ied
 var-ied-ness
var-ie-gate
 var-ie-gat-ed
 var-ie-gat-ing
 var-ie-ga-tion
 var-ie-ga-tor
va-ri-etal
 va-ri-etal-ly
va-ri-ety
 va-ri-e-ties
var-i-ous
 var-i-ous-ly
var-nish
 var-nish-er
var-si-ty
 var-si-ties
vary
 var-ied
 vary-ing
 var-i-er
 vary-ing-ly
vas-cu-lar
 vas-cu-lar-i-ty
va-sec-to-my
 va-sec-to-mies
vas-o-mo-tor
vas-sal
 vas-sal-age
vast-ness
vat

vat-ted
vat-ting
vaude-ville
vault
 vault-ed
 vault-er
vault-ing
vaunt
 vaunt-er
 vaunt-ing-ly
vec-tor
 vec-to-ri-al
veer-ing
veg-e-ta-ble
veg-e-tal
veg-e-tar-i-an
 veg-e-tar-i-an-ism
veg-e-tate
 veg-e-tat-ed
 veg-e-tat-ing
veg-e-ta-tion
 veg-e-ta-tion-al
veg-e-ta-tive
ve-he-ment
 ve-he-mence
 ve-he-men-cy
ve-hi-cle
 ve-hic-u-lar
veil
 veiled
 veil-ing
vein
 veiny
 vein-i-er
 vein-i-est
 vein-ing
vel-lum
ve-loc-i-ty
 ve-loc-i-ties
vel-our
.ve-lum
 ve-la
vel-vet
 vel-vet-ed
 vel-ve-teen
 vel-vety
 vel-vet-i-er
 vel-vet-i-est
ve-nal
 ve-nal-i-ty
 ve-nal-ly
ve-na-tion
 ve-na-tion-al
vend-er
 vend-or
ven-det-ta

vend-i-ble
 vend-i-bil-i-ty
ve-neer
 ve-neer-er
 ve-neer-ig
ven-er-able
 ven-er-abil-i-ty
 ven-er-ably
ven-er-ate
 ven-er-a-tion
 ven-er-a-tor
ve-ne-re-al
venge-ance
venge-ful
 venge-ful-ness
ve-ni-al
 ve-ni-al-i-ty
 ve-ni-al-ness
 ve-ni-al-ly
ven-i-son
ven-om
 ven-om-ous
ve-nous
 ve-nous-ly
vent
 vent-ed
 vent-ing
ven-ti-late
 ven-ti-lat-ed
 ven-ti-lat-ing
 ven-ti-la-tion
 ven-ti-la-tor
ven-tral
 ven-tral-ly
ven-tri-cle
ven-tril-o-quism
ven-tri-lo-qui-al
ven-tril-o-quist
 ven-tril-o-quize
 ven-tril-o-quized
 ven-tril-o-quiz-ing
ven-ture
ven-ture-some
ven-tur-ous
ve-ra-cious
ve-rac-i-ty
 ve-rac-i-ties
ve-ran-da
ver-bal
 ver-bal-ly
ver-bal-ize
 ver-bal-ized
 ver-bal-iz-ing
 ver-bal-i-za-tion
 ver-bal-iz-er
ver-ba-tim

ver-bi-age
ver-bose
  ver-bose-ness
  ver-bos-i-ty
ver-bo-ten
ver-dant
  ver-dan-cy
ver-dict
ver-di-gris
ver-dure
  ver-dured
  ver-dur-ous
verge
  verged
  verg-ing
ver-i-fi-ca-tion
ver-i-fy
  ver-i-fied
  ver-i-fy-ing
  ver-i-fi-abil-i-ty
  ver-i-fi-able
  ver-i-fi-er
veri-si-mil-i-tude
  veri-ta-ble
  veri-ta-bly
ver-i-ty
  ver-i-ties
ver-meil
ver-mic-u-lar
  ver-mic-u-late
  ver-mic-u-lat-ed
ver-mi-fuge
ver-mil-ion
ver-min
  ver-min-ous
ver-mouth
ver-nac-u-lar
  ver-nac-u-lar-ism
ver-nal
  ver-nal-ly
ver-sa-tile
  ver-sa-til-i-ty
versed
ver-si-fy
  ver-si-fied
  ver-si-fy-ing
  ver-si-fi-er
  ver-si-fi-ca-tion
ver-sion
  ver-sion-al
ver-sus
ver-te-bra
  ver-te-brae
ver-te-bral
  ver-te-bral-ly
ver-te-brate

ver-tex
  ver-tex-es
  ver-ti-ces
ver-ti-cal
  ver-ti-cal-i-ty
  ver-ti-cal-ly
ver-ti-go
  ver-ti-goes
  ver-tig-i-nes
ves-i-cant
  ves-i-ca-to-ry
  ves-i-ca-to-ries
ves-i-cate
  ves-i-cat-ed
  ves-i-cat-ing
  ves-i-ca-tion
ves-i-cle
ve-sic-u-lar
ves-pers
ves-sel
ves-tal
vest-ed
ves-ti-bule
  ves-ti-buled
  ves-ti-bul-ing
  ves-tib-u-lar
ves-tige
  ves-tig-i-al
  ves-tig-i-al-ly
vest-ment
vest-pock-et
ves-try
  ves-tries
vet
  vet-ted
  vet-ting
vet-er-an
vet-er-i-nar-i-an
vet-er-i-nary
ve-to
vex
  vex-er
  vex-ing-ly
vex-a-tion
  vex-a-tious
vexed
via
vi-a-ble
  vi-a-bil-i-ty
vi-a-bly
vi-a-duct
vi-al
vi-and
vi-brant
  vi-bran-cy
vi-brate

vi-brat-ed
vi-brat-ing
vi-bra-tion
vi-bra-to
  vi-bra-tos
vi-bra-tor
vi-bra-to-ry
vi-bur-num
vic-ar
  vic-ar-ship
vic-ar-age
vi-car-i-ous
  vi-car-i-ous-ly
vice ad-mi-ral
vice--con-sul
vice--pres-i-dent
vice-roy
  vice-roy-al
vice ver-sa
vi-cin-i-ty
  vi-cin-i-ties
vi-cious
  vi-cious-ly
vi-cis-si-tude
vic-tim
  vic-tim-ize
  vic-tim-ized
  vic-tim-iz-ing
  vic-tim-iz-er
vic-tor
vic-to-ri-ous
  vic-to-ri-ous-ly
vic-to-ry
  vic-to-ries
vict-ual
vid-eo
vie
  vied
  vy-ing
  vi-er
view-er
  view-less
  view-point
vig-il
  vig-i-lance
  vig-i-lant
  vig-i-lan-te
vi-gnette
vig-or
  vig-or-ous
  vig-or-ous-ly
vi-king
vile
vil-i-fy
  vil-i-fied
  vil-i-fy-ing

vil-i-fi-ca-tion
vil-la
vil-lage
vil-lain
  vil-lain-ous
vil-lainy
  vil-lain-ies
vil-lein
vil-lous
vil-lus
  vil-li
vin-ci-ble
  vin-ci-bil-i-ty
vin-di-cate
  vin-di-cat-ed
  vin-di-cat-ing
vin-dic-tive
  vin-dic-tive-ly
  vin-dic-tive-ness
vin-e-gar
vin-e-gary
vine-yard
vi-nous
vin-tage
vint-ner
vi-nyl
vi-ol
vi-o-la
  vi-o-list
vi-o-la-ble
  vi-o-la-bil-i-ty
vi-o-late
  vi-o-lat-ed
  vi-o-lat-ing
  vi-o-la-tor
vi-o-la-tion
vi-o-lence
vi-o-lent
vi-o-let
vi-o-lin
  vi-o-lin-ist
vi-o-lon-cel-lo
  vi-o-lon-cel-list
vi-per
vi-ra-go
vi-ral
vir-eo
  vir-e-os
vir-gin
  vir-gin-al
vir-gin-i-ty
vir-gule
vir-ile
  vi-ril-i-ty
vi-rol-o-gy
  vi-rol-o-gist

vir-tu-al
vir-tue
vir-tu-os-i-ty
  vir-tu-os-i-ties
vir-tu-o-so
vir-tu-ous
  vir-tu-ous-ly
vir-u-lence
  vir-u-len-cy
vir-u-lent
vi-rus
  vi-rus-es
vi-sa
vis-age
vis-cera
  vis-cer-al
vis-cid
  vis-cid-ly
vis-cos-i-ty
  vis-cos-i-ties
vis-count
  vis-count-cy
  vis-count-ship
vis-count-ess
vis-cous
vis-i-bil-i-ty
  vis-i-bil-i-ties
  vis-i-ble
vi-sion
  vi-sion-ary
  vi-sion-ar-ies
vis-it
vis-i-tant
vis-it-a-tion
vis-it-ing
vis-i-tor
vi-sor
vis-ta
vis-u-al
  vis-u-al-ly
  vis-u-al-ize
  vis-u-al-ized
  vis-u-al-iz-ing
  vis-u-al-i-za-tion
vi-tal
  vi-tal-i-ty
  vi-tal-i-ties
vi-tal-ize
  vi-tal-ized
  vi-tal-iz-ing
  vi-tal-i-za-tion
vi-tals
vi-ta-min
vi-ti-ate
vit-re-ous
  vit-re-os-i-ty

vit-ri-fy
  vit-ri-fied
  vit-ri-fy-ing
  vit-ri-fi-a-ble
  vit-ri-fi-ca-tion
vit-ri-ol
  vit-ri-ol-ic
vi-tu-per-ate
  vi-tu-per-at-ed
  vi-tu-per-at-ing
vi-tu-per-a-tion
vi-va
vi-va-cious
vi-vac-i-ty
  vi-vac-i-ties
viv-id
viv-i-fy
  viv-i-fied
  viv-i-fy-ing
vi-vip-ar-ous
vivi-sec-tion
vix-en
vi-zier
vi-zor
vo-cab-u-lar-y
  vo-cab-u-lar-ies
vo-cal
  vo-cal-ic
  vo-cal-ist
  vo-cal-ize
  vo-cal-ized
  vo-cal-iz-ing
  vo-cal-i-za-tion
vo-ca-tion
  vo-ca-tion-al
vo-cif-er-ous
vod-ka
voice
  voiced
  voic-ing
  voice-less
voice-print
void-able
vol-a-tile
  vol-a-til-i-ty
vol-can-ic
  vol-can-i-cal-ly
vol-ca-no
  vol-ca-noes
  vol-ca-nos
vo-li-tion
vol-ley
  vol-leys
vol-ley-ball
volt-age
vol-ta-ic

volt-me-ter
vol-u-ble
  vol-u-bly
  vol-u-bil-i-ty
vol-ume
vo-lu-mi-nous
  vo-lu-mi-nous-ly
vol-un-tary
  vol-un-tar-i-ly
vol-un-teer
vo-lup-tu-ary
  vo-lup-tu-ar-ies
vo-lup-tu-ous
vom-it
voo-doo
vo-ra-cious
vo-rac-i-ty
vor-tex
  vor-tex-es
  vor-ti-ces
vo-ta-ry
  vor-ta-ries
vote
  vot-ed
  vot-ing
vot-er
vo-tive
vouch-er
vouch-safe
  vouch-safed
  vouch-saf-ing
vow-el
voy-age
  voy-aged
  voy-ag-ing
  voy-ag-er
vo-ya-geur
vo-yeur
  vo-yeur-ism
  voy-eur-is-tic
vul-can-ite
vul-gar
  vul-gar-ism
vul-gar-i-ty
  vul-gar-i-ties
vul-gar-ize
  vul-gar-ized
  vul-gar-iz-ing
vul-gate
vul-ner-a-ble
  vul-ner-a-bly
vul-pine
vul-ture
vul-va
  vul-vae
  vul-vas

wab-ble
  wab-bled
  wab-bling
wacky
  wack-i-er
  wack-i-est
  wack-i-ly
wad
  wad-ded
  wad-ding
wad-dle
  wad-dled
  wad-dling
  wad-dler
  wad-dly
  wad-dli-er
  wad-dli-est
wade
  wad-ed
  wad-ing
wad-er
waf-er
waf-fle
wag
  wagged
  wag-ging
  wag-ger
  wag-gish
wage
  waged
  wag-ing
wa-ger
wag-gery
  wag-ger-ies
wag-gle
  wag-gled
  wag-gling
wag-on
  wag-on-er
wain-scot
  wain-scot-ing
wain-wright
waist-band
waist-coat
waist-line
wait-er
wait-ing
wait-ress
waive
  waived
  waiv-ing
  waiv-er
wake
  waked
  wok-en
  wak-ing

wake-ful
  wake-ful-ly
wak-en
wale
  waled
  wal-ing
walk-a-way
walk-er
walk-ie-talk-ie
walk-out
walk-o-ver
walk-up
walk-way
wal-al-by
  wal-la-bies
wall-board
wal-let
wall-eye
  wall-eyed
wall-flow-er
wal-lop
wall-pa-per
wall-to-wall
wal-nut
wal-rus
  wal-rus-es
wam-pum
wan
  wan-ner
  wan-nest
  wan-ness
wan-der
  wan-der-lust
wane
  waned
  wan-ing
wan-gle
  wan-gled
  wan-gling
  wan-gler
want-ing
wan-ton
wa-pi-ti
  wa-pi-ties
war
  warred
  war-ring
war-ble
  war-bled
  war-bling
war-bler
war-den
  war-den-ship
ward-er
ward-robe
ware-house

war-fare
war-head
war-horse
war-like
war-lock
warm
  warm-er
  warm-est
warm--blood-ed
warm-heart-ed
war-mon-ger
warmth
warn-ing
war-path
war-rant
  war-ran-ty
  war-ran-ties
war-ren
war-ri-or
war-ship
war-time
wary
  war-i-er
  war-i-est
  war-i-ly
wash-able
wash-ba-sin
wash-board
wash-bowl
wash-cloth
wash-er
wash-ing
wash-out
wash-room
wash-stand
wash-tub
wasn't
wasp
  wasp-ish
  wasp-ish-ly
was-sail
wast-age
waste
  wast-ed
  wast-ing
  waste-ful
  waste-ful-ly
  waste-ful-ness
waste-bas-ket
waste-land
waste-pa-per
wast-er
wast-rel
watch-dog
watch-ful
watch-man

watch-men
watch-tow-er
watch-word
wa-ter
wat-er-buck
wa-ter-col-or
wa-ter-course
wa-ter-cress
wa-ter-fall
wa-ter-foul
wa-ter-front
wa-ter-less
wa-ter lev-el
wa-ter lily
  wa-ter lil-ies
wa-ter line
wa-ter-llogged
Wa-ter-loo
wa-ter main
wa-ter-man
  wa-ter-men
wa-ter-mark
wa-ter-mel-on
wa-ter moc-ca-sin
wa-ter-proof
wa-ter-re-pel-lent
wa-ter-shed
wa-ter-side
wa-ter ski
  wa-ter-skied
  wa-ter-ski-ing
wa-ter-spout
wa-ter-tight
wa-ter-way
wa-ter-works
wa-tery
watt-age
watt-hour
wat-tle
  wat-tled
  wat-tling
wave
  waved
  wav-ing
wave-length
wave-let
wa-ver
wav-y
  wav-i-er
  wav-i-est
  wav-i-ly
wax
  waxed
  wax-ing
wax-en
wax-wing

wax-work
waxy
  wax-i-er
  wax-i-est
way-far-er
  way-far-ing
way-lay
  way-laid
  way-lay-ing
way-side
way-ward
weak-en
weak-kneed
weak-ling
weak-ly
  weak-li-er
  weak-li-est
weak-mind-ed
weak-ness
wealthy
  wealth-i-er
  wealth-i-est
  wealth-i-ly
wean
weap-on
  weap-on-ry
wear
  wear-ing
wea-ri-some
wea-ry
  wea-ri-er
  wea-ri-est
  wea-ried
  wea-ry-ing
  wea-ri-ly
wea-sel
weath-er
weath-er--beat-en
weath-er-cock
weath-er-glass
weath-er-ing
weath-er-man
  weath-er-men
weath-er-proof
weather vane
weave
  weaved
  wov-en
  weav-ing
  weav-er
web
  webbed
  web-bing
web-foot
  web-foot-ed
wed-ding

wedge
  wedged
  wedg-ing
wed-lock
weedy
  weed-i-er
  weed-i-est
week-day
week-end
week-ly
weep-ing
wee-vil
weigh
weight
weighty
  weight-i-er
  weight-i-est
  weight-i-ly
weird
  weird-er
  weird-est
wel-come
  wel-comed
  wel-com-ing
wel-fare
well--be-ing
well-born
well--bred
well--dis-posed
well--done
well--found-ed
well--groomed
well--ground-ed
well--known
well--mean-ing
well--nigh
well--off
well--read
well--spo-ken
well-spring
well--thought--of
well--timed
well--to--do
well--wish-er
well--worn
wel-ter
  wel-ter-weight
were-wolf
  were-wolves
west-bound
west-er-ly
west-ern
  west-ern-er
west-ern-ize
  west-ern-ized
  west-ern-iz-ing

west-ern-i-za-tion
west-ern-most
west-ward
wet
  wet-ter
  wet-test
wet-back
whale
  whaled
  whal-ing
whale-boat
whale-bone
whal-er
wharf
  wharves
what-ev-er
what-not
what-so-ev-er
wheat
wheat-en
whee-dle
  whee-dled
  whee-dling
  whee-dler
wheel and ax-le
wheel-bar-row
wheel-chair
wheeled
wheel-house
wheel-wright
wheeze
  wheezed
  wheez-ing
wheezy
  wheez-i-er
  wheez-i-est
  wheez-i-ly
whelm
whelp
whence-so-ev-er
where-abouts
where-as
where-by
where-fore
where-in
where-on
where-so-ev-er
where-to
where-up-on
wher-ev-er
where-with
where-with-al
wher-ry
  wher-ries
whet
  whet-ted

whet-ting
wheth-er
whet-stone
whch-ev-er
whim-per
whim-si-cal
whim-sy
  whim-sies
whine
  whined
  whin-ing
whin-ny
  whin-nied
  whin-nying
  whin-nies
whip
  whipped
  whip-ping
whip-lash
whip-per-snap-per
whip-pet
whip-poor-will
whir
  whirred
  whir-ring
whirl-i-gig
whirl-pool
whirl-wind
whisk-er
whis-key
  whis-ky
  whis-keys
  whis-kies
whis-per
whist
whis-tle
  whis-tled
  whis-tling
whis-tler
white
  whit-er
  whit-est
  whit-ish
white--col-lar
white-fish
whit-en
white-wash
white water
whith-er
whit-ing
whit-tle
  whit-tled
  whit-tling
  whit-tler
whiz
  whizzed

whiz-zing
whiz-zes
whoa
who-ev-er
whole-heart-ed
whole-sale
  whole-saled
  whole-sal-ing
  whole-sal-er
whole-some
whole-wheat
whol-ly
whom-ev-er
whom-so-ev-er
whoop-ing
whop-per
whop-ping
whorled
whose-so-ev-er
who-so-ev-er
wick-ed
wick-er
wick-er-work
wick-et
wide
  wid-er
  wid-est
wide--awake
wide--eyed
wid-en
wide-spread
wid-geon
wid-ow
wid-ow-er
wid-ow-hood
width
wield-er
wieldy
wie-ner
wig-gle
  wig-gled
  wig-gling
  wig-gly
  wig-gli-er
wig-gler
wig-wag
  wig-wagged
  wig-wag-ging
wig-wam
wild-cat
  wild-cat-ted
  wild-cat-ting
wild-cat strike
wil-der-ness
wild-fire
wild-fowl

wild--goose chase
wild-life
wild-wood
wile
  wiled
  wil-ing
  wil-i-ly
  wil-i-ness
willed
  will-ful
wil-lies
will-ing
will--o'--the--wisp
wil-low
  wil-lowy
wil-ly--nil-ly
wim-ble
wim-ple
win
  win-ning
wince
  winced
  winc-ing
wind
  wound
  wind-ing
wind-bag
wind-break
wind-ed
wind-fall
wind-flow-er
wind-jam-mer
wind-lass
wind-mill
win-dow
wind-pipe
wind-row
wind-shield
wind-storm
wind-up
wind-ward
windy
  wind-i-er
  wind-i-est
wine
  wined
  win-ing
win-ery
  win-er-ies
wine-skin
winged
wing-span
wing-spread
win-ner
win-ning
win-some

win-ter
win-ter-gree
win-ter-ize
  win-ter-ized
  win-ter-iz-ing
  win-ter-i-za-tion
win-try
wipe
  wiped
  wip-ing
wire-haired
wire-les
wire-tap
wir-ing
wiry
  wir-i-er
  wir-i-est
wis-dom
wise
  wis-er
  wis-est
wise-acre
wise-crack
wish-bone
wish-ful
wishy-washy
wisp
  wispy
wis-ter-ia
wist-ful
witch-craft
witch-ery
  witch-er-ies
witch-ing
with-draw
with-er
  with-ered
  with-er-ing
with-hold
  with-held
  with-hold-ing
with-in
with-out
with-stand
  with-stood
  with-stand-ing
wit-less
wit-ness
wit-ted
wit-ti-cism
wit-ting
  wit-ting-ly
wit-ty
  wit-ti-er
  wit-ti-est
wiz-ard

wi-zard-ly
wi-zard-ry
wiz-en
wiz-ened
wob-ble
woe-be-gone
woe-ful
wolf-hound
wolf-ram
wol-ver-ine
wom-an
wom-en
wom-an-ly
wom-an-hood
womb
wom-bat
wom-en-folk
won-der
won-der-ful
won-der-land
won-der-ment
won-drous
wont-ed
wood-bine
wood-chuck
wood-cock
wood-craft
wood-cut
wood-cut-ter
wood-ed
wood-en
wood-land
wood-man
wood-men
wood-peck-er
wood-pile
wood-shed
woods-man
woods-men
woodsy
woods-i-er
woods-i-est
wood-wind
wood-work
woody
wood-i-er
wood-i-est
woof-er
wool-en
wool-gath-er-ing
wool-ly
wool-li-er
wool-li-est
wool-ly-head-ed
woozy
wooz-i-er

wooz-i-est
word-book
word-ing
word-less
word-less-ly
wordy
word-i-er
word-i-est
work-a-ble
work-a-bil-i-ty
work-a-day
work-bench
work-book
work-day
worked-up
work-er
work-horse
work-house
work-ing
work-ing-man
work-ing-men
work-man
work-men
work-man-like
work-man-ship
work-out
work-room
work-shop
work-ta-ble
world-ly
world-li-er
world-li-est
world-ly--wise
world-wide
worm--eat-en
worm-wood
wormy
worm-i-er
worm-i-est
worn--out
wor-ri-some
wor-ry
wor-ried
wor-ry-ing
wor-ries
wor-ry-wart
wors-en
wor-ship
wor-ship-ful
wor-sted
worth-less
worth-while
wor-thy
wor-thi-er
wor-thi-est
wor-thi-ness

would--be
wouldn't
wound-ed
wraith
wran-gle
wran-gled
wran-gling
wran-gler
wrap
wrapped
wrap-ping
wrap-per
wrath-ful
wreak
wreath
wreathe
wreathed
wreath-ing
wreck-age
wreck-er
wrench
wres-tle
wres-tled
wres-tling
wretch-ed
wrig-gle
wrig-gled
wrig-gling
wrig-gly
wring
wrung
wring-ing
wring-er
wrin-kle
wrin-kled
wrin-kling
wrist-band
write
wrote
writ-ten
writ-ing
write-in
writ-er
writhe
writhed
writh-ing
wrong-do-er
wrong-do-ing
wronged
wrong-ful
wrong-head-ed
wrought
wry
wri-er
wri-est
wry-ly

X

X chro-mo-some
xe-bec
xe-non
xen-o-pho-bia
X-ray
x-sec-tion
xy-lem
xy-lo-phone
xy-lose

Y

yacht
  yacht-ing
  yachts-man
  yachts-men
yak
yam
yank
Yan-kee
yap
  yapped
  yap-ping
yard-age
yard-arm
yard-mas-ter
yard-stick
yarn
yar-row
yawn
year
year-book
year-ling
year-long
year-ly
yearn
  yearn-ing
year--round
yeast
yeasty
  yeast-i-er
  yeast-i-est
yel-low
  yel-low-ish
yel-low-bird
yel-low fe-ver
yel-low-ham-mer
yel-low jack-et
yelp
yen
  yenned
  yen-ning
yeo-man
  yeo-men

ye-shi-va
  ye-shi-vas
yes-ter-day
yes-ter-year
ye-ti
yew
yield
yield-ing
yip
  yipped
  yip-ping
yo-del
  yo-deled
  yo-del-ing
  yo-del-er
yo-ga
  yo-gic
yo-gi
  yo-gis
yo-gurt
yoke
  yoked
  yok-ing
yo-kel
yolk
yon-der
yore
young
young-ling
young-ster
your-self
  your-selves
youth-ful
yowl
yt-ter-bi-um
yt-tri-um
yuc-ca
yule-tide
yum-my
  yum-mi-er
  yum-mi-est

Z

za-ny
  za-nies
  za-ni-er
  za-n-est
  za-ni-ly
  za-ni-ness
zeal-ot
zeal-ous
ze-bra
  ze-bras

ze-bu
ze-nith
zeph-yr
zep-pe-lin
ze-ro
  ze-ros
  ze-roes
zest
  zesty
  zest-i-er
  zest-i-est
zig-zag
  zig-zagged
  zig-zag-ging
zinc
zing
zin-nia
zip
  zipped
  zip-ping
zip-per
zip-py
  zip-pi-er
  zip-pi-est
zir-con
zir-con-ni-um
zith-er
zo-di-ac
  zo-di-a-cal
zom-bie
  zom-bi
zon-al
zone
  zoned
  zon-ing
zoo
  zoos
zo-ol-o-gy
  zo-o-log-i-cal
  zo-o-log-i-cal-ly
  zo-ol-o-gist
zuc-chi-ni
zwie-back
zy-gote